Ksenia Shagal
Participles

Empirical Approaches to Language Typology

Editors
Georg Bossong
Bernard Comrie
Kristine Hildebrandt
Jean-Christophe Verstraete

Volume 61

Ksenia Shagal

Participles

A Typological Study

ISBN 978-3-11-076433-8
e-ISBN (PDF) 978-3-11-063338-2
e-ISBN (EPUB) 978-3-11-062993-4

Library of Congress Control Number: 2019949211

Bibliographic information published by the Deutsche Nationalbibliothek
The Deutsche Nationalbibliothek lists this publication in the Deutsche Nationalbibliografie;
detailed bibliographic data are available on the Internet at http://dnb.dnb.de.

© 2021 Walter de Gruyter GmbH, Berlin/Boston
This volume is text- and page-identical with the hardback published in 2019.
Printing and binding: CPI books GmbH, Leck

www.degruyter.com

Contents

Acknowledgements —— IX
List of figures —— XI
List of tables —— XIII
Abbreviations and glossing conventions —— XV

1	**Introduction** —— 1	
1.1	Introducing participles —— 1	
1.2	Goals of the study —— 3	
1.3	Approach —— 6	
1.4	Sample, data, and methods —— 8	
1.5	Organization of the study —— 12	
2	**Defining participles** —— 14	
2.1	Introduction —— 14	
2.2	Critique of the traditional definitions —— 14	
2.3	Participle as a comparative concept —— 20	
2.3.1	Relative clause —— 21	
2.3.2	Verb form —— 31	
2.3.3	Deranking —— 38	
2.4	Participles and nominalizations —— 41	
2.5	Summary, conclusions, and the core sample —— 45	
3	**Participial orientation** —— 51	
3.1	Introduction —— 51	
3.2	Relativized participants —— 52	
3.3	Orientation towards core participants —— 59	
3.3.1	On patterning of core participants —— 59	
3.3.2	Active participles —— 62	
3.3.3	Passive participles —— 68	
3.3.4	Agentive participles —— 75	
3.3.5	Absolutive participles —— 78	
3.4	Orientation towards non-core participants —— 86	
3.5	Contextual orientation —— 91	
3.5.1	Full contextual orientation —— 91	
3.5.2	Limited contextual orientation —— 100	
3.6	Orientation extension —— 105	
3.6.1	Extension by means of specialized affixes —— 106	

3.6.2	Extension by means of resumptive elements — **109**	
3.6.3	Pragmatic extension — **113**	
3.7	Resumptive pronouns in participial relative clauses — **114**	
3.8	Discussion — **122**	
3.9	Summary and conclusions — **127**	
4	**Desententialization and nominalization — 129**	
4.1	Introduction — **129**	
4.2	Scalar approaches to finiteness — **130**	
4.2.1	Lehmann's (1988) scale of desententialization — **130**	
4.2.2	Cristofaro's (2003) approach — **135**	
4.2.3	Malchukov's (2004) Generalized Scale Model — **138**	
4.2.4	Nikolaeva's (2013) canonical approach — **142**	
4.2.5	Conclusions on the scalar approaches to finiteness — **144**	
4.3	Parameters considered in this study — **145**	
4.3.1	TAM expression — **146**	
4.3.2	Negation — **150**	
4.3.3	Subject agreement — **151**	
4.3.4	Nominal agreement with the modified noun — **152**	
4.3.5	Participant expression — **153**	
4.4	Summary and conclusions — **156**	
5	**Morphological desententialization of participial relative clauses — 157**	
5.1	Introduction — **157**	
5.2	TAM expression — **157**	
5.2.1	Two types of participial markers — **158**	
5.2.2	Restrictions for –TAM participles — **160**	
5.2.3	Restrictions within a paradigm of +TAM participles — **161**	
5.2.4	No TAM contrasts — **164**	
5.2.5	Hierarchical tendencies in TAM constraints — **167**	
5.2.6	Structural factors influencing TAM expression — **172**	
5.3	Expression of negation — **175**	
5.3.1	Non-finite or nominal negation — **175**	
5.3.2	Specialized negative participles — **178**	
5.3.3	No participial negation available — **183**	
5.4	Subject agreement — **184**	
5.5	Nominal agreement with the modified noun — **187**	
5.5.1	Obligatory agreement — **187**	

5.5.2	Conditional agreement —— 191	
5.6	Summary and conclusions —— 193	

6 Participant expression in participial relative clauses —— 194
- 6.1 Introduction —— 194
- 6.2 Subject encoding —— 195
- 6.2.1 Subject as a possessor —— 195
- 6.2.2 Subject as a non-core participant —— 199
- 6.2.3 Language-internal variation in subject encoding —— 201
- 6.2.4 Subject expression unavailable —— 204
- 6.3 Direct object encoding —— 204
- 6.3.1 Direct object as a possessor —— 205
- 6.3.2 Direct object as a non-core participant —— 207
- 6.3.3 Language-internal variation in object encoding —— 207
- 6.4 Encoding of non-core participants —— 210
- 6.5 Summary and conclusions —— 213

7 Participial systems —— 215
- 7.1 Introduction —— 215
- 7.2 Single participle —— 216
- 7.2.1 Inherently oriented participle —— 216
- 7.2.2 Contextually oriented participle —— 218
- 7.3 Orientation-based systems —— 221
- 7.4 TAM-based systems —— 225
- 7.5 Orientation and TAM-based systems —— 226
- 7.5.1 Symmetric systems —— 227
- 7.5.2 Asymmetric systems —— 228
- 7.6 Complex orientation + TAM systems —— 231
- 7.7 Other criteria for classification —— 234
- 7.8 Summary and conclusions —— 236

8 Conclusions and further prospects —— 244
- 8.1 Summary of the findings —— 244
- 8.2 Further prospects —— 246

Appendix 1. Languages investigated in the study —— 252
Appendix 1a. Languages of the core sample —— 252
Appendix 1b. Languages with little information on presumably participial forms —— 257

Appendix 1c. Languages without participles —— 259

Appendix 2. Properties of the languages in the core sample —— 272

Appendix 3. Forms considered in the study —— 276
Appendix 3a. Relativizing capacity —— 276
Appendix 3b. Position and desententialization —— 285
Appendix 3c. Argument expression —— 297

References —— 305
General references —— 305
References on languages outside the core sample —— 325

Index of subjects —— 339
Index of languages —— 343

Acknowledgements

This book is a revised version of my doctoral dissertation "Towards a typology of participles", which I defended at the University of Helsinki in April 2017 and published as Shagal (2017). Many people have helped me in one way or another during my work on this book, and I would like to express my sincere gratitude to all of them.

I am extremely grateful to Seppo Kittilä, the supervisor of the original dissertation, for all the feedback he provided over the years, and for his amazing ability to cheer me up no matter what. Many thanks to Maria Koptjevskaja-Tamm and Sonia Cristofaro, the preliminary examiners of the dissertation, for their encouraging reviews and suggestions for improvement, which I tried to implement in the revised version of the book. I am also indebted to Peter Arkadiev for his careful reading and valuable comments on the manuscript.

I would like to thank Jean-Christophe Verstraete, the responsible editor of the series Empirical Approaches to Language Typology, for all the work he did throughout the revision stage, and for his incredible patience. I am also thankful to Katja Schubert, the production editor of the book, for her technical help, and to all the others at De Gruyter Mouton involved in the publication process. Special thanks to Eduard Shagal for preparing the maps and figures for this book, and for all the other help.

Most of the time I spent working on this book, I was lucky to be a member of the Department of (Modern) Languages at the University of Helsinki, and I benefited greatly from its research environment. I wish to thank all my colleagues in General Linguistics and Finno-Ugrian Language Studies, in particular those behind the Helsinki Area & Language Studies initiative, for building up a lively research community that has so many inspiring activities to offer. Financial support for my research was provided mainly by the University of Helsinki and the Langnet Doctoral Programme.

I am deeply indebted to all those who assisted me in different ways in obtaining information on individual languages. Many thanks to the numerous language experts who shared their knowledge and data, and to the speakers of Kalmyk, Nanai, Nivkh, Uilta, Erzya and Hill Mari who worked with me on different occasions. I also wish to express my gratitude and admiration to all authors of descriptive grammars, without whom typological studies like this one would hardly be possible.

Finally, I would like to thank all those wonderful people in and outside of academia who have supported me throughout these years. This book would have never been completed without them.

List of figures

Fig. 1: All the languages investigated in the study —— 10
Fig. 2: Languages of the core sample —— 47
Fig. 3: Orientation of active participles —— 62
Fig. 4: Languages with active participles —— 65
Fig. 5: Orientation of passive participles —— 68
Fig. 6: Languages with passive participles —— 73
Fig. 7: Orientation of agentive participles —— 75
Fig. 8: Languages with agentive participles —— 77
Fig. 9: Orientation of absolutive participles —— 78
Fig. 10: Languages with absolutive participles —— 84
Fig. 11: Languages with participles oriented towards non-core participants —— 90
Fig. 12: Languages with contextually oriented participles: full contextual orientation —— 97
Fig. 13: Languages with contextually oriented participles: limited contextual orientation —— 104
Fig. 14: Languages with resumptive pronouns in participial relative clauses —— 120
Fig. 15: Participial systems in the languages of the core sample —— 238

List of tables

Tab. 1: Non-finite verb forms and their core syntactic functions —— 6
Tab. 2: Defining features of participles —— 46
Tab. 3: Languages of the core sample by genealogical groups and macroareas —— 47
Tab. 4: Languages with active participles —— 66
Tab. 5: Languages with passive participles —— 74
Tab. 6: Participial markers for relativizing core participants in Matsés —— 76
Tab. 7: Languages with agentive participles —— 77
Tab. 8: Languages with absolutive participles —— 85
Tab. 9: Languages with participles oriented towards non-core participants —— 90
Tab. 10: Languages with contextually oriented participles: relativization up to P —— 97
Tab. 11: Languages with contextually oriented participles: relativization up to IO —— 98
Tab. 12: Languages with contextually oriented participles: relativization up to OBL —— 98
Tab. 13: Languages with contextually oriented participles: relativization up to POSS —— 99
Tab. 14: Languages with participles demonstrating limited contextual orientation —— 105
Tab. 15: Resumptive pronouns in participial relative clauses —— 121
Tab. 16: Finite relative clauses in languages with different participial types —— 126
Tab. 17: Different types of participial orientation across languages —— 127
Tab. 18: Indicative and participial forms in Nanai —— 162
Tab. 19: Participial system in Yakut —— 179
Tab. 20: Negative participles in the languages of the sample —— 182
Tab. 21: Subject encoding in participial relative clauses in Meadow Mari —— 203
Tab. 22: Participial system in Standard Russian —— 227
Tab. 23: Participial system in Modern Standard Arabic —— 228
Tab. 24: Participial system in Tümpisa Shoshone —— 229
Tab. 25: Participial system in Koorete —— 229
Tab. 26: Participial system in Meadow Mari —— 231
Tab. 27: Participial system in Tundra Nenets —— 231
Tab. 28: Participial system in Kalmyk —— 232
Tab. 29: Participial system in Matsés —— 234
Tab. 30: Different types of participial systems across languages —— 239
Tab. 31: Languages with a single inherently oriented participle —— 239
Tab. 32: Languages with a single contextually oriented participle —— 240
Tab. 33: Languages with an orientation-based system —— 241
Tab. 34: Languages with a TAM-based system —— 241
Tab. 35: Languages with an orientation- and TAM-based system —— 242
Tab. 36: Languages with other oppositions and unclassified languages —— 243
Tab. 37: Constituent order in languages with different participial types —— 247
Tab. 38: Position of participial relative clauses in languages with different participial types —— 247

Abbreviations and glossing conventions

(For information on the standardization of the glosses see Section 1.4.)

||	long pause (Nias)
(*…)	ungrammatical if a specific segment is added
*(…)	ungrammatical without a specific segment
___	gap in a relative clause (where the relativized participant would be if expressed overtly)
1	first person
2	second person
3	third person
I–V	gender classes
A	agent-like argument of canonical transitive verb
ABL	ablative
ABS	absolutive
ACC	accusative
ACT	active
ACTUAL	actual
AD	'at', location typically associated with a particular entity (Tanti Dargwa)
ADF	AD-form, i.e. form referring to a property (Panare)
ADJR	adjectivizer
ADV	adverbializer
AFF	affirmative
AFR	aforementioned
AGR	agreement
ALL	allative
ALN	alienable
AN	animate
ANT	anterior
AOR	aorist
APP	affected peripheral participant
ART	article
ASP	aspect
ASSINV	assertor's involvement
ASSOC	associative
ATTR	attributive
AUG	augmentative
AUGM	augment
AUX	auxiliary
CAR	caritive
CAUS	causative
CHAR	characteristic
CL	classifier
CL1, CL2, etc.	noun classes
CM	compact

XVI — Abbreviations and glossing conventions

CNG	connegative
CNT	location with contact
COM	comitative
COMPL	completive, completion
CONC	concord suffix
CONJ	conjunctive
CONN	connector
CONS	consequential case
CONSTR	construct state
CONT	continuous
COORD	coordinator
COP	copula
CVB	converb
D	gender class /d/ (Ingush)
DAT	dative
DEB	debitive
DEC	declarative
DEF	definite
DEM	demonstrative
DEP	dependent marker
DET	determiner
DETR	detransitivizer
DIR	directional
DISC	discontinuity marker
DIST	distal demonstrative
DO	direct object
DOM	differential object marking
DS	different-subject marker
DU	dual
DUR	durative
DX	deictic prefix to verb
DYN	dynamic
ELA	elative
EMP	emphatic
END	ending
EP	epenthetic
ERG	ergative
ESS	essive
EVD	evidential
EVT	eventual mood
EX	exclusive person
EXIST	existential particle
EXP	experiential
EXT	extension
F	feminine gender
FIN	finite
FOC	focus

FUT	future
GEN	genitive
GEN1	first genitive (Hinuq, Komi-Zyrian)
GEN2	second genitive (Beserman Udmurt, Komi-Zyrian)
GNMCC	general noun-modifying clause construction
GNO	gnomic time reference (Panare)
HA	suffix -*ha*- (Muna)
HAB	habitual
HAVE	'have', verb-forming prefix (Nias)
HERE	'here', deictic element (Pitta Pitta)
HOLLOW	a hollow object (Tariana)
HPL	human plural
HTR	half-transitive (West Greenlandic)
ILL	illative
IMM	immediate
IMP	imperative
IN	'inside'
INAL	inalienable
INAN	inanimate
INC	inclusive
INCH	inchoative
IND	indicative
INESS	inessive
INF	infinitive
INFR	inferential
INS	instrumental
INT	intensifier
INTR	intransitive
INTRJ	interjection
IO	indirect object
IPFV	imperfective
IRR	irrealis mood
ITER	iterative
ITG	intangible
J	gender class /j/ (Ingush)
L	low tone
LAT	lative
LIG	ligature
LK	linker
LOC	locative
M	masculine gender
MID	middle voice
MLOC	modal locative
MOD	modal
MS	male speech
MUT	mutated nominal
N	neuter gender

NARR	narrative
NEC	necessitative
NEG	negation, negative
NEUT	neutral tense-aspect suffix
NEW	newly-learned information (Panare)
NF	non-finite
NFUT	non-future
NHPL	non-human plural
NMZ	nominalization
NOM	nominative
NOMFUT	nominal future marker
NOMPST	nominal past marker
NON3	non-3rd person (Barasano)
NONF	non-feminine gender
NP	noun phrase
NPL	non-personal plural class
NPST	non-past
NS	non-subject
NUC	nuclear case
O	patient-like argument of canonical transitive verb
OBJ	object
OBL	oblique
OCOMP	object of comparison
ORD	ordinal number
ORIG	origin case
P	patient-like argument of canonical transitive verb
PASS	passive
PFV	perfective
PL	plural
PLR	plurality
POL	polarity clitic (Finnish)
POSS	possessive
POSTER	posterior
POT	potential
PP	prepositional phrase/postpositional phrase
PPERF	immediate past-perfective aspect
PREP	prepositional case
PRET	preterite
PREV	preverb
PRF	perfect
PRIV	privative
PROG	progressive
PRON	pronominal
PROP	proprietive
PROX	proximal, proximate
PRS	present
PST	past

PSTFAR	far past (Barasano)
PTCP	participle
PTV	partitive
PURP	purpose, purposive
Q	question word or particle
R	recipient-like argument of ditransitive verb
RC	relative clause
REAL	realis mood
REAS	reason
REC	recent past
REFL	reflexive
REL	relative clause marker/relativizer
REM	remote past
REP	repetitive aspect
RES	resultative
RET	retrospective
RPTD	reported
S	single argument of canonical intransitive verb
SG	singular
SGT	singulative
SIM	simultaneous
SJV	subjunctive
SPEC	specifier
SPR	location 'on'
SR	subordinator
SRC	source postposition
SRESS	superessive
SS	same-subject marker
STAT	stative
SUB	subordinated form
SUBJ	subject
SUP	superlative
SURPR	surprisive (Muna)
T	theme-like argument of ditransitive verb
TAM	tense-aspect-modality
TEL	telic
TH	thematic consonant
TOP	topic marker
TR	transitive
TS	thematic suffix
UWPST	unwitnessed past
V	verb
VLD	validator
VN	verbal noun
WPST	witnessed past

1 Introduction

1.1 Introducing participles

This book is a typological study of participles, that is, deranked verb forms that can be employed for adnominal modification. An illustration of their use as relative clause predicates is provided in (1a) and (1b), both by Russian participial constructions and their English translations:[1]

(1) Russian (Indo-European)
    a. *devočk-a*   [***piš-ušč-aja***   *pis'm-o*]
        girl(F)-NOM.SG   write-PTCP.PRS.ACT-F.NOM.SG   letter(N)-ACC.SG
        'the girl [writing a letter]'
    b. *pis'm-o*   [***na-pisa-nn-oe***   *devočk-oj*]
        letter(N)-NOM.SG   PFV-write-PTCP.PST.PASS-N.NOM.SG   girl(F)-INS.SG
        'the letter [written by the girl]'

The category of participle as defined here is not universal, in the sense that not all languages have the relevant forms. Nevertheless, it is clearly cross-linguistically valid, since forms that fall under this definition have been described for numerous genealogically and geographically diverse languages. At the same time, as a consequence of such diversity, the forms referred to by this label also demonstrate a significant degree of variation.

Participles, thus, form a rather heterogeneous group. For instance, in most European languages, such as Russian, English, or Finnish, each participial form is specialized in relativizing one specific participant of the situation. To put it simply, the forms that relativize agents, as in (1a), are referred to as *active participles*, while the forms that relativize patients, as in (1b), are referred to as *passive participles*. Using the notion of *orientation* introduced by Lehmann (1984: 152) and later adopted by Haspelmath (1994: 153–154), we can say that participles of the European type are *inherently oriented*. On the other hand, in many other languages, such as Mongolic, Turkic, Nakh-Daghestanian, or Dravidian, participles can be *contextually oriented*, which means that one and the same form can be used to relativize several participants, e.g. the agent (2a), the patient (2b), and the location (2c):

---

[1] Square brackets in example sentences will be used to highlight the borders of subordinate (primarily relative) clauses, unless indicated otherwise.

(2) Kalmyk (Mongolic)
 a. [*bičəg* **bič-ǯä-sən**] *küükə-n*
  letter write-PROG-PTCP.PST girl-EXT
  'the girl who is writing a letter'
 b. [*küük-n-ä* **bič-ǯä-sən**] *bičəg*
  girl-EXT-GEN write-PROG-PTCP.PST letter
  'the letter which the girl is writing'
 c. [*küük-n-ä* *bičəg* **bič-ǯä-sən**] *širä*
  girl-EXT-GEN letter write-PROG-PTCP.PST desk
  'the desk at which the girl is writing a letter'

Despite this difference, inherently and contextually oriented participles share an important feature that is crucial for the definition of participles, namely they have to be *deranked*. In the linguistic literature, participles are commonly described as *non-finite* forms; this notion, however, is notoriously hard to operationalize. As has been recently shown in many typological studies, finiteness from a cross-linguistic perspective is best regarded as a gradual and multifactorial phenomenon; see Givón (2001), Cristofaro (2003, 2007), Nikolaeva (2013), and Chapter 4 of the present study for further discussion. For this reason, I choose to refer here to the distinction between *deranking* and *balancing* introduced by Stassen (1985: 76–83); see also Koptjevskaja-Tamm (1993), Cristofaro (1998, 2003), and van Lier (2009).[2] Dependent clause predicates that exhibit morphological or syntactic deviation from the standard of the independent clause predicate in a given language and bear some formal marking of their dependent status are referred to here as *deranked*, as well as the dependent clauses featuring such verb forms. In contrast, *balanced* verb forms are predicates of balanced dependent clauses, which structurally resemble independent clauses in the language in question. Balanced relative clauses as opposed to deranked participial ones can be illustrated by the primary relativization strategy in many European languages, where a relative clause is introduced by a relative pronoun (3a), and otherwise the structure of the clause and the form of the predicate is exactly the same as in the corresponding independent sentence (3b):

---

[2] That being said, for convenience I will sometimes use the term "non-finite" as a synonym for "deranked", especially when referring to studies where this term is used, or when discussing languages in which the contrast between finite (=balanced) and non-finite (=deranked) forms is uncontroversial.

(3) Russian (Indo-European)
   a. *devoč-a*   [*kotor-aja*   ***piš-et***   *pis'm-o*]
      girl(F)-NOM.SG   which-F.NOM.SG   write-PRS.3SG   letter(N)-ACC.SG
      'the girl [who is writing a letter]'
   b. *Devoč-a*   ***piš-et***   *pis'm-o.*
      girl(F)-NOM.SG   write-PRS.3SG   letter(N)-ACC.SG
      'The girl is writing a letter.'

The differences between participial relative clauses and regular independent clauses in a given language can take various forms, such as lack of the categorial distinctions pertaining to finite verb forms (e.g. tense, aspect, mood or person agreement), use of special categories not pertaining to finite verb forms (e.g. nominal agreement), or changes in the encoding of verbal arguments (e.g. subjects or direct objects). For instance, in Standard Russian the tense distinction in participial relative clauses is twofold (past vs. present) instead of threefold in independent clauses (past vs. present vs. future), while in Kalmyk there is no specialized present participle whatsoever, although a present tense form exists in the verb paradigm for independent clauses.[3] The agent is also often expressed differently with participles when compared to finite predicates, for example by the instrumental in Russian, as in (1b),[4] or by the genitive in Kalmyk, as in (2b) and (2c).

1.2 Goals of the study

Although participles have been studied extensively in various individual languages, so far no systematic effort has been made to list the genealogical units and geographical areas where they are especially common or at least attested. Probably the best information available on the matter is given in Haspelmath (1994: 153), but the author himself comments that his "impressionistic remarks are only meant to be suggestive, and much more comparative work needs to be done before any firm conclusions can be reached". Therefore, the first practical goal of this book is to fill this gap and provide preliminary information on the

---

[3] The corresponding meaning in Kalmyk relative clauses is expressed by the past participle with a progressive marker; see Section 5.2.3 and example (142) for more information.
[4] In Russian, this type of agent encoding is not specific to participial relative clauses, but is characteristic of independent passive clauses as well; see Section 6.2.2. However, in this study, I consider all agents of passive participles together because of the semantic properties they share; see Sections 3.3.3 and 4.3.5.

representation of participles in the world's languages and their geographical distribution.

The broader and the more important aim of the study is to map out the space of variation demonstrated by participles in the world's languages. In order to do that, I investigate three major topics:

1) As shown above, participles can differ in their relativizing capacity: an inherently oriented form only serves to relativize a specific participant or a set of participants, while a contextually oriented form can relativize different participants depending on the context. The questions for this part of the study are: What types of inherently oriented participles are attested, and what types are not? What are the limits of contextual orientation? What are possible motivations for the restrictions on participial orientation observed across languages? What kinds of paradigms based on orientation can participles form in individual languages?

2) The manifestations of deranking in participial relative clauses can be very different in different languages. Many typologists have discussed the properties that need to be eliminated or introduced in order to derive a deranked dependent clause from an independent one, as the scale of desententialization in Lehmann (1988), cross-linguistic parameters for the coding of subordination in Cristofaro (2003), the Generalized Scale Model in Malchukov (2004), criteria for finiteness in canonical typology in Nikolaeva (2013), and many others. There is, however, no typological study on these manifestations specifically in relative clauses. It is, therefore, reasonable to ask the following questions: What signals of deranking are available in participial relative clauses, and how are they related to each other? Which of these signals are especially relevant for participial relative clauses if compared to other types of dependent clauses? How can we explain the variation and tendencies observed in this domain?

3) It is possible for a language to have either one participial form, or several of them. Both situations raise questions that I will try to answer in this study: In case a language has only one participle, what are the typical characteristics of this form? How is it different from participles that belong to a paradigm? If a language has more than one participle, what are possible criteria for the formation of the participial paradigm? Are the criteria independent, or do they show any interaction? Are there any restrictions regarding the organization of a participial paradigm, and if yes, then how can they be explained?

It is important to emphasize that this study cannot be considered a cross-linguistic study of all aspects of use of participles. In many languages, forms employed for adnominal modification and traditionally referred to as participles appear to be extremely multifunctional. For instance, in most European languages, as well as in some Indic and Iranian languages, the passive construction is formed analytically by means of an auxiliary verb and a passive participle (Haspelmath 1990; Siewierska 1984: 126), as in (4), while in many languages featuring contextually oriented participles these forms are also commonly used as predicates in complement and adverbial clauses; see (5a) and (5b) respectively and Section 2.4 on this issue.

(4) Russian (Indo-European)
Pis'm-o **by-l-o** **na-pisa-n-o** *devočk-oj.*
letter(N)-NOM.SG be-PST-N.SG PFV-write-PTCP.PST.PASS-N.SG girl(F)-INS.SG
'The letter was written by the girl.'

(5) Kalmyk (Mongolic)
a. [*küükə-n* *bičəg* **bič-ǯä-s-i-n'**] *bi* *üz-lä-v*
girl-EXT letter write-PROG-PTCP.PST-ACC-POSS.3 1SG see-REM-1SG
'I saw that the girl was writing a letter.'
b. *küükə-n* [*bičəg* **bič-ǯä-sən-d-än**] *cä* *uu-v*
girl-EXT letter write-PROG-PTCP.PST-DAT-POSS.REFL tea drink-PST
'The girl was drinking tea while writing a letter.'

A cross-linguistic survey of such forms in all their functions would be exceedingly broad. Therefore, as the first attempt of a wide-scale typological study dealing with participles, this study focuses on the function that can be regarded as the core one for participles as a cross-linguistically applicable notion, namely the function of predicate of a relative clause. Forms that qualify as participles can have many other syntactic functions as well, but adnominal modification is something that they all have in common. Thus, investigating relative clauses with participial predicates can reveal the properties and distinctions that are relevant for participles as a typologically valid category and that can be further manifested in other constructions. I will occasionally refer to other uses of participial forms whenever this is relevant, but this study will not incorporate this question in a systematic way.

Apart from its own practical and theoretical value, the typological study of participial relative clauses fits very naturally into a general interest in subordinate structures that has been evident among typologists in recent years (see Cristofaro 2003, van Lier 2009, Gast and Diessel 2012, van Gijn 2014, Ross 2016, and many others). This book contributes to the general study of variation found in deranked structures in the languages of the world. In fact, it fills an important gap in the study of deranked forms. Table 1 below, which is a combination of the tables presented by Haspelmath (1995: 4) and van Lier (2009: 68), situates the study of participles in the broader context of other deranked verb forms specialized in a specific type of subordination. Deranked verb forms specializing in argument functions, viz. *action nominals* or *verbal nouns*, were extensively discussed in Koptjevskaja-Tamm (1993), while deranked forms specializing in adverbial functions, or *converbs*, were studied in Haspelmath (1995). As a result of these studies, the categories they investigated became more widely recognized as cross-linguistically valid, and the use of the labels became more uniform in both descriptive and theoretical studies. The problem of uniformity in terminology is relevant to the study of participles, as will be shown in Section 2.2, and a cross-linguistic study like this one is a good way to provide a grounded solution.

Tab. 1: Non-finite verb forms and their core syntactic functions

Syntactic function	Word class	Non-finite verb form	Dependent clause
argument	noun	verbal noun (masdar), infinitive	complement clause
adnominal modifier	adjective	participle	relative clause
adverbial modifier	adverb	converb	adverbial clause

1.3 Approach

This book is a typical study in functional-typological linguistics, the framework that became widespread after the seminal work by Joseph Greenberg (1963), and has been later developed by many other linguists (see Comrie 1981, Croft 1990, Givón 2001, among others). Research conducted within this framework aims at establishing the range of cross-linguistic variation – which properties are shared by all or most languages, which features are common, and which are extremely rare or, presumably, impossible in natural language – and accounting for such tendencies in terms of basic principles of language function.

The approach adopted in this study can be characterized as *non-aprioristic* because no a priori assumptions are made with respect to the kinds of categories and constructions that languages may have (Haspelmath 2014: 492). The data for typological comparison comes primarily from the sources provided by descriptive linguists, but the analysis does not have to be based on the categories established for individual languages. Instead, the idea is to develop universally applicable *comparative concepts*, which do not necessarily correspond to any *descriptive categories* used in the analysis of particular languages (Haspelmath 2010). Comparative concepts are not necessarily psychologically real; the only requirement is that they allow for meaningful cross-linguistic comparison and the formulation of relevant statements concerning the languages of the world and natural language in general. The key comparative concept for the present study is, naturally, the concept of participle discussed in detail in Chapter 2.

Apart from determining the limits of cross-linguistic variation, functional typologists are also interested in interpreting the results. The assumption underlying this approach is that many aspects of language structure can be explained with reference to language function. In other words, universal tendencies regarding language structure can be accounted for in terms of the meaning and use of certain structures in human communication (Croft 1990, 1995; Cristofaro 2003). Functional motivations governing the emergence, development and use of particular structures are commonly proposed based on synchronic distributional evidence. Over recent decades, however, a number of linguists (e.g. Bybee 1988, 2008; Dryer 2006) have argued that the explanations proposed for given distributional patterns should refer to the diachronic processes that give rise to these patterns, rather than to the functions of the patterns themselves; see Cristofaro (2012: 647). In a more moderate view, the diachronic processes are regarded as a valuable source of evidence for particular principles that might motivate certain observed linguistic phenomena. Unfortunately, in many cases this approach is hard to implement due to a lack of relevant diachronic data, which is exactly the case with the participial relative constructions addressed here. Therefore, most explanations proposed throughout this book will refer to diachrony only to a very limited extent.

In the past decades, at least since Nichols (1992), more typologists are also getting interested in explaining the patterns of linguistic diversity from a geographical point of view. This typological paradigm is commonly referred to as "what's where why?", which includes investigating universal preferences and geographical skewings ("what's where?"), as well as explaining them as historically grown and interrelated among themselves and with social, cognitive, and genetic patterns ("why?"); see Bickel (2007) for a general overview and further references. Nevertheless, before this kind of research can be done, it is necessary to establish a set of fine-grained variables that would later allow one to capture similarities and differences of structures across languages. In order to do this, a qualitative study like the present one is a necessary first step. Therefore, apart from being a contribution to functional typology, this book can also be considered as a foundation for further typological work in this domain, specifically as regards diachronic and areal typology.

1.4 Sample, data, and methods

As a typological study, this book aims to make claims about natural language in general and thus, in principle, has all the languages of the world as its object of study. However, since it is clearly impossible to examine all human languages ever spoken (according to an estimate given in Bickel 2013, there have been at least half a million languages on earth so far), it is necessary to create a sample of languages that is most adequate for the goals set in the study.

Given that this study of participles is the first attempt to approach a phenomenon that has not been extensively investigated from a typological point of view, the sampling strategy should aim at capturing the greatest possible linguistic diversity. As mentioned above, we do not even know precisely in which language families or geographical areas participles are attested and where not. Therefore, the investigation should be based on a *variety sample* (as opposed to *probability samples* and *random samples*, which are commonly employed for statistical analysis; see Rijkhoff et al. 1993, Rijkhoff and Bakker 1998). Since we did not have much preliminary information on the typology of participles before this study, it is not possible to control for any factors that may refer to such variables, i.e. types of participles and participial constructions that can be distinguished in the world's languages, or the parameters with respect to which they might differ. Also, for the same reasons, we cannot estimate the number of such variables beforehand; this implies that it is impossible to apply the sampling procedure introduced by Rijkhoff and Bakker (1998), which includes a method for calculating the ideal sample size for a certain object of study.

Taking all this into account, the optimal strategy for this study is simply to build a sample that is as large as possible and aims at maximal independence of languages, i.e. trying to avoid bias in their choice. As noted by Rijkhoff et al. (1993: 172), the most important bias a typologist should avoid when creating a language sample is genetic, which, in turn, can generate other sources of bias, namely geographic, typological, and cultural. It is necessary, therefore, to stratify the sample on some level of genealogical classification.

The sample used in this study is genealogically stratified at the level of *genus*, as explained in Dryer (1989) and used in The World Atlas of Language Structures (henceforth WALS, Dryer and Haspelmath 2013), i.e. a level of classification that is intended to be comparable in time depth across language families all around the world. The genus has a time depth of 3500–4000 years or less, and classic examples of genera are the standard subfamilies of Indo-European, such as Germanic, Slavic, or Celtic. Each language isolate is regarded as constituting a genus by itself. The genealogical classification employed in this study is the one represented in WALS, which is mostly based on the classification in the 14th edition of Ethnologue (Grimes 2000). If a language considered in this study is not present in the WALS database, the genus it belongs to is determined on the basis of the source on this language and/or Glottolog 4.0 (Hammarström, Forkel, and Haspelmath 2019). Glottolog 4.0 was also used in this study as a source of information on top-level language families.

The choice of languages representing particular genera was determined by several factors. Since the first step of the study was to check the existence of relevant forms in as many languages as possible, all sources providing information on the existence of deranked relative clauses in certain languages were taken into account. These were mostly typological works dealing with various subordinate structures, such as Koptjevskaja-Tamm (1993), Cristofaro (2003), Malchukov (2004), van Lier (2009), Wu (2011), and van Gijn (2014), among others. In addition, there is also the classic problem of insufficient documentation. For many languages, no adequate description is available, especially concerning subordinate structures, so for some genera, searching for information on deranked relative clauses simply implied searching for the fullest description of a language belonging to this genus. In some cases, specific genera could not be investigated in this study, because of a lack of such descriptions.

As a result of this preliminary work, it was possible to find relatively reliable information on the presence or absence of participial relative clauses for 360 genera out of the 544 included in WALS. In some cases, more than one language per genus was considered, mainly if a particular genus featured languages both with and without participial relative clauses (e.g. Mẽbengokre and Canela-Krahô > Ge-Kaingang; Nias and Karo Batak > Northwest Sumatra-Barrier Islands), or if it was known beforehand that participles or participial systems in two closely related languages show considerable differences (e.g. Beng and Wan > Eastern Mande; Imbabura Quechua and Tarma Quechua > Quechuan; Even and Nanai > Tungusic). In addition, some points in the book are illustrated by data from languages that are not included in the sample. This is the case mainly if a particular feature described for participles in a given language appears to be typologically rare or unique, but deranked clauses are otherwise not described in sufficient detail in this language. It should be emphasized that since the goals of the present book are qualitative rather than quantitative, the inclusion of additional languages does not invalidate the sample in any way.

The map of all 388 languages investigated in the preliminary phase of this work is presented in Figure 1 below (black dots stand for the languages that have participial relative clauses, whereas white dots represent the languages that do not have participial relative clauses). The 253 languages that were found to lack participles are listed in Appendix 1c, along with the sources of information. Of the remaining 135 languages, there are 35 languages that seem to have participles, but for which information on the relevant forms is very limited. A list of these languages and their descriptions is provided in Appendix 1b. As a consequence, the core sample used for this study will consist of 100 languages. This will be discussed in more detail in Section 2.6; some additional information is also provided in Appendix 1a. In all, we can say that participles were found in 34.8% of the languages sampled. Due to the imperfect sampling procedure, this figure cannot be taken as fully representative of the overall share of languages with participles, but at least it gives a general impression of how common they are.

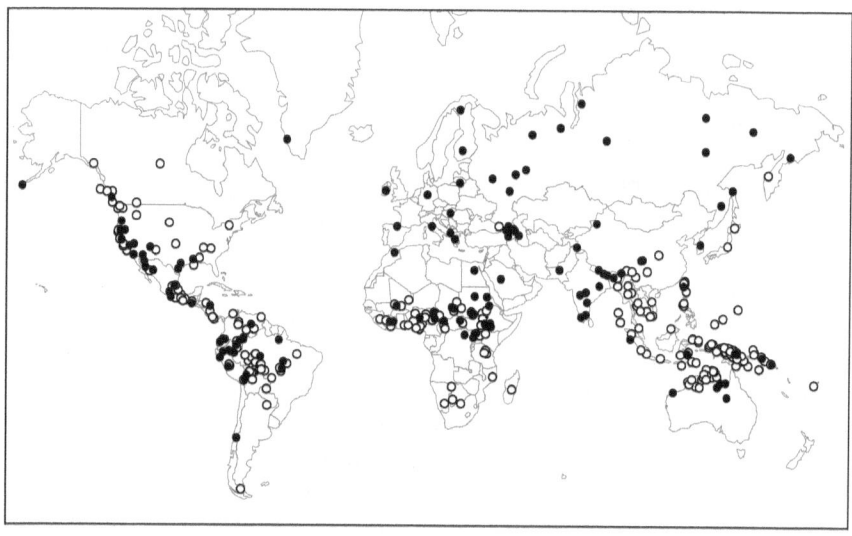

Fig. 1: All the languages investigated in the study

As can be seen from the map, forms classified as participles can be found in languages all over the world. As it was noticed by Haspelmath (1994), they are indeed most typical for Eurasia, with the exception of South-East Asia. Among the big language families in Eurasia, participles are typical for Indo-European, Uralic, Nakh-Daghestanian and Dravidian languages, as well as for Turkic, Mongolic and Tungusic. In fact, they can be regarded as an areal feature common for at least the languages of Northern Eurasia (see Pakendorf 2012, Shagal 2016). On the other hand, among Austroasiatic languages, which are generally poor in inflectional morphology, only Kharia in my sample possesses forms that can be classified as participles.

In Papunesia and Australia, participial relative clauses are attested only occasionally, while most languages in these areas do not exhibit this type of forms. Austronesian languages, for instance, mostly employ linking particles rather than specialized non-finite forms for relativization (see Foley 1980). Most of Australian languages use so-called *adjoined relative clauses* (a term introduced in Hale 1976), a generalized subordinate clause type, which can receive different interpretations depending on the syntactic and pragmatic context. Fairly often the relative clause is not adjacent to its nominal head, and in most languages, the predicates of relative clauses are fully finite, even though some of them are able to take case morphology (see Nordlinger 2002: 4).

Participles are characteristic of about half of the languages examined in Africa, all of them north of the equator, although for most of them very little data is available. Participial forms are fairly well represented in the Afro-Asiatic language family (I was able to find them in more than half of the genera that I examined), while for other families they are relatively infrequent.

In the Americas, participial forms are mostly observed in the languages of the western coast, although some languages of the Amazon use deranked relative clauses as well. The existence of participles in South America is, in fact, expected, since many languages there are known to use nominalization (including non-finite nominalization) as a subordination strategy; see Dixon and Aikhenvald (1999) for the Amazon basin, Crevels and van der Voort (2008) for the Guaporé-Mamoré area in Bolivia and Brazil, and van Gijn (2014) for the Andean linguistic area, with reference to Torero (2002) and Adelaar (2004). Moreover, van Gijn (2014) shows that languages possessing nominalized structures are significantly more common in South America, when compared to their global distribution, as calculated on the basis of Cristofaro (2003). Unfortunately, for many American (especially North American) languages that appear to have participial forms, no good sources are available, or non-finite subordination is only touched upon very briefly. All in all, according to the map resulting from my survey, participles appear to be a more widespread phenomenon than traditionally assumed.

The sources used in the study are descriptive grammars of the languages included in the sample, typological and language-specific articles dealing with the relevant topics, as well as first-hand data obtained from specialists in particular languages and collected during several field trips.[5] In most cases in the book, I have reproduced the orthography and the glosses used in the sources from which the language data is taken. As a result, many forms treated as participles in this study can have other glosses, since they may represent other descriptive categories in particular languages. The only standardization procedure that has been applied concerned cases where different abbreviations were employed by different authors for the same category. Some minor changes have also been made in order to avoid confusion where it might have occurred.

The methods used in this study are predominantly qualitative. Because of considerable data limitations and the resulting unbalanced nature of the sample, I do not employ any quantitative methods to account for the geographical distribution of participles. Neither is it possible to conduct any consistent statistically grounded comparison of all languages of the sample, since on many of the significant parameters no data is available for at least several languages. Because of this, for each aspect of participles or participial relative clauses discussed in this study, I only discuss (and count) the languages for which the relevant information is available in descriptive grammars.

1.5 Organization of the study

The book is organized as follows. In Chapter 2, I develop a typologically oriented definition (or comparative concept) of participle which is based on several other comparative concepts, such as relative clause, verbal paradigm, and deranking. I further specify the range of forms and constructions that fall within the scope of the present study. Chapters 3–6 are devoted to various properties pertaining to individual participial forms, while in Chapter 7, I address the topic of their interaction within participial paradigms.

Chapter 3 discusses the phenomenon of participial orientation, i.e. the range of participants that can be relativized by a particular participle. Based on the available data on the languages of the sample, I propose a list of typologically

---

[5] The data on Kalmyk (Mongolic) comes from three field trips to the Republic of Kalmykia organized by Saint Petersburg State University in 2006–2008. The data on Nanai (Tungusic) comes from two field trips to the Khabarovsk Krai in 2007 and 2009. The data on Erzya (Uralic) partly comes from a field trip to the Republic of Mordovia organized by the Helsinki Area and Language Studies group in 2013. The data on Nivkh (Nivkh) and Uilta (Tungusic) partly comes from a field trip organized by the Helsinki Area and Language Studies group in 2014. Unless indicated otherwise, examples from these languages come from my personal field notes. Examples from Russian, English, Finnish and German are mostly based on my personal knowledge.

relevant orientation types. In particular, I distinguish between participles used to relativize specific core or peripheral participants (e.g. active and passive, or instrumental and locative participles), and participles that can relativize a wider range of participants depending on the context (the available range varies cross-linguistically and can sometimes be extended by certain means). I also discuss possible motivations for different orientation types, and highlight the importance of semantic and pragmatic motivations in this domain.

In Chapters 4–6, I discuss deviations in participial relative clauses in comparison to independent clauses in individual languages. In Chapter 4, I provide an overview of several recent theoretical approaches to the topic (Lehmann 1988; Cristofaro 2003; Malchukov 2004; Nikolaeva 2013), and identify the criteria relevant for cross-linguistic comparison, which can be roughly divided into those pertaining to the participial form itself and those involving the encoding of its dependents. Chapters 5 and 6 then deal with these two sets of criteria in turn.

Chapter 5 discusses a variety of ways in which participles can differ morphosyntactically from independent clause predicates: how they encode verbal categories, such as tense, aspect and modality (TAM), how they express negation, and whether or not they agree with the subject of the participial relative clause (verbal agreement) or with the noun they modify (nominal agreement).

Chapter 6 considers the deviations manifested in argument marking, primarily in the encoding of subjects and direct objects in participial relative clauses. I show that in addition to retaining standard encoding, participles can encode core arguments as possessors or non-core participants, or they show language-internal variation in their expression. I also briefly comment on the rare cases where deranking leads to non-standard expression of peripheral participants in the relative clause.

In Chapter 7, I provide an overview of participial systems, and formulate some generalizations concerning their possible organization. In languages that have more than one participle, the paradigm is usually based on either orientation, or TAM properties of the forms, but commonly also on the combination of the two criteria. Notably, these criteria are rarely independent, so I will pay special attention to their interaction.

A summary of the results, prospects for future research and concluding remarks are presented in Chapter 8.

2 Defining participles

2.1 Introduction

Although the label "participle" is widely used in the linguistic literature, the term is far from well-defined. For a typological study like this one, however, providing a precise definition of the object of investigation is of utmost importance. The goal of the present chapter is to develop such a definition, against a background of potential problems in defining the category for cross-linguistic comparison.

I will start by presenting several traditional definitions of participles and the conceptions they are based upon. I will also show why these definitions appear to be problematic for a wide-scale typological study. This discussion constitutes the topic of Section 2.2. As an alternative to existing definitions, in Section 2.3 I will propose a cross-linguistically applicable comparative concept of participle based on several other comparative concepts, namely the concepts of relative clause (Section 2.3.1), verb form (Section 2.3.2), and deranking (Section 2.3.3). Section 2.4 is specifically devoted to participle/nominalization syncretism, a very widespread phenomenon in the languages of the world, which has been pointed out in many studies, such as DeLancey (2002), Comrie and Thompson (2007), Genetti et al. (2008), and others. Finally, in Section 2.5, I summarize the main points discussed in this chapter.

2.2 Critique of the traditional definitions

Most linguistic dictionaries and encyclopedias give quite vague definitions of participles, which often cover all non-finite forms, as in (6), sometimes with the exception of infinitives, as in (7):

(6) A traditional term for a non-finite form of the verb. (Hartmann and Stork 1972: 165)
(7) A traditional grammatical term referring to a word derived from a verb and used as an adjective, as in *a laughing face*. ... In linguistics the term is generally restricted to the non-finite forms of verbs other than the infinitive. (Crystal 2003: 337–338)

Furthermore, Trask (1993: 200–201) notes that this label can also be extended to non-finites that do not function as adjectival or adverbial modifiers, but only serve to combine with auxiliaries in the formation of periphrastic verb forms, such as the so-called "perfect participle" *finished* in *Lisa has finished her translation*. This last extension in particular seems to make the category unreasonably broad. Such definitions, however, do not appear out of nowhere. They should rather be seen as an attempt to unite under one term the properties of all the forms that bear the label "participle" in numerous descriptions of individual languages. Thus, the concept represented in dictionaries is the result of numerous successive extensions. But what are the mechanisms of these extensions?

Participles in the narrowest sense are traditionally regarded as verb forms that "behave like adjectives with respect to morphology and external syntax" (Haspelmath 1994: 152). Indeed, for some languages this definition works perfectly. For example, in Finnish, there is a distinct class of adjectives neatly determined from both a morphological and a syntactic point of view, and Finnish participles fit faultlessly into this class, compare (8a) with an adjective as adnominal modifier and (8b), where the same noun is modified by a participle:

(8) Finnish (Uralic)
    a. *Keitto-a*   *voi*   *tehdä*   **tuore-i-sta**   *sien-i-stä.*
        soup-PTV.SG   can.3SG   do.INF   fresh-PL-ELA   mushroom-PL-ELA
        'One can cook soup with fresh mushrooms.'
    b. *Keitto-a*   *voi*   *tehdä*   **kuiva-tu-i-sta**
        soup-PTV.SG   can.3SG   do.INF   dry-PTCP.PST.PASS-PL-ELA
        sien-i-stä.
        mushroom-PL-ELA
        'One can cook soup with dried mushrooms.'

There are two problems with taking the notion of "adjective" as a basis, however. One is that participles often have a broader range of functions than regular adjectives, and the other is that many languages do not have a separate class of adjectives to measure participles against. I will deal with these in turn. First, in many languages with a well-defined class of adjectives, the distribution of non-finite verb forms that can function as an adnominal modifier appears to be broader than that of regular adjectives. For instance, the English *-ing* form, which can be considered a participle due to adjectival uses like the one illustrated in (9a), also occurs in adverbial and complement clauses, as shown in (9b) and (9c) respectively:

(9) English (Indo-European)
    a. *The note was addressed to the girl* [**sitting** *in the back row*].

b. *During my first years in college, I mostly read comics [**sitting** in the back row].*
c. *I hate [**sitting** in the back row], because I can't see anything from there.*

This is confirmed by Hendery (2012: 171), who estimates that in the majority of cases, non-finite verb forms used for adnominal modification are actually not specific to this function, but can be found in other subordinate constructions as well. This observation is also supported by the data provided in Appendix 4 of Cristofaro's (2003) typological study of subordination. Van Lier (2009: 206–210) shows that in a genealogically and geographically balanced sample of 50 languages all logically possible combinations are attested, when it comes to the types of dependent clauses in which certain non-finite verb form can function as a predicate. The function of adnominal modification can, therefore, combine with either the function of adverbial modification, the reference function, or both (see Table 1 in Section 1.2).

An example of the most flexible case is the verb form with the *-n-* marker in Kayardild, which can function as a predicate of a relative clause (10a), a predicate of a complement clause (10b), or a predicate of an adverbial clause (10c):

(10) Kayardild (Tangkic)
  a. *nga-ku-l-da* [**wirr-n-ku**] *dangka-wu kurri-ju*
     1-INC-PL-NOM dance-NMZ-PROP.MOD man-PROP.MOD see-POT
     'We will watch the dancing man.' (Evans 1995: 474)
  b. *ngada kurri-ja* [*niwan-ji* **budii-n-marri**]
     1SG.NOM see-ACTUAL 3SG.POSS-MLOC run-NMZ-PRIV
     'I saw that he was not running.' (Evans 1995: 476)
  c. [*bilaangka-nurru* **kari-i-n-da**] *ngada warra-j*
     blanket-ASSOC cover-MID-NMZ-NOM 1SG.NOM go-ACTUAL
     'I went along, covering myself in a blanket.' (Evans 1995: 474)

In Krongo, the marker *n-* is used in non-finite relative clauses (11a), and in non-finite adverbial clauses (11b):

(11) Krongo (Kadugli-Krongo)
  a. *n-úllà à?àŋ kí-ǹt-àndìŋ* [**n-úufò-ŋ**] *kò-níimò*
     1/2-IPFV.love I LOC-SGT-clothes CONN.N-IPFV.sew-TR POSS-mother
     kàtí]
     my
     'I love the dress that my mother is sewing.' (Reh 1985: 256)

b. *n-áa*   *t-ánkwà-ànì*   [***n-úrùná-ŋ***]
CONN.N-COP   INF-go.round-DETR   CONN.N-IPFV.watch-TR
úuní   *kànáày*]
footprint   POSS.3PL
'She goes round, watching their footprints.' (Reh 1985: 333)

Forms that combine the function of predicate of a relative clause with that of predicate of a complement clause are especially common. Van Lier (2009: 209–210) provides an example from Turkish, but this combination is attested in other languages of the proposed Altaic family as well, for example in Nanai, compare the relative clause in (12a) and the complement clause in (12b), which both have one and the same *-xə(m)-* form as a predicate. This last pattern is so common that it deserves to be discussed separately; see Section 2.4 of the present chapter.

(12) Nanai (Tungusic)
    a. [*si*   ***niru-xə-si***]   *daŋsa-wa*   *mi*   *xola-xam-bi*
       2SG write-PTCP.PST-POSS.2SG   book-ACC   1SG read-PTCP.PST-POSS.1SG
       'I have read a book that you had written.'
    b. [*si*   *daŋsa-wa*   ***niru-xəm-bə-si***]   *mi*   *xola-xam-bi*
       2SG book-ACC   write-PTCP.PST-ACC-POSS.2SG   1SG read-PTCP.PST-POSS.1SG
       'I have read that you had written a book.'

Taking such multifunctionality into account, it is not at all surprising that the term "participle" got reinterpreted as referring to virtually any non-finite verb form that can be used in at least some of the functional syntactic slots discussed above. This especially concerns the forms that are used for adverbial modification, presumably because due to the lack of such specialized forms in Latin or Classical Greek, the Eurocentric linguistic tradition did not provide a separate term for this notion (see Haspelmath 1995: 2 for this observation and König and van der Auwera 1990 for an overview of "adverbial participles" in European languages). The latter fact is reflected, for example, in the use of the term "participle" to refer to non-finite adverbial modifiers in many Australian languages (see Cook 1987: 232–267 for Wagiman, Furby and Furby 1977: 87–93 for Garrwa, Birk 1976: 129–131 for Malakmalak, and many later works), as well as in many other languages (see the term "processual participle" in the grammar of Eastern Armenian by Dum-Tragut 2009: 205–206).

Even if there are typological extensions, however, adjective-like functions are always present in participles. So would it be an option to disregard these extensions and simply take adjective-like behaviour as the basis for a definition, that is, to define participle as a non-finite verb form that behaves like adjectives in a particular language? This approach appears to be used by Haspelmath (1994) in a paper on passive participles, although it is not expressed overtly. However, it turns out that formulating a definition of participles based on the concept of adjective is equally problematic, as shown in what follows.

First, it is not uncommon that verb forms used for adnominal modification, which clearly correspond to prototypical participles in the languages that have them, may demonstrate certain (minor) differences from adjectives in a given language. For instance, in Hup, relative clauses with non-finite predicates always precede the modified noun, while adjectives follow it (see Epps 2008: 828); compare (13a) and (13b) (modified nouns are underlined):

(13) Hup (Nadahup)
   a. *yúp*   [*hɨd*   **key-ʔĕ-p**]   <u>hɔhɔ́h=b'ay</u>, *ham-yiʔ*   *ní-ay-áh*
       that.ITG   3PL   see-PFV-DEP   toad=REP   go-TEL   be-INCH-DEC
       'That toad they were looking at, (it) went away.'
       (Epps 2008: 829)
   b. *hɨd*   <u>nɔg'od</u> *j'á*   *pæm-hi-ham-tég*
       3PL   mouth black   sit-descend-go-FUT
       'They'll all be sitting around with black mouths (from eating coca).'
       (Epps 2008: 326)

In addition, as explicitly stated in Haspelmath (1994: 152), a definition of participles referring to adjectives can obviously only work for those languages that have adjectives as a primary word class. This approach, thus, would rule out all languages that resort to non-lexical strategies for expressing adnominal modification, i.e. mainly languages where functional equivalents of adjectives are a subclass of verbs, or verb-like adjectives (see Dixon 2004a). An example of such language is Lakhota, where they are a subset of stative verbs (Van Valin 1977: 41). Consequently, the most common way to modify a noun is by a stative verb in the same form as found when heading an independent sentence; see (14):

(14) Lakhota (Siouan)
   a. **kha'ta**
       hot
       'he is hot' (Van Valin 1977: 9)
   b. *mni'*   **kha'ta**   *el*   *owa'gnáka*   *cha*   *nable'che*
       water   hot   into   I.put   and.so   it.breaks
       'I put it in hot water, and so it broke.' (Van Valin 1977: 23)

Nevertheless, if we have a closer look at languages with verb-like adjectives, we will see that excluding them would imply overlooking a significant number of forms that show striking similarities with forms that are incontrovertibly classified as participles in other languages. Let us consider forms of this kind in three languages without primary adjectives from different parts of the world, namely Garo (15), Seri (16), and West Greenlandic (17). In the examples below, sentences in (a) illustrate regular independent clauses in each language, while constructions in (b) are deranked relative clauses modifying nouns:

(15) Garo (Sino-Tibetan)
    a. *Me·chik   skang-o   rua-cha a·bol-ko   den·-a-ming.*
       women   previously-LOC axe-INS firewood-ACC cut-NEUT-PST
       'Women previously chopped the firewood with an axe.'
       (Burling 2004: 299)
    b. [*me·chik-ni skang-o   rua-cha **den·-gipa**] a·bol*
       women-GEN previously-LOC axe-INS cut-NMZ   firewood
       'firewood that the women previously cut with an axe'
       (Burling 2004: 299)
(16) Seri (Seri)
    a. *Hapxa   quij   ih-mii-ho.*
       cottontail the.CM 1SG.SUBJ.TR-PROX-see
       'I saw the cottontail rabbit.' (Marlett 2012: 215)
    b. [*hapxa   **h-oco-ho**]   quij*
       cottontail 1.POSS-NMZ.OBJ-see the.CM
       'the cottontail rabbit that I saw' (Marlett 2012: 215)
(17) West Greenlandic (Eskimo-Aleut)
    a. *Ippassaq   angut   naapip-para.*
       yesterday   man   meet-1SG.SUBJ.3SG.OBJ.IND
       'Yesterday I met the man.' (van der Voort 1991: 20)
    c. *angut   [ippassaq   **naapi-ta-ra**]*
       man.ABS.SG yesterday   meet-PTCP.PASS-POSS.1SG.ABS.SG
       'the man I met yesterday' (van der Voort 1991: 20)

As can be seen from these examples, the forms functioning as predicates in relative clauses (in bold) clearly differ from independent clause predicates in their morphology and syntax. First, all of them have special subordinating morphemes marked as NMZ 'nominalization' (Garo), NMZ.OBJ 'object nominalization' (Seri), or PTCP.PASS 'passive participle' (West Greenlandic). Second, they do not allow certain affixes characteristic of finite verb forms, such as tense markers (Garo), or markers referring to the core participants (Seri, West Greenlandic). Finally, all of these forms differ from finite verbs in the corresponding languages in their subject encoding. In all cases, subjects are expressed as possessors, which can be seen from the genitive case marking on the word *me·chik-ni* 'women-GEN' in the Garo examples, and from the possessive affixes on the relative clause predicates in Seri and West Greenlandic. In addition to that, the non-finite predicate of the relative clause in West Greenlandic shows agreement with the modified noun in case and number (ABS.SG 'absolutive singular'). All of these features bring the forms in question very close to participles in languages where adjectives and participles are clearly distinct from other word classes. For example, in Finnish, the so-called "agentive participle" used for direct object relativization also has its own segmental marker *-ma*, lacks the possibility to express tense, and encodes the agent as a possessor. Moreover, exactly like the *-ta-* form in West Greenlandic, it agrees with the modified noun in case and number, as shown in the translation of the West Greenlandic construction into Finnish in (18):

(18) Finnish (Uralic)
[*eilen* **tapaa-ma-ni**] *mies*
yesterday meet-PTCP.A.NOM.SG-POSS.1SG man.NOM.SG
'the man I met yesterday'

In fact, predicates of relative clauses in West Greenlandic are of particular interest for the typological study of participles. The reason is that they are only used in headed (and only marginally headless; see van der Voort 1991: 33) relative clauses, hence adnominal modification is their primary syntactic function. In many other languages with the same word class pattern, relative clause predicates are also widely used in headless relative clauses and complement clauses, so it is possible to simply classify them as lexical or clausal nominalizations (although in Section 2.4 I will argue that this should not prevent regarding them as genuine participles in a typological study). By contrast, non-finite adnominal modifiers in West Greenlandic are participles in their own right, so the comparative definition of participle should be formulated so that they would be included in the scope of investigation.

2.3 Participle as a comparative concept

Taking into account the diversity outlined in the previous section, it is most reasonable for a typological study to formulate a comparative concept of participle in the sense of Haspelmath (2010). Since the primary goal of such comparative concepts is to allow for cross-linguistic comparison, it does not have to be psychologically real, and it does not have to correspond to any language-particular categories. Nevertheless, the ultimate goal is to study a cross-linguistic category whose members are similar enough to warrant a scholarly comparison. For this purpose, I apply the method introduced in Rijkhoff (2016), which requires that defining a category starts with functional criteria, since they have the widest cross-linguistic applicability, and then uses formal and semantic restrictions to ensure that the items included in the scope of investigation form a cross-linguistically meaningful morphosyntactic category.

The typological definition of participle introduced in this study is based on three comparative concepts that are consistently identifiable from a cross-linguistic perspective, namely the concepts of *relative clause*, *verb form* and *deranking*. The first concept, relative clause, is primarily defined functionally, while the other two, verb form and deranking, are based on formal criteria. The three concepts will be discussed separately in the following sections.

2.3.1 Relative clause

As has already been mentioned above, the prototypical syntactic function of participles is that of adnominal modification. Since a participle is verbal in nature, it can obviously serve as a predicate of a verbal clause. Therefore, it seems reasonable to base the comparative concept of participle on the type of clauses for which the function of adnominal modification is a defining feature, i.e. relative clauses (RCs). The definition of relative clause adopted in this study is very straightforward, and based on the one provided by Lehmann (1986: 664). The relative construction is understood here as a construction consisting of a nominal (head) and a subordinate clause interpreted as attributively modifying the nominal (relative clause). However, since the definition is so concise, several very important clarifications will be made in the following subsections. In subsection (a), I show that it is reasonable to take into account both restrictive and non-restrictive relative clauses. Subsection (b) explains why the ability to introduce headed relative clauses is crucial for the definition of participles. Subsections (c) and (d) clarify the requirements for the participle to be the locus of subordination marking and to act as a general means of relative clause formation.

a) Restrictive and non-restrictive relative clauses

It is fairly common among typologists to define relative clauses in a more semantic way, consider definitions in (19) and (20) below:

(19) We consider any syntactic object to be an RC if it specifies a set of objects (perhaps a one-member set) in two steps: a larger set is specified, called the domain of relativization, and then restricted to some subset of which a certain sentence, the restricting sentence, is true. (Keenan and Comrie 1977: 63–64)
(20) A relative clause (RC) is a subordinate clause which delimits the reference of an NP by specifying the role of the referent of that NP in the situation described by the RC. (Andrews 2007: 206)

The reason why I prefer not to use such definitions is because they narrow the scope down to *restrictive* (or defining) relative clauses, thus excluding *non-restrictive* (or non-defining/appositive) ones. In the latter type, the subordinate clause does not delimit the reference of the noun phrase, but rather provides the listener with additional information about the referent. At the same time, the distinction between restrictive and non-restrictive relative clauses appears to be of some relevance for the distribution of participial relative clauses. For instance, Lehmann (1984: 270–280) formulated a typological prediction that if a language has two relativization strategies one of which is prenominal and participial and the other one is postnominal and finite, the participial strategy will be mostly used for restrictive relative clauses. The proposed explanation is based on the fact that the semantic integration associated with referent identification is parallel to syntactic integration into the noun phrase due to nominalization, which is characteristic of participial relative clauses. This claim, however, has not been tested on a representative sample of languages, and the illustrative example from Turkish provided by Lehmann (1984: 278) has been criticized by Haig (1998: 126–128), so Lehmann's hypothesis clearly requires further investigation. In my sample, I did not find any direct counterexamples to Lehmann's hypothesis, i.e. a participial strategy that would mostly be used for non-restrictive relative clauses, let alone limited to those. However, Marathi is remarkable in this sense, because in this language, sentential relative clauses (using a correlative strategy; see Pandharipande 1997: 76–80) are usually restrictive, while participial relative clause can be both restrictive (or ambiguous) and non-restrictive, compare (21a) and (21b):

(21) Marathi (Indo-European)
    a. [*paḷūn* **gelelā**] *mulgā sāpḍlā*
       run.PTCP.CONJ go.PTCP.PFV.SG.M boy find(INTR).PST.3SG.M
       'The boy who had run away was found.'
       (Pandharipande 1997: 80)
    b. [*nāgpurlā* **rāhṇārā**] *mādzhā bhāū dilip*
       Nagpur.ACC live.PRS.PTCP.REL.3SG.M I.POSS.SG.M brother Dilip
      wakil āhe
       lawyer is
       'My brother Dilip, who lives in Nagpur, is a lawyer.'
       (Pandharipande 1997: 81)

In general, the information on this matter is, unfortunately, extremely limited, and is usually only available for the most thoroughly documented languages. In most cases, the lack of information in descriptions is probably due to the fact that the language makes no morphosyntactic distinction between the two constructions (though it can be intonational; see Comrie 1981: 139), but it is also commonly the case that authors only take restrictive relative clauses into account. Nevertheless, there seems to be no need to exclude non-restrictive relative clauses in general. Therefore, the comparative concept of relative clause used here as a basis for the concept of participle includes both restrictive and non-restrictive relative clauses, and both of these will be considered in this study.

b) Headed and headless relative clauses

Another clarification concerns headless (or free) relative clauses, i.e. constructions that lack a head nominal. An example of such a construction from Hup is given in (22a). Commonly, syntactic typologies only recognize a binary distinction between headed and headless relatives, but it has been recently shown by Epps (2012) that the ability of relative clauses to appear with or without a head nominal can be best understood as a continuum, based on the degree to which the element appearing in the role of the modified nominal can be understood as a lexical or a grammatical entity. For instance, apart from headless (22a) and headed relative clauses (22b), Hup also has several intermediate constructions exhibiting varying degrees of grammaticalization of the head nominal. One of such constructions, a relative clause with a bound noun =*teg* 'tree' cliticized to the dependent verb form, is given in (22c):

(22) Hup (Nadahup)
    a. tih   tɔhɔ-yɨ́ʔ-ay=mah,   [tinɨ̌h   hǔ   ni-ʔĕ-p],   [húp
       3SG   finish-TEL-INCH=REP   3SG.POSS   animal   be-PFV-DEP   person
       nɨ̌h   hǔ   ni-ʔĕ-p]
       POSS   animal   be-PFV-DEP
       'It was all gone, that which had been his game animal, that which had been the person's game animal.' (Epps 2012: 195)
    b. ʔã́h=yiʔ   [ʔám=tœ̆hʔĭn   tih   ní-ĭp]   **hayám-ăn**   kéy-éh
       1SG=FOC   2SG=wife   3SG   be-DEP   village-OBJ   see-DEC
       'I have seen the village [that your wife is living in]!' (Epps 2012: 195)
    c. [ʔin   wǽd-œp]=**teg**   ʔám   b'ɔt-yɨ́ʔ-ɨy!
       1PL   eat-DEP=tree   2SG   chop.down-TEL-DYN
       'You've chopped down the tree we eat from!' (Epps 2012: 198)

This phenomenon of gradual "headedness", as noted by Epps (2012: 210), is likely to be relevant for languages that use nominalization as a relativization strategy, as is the occurrence of headless relative clauses in general. Indeed, if a predicate of a relative clause exhibits some features of a noun, it is expected that it will be able to function as a participant of the main clause on its own or by attaching some minor grammatical material. The problem that arises in such languages is to distinguish between headless relative clauses and various kinds of participant nominalizations, such as, for example, agent nominalization, patient nominalization, or locative nominalization (see Section 2.4 below). Since many languages with deranked relative clauses belong to this type, in the present study I will only consider the forms that can introduce headed relative constructions of the type illustrated in (22b), in which the head is explicitly expressed by a full nominal element. This excludes participant nominalizations that cannot co-occur with a head noun, such as agentive nominalizations in Mongsen Ao (-əɹ), Dongwang Tibetan (-nə), or Zhuokeji rGyalrong (-kə); see Genetti et al. (2008: 108–113). I also did not include some forms that are labelled as relative clause predicates, but without an explicit statement that they can introduce headed relative clauses or language data to support this label. An example of such forms are nominalizations in Apalaí (Cariban, Koehn and Koehn 1986). As a result, in this study, Apalaí is listed among the languages that presumably have participles, but more data is needed to confirm it; see Appendix 1b.

As long as the relative clause is headed, it does not matter whether the head noun occurs within the main clause (the relative clause in this case is referred to as *externally headed*), or within the relative clause itself (the relative clause is then labelled *internally headed*). An illustration of both types of constructions can be taken from Imbabura Quechua, where a deranked relative clause can have either external head (23a), or internal head (23b):

(23) Imbabura Quechua (Quechuan)
    a. [Juzi ri-ju-j] **llajta**
       José go-PROG-NMZ.PRS town
       'the town José is going to'
       (Cole 1985: 54)
    b. [Juzi **llajta-man** ri-ju-shka]-ka maymi karu-mi ka-rka
       José town-to go-PROG-NMZ.PST-TOP very big-VLD be-PST.3
       'The town José was going to was very big.'
       (Cole 1985: 55)

It should be noted that internally headed relative clauses are in general a fairly rare phenomenon (according to Dryer 2013b, only 24 languages in the sample of 824 employ them as primary relativization strategy). When it comes to participial relative clauses, they may be even more restricted. In the core sample of 100 languages examined for the current study, I have not found a single language where internally headed participial relative clauses are the primary strategy. In the languages that allow them at all, they tend to be subject to various semantic restrictions, or they simply appear to be less frequent than other types of participial constructions (see, for instance, Genetti et al. 2008: 128 on Tibeto-Burman languages).

On a final note, as regards the relationship between the modifying clause and the head noun, I make no distinction here between relative clauses in a strict sense, which are only employed to relativize arguments and adjuncts, and *general noun-modifying clause constructions*, or GNMCC, in which the relationship between the modified noun and the clause is different; see Matsumoto, Comrie, and Sells (2017). For instance, many Eurasian languages belonging to the sample, such as Hinuq, Korean or Tundra Nenets, use the same type of deranked clauses to form both relative clauses and 'smell of' or 'fact S' constructions. The verb forms featuring in these constructions are naturally regarded as participles.

c) Participle as the locus of subordination marking

The third important specification is that I will only take into consideration forms that can by themselves signal relative clause status. What is implied here is that I do not regard as participles non-finite predicates that require other markers of subordination to let the clause function as an adnominal modifier. An example of the latter case comes from the Miya language, where relative clauses with non-finite predicates are obligatorily introduced by clause-initial relativizers agreeing in gender with the modified noun; see (24):

(24) Miya (West Chadic)
    mbə̀rgu   [*bá*   *pəráw*]
    ram   REL.M   slaughtered.NF
    'a slaughtered ram' (Schuh 1998: 111)

It should be noted though, that constructions of this kind can develop into genuine participial relative clauses, as it apparently happened in Armenian. According to Hewitt (1978), relative clauses of the type illustrated in (25), where a nonfinite form co-occurs with the relative clause marker *or*, represent the transitional structure between fully finite relative clauses attested on earlier stages, which combined the relative clause marker with a participle accompanied by an auxiliary verb, and prenominal participial relative clauses employed in modern variants of Armenian; see (26):

(25) Classical Armenian (Indo-European)
    es   *em*   *haçn*   *kendani*   [*or*   *jerkniç*   **idž-eal**]
    I   am   bread.the living which from.heaven descend-PTCP
    'I am the living bread which has descended from heaven.'
    (Thomson 1975: 71, as cited in Hewitt 1978: 128)
(26) Modern Eastern Armenian (Indo-European)
    Sa   [*lav*   **kardac'-oł**]   *ašakert-n*   *ē.*
    DEM   well   read-PTCP.SUBJ   pupil.NOM-the   it.is
    'This is the pupil who reads well.'
    (Dum-Tragut 2009: 211)

The languages excluded from this study by this specification are not numerous, however: as predicted by Andrews (2007: 208–209), relative clauses that demonstrate at least some degree of nominalization (which is characteristic of participial relative clauses; see Chapters 4–6), tend to employ no relative pronouns or complementizers whatsoever.

    This part of the definition appears to be slightly problematic in the case of Austronesian languages. In many of them, nominal modifiers, such as deictic elements, quantifiers, adjectives and relative clauses, are commonly connected to the head noun by special particles, or ligatures (Foley 1980: 171); see examples in (27) from Palauan, where the ligature *el/'l* is given in bold:

(27) Palauan (Austronesian)
    a. *tirikey*   *'l*   *ʔekebil*
        those   LIG   girl
        'those girls' (Foley 1976: 15)
    b. *betok*   *el*   *ʔad*
        many   LIG   man
        'many men' (Foley 1976: 15)
    c. *a*   *odelekelek*   *el*   *bil-ek*
        ART   black   LIG   clothes-POSS.1SG
        'my black clothes' (Foley 1976: 16)
    d. *a*   [*mley*   *ʔelʔang*]   *el*   *ʔad*
        ART   came   today   LIG   man
        'the man who came today' (Foley 1976: 16)

If in the definition of participle we adhere to the requirement that the participial form has to be the main locus of subordination, we cannot include any verb forms that have to be accompanied by a ligature, because it is at least partly the ligature that performs the subordinating function. On the other hand, if the ligature has to be used with any modifier of a noun, this restriction does not make much sense. Fortunately, in a thorough study of the Austronesian noun phrase structure, Foley (1976) mentions only one language that uses ligature with participles, namely Palauan, examples from which were given above. Moreover, it is not at all clear from Foley's analysis whether the forms that he regards as participles do indeed have any clear differences from independent clause predicates. The reference grammar of Palauan by Josephs (1975) does not mention any participial forms at all. Therefore, I do not consider Palauan in this study.

In the only other Austronesian language with participles mentioned by Foley (1976), namely Wolio, the use of ligature is actually one of the differences between deranked and balanced relative clauses. Relative clauses introduced by participles do not require a linking particle, as shown in (28a), while for finite relative clauses its use is obligatory; cf. (28b). Apart from that, participles have special prefixes, which finite verbs do not have, and do not take prefixes for concord with the agents:

(28) Wolio (Austronesian)
    a. *rampe*   [*i-tau-na*   *mawa*]
        flotsam   PTCP.PASS-carry-3SG   flood
        'flotsam carried down by the flood'
        (Anceaux 1952: 41, as cited in Foley 1980: 192)

b. *wakutuu* **na** [*a-umba-mo*]
　　time　　LIG　3SG-come-DEF
　　'the time he came'
　　(Anceaux 1952: 41, as cited in Foley 1980: 192)

Another language group for which postulating a class of participles is problematic are Abkhaz-Adyge languages. In traditional grammars of these languages, relative clause predicates are usually referred to as participles; see an overview and further references in Lander (2012: 61–65). Indeed, these predicates do show certain morphosyntactic differences from the predicates of independent sentences, especially in Abkhaz, which basically has a separate set of non-finite forms (see Hewitt 1979: 201–208). However, an important aspect of relative clause formation in Abkhaz and Adyghe is replacing the pronominal element corresponding to the relativized participant by the appropriate relative marker; compare (29a) and (29b):

(29) Abkhaz (Abkhaz-Adyge)
　a. *a-xàc'a*　　*a-pħ°əs*　　*a-š°q°'ə*　　*(Ø-)là-y-te-yt'*
　　　DEF-man　　DEF-woman　　DEF-book　　it-she.IO-he-give-FIN
　　　'The man gave the book to the woman.'
　　　(Hewitt 1979: 36)
　b. [*a-xàc'a*　　*a-š°q°'ə*　　*(Ø-)zə-y-tà(-z)*]　　*a-pħ°əs*
　　　DEF-man　　DEF-book　　it-REL.IO-he-give-NF　　DEF-woman
　　　də-z-dàr-we-yt'
　　　her-I-know-DYN-FIN
　　　'I know the woman to whom the man gave the book.'
　　　(Hewitt 1979: 36)

Functionally, such relative markers are equivalent to relative pronouns in European languages (e.g. English *which* or Russian *kotoryj*); see Lander (2012: 194–195). Since Abkhaz-Adyge languages are polysynthetic, these markers are incorporated in the verbal complex and thus belong to morphology rather than syntax. However, these affixes occupy the slots that are clearly meant for participant expression, which means that they cannot themselves be regarded as markers of specialized participial forms in the verbal paradigm (see also Lander 2012: 119–120, 187–188 on the problems with the notion of paradigm in Adyghe as a polysynthetic language). Based on this, I regard relative affixes here as additional markers required for signaling the relative relation and, therefore I exclude respective forms in Abkhaz-Adyge languages from the sample.

d) Participles as a general means of forming relative clauses

Finally, participles as predicates of relative clauses should be general, that is, they should not themselves bring in any additional meaning to the construction. This requirement implies that I do not consider infinitival relative clauses, even though they are instances of non-finite adnominal modifiers. As shown in Haspelmath (1989), infinitives as a word class are closely related to purposive constructions. Arguably, this connection is also present in constructions where infinitives are used for adnominal modification; see examples in (30) from English:

(30) English (Indo-European)
  a. *He bought this book **to read** it in the train.*
     (Infinitival purpose construction)
  b. *He bought a book [**to read** in the train].*
     (Infinitival relative clause)

Lehmann (1984: 157–159) noted a general lack of knowledge about infinitival relative clauses, with the exception of English and Italian, and even after 35 years this statement is still true to a large extent. Constructions of this type are, however, attested in a number of typologically and geographically diverse languages; see examples (31a) and (31b) from Ingush (example (31c) representing a participial relative clause is given for comparison), and examples (32a) and (32b) for Tamil:

(31) Ingush (Nakh-Daghestanian)
  a. *Aaz   cynna   [**diesha**]   kinashjka   iicar*
     1SG.ERG   3SG.DAT   D.read.INF   book   bought
     'I bought him a book to read.'
     (Nichols 2011: 594)
  b. [***mala***]   *xii*
     drink.INF   water
     'water to drink'
     (Nichols 2011: 594)
  c. [***mola***]   *xii*
     drink.PTCP.PRS   water
     'drinking water, water that is drunk, water that people drink'
     (Nichols 2011: 594)

(32) Tamil (Dravidian)
   a. [*naaval* **paṭi·kk-a**] neeram kumaar-ukku ippootu kiṭai-tt-atu
      novel read-INF time Kumar-DAT now get-PST-3SG.N
      'Now Kumar has got time to read novels.'
      (Lehmann 1993: 262)
   b. [**kuṭiyiru·kk-a**] vacati·y-aaṉa viiṭu aṅkee iru-kkir̠-atu
      live-INF comfort-ADJR house there be-PRS-3SG.N
      'There are comfortable houses to live in.'
      (Lehmann 1993: 262)

As can be seen from these examples, infinitival relative clauses, in addition to modifying the noun, convey the meaning of purpose. This is a significant augmentation in semantics that considerably restricts the number of contexts in which the use of such relative clauses is possible. Therefore, infinitival relative clauses do not fall into the scope of this study and will further be disregarded. Importantly, these constructions are usually described separately from other non-finite relative clauses in grammars, which facilitates their identification in the languages of the sample.

To summarize the relationship between participles and relative clauses as comparative concepts, in the present study the label "participle" will only be used to refer to forms that can introduce headed relative clauses (both restrictive and non-restrictive) without any semantic restrictions, and do not require any additional marking, such as relative pronouns or complementizers. In general, the notion of relative clause is largely equivalent to adnominal modification using clauses, but there are two substantial reasons why I use the concept "relative clause". First, the domain of relativization is relatively well studied cross-linguistically, which also means that the terminology is fairly established and abundant. Therefore, it is convenient to describe participles using the existing set of terms, and taking into account the recognized distinctions. Second, stating that a participle can function as a predicate of a clause, though deranked, emphasizes its verbal properties and the ability to have verbal valency in spite of deranking.[6]

---

[6] In this study, preserving verbal valency is not considered as a defining feature for participles, since deranked relative clause predicates can block the expression of various dependents for a number of reasons, which are further discussed in Chapter 6. Nevertheless, failing to preserve it appears to be a good diagnostic criterion for lexicalized units, which should rather be regarded as verbal adjectives; see criterion (b) in the next section.

2.3.2 Verb form

Defining participles as verb forms implies that they have to belong to a verbal paradigm. This statement, in turn, implies two things. First, the marker of participial status has to function on the verbal rather than the clausal level, which in most cases means distinguishing a subordinating participial affix from a subordinating conjunction. On the other hand, participles as an inflectional form have to be distinguished from derivational verbal adjectives and in some cases also from verbal nouns, hence we need to differentiate between inflection and derivation in general. Both distinctions are notoriously hard to formulate from a theoretical point of view. There are, however, several operational criteria that can be used in a cross-linguistic study like this one to make decisions regarding what should and what should not be taken into account. These are discussed in subsections (a) and (b) below.

a) Verbal level vs. clausal level

As mentioned above, in the present study, the contrast between verbal level and clausal level is primarily relevant in order to distinguish between subordinating participial affixes affecting the categorical status of the relative clause predicate, and subordinating conjunctions functioning at the level of the clause as a whole. Generally, these two ways of encoding relativization are easy to distinguish, since relative pronouns and complementizers tend to occupy clause-initial position, and they are rarely obligatorily in contact with the relative clause predicate. However, making this distinction can be problematic in cases where the conjunction is attached to the predicate of the relative clause and looks like it pertains to the verb, while in fact it functions on the level of clause as a whole, just like a freestanding subordinating conjunction (see Cristofaro 2003: 58). This issue is discussed in detail in Fischer and van Lier (2011) in connection with different types of subordinate clauses in Cofán. It is shown by the authors that the two relative clause markers attested in Cofán, ='*cho* and -'*su*, differ in their morphosyntactic status, although they seem to occur in similar positions. The element ='*cho* is a subordinating conjunction, but it always appears cliticized to the relative clause predicate because it attaches to the last element of its host constituent, and subordinate clauses are obligatorily predicate-final; see (33a). The marker -'*su*, on the other hand, is a suffix forming a non-finite verb form that can be used for adnominal modification, as illustrated in (33b). The differences between the two forms with regard to their status are twofold. First, ='*cho* clauses can be marked for all verbal categories (although, as it can be seen from (33c), none of them are obligatory in Cofán, so it is not unusual for ='*cho* to attach to a bare verb stem). By contrast, in -'su clauses none of the verbal inflectional categories expressed in independent clauses can be expressed. Second, ='cho fulfills the phonological criteria for clitichood in Cofán (in particular, it does not alter the stress of its host word), while -'su in this respect is rather a suffix.

(33) Cofán (Cofán)
    a. [yori-'ye   [ke'i   su-je]=**'cho**=ja]
       Yori-NOMPST you.all say-IPFV=SR=DEF
       'the late Yori you are talking about'
       (Fischer and van Lier 2011: 236)
    b. [ingi=ma atesian-**'su**] pushe'su
       we=ACC   teach-PTCP woman
       'the woman that teaches us' (=our teacher)
       (Fischer and van Lier 2011: 242)
    c. [[ke kanse]=**'cho** ande]=nga=tsu napi-ya
       you live=SR   land=DAT=DISC.3 arrive-IRR
       '(It) will reach the country you live in.'
       (Fischer and van Lier 2011: 235)

One of the main problems in identifying participles is, therefore, distinguishing between morphological and syntactic expression (affix vs. conjunction). As shown in Haspelmath (2011b), it is not always possible to draw the border between the two in a coherent way across languages, since none of the criteria that have been employed by linguists so far are uniformly applicable across contexts and languages (and where they are applicable, they do not always converge). For this reason, in the current study I prefer to keep the distinction language specific, stating that in order to qualify as a participial marker, an affix has to fulfill the basic criteria for being an affix in this particular language (in this case, I rely on the analysis provided by the authors of language descriptions). Non-affixal ways of forming participles, which are much less common, are discussed towards the end of this subsection.

Formal means that languages can use to form participles are fairly diverse. While most languages that are known to have participles are predominantly or strictly suffixing (e.g. Indo-European, Uralic, Turkic, Mongolic, Tungusic, or Dravidian), there are also languages in which participial markers belong to other positional types of affixes. For example, prefixal participial forms are attested in Georgian (34), Tariana (35), and Santiam Kalapuya (36), whereas Muna exhibits, among other options, circumfixal marking in deranked relative clauses (37):

(34) Georgian (Kartvelian)
[bavšv-is-tvis   pul-is   **mi-m-c-em-i**]   kal-i
child-GEN-for   money-GEN   PREV-PTCP.ACT-give-TS-AGR   woman-NOM
'the woman giving money to the child'
(Hewitt 1995: 540)

(35) Tariana (Arawakan)
[diha   hiwaru-pukwi   **ka-de**]   kuphe-nuku   di-ka
ART   gold-CL:HOLLOW   REL-have   fish-TOP.NS   3SG.NONF-see
di-anhi-pidana
3SG.NONF-know-REM.RPTD
'(The cat) recognized the fish who had the golden ring.'
(Aikhenvald 2003: 542)

(36) Santiam Kalapuya (Kalapuyan)
lauʔmdɛ guš   an-ʔuihi   [**gi·-ʔwai-ni**]   guš   aʔ-waiʔwa]
then   DIST   ART-man   INF-lie-3.OBJ   DIST   ART-woman
d-ɛ-m-wu·ʔ-yωʔ-q
HAB-IRR-FIN-get-INCH-PASS
'And then the man who had had sexual intercourse with the woman was fetched.' (Banks 2007: 50)

(37) Muna (Austronesian)
ana-no   [**mo-saki-no**]   naando   ne-ndo-ndole
child-his   PTCP.ACT-sick-PTCP.ACT   be   3SG.REAL-INT~lie
'His sick child was still lying down.'
(van den Berg 2013: 232)

Moreover, some languages feature forms that can be classified as periphrastic participles, i.e. consisting of a lexical verb in a certain form and a participial form of an auxiliary.[7] For instance, in Nanga, the perfective participial suffix -sè, which normally attaches to lexical verb stems, as in (38a), can also attach to the experiential perfect auxiliary tá:- preceded by the bare stem of the lexical verb, as in (38b):

---

[7] Note that in this case participial marker still functions on the verbal and not clausal level, since the lexical verb stem and the auxiliary containing the participial suffix constitute an analytic verb form.

(38) Nanga (Dogon)
  a. [àrⁿà   bǎ: nɔ̀   ǹnè-sɛ̀   nɛ́]
     man.L   father   3SG.POSS   go-PTCP.PFV.L   DEF.AN.SG
     'the man whose father has gone' (Heath 2008: 287)
  b. [yà: ìsè   gó   ńné   tá:-sɛ̀]
     woman.L village.L   in   go   PRF.EXP-PTCP.PFV
     'a woman who has (ever) gone to the village' (Heath 2008: 273)

Other examples of such forms are attested, for instance, in Krongo (Kadugli-Krongo) and Russian (Indo-European), even though in the latter they are very marginal. In these languages, auxiliaries take participial markers to refer to future events in non-finite relative clauses. In Krongo, the periphrastic future participle consists of a future auxiliary in the participial form and an infinitive of a lexical verb in the locative form, e.g. *ŋ-ákká k-áadìyà* CONN.M-FUT LOC-come.INF 'the one who will come' (Reh 1985: 253). In Russian, it is formed by a participle of the verb *byt'* 'to be' and an infinitive of a lexical verb, e.g. *budu-šč-ij sid-et'* be.FUT-PTCP.PRS-NOM.SG.M sit-INF 'the one who will be sitting' (Krapivina 2009b: 24–25). In both cases, this formation is parallel to the formation of main clause future forms.

Similarly, it does not matter either whether the formation of a participle involves a segmental morpheme or not. For instance, in Margi (Afro-Asiatic, Hoffmann 1963: 160–166), participles[8] are formed by complete or partial reduplication, e.g. *pìdà* 'to lie down' > *pìdàpìdà* 'lying down', *dzə̀gà* 'to puncture' > *dzə̀dzə̀gà* 'punctured'. Reduplication is also employed for the formation of participles in Kharia, as illustrated in (39):

(39) Kharia (Austroasiatic)
  a. [iɲ=te   **yo~yo**]   lebu
     1SG=OBL   see~PTCP   person
     'the person who saw/sees/will see me'
     (Peterson 2011: 413)

---

8 These Margi forms are not included in the sample used for this study, since it is not clear from Hoffmann's grammar if they are inflectional (general and regular; see discussion in subsection (b) below) and can thus be regarded as participles rather than verbal adjectives. According to Hoffmann (1963: 166), participles formed by reduplication are also attested in some languages related to Margi, e.g. Bura, Pabir, Cibak, and Kilba, but I was not able to find sufficient information on them either.

b. [iɲ=aʔ   dura=te   **ruʔ~ruʔ**]   kuɲji
   1sg=GEN door=OBL   open~PTCP   key
   'the key I opened/open/will open the door with'
   (Peterson 2011: 413)

In Kambaata (Afro-Asiatic, Treis 2008: 165–168), affirmative relative verbs are primarily marked by the final accent as opposed to main verbs, in which the accent is always located in a non-final position; compare the independent sentence in (40a) and the relative construction in (40b):

(40) Kambaata (Afro-Asiatic)
    a. *adab-óo*   **xúujj-o-se**
       boy-M.NOM see-3M.PFV-3F.OBJ
       'The boy saw her.' (Treis 2008: 167)
    b. [***xuujj-o-sé***]   *adab-áa*
       see-3M.PFV-3F.OBJ.REL boy-M.ACC
       'the boy who saw her' (Treis 2008: 167)

Similarly, in Tanti Dargwa, the so-called "short attributive forms" segmentally coincide with verb forms heading the corresponding independent clauses, but stress shifts from the stem to the inflection; compare (41a) and (41b):

(41) Tanti Dargwa (Nakh-Daghestanian)
    a. [*murad-li*   **ix-úb**]   *q:arq:a*
       Murad-ERG throw.PFV-PRET[PTCP] stone
       'the stone that Murad threw'
       (Sumbatova and Lander 2014: 215)
    b. *murad-li*   *q:arq:a*   **ix-ub**
       Murad-ERG stone throw.PFV-PRET
       'Murad threw a stone'.
       (Sumbatova and Lander 2014: 215)

Nivkh, instead of a segmental morpheme, developed a morphophonemic rule that affects the modified noun following the relative clause predicate. It is assumed that participial forms in Nivkh used to end in a weak nasal, which was lost in the Amur dialect of Nivkh (Mattissen 2003: 51). Now, this is reflected in regular alternations. For instance, although the basic form of the noun *təf* 'house' begins with a voiceless plosive /t/, it changes into /d/ when preceded by a relative clause, as in (42):

(42) Nivkh (Nivkh)
ətək [t'am **lu**] dəf-toχ vi-ḍ
father shaman sing.PTCP house-DAT go-IND
'Father went into the house where the shaman sang.'
(Nedjalkov and Otaina 2013: 276)

The important thing for the comparative concept in question is, therefore, that the participial status and morphosyntactic deranking of given forms are not manifested exclusively in their distribution or their ability to take certain morphological material (this approach to finiteness, referred to as constructional, will be briefly discussed in Section 2.3.3), but have to be marked with certain formal means. These means, on the other hand, do not necessarily have to be segmental, that is, suprasegmental marking and morphophonemic rules are regarded as valid participial markers.

b) Inflection vs. derivation

As mentioned above, the problem of distinguishing between participles and verbal adjectives or derived verbal nouns boils down to the more basic problem of distinguishing between inflection and derivation. This issue has been discussed in numerous books in typology, and many authors have suggested various criteria relevant for the distinction (Bybee 1985; Plank 1991; Payne 1997, among others). Most linguists, however, tend to agree that instead of a binary contrast, it is more reasonable to think of this as an inflection–derivation continuum (Bybee 1985; Corbett 1987; Plank 1994), or even a multidimensional space (Spencer 2013); see also Haspelmath (1994: 152) where this issue is discussed specifically in relation to participles and verbal adjectives. Nevertheless, if we need to define a range of forms that we are going to regard as participles, we can use some of the criteria proposed in the literature to distinguish them from words formed by means of derivation. In this section, I will only focus on verbal adjectives, since this is the topic that has received most attention in this respect. Deverbal adnominal modifiers that can be classified as nouns are treated in some detail in Section 2.4, and the same criteria as discussed here are relevant for them as well.

It should be noted from the outset that one of the most commonly mentioned criteria in the polemics about the differences between inflection and derivation is that derivational morphemes can change the word class of the stem they attach to, while inflectional morphemes cannot (see Langacker 1972: 75, Scalise 1988: 562, Payne 1997: 25, among others). As should be clear from the discussion above, I do not recognize this property as defining for the distinction. Haspelmath (1996) has convincingly shown that it is reasonable to admit the existence of such thing as word-class-changing inflectional morphology, and participial affixes fit neatly into this type. Apart from an inability to change the word class of the stem, Haspelmath and Sims (2010: 90) propose a list of other properties that can differentiate inflection and derivation. Here is a brief overview of the two commonly recognized properties that appear to be most relevant for the difference between participles and verbal adjectives, and can, therefore, be used as criteria for the distinction:

1) Participles are *general* (i.e. they can be formed from all or almost all verbs in a given language), while verbal adjectives are not. For instance, in Garo, a suffix *-a* can be used to transform a verb into an adnominal modifier, but it is restricted to stative verbs denoting qualities, such as 'to be big', as in example (43a). As shown in (43b), this suffix cannot be used with non-stative verbs, such as 'run'; in order to form an adnominal modifier from such verbs, an alternative fully productive suffix *-gipa*, which can attach to any kind of verbs, has to be used; see (43c) and (43d). The adnominal modifier formed with *-gipa* is thus considered participial, while the *-a* form is considered a verbal adjective.

(43) Garo (Sino-Tibetan)
    a. *Ang-a*   **dal·-a**   *ma·su-ko*   *nik-a.*
        I-NOM   big-ADJR   cow-ACC   see-NEUT
        'I see the big cow.' (Burling 2004: 135)
    b. **Ang-a*   **kat-a**   *ma·su-ko*   *nik-a.*
        I-NOM   run-ADJR   cow-ACC   see-NEUT
        'I see the running cow.' (Burling 2004: 136)
    c. *Ang-a*   [**dal·-gipa**]   *ma·su-ko*   *nik-a.*
        I-NOM   big-NMZ   cow-ACC   see-NEUT
        'I see the cow that is big.' (Burling 2004: 136)
    d. *Ang-a*   [**kat-gipa**]   *ma·su-ko*   *nik-a.*
        I-NOM   run-NMZ   cow-ACC   see-NEUT
        'I see the running cow.' (Burling 2004: 136)

2) Participles are *regular* (i.e. the meaning of participles is derived from the meaning of the corresponding verbal stems in a straightforward way), while verbal adjectives can have idiosyncratic semantic connections with the verbs. This criterion is very important for the category of *pseudoparticiples* introduced by Plungian (2010) for Russian. This label was proposed for the forms that are diachronically participial, but have developed certain morphological, syntactic and/or semantic properties that allow us to classify

them as lexicalized adjectives. For example, possible semantic augmentations of the *-uč-/-ač-* pseudoparticiples include 'the one which is constantly X-ing', e.g. *viset'* 'to hang' – *visjačij* 'the one which is constantly hanging'; 'the one which is constantly X-ing intensively', e.g. *paxnut'* 'smell' – *paxučij* 'the one which constantly has an intensive smell'; 'the one that can X a lot', e.g. *pisat'* 'write' – *pisučij* 'the one that can write a lot', and some others. The meaning introduced to the verb by a prototypical participial affix is usually simpler than those exemplified above, and it is roughly the same for all the verbs, which is clearly not the case for pseudoparticiples in Russian, as well as for other verbal adjectives in the world's languages.

This being said, distinguishing between participles and verbal adjectives can still be problematic, and an individual decision has to be made for every particular language. Therefore, in order not to leave out any forms that might be relevant for this study, when there is little evidence regarding the status of specific forms, I will include them in the analysis.

2.3.3 Deranking

Finally, the comparative concept of participle proposed in this study is based on the opposition between balancing and deranking introduced by Stassen (1985: 76–83), which is commonly used for distinguishing between two types of constructions containing subordinate clauses. In balanced constructions the predicates of both the main and the subordinate clause are structurally the same, while in deranked constructions the predicate of the subordinate clause exhibits structural differences from the main clause predicate; compare examples (1) and (3) discussed in the introductory chapter. Different authors have understood this opposition in slightly different ways (see, for instance, Koptjevskaja-Tamm 1993: 23–24, Cristofaro 2003: 57, and van Lier 2009: 87). In the present study, I adopt van Lier's (2009) version of the distinction, which requires deranked forms in a given language to exhibit certain deviations in their behavioural potential from the prototypical predicate of an independent clause in this language. These deviations can be manifested in restrictions imposed on verbal morphological categories or total loss thereof, acquisition of nominal morphological categories, or change in the encoding of various dependents (all of these features in connection to participial relative clauses will be discussed in detail in Chapters 4–6).

This requirement is meant to exclude the forms that follow the independent clause pattern in subject encoding and have the same or almost the same range of verbal categories as independent clause predicates, but express some of these by means of a special dependent paradigm. For example, Yurok (Algic, Robins 1958: 59–69) has a specialized attributive paradigm, which is used almost exclusively for the formation of headed and headless relative clauses. Attributive forms differ from indicative forms in that they use a special set of affixes for person marking. The distinctions included in the attributive paradigm are, however, exactly the same, and these forms should not, therefore, be regarded as deranked.

Obviously, I also do not consider cases where a relative clause predicate is formed by adding an appropriate affix to a regular finite form. This situation seems to be especially common among the languages of North America, e.g. Ineseño Chumash (Chumashan), where predicates of relative clauses are formed by a prefixal article *ma-/ha-* (Applegate 1972: 204), or Cherokee, which has a specialized affix *ts-* for this purpose, as shown in (44):

(44) Cherokee (Iroquoian)
    a. *U:-li:ye:t-iha.*
        3SG-moan-PRS
        'S/he's moaning.'
        (Lindsey and Scancarelli 1985: 210)
    b. *na   ake:hy   [**ts**-u:-li:ye:t-íha]*
        that   woman REL-3SG-moan-PRS
        'the woman who is moaning'
        (Lindsey and Scancarelli 1985: 211)

It is, however, important to emphasize once again (see the discussion in Section 2.3.2 above) that participles have to be formally distinct from the prototypical predicates of independent sentences. I refer to prototypical predicates of independent sentences here as opposed to the relatively rare cases where morphosyntactically clearly deranked forms function as predicates in independent sentences. As shown by Kalinina (2001), such uses are commonly limited by certain pragmatically marked contexts; see also Evans (2007) and Evans and Watanabe (2016) on the notion of *insubordination*.

The requirement for participles to bear formal marking different from what is found on independent clause predicates is in line with Stassen's (1985: 80) original formulation of the balancing–deranking distinction. This is opposed to a constructional approach to finiteness proposed in Creissels (2009), according to which finiteness is a feature of predicative constructions not necessarily correlated in a simple way with the morphological structure of the verb forms involved.

Creissels illustrates this approach by the pattern of relativization demonstrated by Akhvakh (Nakh-Daghestanian).

In Akhvakh, the perfective form *-ada* can be used both as the predicate of an unmarked relative clause (45a), and as the predicate of an independent sentence (45b). The difference is, however, that in relative clauses it is the only way to express perfective meaning (hence it is glossed here as PTCP.PFV 'perfective participle'),[9] while in independent clauses, *-ada* implies a 1st person A/S argument in declarative clauses and a 2nd person A/S argument in questions (hence it is glossed as PFV.ASSINV 'perfective and assertor's involvement'). If this condition is not met, perfective in independent sentences is marked by the suffix *-ari*; cf. (45c):

(45) Akhvakh (Nakh-Daghestanian)
    a. *di-ƛa   harigw-iƛa   [lãga   r-eχ-ada]   ek'wa*
       1SG.O-DAT   see-PFV.NEG   sheep.PL   N.PL-buy-PTCP.PFV   man
       'I did not see the man who bought sheep.'
       (Creissels 2009: 125)
    b. *de-de   lãga   r-eχ-ada*
       1SG-ERG   sheep.PL   N.PL-buy-PFV.ASSINV
       'I bought sheep.'
       (Creissels 2009: 125)
    c. *ek'wa-ṣw-e   lãga   r-eχ-ari*
       man-O.M-ERG   sheep.PL   N.PL-buy-PFV
       'The man bought sheep.'
       (Creissels 2009: 125)

A very similar situation can be observed in another Nakh-Daghestanian language, Udi, and it is discussed as *unmarked relative subordination* in Lander (2014). This label is used for situations when a relative clause does not have any overt marking of its subordinate status (neither within the predicate nor by means of any other markers), but the construction shows significant structural differences when compared to independent sentences. For example, in Udi, the *-i* form can function as a predicate of both dependent and independent clauses, but it is only in the latter case that it can take subject agreement markers; compare (46a)

---

[9] The verb forms in Udi functioning as predicates of relative clauses are also often referred to as participles; see, for example, Harris (2002), Maisak (2008).

and (46b) below. In addition, unmarked relative clauses in Udi differ from independent clauses in the rigidity of their word order, number of available temporal distinctions, and expression of negation (see Lander 2008 for details).

(46) Udi (Nakh-Daghestanian)
    a. [zu   iz   boš   **arc-i**]   aft:obus
       I   POSS.REFL inside sit-i   bus
      'the bus which I entered'
      (Lander 2008: 60)
    b. šähär-e   **cir-i=z**
      city-DAT go.down-i=1SG
      'In the city I went out (of the car).'
      (Lander 2008: 63)

As Creissels (2009: 128–129) states, a constructional approach to finiteness may result in a situation that requires positing the notion of participial clause (defined in constructional terms) as logically anterior to the notion of participial form. However, in this study, I am primarily interested in the cross-linguistic functioning of forms exhibiting certain morphosyntactic properties rather than in a certain type of clauses. Therefore, I will only take overtly marked deranked verb forms into account, and not unmarked predicates of constructionally defined non-finite clauses, as proposed by Creissels.

2.4 Participles and nominalizations

As already stated in the introduction, in this study a participle is defined as a deranked verb form that can be employed for adnominal modification. However, as has often been noted by typologists, it is very common for non-finite forms that can function as adnominal modifiers to have other syntactic functions as well, especially that of a verbal argument (see Koptjevskaja-Tamm 1993: 42–44, Serdobolskaya and Paperno 2006, Shibatani 2009, among others). In other words, many languages do not distinguish between participles and nominalizations. This fact has been particularly widely discussed for Uralic and Altaic languages; see examples from Komi-Zyrian (47), and Yakut (48), where constructions in (a) illustrate adnominal modification, while examples in (b) show the same form as a predicate of a complement clause:

(47) Komi-Zyrian (Uralic)
    a. [mama-liʃ **vur-əm**] dərəm me koʃal-i.
       mother-GEN2 sew-PTCP.PFV shirt I tear-PST
       'I've torn the shirt mother gave.'
       (Serdobolskaya and Paperno 2006: 1)
    b. [mama-lən dərəm **vur-əm**] menim kaʒitʃʼ-ə.
       mother-GEN1 shirt sew-PTCP.PFV I.DAT like-PRS.3
       'I like the way mother has sewn the shirt.'
       (Serdobolskaya and Paperno 2006: 1)

(48) Yakut (Turkic)
    a. [ikki ojoy-o **öl-büt**] kïrdjayas
       two wife-POSS.3SG die-PTCP.PST old.man
       'the old man whose two wives died'
       (Ubrjatova 1976: 143, as cited in Kalinina 2001: 66)
    b. [Narïja **sïraj-bït-a**] billi-bet-Ø
       Nariya get.tired-PTCP.PST-POSS.3SG not.see-PTCP.PST-3SG
       'It could not be seen that Nariya got tired.'
       (Čeremisina 1995: 222, as cited in Kalinina 2001: 66)

The examples provided above are instances of participle/action (event) nominalization syncretism, but in many languages syncretism of participles and argument (participant) nominalizations is also attested (this type is especially common for instrumental and locative participles/nominalizations; see Section 3.4). Illustrations for this type of situation can be found in Tibeto-Burman languages, where it has been observed many times (see Matisoff 1972, DeLancey 1999, 2002, Genetti et al. 2008, and many others). For instance, in Chantyal, the marker -wa is used to create forms that can be classified as participles (49a), action nominalizations (49b), or argument nominalizations (49c), based on the functions they can perform:

(49) Chantyal (Sino-Tibetan)
    a. [gay-ye sya **ca-si-wa**] mənchi
       cow-GEN meat eat-ANT-NMZ person
       'the person who ate beef'
       (Noonan 1997: 376)
    b. [nɦi-i tɦem-əŋ pali-ri mi **phur-si-wa**] puttə
       we-GEN house-LOC veranda-LOC fire blow-ANT-NMZ smoke+rising

	dḫwãl	**wurə-wa**]	mãra-i		
	smoke	fly-NMZ	see-PFV		

'We saw a fire set and smoke rising on the veranda of our house.'
(Noonan 1997: 375)

c. na-sə   [capa   **ca-wa-ra**]   kwi   pin-ji
   I-ERG   meal   eat-NMZ-DAT   water   give-PFV

'I gave water to the one who was eating'
(Noonan 1997: 379)

Typologists generally approach forms exhibiting participle/nominalization syncretism from two different points of view. The first option is to state that the argument function is primary, and, therefore, they should be treated as nominalizations. In this case, the use of these forms for adnominal modification should be explained as an extension of the primary nominal function. This approach is represented, for instance, in Givón (2012). Comrie and Thompson (2007) propose the following mechanism:

(50) It is not difficult to understand how a nominalization can function as a relative clause: the nominalization and the noun with which it is in construction can be thought of as two juxtaposed nominal elements [nom] [nom], the modifying relationship between them being inferred by the language users (rather than being specified by the grammar, as it is in languages with specific relative clause morphology), just as the modifying relationship is inferred in a noun–noun compound such as *tree-house*, in which the two nominal elements simply happen to be single nouns. (Comrie and Thompson 2007: 378)

The second option is to regard the function of adnominal modification as primary, and thus treat such forms as participles. If we accept this viewpoint, the use of these forms as arguments should be described as involving headless relative clauses. The participle is, therefore, regarded as contextually substantivized, and in this way it acquires the ability to function as an argument. This approach is presented in many traditional descriptions of individual languages (see, for instance, Pengitov 1951 on Mari (Uralic), Sat 1980 on Tuvan (Turkic), and Sunik 1947 on Tungusic languages).

In this study, I prefer not to adopt any of the outlined approaches. If a choice between them had to be made, it would be most reasonable to base it on the primary function of the investigated forms in every particular language. Most descriptive grammars, however, do not provide any information concerning the synchronically primary, or most frequent, function of forms demonstrating participle/nominalization syncretism, or any diachronic evidence based on which the decision concerning their original function could have been made. An additional argument in favour of this decision is that argument clauses and relative clauses introduced by one and the same form are usually identical with respect to their structure and the morphosyntactic properties of their predicate. Therefore, if we simply accept the syncretism and approach the forms in general, in most cases it is possible to use evidence from all kinds of subordinate clauses with these forms. A rare example of an exception is provided by Permic languages, where the subject of a non-finite relative clause predicate can be encoded by either genitive/nominative case or instrumental case, while for complement clauses with the same predicate genitive/nominative is the only option (Serdobolskaya 2005: 23). Some other peculiarities in argument encoding demonstrated by deranked relative clauses in comparison to deranked complement clauses will be further addressed in Chapter 6. Finally, sometimes it is simply impossible to tell apart cases where a participle introduces a relative clause and cases where a participle is a predicate of a complement clause. This is especially common among Australian languages, which typically have multifunctional subordinate clauses (Hale 1976; Nordlinger 2006), like the one in example (51) from Pitta Pitta:[10]

(51) Pitta Pitta (Pama-Nyungan)
  ṉatʸi-ka ŋa-ṭu i-ṉa-ka piyawaḷi-ṉa [patʸa-ka-ṉa ṭakuku-ṉa]
  see-PST I-ERG he-ACC-HERE dog-ACC bite-PST-ACC child-ACC
  'I saw the dog bite the child./I saw the dog that bit the child.'
  (Blake 1979: 217)

In sum, in the current study I will not propose any way of distinguishing between participles and nominalizations, but rather investigate all kinds of relative clauses introduced by either strictly participial forms or forms demonstrating the participle/nominalization syncretism discussed above. All restrictions imposed on prototypical participles that were discussed in previous sections apply to the forms labeled as nominalizations in individual languages.

---

10 In the examples from Pitta Pitta, I have preserved the original glosses used in Blake (1979), where the suffix -*ka*- is glossed as PST 'past tense' regardless of the function it has in a particular context. However, Blake himself notes that the connection of -*ka*- used to introduce dependent clauses and -*ka*- as a past tense marker is a diachronic one (Blake 1979: 219).

2.5 Summary, conclusions, and the core sample

In the present chapter, I have given a brief overview of traditional definitions of participles. I have shown that many of these definitions appear to be extremely broad, which presumably can be explained by the multifunctionality of the forms used for adnominal modification, especially in languages whose description most influenced the European linguistic tradition. I have further shown that narrower definitions, which take the notion of adjective as a starting point, also turn out to be fairly problematic. Although these work perfectly for the languages with primary adjectives, they fail to include some relevant verb forms in languages that lack them, for instance in languages with verb-like adjectives, such as West Greenlandic, Seri, and Garo.

As an alternative, I have proposed to create a comparative concept, which would allow to study the similarities and differences of the forms that are functionally and structurally close to each other in all kinds of typologically diverse languages. The proposed concept of participle is based on the following features of the form:
- the ability to introduce a headed relative clause, while being itself the locus of subordination marking and conveying no additional meaning;
- pertaining to the verbal paradigm, i.e. being formed by morphological rather than syntactic means, and at the same time demonstrating enough regularity and generality to qualify as inflection rather than derivation;
- being deranked, i.e. demonstrating some degree of morphosyntactic deviation from the prototypical predicate of an independent sentence in a given language.

I have further shown that typologically it is extremely common that verb forms used for adnominal modification, i.e. qualifying as participles in this study, also function as arguments, and therefore receive the label "nominalization" in the descriptions of individual languages. I argue that although in an in-depth analysis of a particular language it may be valuable to determine the primary function of the forms demonstrating such syncretism, for a typological study like this one it is more reasonable to consider these forms as participial and hence investigate them together with the other participial forms. However, I do exclude infinitival relative clauses from my study, because of the considerable semantic augmentation typically associated with them.

Table 2 summarizes all of the features relevant for the definition of participles and provides examples of forms taken into account and forms excluded from the sample based on these features.

Tab. 2: Defining features of participles

Features	Examples of included forms	Examples of excluded forms
Relative clause		
– restrictive or non-restrictive	relative participles in Marathi	—
– headed (including GNMCC)	nominalizations in Imbabura Quechua (external or internal head)	agentive nominalizations in -ɤʌ in Mongsen Ao, in -na in Dongwang Tibetan and in -ka in Zhuokeji rGyalrong (headless only)
– locus of subordination marking	participles in Modern Eastern Armenian (no separate relativizer); participles in Wolio (no ligature)	"participles" in Classical Armenian (obligatory clause-initial relativizer); relative clause predicates in Palauan (ligature); relative forms in Abkhaz and Adyghe (additional relative marker)
– no additional meaning	participles in English, Ingush, Tamil, etc. (general means of forming relative clauses)	infinitives in English, Ingush, Tamil, etc. (purposive meaning)
Verb form		
– verbal, not clausal	predicates with marker -'su in Cofán (verbal scope)	predicates with marker ='cho in Cofán (clausal scope)
– formal marking	participles marked by: prefix in Georgian; circumfix in Muna; participial auxiliary in Nanga; reduplication in Kharia; accent in Kambaata; morphophonemic rule in Nivkh	form in -ada in Akhvakh and form in -i in Udi (=independent clause predicates)
– inflectional (general and regular), not derivational	participles in -gipa in Garo (from any verbs); participles in Russian (predictable meaning)	verbal adjectives in -a in Garo (from stative verbs only); pseudoparticiples in Russian (semantic augmentations)
Deranking	discussed in Chapters 5 and 6	Yurok attributive paradigm (same distinctions as in independent clauses); Cherokee RC predicates (affix + finite form)

Using the comparative concept of participle discussed above, we can now draw up the final sample that will be used in this study, containing all the languages that have forms qualifying as participles and for which enough data is available.

This sample is provided in the Table 3 below and represented on the map in Figure 2.

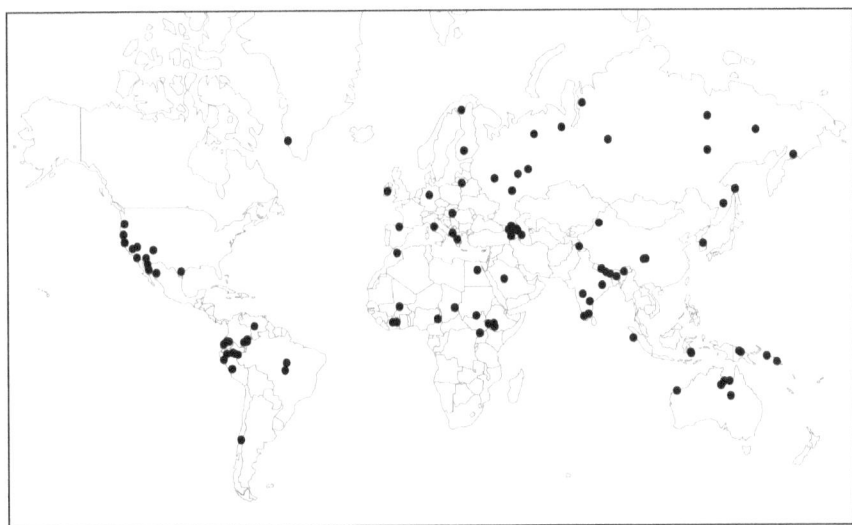

Fig. 2: Languages of the core sample

The languages in the table are organized both geographically (according to macroareas) and genealogically (according to language families and genera). The sources of information on all the languages, as well as the countries where the languages are spoken, are listed in Appendix 1a. The list of languages that have been investigated, but appeared to lack participial forms as defined in the current study is provided in Appendix 1c. The question why some languages have this kind of structures and others do not is very interesting in its own right, but it is outside the scope of the current research.

Tab. 3: Languages of the core sample by genealogical groups and macroareas

Family	Genus	Language
Australia (5)		
Garrwan	Garrwan	Garrwa
Mirndi	Wambayan	Wambaya
Pama-Nyungan	Central Pama-Nyungan	Pitta Pitta

Family	Genus	Language
Pama-Nyungan	Western Pama-Nyungan	Martuthunira
Tangkic	Tangkic	Kayardild
Papunesia (7)		
Austronesian	Celebic	Muna
Austronesian	Celebic	Wolio
Austronesian	Northwest Sumatra-Barrier Islands	Nias
Lower Sepik-Ramu	Lower Sepik	Yimas
Nuclear Trans New Guinea	Madang	Kobon
Savosavo	Savosavo	Savosavo
South Bougainville	East Bougainville	Motuna
North America (13)		
Chimariko	Chimariko	Chimariko
Coahuilteco	Coahuiltecan	Coahuilteco
Cochimi-Yuman	Yuman	Maricopa
Eskimo-Aleut	Eskimo	West Greenlandic
Kalapuyan	Kalapuyan	Santiam Kalapuya
Seri	Seri	Seri
Uto-Aztecan	California Uto-Aztecan	Luiseño
Uto-Aztecan	Hopi	Hopi
Uto-Aztecan	Numic	Tümpisa Shoshone
Uto-Aztecan	Tarahumaran	Guarijío
Uto-Aztecan	Tepiman	Nevome
Yokutsan	Yokuts	Wikchamni
Yuki-Wappo	Wappo	Wappo
South America (16)		
Araucanian	Araucanian	Mapudungun
Arawakan	Inland Northern Arawakan	Tariana
Barbacoan	Barbacoan	Tsafiki
Cariban	Cariban	Panare
Chicham	Jivaroan	Aguaruna
Cofán	Cofán	Cofán
Mochica	Chimúan	Mochica
Nadahup	Nadahup	Hup

Summary, conclusions, and the core sample — 49

Family	Genus	Language
Nuclear-Macro-Je	Ge-Kaingang	Mẽbengokre
Pano-Tacanan	Panoan	Matsés
Quechuan	Quechuan	Imbabura Quechua
Quechuan	Quechuan	Tarma Quechua
Tucanoan	Tucanoan	Barasano
Tupian	Tupí-Guaraní	Cocama
Tupian	Tupí-Guaraní	Kamaiurá
Urarina	Urarina	Urarina
Africa (12)		
Afro-Asiatic	Berber	Rif Berber
Afro-Asiatic	Egyptian-Coptic	Middle Egyptian
Afro-Asiatic	Highland East Cushitic	Kambaata
Atlantic-Congo	Northern Atlantic	Fula
Central Sudanic	Moru-Ma'di	Ma'di
Dizoid	North Omotic	Sheko
Dogon	Dogon	Nanga
Kadugli-Krongo	Kadugli	Krongo
Maban	Maban	Maba
Mande	Eastern Mande	Beng
Mande	Eastern Mande	Wan
Ta-Ne-Omotic	North Omotic	Koorete
Eurasia (47)		
Afro-Asiatic	Semitic	Modern Standard Arabic
Austroasiatic	Munda	Kharia
Basque	Basque	Basque
Burushaski	Burushaski	Burushaski
Chukotko-Kamchatkan	Northern Chukotko-Kamchatkan	Koryak
Dravidian	South-Central Dravidian	Telugu
Dravidian	Southern Dravidian	Malayalam
Dravidian	Southern Dravidian	Tamil
Indo-European	Albanian	Albanian
Indo-European	Armenian	Eastern Armenian
Indo-European	Baltic	Lithuanian
Indo-European	Celtic	Irish
Indo-European	Germanic	German

Family	Genus	Language
Indo-European	Greek	Modern Greek
Indo-European	Indic	Marathi
Indo-European	Iranian	Apsheron Tat
Indo-European	Romance	Italian
Indo-European	Slavic	Russian
Kartvelian	Kartvelian	Georgian
Koreanic	Korean	Korean
Mongolic	Mongolic	Kalmyk
Nakh-Daghestanian	Avar-Andic-Tsezic	Hinuq
Nakh-Daghestanian	Lak-Dargwa	Tanti Dargwa
Nakh-Daghestanian	Lezgic	Lezgian
Nakh-Daghestanian	Nakh	Ingush
Nivkh	Nivkh	Nivkh
Sino-Tibetan	Bodic	Manange
Sino-Tibetan	Bodo-Garo	Garo
Sino-Tibetan	Dhimalic	Dhimal
Sino-Tibetan	Mahakiranti	Dolakha Newar
Sino-Tibetan	Qiangic	Ronghong Qiang
Sino-Tibetan	rGyalrong	Japhug rGyalrong
Sino-Tibetan	Tani	Apatani
Tungusic	Tungusic	Even
Tungusic	Tungusic	Nanai
Turkic	Turkic	Yakut
Uralic	Finnic	Finnish
Uralic	Mari	Meadow Mari
Uralic	Mordvin	Erzya
Uralic	Permic	Beserman Udmurt
Uralic	Permic	Komi-Zyrian
Uralic	Saami	North Saami
Uralic	Samoyedic	Tundra Nenets
Uralic	Ugric	Hungarian
Uralic	Ugric	Northern Khanty
Yeniseian	Yeniseian	Ket
Yukaghir	Yukaghir	Kolyma Yukaghir

3 Participial orientation

3.1 Introduction

The notion of *orientation* was introduced to the typology of participles by Haspelmath (1994: 153) in order to describe different possible relations between the participle, which is a verb form, and the nominal it modifies, which is a participant related to this verb.[11] Indeed, the transitive German verb *fangen* 'catch' has at least two participants, the agent and the patient, and each of the two participles that can be formed from this verb are oriented towards one of the participants. The noun modified by the active participle is understood to be the agent (52a), whereas the noun modified by the passive participle is understood to be the patient (52b):

(52) German (Indo-European)
    a. *die*   [*Mäuse*   **fang-end-e**]   *Katze*
        DEF.F.NOM.SG   mouse.PL   catch-PTCP.PRS-DEF.F.NOM.SG   cat(F)
        'the cat who cathes mice'
    b. *die*   [*von der*   *Katze*   **ge-fang-en-e**]
        DEF.NOM.PL   by   DEF.F.DAT.SG   cat(F)   PTCP.PST-catch-PTCP.PST-DEF.NOM.PL
        Mäuse
        mouse.PL
        'the mice caught by the cat'

Both active and passive participles are instances of *inherently oriented participles*, which means that each form can be used to modify only one particular participant of the verb. Such forms are common in most European languages, e.g. also in English, Russian, or Finnish. On the other hand, many languages are able to employ one and the same participial form for relativizing several participants of the verb. Participles of this kind are referred to as *contextually oriented*, and they have been shown to be the dominant type in the languages of Siberia and beyond (Pakendorf 2012; Shagal 2016). Haspelmath exemplifies the functions of a contextually oriented participle by several constructions from Lezgian, where the imperfective participle *kẋizwaj* can be oriented towards the agent (53a), towards the patient (53b), or towards peripheral participants (53c)–(53d):

---

[11] Haspelmath himself refers to Lehmann (1984: 152) as the source of this term, although Lehmann only uses this notion (*Ausrichtung*) in connection with verbal nouns.

https://doi.org/10.1515/9783110633382-003

(53) Lezgian (Nakh-Daghestanian)
 a. [čar **k̂i-zwa-j**] ruš
    letter.ABS write-IPFV-PTCP girl
    'the girl who is writing a letter' (Haspelmath 1994: 154)
 b. [ruš-a **k̂i-zwa-j**] čar
    girl-ERG write-IPFV-PTCP letter.ABS
    'the letter which the girl is writing' (Haspelmath 1994: 154)
 c. [ruš-a čar **k̂i-zwa-j**] stol
    girl-ERG letter.ABS write-IPFV-PTCP table
    'the table on which the girl is writing a letter' (Haspelmath 1994: 154)
 d. [ruš-a čar **k̂i-zwa-j**] juğ
    girl-ERG letter.ABS write-IPFV-PTCP day
    'the day on which the girl is writing a letter' (Haspelmath 1994: 154)

The goal of this chapter is to provide a systematic description of all the types of participial orientation attested in the languages of the sample, to propose possible motivations for these types, and to establish, where possible, correspondences of certain patterns with other aspects of language structure. In Section 3.2, I discuss the range of participants that demonstrate significant distinctions with respect to relativization and should be taken into account in investigating participial orientation. Sections 3.3 and 3.4 discuss all types of participles demonstrating inherent orientation, namely participles oriented towards core and peripheral clause participants respectively. Section 3.5 provides an overview of contextually oriented participles. In Section 3.6, I discuss the most widely attested means of extending participial orientation, in particular specialized affixes and resumptive pronouns. The use of resumptive pronouns is further discussed in Section 3.7 from a more general perspective. Section 3.8 is devoted to a discussion of possible functional motivations underlying the development of attested types of orientation. The major findings of the chapter are summarized in Section 3.9.

3.2 Relativized participants

If we define participles as deranked predicates of a relative clause (see Section 2.3.1), then the participant towards which the participle is oriented is in essence the participant relativized by this clause. Therefore, it is convenient to link the discussion of possible participial orientations to the range of relativizable positions presented in the form of the Noun Phrase Accessibility Hierarchy, an implicational scale introduced by Keenan and Comrie (1977). The general idea of this hierarchy is that noun phrases can be more or less accessible to relativization depending on their role in the relative clause. The original formulation of the Accessibility Hierarchy is as follows (subsequent modifications will be discussed below):

(54) Subject (SUBJ) >
 Direct Object (DO) >
 Indirect Object (IO)>
 Oblique (OBL) >
 Genitive (POSS) >
 Object of Comparison (OCOMP)

The main prediction regarding this hierarchy is that if a language allows relativization for a certain position, then it must also allow relativization for all positions to the left, up to the subject. Different relativization strategies (e.g. employing relative pronouns, resumptive pronouns, complementizers, or non-finite verb forms) can be used for different positions, but each strategy has to apply to a continuous segment of the hierarchy. Apart from the basic implicational relations, the relative accessibility to relativization of different grammatical roles was later also shown to be reflected in a number of tendencies. For instance, Maxwell (1982) formulated several diachronic typological generalizations based on the Accessibility Hierarchy, Herrmann (2003) used a corpus of British dialect data to demonstrate a correlation between the position of a noun phrase on the hierarchy and the frequency of corresponding relative clauses, while Diessel and Tomasello (2005) showed the relevance of the hierarchy for the acquisition of relative clauses by English- and German-speaking children.

Numerous additions and elaborations have been proposed since the Accessibility Hierarchy was first introduced; see, for instance, Keenan and Comrie (1979), Keenan (1985), Lehmann (1986), and Fox (1987), among others. In what follows, I present an overview of problems with the original formulation of the hierarchy and propose solutions. As a result of this discussion, I will develop my own version of the Accessibility Hierarchy to be used in this study.

One of the most important modifications concerns the notions of subject and object as positions on the hierarchy. The concepts themselves are known to be problematic, and there has been a lot of discussion among typologists concerning their cross-linguistic applicability (Li 1976; Comrie 1981; Foley and Van Valin 1984; Croft 1991; Dixon 1994, and others). As regards the Accessibility Hierarchy, the problem with the positions of subject and object is primarily connected to the difference between accusative and ergative languages. It was proposed as early as Johnson (1974) and Woodbury (1975) that in ergative languages it is not the subject in the traditional sense that is most accessible to relativization, but rather the absolutive argument. Parallel to this, Fox (1987) showed that for accusative languages the distinction between transitive and intransitive subjects can also be relevant, since in a corpus of conversational English the instances of both instransitive subject relativization and object relativization are significantly more frequent than those of transitive subject relativization. This distinction is thus of general relevance to the study of relativization. Therefore, in a study of participial orientation, it makes sense to distinguish three core participants instead of two, i.e. to treat subjects of transitive and intransitive clauses separately. Following Comrie (1981), I will henceforth use the labels A, P and S, where A stands for the subject of the transitive clause, P denotes the object of the transitive clause (also referred to as O in some studies), and S is the label for the single participant of the intransitive clause. It should be emphasized that A, P and S in this approach are conceived of as syntactic functions, not generalized semantic roles, even though A and P are defined based on the coding properties of the agent and the patient of the construction expressing an action (see discussion in Haspelmath 2011a). That said, some participles can be sensitive to the semantic role of the relativized participant; see in particular Section 3.3.5 on absolutive participles. Unfortunately, it is not always clear from descriptions of particular languages whether it is syntax or semantics that plays a crucial role. However, when the nature of orientation is obviously semantic, I will explicitly mention this in the analysis.

Another position on the Accessibility Hierarchy that appears to be problematic is that of the indirect object. This label is used by Keenan and Comrie (1977) to refer to the recipient participant in the ditransitive construction. The authors themselves remark that this position is the subtlest, since many languages assimilate it either to other oblique cases, or to direct objects (Keenan and Comrie 1977: 72).[12] English, in principle, provides examples for both kinds of cases, compare the sentence *John gave a book to Mary*, where the recipient is encoded by a prepositional phrase, and the double object construction in *John gave Mary a book*. At the same time, some languages do have a grammatical role of indirect object which is distinct from both direct objects and obliques, which is reflected in the relativization pattern. For instance, in Apatani, indirect objects are encoded differently from direct objects, namely as datives, as shown in (55a). At the same

---

[12] In languages showing a distinction between primary objects and secondary objects, indirect objects pattern with direct objects in monotransitive constructions on a more general level, including encoding in independent sentences (see Dryer 1986).

time, they behave differently from obliques in that they can be relativized using contextually oriented nominalization (55b), which otherwise only allows relativization of subjects (55c), and direct objects (55d):

(55) Apatani (Sino-Tibetan)
 a. ání **hime mi** ude ho ó bibine
    mother child DAT house LOC beer give.PST
    'Mother gave beer to the child in the house.' (Abraham 1985: 123)
 b. [ñika digotaṅgo bini] alyi mi mó latubine
    I.GEN food give.NMZ pig ACC he catch.PST
    'He caught the pig to which I gave food.' (Abraham 1985: 132)
 c. [alyi mi ka lanibo] nyimi hi aya do
    pig ACC GEN catch.NMZ woman DET good exist
    'The woman who caught the pig is good.' (Abraham 1985: 131)
 d. mólu [ñika labine] alyi mi medo a?
    they I.GEN bring.NMZ pig ACC search.exist Q
    'Did they search for the pig that I brought?' (Abraham 1985: 132)

In addition, Apatani also features an inherently oriented nominalization used to relativize instruments (see example (84) and the discussion in Section 3.4), whereas no other positions of the Accessibility Hierarchy can be relativized in the language.[13]

Restrictions like the ones in Apatani seem to be very rare. However, they are not the only evidence for the relevance of the indirect object position for the Accessibility Hierarchy. In Sheko (Dizoid), quite in line with the prediction of Keenan and Comrie (1977: 92), the frequency of resumptive pronoun use increases towards the rightward end of the hierarchy. In the case of direct object relativization it is almost prohibited, for obliques it is strongly preferred, while for indirect objects both strategies appear to be available (see Hellenthal 2010: 349–350), which once again singles out this grammatical role as a separate position. The use of resumptive pronouns is further discussed in Section 3.7.

---

[13] Keenan and Comrie (1977: 72) illustrate the relevance of the indirect object position by several examples from Tamil (Dravidian), claiming that it only uses the participial relativization strategy for relativizing subjects, direct objects and indirect object, whereas lower positions are relativized by means of the correlative strategy. This information, however, contradicts Lehmann's (1993) descriptive grammar of Tamil which I use as a primary source of information on Tamil in this study. According to Lehmann (1993: 288–293), various kinds of obliques, such as instruments and locatives, can also be relativized using the participial strategy.

The options for relativization united under the label "oblique" in the Accessibility Hierarchy are in reality very diverse, both from a semantic and a syntactic point of view. A good example of the syntactic heterogeneity found in individual languages is provided by Kalmyk. As shown in Krapivina (2009a: 499–504), Kalmyk uses two participial relativization strategies. The first one, where the relativized noun phrase is not represented in any way within the relative clause (the so-called *gap strategy*),[14] can be used to relativize subjects, direct and indirect objects, and all kinds of obliques; see an example of locative relativization in (56a). The second strategy, where the role of the relativized noun phrase in the relative clause is indicated by a resumptive element, is used to relativize lower positions of the Accessibility Hierarchy. The important thing here is that the resumptive element used in the second strategy is in essence a possessive marker, which needs to attach to a participant encoded as a possessor. Therefore, this strategy only applies to the cases of possessor relativization, and also to the relativization of obliques expressed by postpositional phrases, which in Kalmyk are syntactically identical to possessive constructions; compare (56b) and (56c). For the relativization of the obliques expressed by case forms, only the first strategy is applicable. As a result, in the analysis of Kalmyk relativization, it makes sense to divide obliques into two separate positions on the hierarchy, case-marked obliques and postpositional obliques.

(56) Kalmyk (Mongolic)
    a. *kuuxən^j-də* [*mini suu-xə*] *stul av-ad irə-Ø*
        kitchen-DAT 1SG.GEN sit-PTCP.FUT chair take-CVB.ANT come-IMP
        'Bring the chair on which I am going to sit to the kitchen.'
        (Krapivina 2009a: 501)
    b. [***dotrə-n^j*** *määčə kevt-sən*] *avdər orə-n dor bää-nä*
        inside-POSS.3 ball lie-PTCP.PST chest bed-EXT under be-PRS
        'The chest in which there is a ball is under the bed.'
        (Krapivina 2009a: 503)
    c. [*gerə-n^j* *šat-žə od-sən*] *övgə-n Elstə*
        house-POSS.3 burn-CVB.IPFV leave-PTCP.PST old.man-EXT Elista

---

[14] It should be emphasized that in this book the broad definition of gap strategy is adopted, that is, this term refers to any strategy in which the relativized argument is not overtly represented within the relative clause (see Comrie and Kuteva 2013b).

bää-xär   jov-la
be-CVB.PURP   go-REM
'The old man whose house had burned down moved to Elista.'
(Krapivina 2009a: 503)

As regards the semantic heterogeneity of obliques, basically all non-core participants of the clause fall into this class, in many cases including recipients if they pattern syntactically with other peripheral participants. Apart from that, the relativized oblique roles most commonly discussed in the descriptions of individual languages are comitatives, instrumentals, locatives, and time adverbials.

The position of possessor is not homogeneous either. In some languages, the availability of a certain relativization strategy or possessor relativization in general depends on the role of the possessed participant. For instance, in Kalmyk, it is totally acceptable to relativize a possessor of a subject, while relativizing a possessor of a direct object is problematic for many speakers; compare the problematic example (57) with the fully grammatical sentence (56c) above:

(57) Kalmyk (Mongolic)
$^{??}$[*čonə   ükr-i-n^j id-sən]   övgə-n   xö*
wolf   cow-ACC-POSS.3 eat-PTCP.PST   old.man   sheep
xuld-ӡə   avə-v
sell-CVB.IPFV   take-PST
'The old man whose cow a wolf had eaten bought a sheep.'
(Krapivina 2009a: 504)

Almost the same restriction applies to Kolyma Yukaghir, where only a possessor of an intransitive subject can be relativized, but not other types of possessors (Maslova 2003: 417). In this study, I do not make a consistent distinction among different types of possessors, primarily because for many languages in my sample such detailed information is simply not available. I will, nevertheless, emphasize the role of the possessum in the relative clause when it appears to be relevant.

The object of comparison as a position on the Accessibility Hierarchy is not considered in this study, primarily due to a lack of data. The same concerns various cases of relativization from a subordinate clause illustrated by the sentence from Imbabura Quechua in (58), where it is the indirect object of a complement clause that gets relativized (the position where the indirect object would be in the clause if not for relativization is indicated by an underscore):

(58) Imbabura Quechua (Quechuan)
 NP[*chay*   s[*Marya*   s[*Juzi   libru-ta* ___ *kara-shka*]-*ta*   *kri-j*]
    that   María   José   book-ACC   give-NMZ.PST-ACC believe-NMZ.PRS
 wawa]NP   *ña-mi*   *ri-rka*
    child   already-VLD go-PST
'The child to whom María believes José gave the book already left.'
(Cole 1985: 57)

Examples like the one above are important if we aim to evaluate the capacity of a certain relativization strategy, but they are of very little use in connection with the notion of participial orientation, which is the focus of this chapter. Indeed, it is hard to imagine a language which would have a specialized participial form oriented towards the indirect object of a subordinate clause and not capable of relativizing any other position. Therefore, I do not include such constructions within the framework of this study.

To summarize, I will further take into account the following types of participants, determined based on both their grammatical and semantic properties:
- S, or the single participant of the intransitive clause;
- A, or the agent-like participant of the transitive clause;
- P, or the patient-like participant of the transitive clause;
- indirect object, or the recipient in the ditransitive construction (if treated differently from direct objects and obliques in a given language);
- obliques, or peripheral participants, such as instrumental and locative (differentiating between various semantic types where appropriate);
- possessor, or the participant encoded in the same way as prototypical possessors in a given language (i.e. including inanimate possessors and the like).

All participial forms in the languages of the sample can be classified into several groups according to the combinations of positions that they are able to relativize. In the following sections, I will discuss all attested combinations and the resulting groups formed by participles, which constitute the typology of participial orientation.

Before proceeding to the examination of the data, two final clarifications are in order. The first one concerns the difference between inherent and contextual orientation. Although active participles can relativize two of the participant types listed above (A and S), they are, of course, considered inherently oriented. This is justified by the fact that in each clause there is only one participant that can be relativized using an active participle, namely S in an intransitive clause, and A in a transitive clause. The same argument concerns participial forms that can relativize both S and P participants, which will be discussed in Section 3.3.5. On the other hand, if a participle can relativize both A and P participants, its orientation can only be regarded as contextual, since both of these participants typically occur together within one transitive clause.

The second clarification concerns the use of valency-changing operations on participles. In some languages, participles regularly take specialized affixes allowing the relativization of participants that cannot be relativized otherwise. These affixes can be either valency-reducing, such as a detransitivizing suffix in West Greenlandic discussed in Sections 3.3.2 and 3.6.1, or valency-increasing, such as various causative and applicative markers described in Section 3.6.1. Wherever appropriate, I will discuss these markers as means of extending orientation, but when typologizing orientation of participles as such, I will disregard any additional morphology and only consider the properties of "bare" participial forms. Naturally, this rule cannot be applied to the majority of participles traditionally labelled as passive, since they are typically formed by affixes that combine the relativizing function with the passive meaning (e.g. -n-/-t- in Russian, -t- in Latin). In principle, such forms can be seen either as relativizing the P participant of the original transitive clause, or as relativizing the S participant of the passivized clause. In what follows, I will determine their orientation based on the original valency of the verb, thus adopting the first approach. Consequently, I will consider prototypical passive participles together with other forms oriented towards the P participant (and use the label "passive" for all of them); see further argumentation in Section 3.3.3. The same approach also applies to resultative participles discussed in Section 3.3.5.

3.3 Orientation towards core participants

Out of 125 inherently oriented participles in my sample, 113 are oriented towards either a particular core participant (A, P, or in very rare cases S) or a combination thereof. This section focuses on the attested combinations of core participants in participial orientation and their underlying motivation.

3.3.1 On patterning of core participants

It is a well-known fact that in many languages either the A or the P argument of a main verbal clause is treated in the same way as the S argument. The identity of treatment can be manifested in the marking of full noun phrases or in the marking of pronouns (see Comrie 2013a and 2013b respectively), or in the verbal person marking (see Siewierska 2013). The situation when the A argument is treated in the same way as the S argument is commonly referred to as a *nominative–accusative* (or simply: *accusative*) system, while the system where the P argument is treated in the same way as the S argument is called *ergative–absolutive* (or simply: *ergative*). The first type of patterning for noun phrases is illustrated by the Russian example in (59), and the second is exemplified by the sentences in (60) with the same meaning from Hunzib (identically encoded participants are shown in bold):

(59) Russian (Indo-European)
    a. **devočk-a**   spa-l-a
       girl(F)-NOM.SG sleep-PST-F.SG
       '**The girl** slept.'
    b. **mal'čik-Ø**   udari-l-Ø   devočk-u
       boy(M)-NOM.SG hit-PST-M.SG girl(F)-ACC.SG
       '**The boy** hit the girl.'
(60) Hunzib (Nakh-Daghestanian)
    a. **kid**   y-ut'-ur
       girl.ABS CL₂-sleep-PST
       '**The girl** slept.' (van den Berg 1995: 122)
    b. oždi-l   **kid**   hehe-r
       boy-ERG girl.ABS hit-PST
       'The boy hit **the girl**.' (van den Berg 1995: 122)

The labels "accusative" and "ergative" are also commonly used to refer to S/A and S/P patterning in the construction of complex sentences, such as coordinate constructions or sentences with purposive clauses. A language is accusative in this respect if it requires a common argument of two clauses to be in S or A function in each, and it is considered ergative if this common argument can have S or P function. A concise overview of the main features of ergative and accusative systems for marking core syntactic relations and clause linking can be found in Aikhenvald and Dixon (2011: 144–150).

In addition, many languages show other associations between S and A participants and S and P participants, which are not necessarily related to the syntactic structure of the respective languages, but should rather be explained from a semantic/pragmatic point of view. This type of association between S and A arguments is widely known; see Du Bois (1987: 839–843) and Dixon (1994: 131–

142), among others. It is commonly manifested, for example, in reflexive constructions (S or A argument is the controller of the reflexive pronoun), in imperative constructions (S or A argument is commonly second person and can be left without overt expression), as well as in constructions with verbs like 'can', 'try' or 'begin' (these verbs usually have the same S or A argument as the verbs to which they are linked) and in serial verb constructions (see Aikhenvald 2006). Recurrent associations between S and P participants have received relatively little attention in the literature, although some of them were discussed in Keenan (1984), Dixon (1994), and Mithun and Chafe (1999). These include nominal incorporation (if nominal incorporation relates to a core function, this is almost always S or P); see Mithun (1984), Fortescue (1992), de Reuse (1994); suppletive verb forms (the choice often depends on the number reference of the S or the P argument); see Durie (1986); verbal classifiers (which typically categorize S and P arguments); see Aikhenvald (2000: 149–161); and demonstratives with limited syntactic function (the functions to which the use of particular demonstratives is limited are commonly S and P); see Daguman (2004: 207).

Crucially, the associations listed above are not directly dependent on the type of syntactic organization, that is, they apply equally to languages with accusative or ergative marking of core syntactic functions. As proposed by Du Bois (1987: 839), instances of the S/A association relate to the fact that the topic around which a discourse is organised is in the great majority of instances human, and generally the controller of an activity, and thus in S or A function. The S/P association can be explained by the existence of a close semantic link between a transitive verb and its P argument and between an intransitive verb and its S argument, as discussed, for instance, in Keenan (1984: 200–205), or Aikhenvald and Dixon (2011: 160). In addition, as suggested in Du Bois (1987: 805), arguments comprising new information appear preferentially in the S or P roles, and not in the A role. This observation might be relevant for the aforementioned pattern in demonstratives, but also in the context of relativization, as I will suggest in Section 3.8.

The subsequent sections are devoted to four categories of participles oriented towards certain core participants in different combinations. Sections 3.3.2 and 3.3.3 discuss active (A/S) and passive (P) participles, the two types widely known and accepted in linguistic literature, largely due to their presence in many European languages. Section 3.3.4 presents data on agentive (A) participles attested in the languages of South America. Finally, in Section 3.3.5, I will discuss absolutive (S/P) participles. The latter two types have so far received very little attention in the literature, but, as I will show, they deserve to be considered more closely.

In each of these sections, I will also consistently test whether the inherent orientation of participles attested in a language tends to correspond to the morphosyntactic alignment in its basic clause structure. For this purpose, I contrast languages that show at least some ergativity in either argument marking or verbal agreement (24 languages in my sample, see Appendix 2) to languages that do not show any ergativity in these domains (76 languages in my sample). As I will show, there is no clear connection either between nominative–accusative alignment and a pattern of A/S vs. P in participial orientation, or between absolutive–ergative alignment and a pattern of A vs. S/P. Therefore, participial orientation cannot be regarded as an epiphenomenon of the syntactic organization of a language on a more general level, but rather requires a functional motivation of its own. In other words, there is a reason to look for semantic/pragmatic associations in the spirit outlined above; see Section 3.8 for further discussion.

3.3.2 Active participles

The term *active participles* is commonly used to refer to non-finite forms that can relativize both S and A participants (see Figure 3 below). However, as I will further show, there are some reasons to consider forms specialized in S relativization under this label as well.

Fig. 3: Orientation of active participles

Prototypical active (S/A) participles are characteristic of many languages of the Standard Average European type (henceforth SAE; see Haspelmath 2001 on this notion), both Indo-European (see example (61) from Lithuanian), and non-Indo-European (see example (62) from Hungarian):

(61) Lithuanian (Indo-European)
[Iš   mokykl-os   **parėj-us-io**]   vaik-o
from school-GEN.SG come.home-PTCP.PST.ACT-GEN.SG.M child-GEN.SG
skub-a-me   pa-klaus-ti   apie   pažymi-us...
hurry-PRS-1PL PREV-ask-INF about   mark-ACC.PL
'We hurry to ask the child who has come back from school about marks...'
(Arkadiev 2014a: 85)

(62) Hungarian (Uralic)
A   [könyv-et   a   fiú-nak   gyorsan **olvas-ó**]   lány itt   van.
the   book-ACC   the   boy-DAT   fast   read-PTCP.ACT   girl here   is
'The girl who reads the book to the boy fast is here.'
(Kenesei, Vago, and Fenyvesi 1998: 45)

Most of the subject-oriented forms in my sample relativize both S and A participants: forms specializing in S participants are only attested in three languages, West Greenlandic (Eskimo-Aleut), Kamaiurá (Tupian) and Fula (Atlantic-Congo). In West Greenlandic, the participial marker -*soq* on its own only allows relativization of intransitive subjects, as illustrated in (63a). However, this marker can also attach to transitive verb stems, which in this case need to take a detransitivizing suffix. The original direct object is then either not expressed at all, or it receives instrumental marking, as shown in (63b). Therefore, the language has a regular way of relativizing both S and A participants using one and the same form, even though the latter option is only available with additional morphology.[15]

(63) West Greenlandic (Eskimo-Aleut)
  a. *arnaq*   [**suli-soq**]
     woman   work-PTCP.ACT.3SG
     'the/a woman who is working' (van der Voort 1991: 17)
  b. *angut*   [(*uannik*)   **naapit-si-soq**]   *sianiip-poq*
     man   I-INS   meet-HTR-PTCP.ACT.3SG   be.stupid-IND.3SG
     'The man who met me is stupid.' (van der Voort 1991: 21)

---

[15] This case is slightly different from other cases of orientation extension attested in my sample, since usually the use of valency-changing affixes creates forms with very wide relativizing capacity (see Section 3.6.1 for further discussion), while here the resulting relativizing capacity of the participial form equals that of a prototypical active participle. Due to this, functionally, the -*soq* form can be seen as belonging in this section despite its inherent orientation towards S participants.

The second instance of a participle specialized in S relativization is attested in Kamaiurá, which employs different means for relativizing each of the core participants, -*ama'e* being the marker for S relativization (64a), -*tat* for A relativization (64b), and -*ipyt* for P relativization (64c):

(64) Kamaiurá (Tupian)
   a. *a-mo-y'u*   rak   *akwama'e-a*   [*i-'ywej-ama'e-her-a*]
      1SG-CAUS-drink at   man-NUC   3-be.thirsty-NMZ.S-PST-NUC
      'I made the man who was thirsty drink.' (Seki 2000: 179)
   b. *akwama'e-a*   *o-juka* *wyrapy-a* [*kunu'um-a* **pyhyk-ar-er-a**]
      man-NUC   3-kill   hawk-NUC   boy-NUC   catch-NMZ.A-PST-NUC
      'The man killed the hawk that caught the boy.' (Seki 2000: 179)
   c. *o-yk*   *akwama'e-a* [*i-mono-pyr-er-a*   *morerekwar-a*   *upe*]
      3-come   man-NUC   3-send-NMZ.P-PST-NUC   boss-NUC   DAT
      'The man who was sent by the boss came.' (Seki 2000: 179)

Kamaiurá is the only language in my sample with a tripartite distinction of this type. As shown in Seki (1990), the crucial opposition in independent clauses in Kamaiurá is the semantic opposition between active and inactive participants, that is, primarily A and P participants respectively. The same semantic opposition is presumably the reason for the existence of separate participles for A and P relativization. On the other hand, the form used for S relativization conceivably is not grounded in semantics on its own, but rather fills the gap in the relativizing capacity of the language. This assumption is supported by the fact that no other languages in the sample have participial forms specialized in S relativization to the total exclusion of any other participants. The other option, namely a specialized form for A relativization, is more common, as I will show in Section 3.3.4 below. The lack of semantic basis of their own and the rarity of S-oriented forms can be seen as further reasons not to consider them as a distinct type of participles.

Finally, Fula (Atlantic-Congo) has different participial forms for three different voices, active, middle and passive (see Arnott 1970: 373–374). Middle participles naturally have reflexive meaning, e.g. '(one) who has hidden himself' or '(one) who is hiding himself', so in Fula they are instances of intransitive subject (S) relativization. This three-way distinction, however, is prominent in the whole verbal system of the language, and is in no way specific to participles. I will not, thus, discuss it in detail here.

Among the languages of the sample, at least 46 have forms that can qualify as active participles. In nine of these languages (Cofán, Garrwa, Kobon, Krongo,

Maba, Martuthunira, Rif Berber, Wambaya and Yimas) the active participle is the only (affirmative) participial form (there is also a contextually oriented negative participle in Yimas). In 13 languages the single (affirmative) active participle forms a binary opposition with a passive (P), an absolutive (S/P), or a non-subject participle (Aguaruna has both an affirmative and a negative active participle). In all the others, active participles belong to a more complex participial system. I will discuss this topic in detail in Chapter 7.

Out of 46 languages with active participles, 10 show certain ergative features in either argument marking or verbal agreement, such as Garrwa and Wambaya (ergative case marking on full noun phrases), or Yimas (ergative behaviour of 3rd person prefixes; see Foley 1991: 201). The proportion of such languages among languages with active participles (21.7%) is, thus, roughly the same as in the sample in general (24%). In other words, the existence of active participles in a language does not mean that this language cannot show ergativity in other domains (the observed situation could, in fact, be expected, since morphologically ergative languages commonly have accusative syntax, in particular in the domain of relativization; see, for example, Dixon 1994: 15, McGregor 2009: 485).

The list of sample languages that have active participles is given in Table 4. A map is presented in Figure 4.

Fig. 4: Languages with active participles

Tab. 4: Languages with active participles (% per macroarea)

Family	Language	Form(s)
Australia (4/5, 80%)		
Garrwan	Garrwa	NMZ.CHAR -*warr*
Mirndi	Wambaya	NMZ.A
Pama-Nyungan	Martuthunira	REL.PRS -*nyila*
Tangkic	Kayardild	NMZ-CONS -*n-ngarrba*
Papunesia (4/7, 57.1%)		
Austronesian	Muna	PTCP.ACT *mo-V-no*
	Wolio	PTCP.ACT *mo-*
Lower Sepik-Ramu	Yimas	NF -*ru*
Nuclear Trans New Guinea	Kobon	NMZ/ADJR -*eb*/-*ep*
North America (7/13, 53.8%)		
Cochimi-Yuman	Maricopa	REL *kw-*
Eskimo-Aleut	West Greenlandic	PTCP.ACT -*soq*
Seri	Seri	NMZ.SUBJ
Uto-Aztecan	Guarijío	NMZ.S/A -*me*
	Nevome	NMZ -*cama*
	Tümpisa Shoshone	PTCP.PRS -*tün*
Yokutsan	Wikchamni	VN.SUBJ {-*ač̓*/}/{-*ič̓*/}
South America (9/16, 56.3%)		
Araucanian	Mapudungun	PTCP.ACT -*lu*
Arawakan	Tariana	REL *ka-*, REL.PST *ka-V-kari* (M)/ *ka-V-karu* (F)/*ka-V-kani* (PL), REL.FUT *ka-V-pena*
Barbacoan	Tsafiki	PTCP.IPFV -*min*
Chicham	Aguaruna	REL.SUBJ -*u*, REL.NEG -*tʃau*
Cofán	Cofán	PTCP -ʼ*su*
Pano-Tacanan	Matsés	NMZ.A/S -*quid* (REC), NMZ.NEG.S/A.HAB -*esa*
Quechuan	Tarma Quechua	NMZ.SUBJ -*q*
Tucanoan	Barasano	PTCP -*ri*
Tupian	Kamaiurá	NMZ.S -*ama'e*, NMZ.NEG.S -*uma'e*

Family	Language	Form(s)
Africa (7/12, 58.3%)		
Afro-Asiatic	Middle Egyptian	PTCP.SUBJ
	Rif Berber	PTCP.ACT
Atlantic-Congo	Fula	PTCP.PST.ACT -u/-Ø, PTCP.PST.MID -ii/-i, PTCP.FUT.ACT -oo/-ay, PTCP.FUT.MID -otoo/-oto
Central Sudanic	Ma'di	SR.S/A -rē̂ (SG)/-bá (PL)
Kadugli-Krongo	Krongo	CONN ŋ-
Maban	Maba	PTCP n-
Ta-Ne-Omotic	Koorete	PTCP.PFV.SUBJ -a
Eurasia (15/47, 31.9%)		
Afro-Asiatic	Modern Standard Arabic	PTCP.ACT
Indo-European	Eastern Armenian	PTCP.SUBJ -oł
	German	PTCP.PRS -end
	Lithuanian	PTCP.PST.ACT -us-, PTCP.PRS.ACT -nt-
	Russian	PTCP.PST.ACT -vš-/-š-, PTCP.PRS.ACT -ušč-/-ašč-
Kartvelian	Georgian	PTCP.ACT m-V(-el)
Sino-Tibetan	Dolakha Newar	NMZ.SUBJ -gu/-ku/-u
	Japhug rGyalrong	NMZ.S/A kɯ-
Uralic	Beserman Udmurt	PTCP.PRS -š'
	Erzya	PTCP.PRS -i(c'a)
	Finnish	PTCP.PST.ACT -nut, PTCP.PRS.ACT -va
	Hungarian	PTCP.ACT -ó
	Komi-Zyrian	PTCP.ACT -iš'
	Meadow Mari	PTCP.ACT -še
	North Saami	PTCP.PRS -i/-(jead)dji, PTCP.PST -n

3.3.3 Passive participles

In this study, I use the label *passive participles* to refer to non-finite forms that relativize P participants, as shown in Figure 5:

Fig. 5: Orientation of passive participles

As mentioned earlier in Section 3.2, this label encompasses two different types of forms. Passive participles of the first type actually have properties that are characteristic of prototypical passives as listed, for example, in Dixon and Aikhenvald (2000: 7). The most prominent of these properties is demoting the original A argument to some peripheral position (e.g. instrumental) or omitting it altogether ("agentless passive"); see further discussion in Sections 6.2.2 and 6.2.4 respectively. This type of passive participles can be found in many European languages, such as, for instance, Russian or Lithuanian. Relative clauses introduced by these forms can be regarded as a direct equivalent of finite passive clauses. In fact, these passive participles are commonly used to form passives in independent sentences, compare examples (1b) and (4) from Russian repeated here as (65a) and (65b) respectively:

(65) Russian (Indo-European)
 a. *pis'm-o* [*na-pisa-nn-oe* *devočk-oj*]
 letter(N)-NOM.SG PFV-write-PTCP.PST.PASS-N.NOM.SG girl(F)-INS.SG
 'the letter written by the girl'
 b. *Pis'm-o* *by-l-o* *na-pisa-n-o* *devočk-oj.*
 letter(N)-NOM.SG be-PST-N.SG PFV-write-PTCP.PST.PASS-N.SG girl(F)-INS.SG
 'The letter was written by the girl.'

Because of this, such participial relative clauses are usually considered instances of subject relativization in the generative tradition (see, for example, de Vries 2002: 58). In some languages, relative constructions featuring passive participles of this type can actually be shown to be instances of subject relativization from a syntactic point of view. For instance, in Modern Standard Arabic, passive participles agree in gender and number with the patientive participant of the relative clause, which is a valid criterion for subjecthood in the language; see example (66) below and the discussion of passive participles in Modern Standard Arabic in Section 5.4.

(66) Modern Standard Arabic (Afro-Asiatic)
 ʔal-jihat-u [l-manūṭ-u bi-hā
 the-agency.F.SG-NOM the-trust.PTCP.PASS.**M.SG**-NOM in-F.SG
 xtiyār-u l-musāfir-īna]
 CONSTR.choice(**M**).**SG**-NOM the-traveller-M.PL.GEN
 'the agency with which the choice of travellers has been entrusted'
 (Badawi, Carter, and Gully 2004: 114)

For most languages, however, we do not have enough syntactic evidence to support an analysis of these constructions either as subject relativization or as direct object relativization. Therefore, in this study I rely on the structure of the clause before relativization, which means that all the participles used for relativizing the P participant will be considered together, irrespective of whether the underlying clause has presumably undergone passivization prior to relativization or not. As explained in Section 3.2, I will not, however, consider forms containing a separate passive marker in addition to a participial marker. These cases (which are, as a matter of fact, quite rare) will be briefly discussed towards the end of this section. Also, due to the syntactic ambiguity that has just been mentioned, when dealing with participles oriented towards P participants, I will avoid referring to the original A participant as the subject of the relative clause, and use the term *agent* instead.

The second type of passive participles are forms that cannot be regarded as non-finite equivalents of independent passives, since the languages they are attested in do not have well-established finite passives whatsoever. One such language is Nias, where the only participle in its default form is used for relativizing P participants; see (67):

(67) Nias (Austronesian)
 U-fake zekhula [**ni-rökhi-nia**].
 3SG.REAL-use coconut.MUT PTCP.PASS-grate-3SG.POSS
 'I used the coconut which she grated.' (Brown 2001: 420)

In relative clauses introduced by participles of the second type, the agent is usually expressed, since demoting it is not among the primary functions of these forms. Moreover, in some languages it is even obligatory to express the agent in a passive participial relative clause, at least under certain circumstances. For instance, the example from Nias would be ungrammatical without the possessive marker on the participle denoting the agent, since agents in Nias participial relative clauses always have to be expressed if they are human, and otherwise are also very common (Brown 2001: 421).

It should be emphasized once again that in this book both types presented above are regarded as passive participles, irrespective of their label and status in the language. The only thing that matters is that all of them are inherently oriented towards original P participants of the clause. Interestingly, both types of passive participles can be attested in a single language. In Finnish, there are three participles inherently oriented towards the P participant, namely the present passive participle in *-tava*, the past passive participle in *-tu*, and the so-called "agentive participle" in *-ma*. The first two of these do not allow for the expression of the agent, even though they can easily take other verbal dependents, such as temporal or quality adverbials, as illustrated in (68a) and (68b). The participle in *-tu* is also the most important means of forming perfective passives in independent clauses, as in (68c). The form in *-ma*, by contrast, requires the agent to be expressed, as shown in (68d):

(68) Finnish (Uralic)
    a. *use-ita*   [pian **järjeste-ttäv-iä**]   *tilaisuuks-ia*
       many-PTV.PL   soon organize-PTCP.PASS.PRS-PTV.PL occasion-PTV.PL
       'many events that will be/have to be organized soon'
    b. *use-ita*   [hyvin **järjeste-ttäv-iä**]   *tilaisuuks-ia*
       many-PTV.PL   well organize-PTCP.PASS.PRS-PTV.PL occasion-PTV.PL
       'many well organized events'
    c. *Tilaisuude-t*   on   hyvin **järjeste-tty**.
       occasion-NOM.PL be.PRS.3SG well organize-PTCP.PASS.PST
       'The events are organized well.'
    d. *use-ita*   [**järjestä-m-iä-*(mme)**]   *tilaisuuks-ia*
       many-PTV.PL   organize-PTCP.A-PTV.PL-POSS.1PL occasion-PTV.PL
       'many events organized by us'

A similar situation is found in Japhug rGyalrong. In this language, the only non-finite form that can relativize P participants is the participle in *kɤ-*. What is interesting, however, is that this participle can appear in two different types of constructions. The first type has a TAM marker but no possessive prefix referring to the agent (69a). The second type, by contrast, has no TAM prefix but requires a possessive prefix coreferential with the A participant of the relative clause (69b).[16]

(69) Japhug rGyalrong (Sino-Tibetan)
    a. [chɤmdɤru   tɤ-kɤ-sɯ-ɤzgɯr]   nɯ   ɲɤ-sɯ-ɤstu-nɯ   qhe,
       drinking.straw PFV-NMZ.P-CAUS-bent TOP EVD-CAUS-straight-PL COORD
       tɕe   to-mna
       COORD EVD-recover
       'He put straight the straw that had been bent, and (her son) recovered.'
       (Jacques 2013: 22)
    b. [aʑo a-mɤ-kɤ-sɯz]   tɤjmɤɣ   nɯ   kɤ-ndza   mɤ-naz-a
       1SG POSS.1SG-NEG-NMZ.P-know mushroom DEM INF-eat NEG-dare-1SG
       'I do not dare to eat the mushrooms that I do not know.'
       (Jacques 2016: 10)

Passive participles sometimes serve as a basis for orientation extension, i.e. they can be modified by some formal means in order to allow the relativization of certain lower positions of the Accessibility Hierarchy; see Section 3.6 for a more detailed discussion of this topic. Apart from this, in some languages passive participles can also allow for relativization of a limited number of peripheral participants without any additional morphology. For instance, in both Russian and Finnish the locative argument of the verb meaning 'to live' can be relativized by a regular passive participle; compare examples (70) and (71) respectively. Presumably, in both cases the range of relativizable participants is chiefly restricted to arguments belonging to the valency of the verb, i.e. it does not concern "genuine" peripheral participants (see Section 3.5.1 for further discussion of this matter). It is noteworthy, however, that most of such "extended passive" participles are lexicalized, so this observation might belong to the domain of adjectival rather than participial orientation; see Generalova (2016) on the orientation of Russian deverbal adjectives.

---

[16] Another difference between these two constructions is that in the first type the relative clauses are usually internally headed, while in the second type they are either prenominal or headless (Jacques 2016: 22). This difference is not relevant for the current discussion, however.

(70) Russian (Indo-European)
[*obita-em-yj*]   *ostrov*
live-PTCP.PRS.PASS-M.NOM.SG   island(M).NOM.SG
'an island where someone lives (an inhabited island)'

(71) Finnish (Uralic)
[*asu-ttu*]   *saari*
live-PTCP.PST.PASS.NOM.SG   island.NOM.SG
'an island where someone lives (an inhabited island)'

As mentioned above, specialized passive participles can also be derived, especially in languages which have other participial forms and a passive marker. For instance, in Seri, it is possible to derive a passive participle from the active one by adding a special prefix, as shown in (72), even though there exists a specialized non-finite form for relativizing the P participant, illustrated by example (16) in Section 2.2.

(72) Seri (Seri)
a. [*k-i-asi*]
NMZ.SUBJ-TR-drink
'who drinks/drank it' (Marlett 2012: 220)
b. [*ʔa-p-asi*]
NMZ.SUBJ-PASS-drink
'that/what is/was drunk' (Marlett 2012: 220)

In Kalmyk (Mongolic), contextually oriented participles can in very rare cases optionally take the regular passive affix, which results in an inherently oriented passive form. I have, however, never encountered a grammatical description where the properties of such forms and their distribution are discussed in detail, and therefore, this topic will not be considered in this study.

Passive participles are not as common as active forms, but according to the data on the languages of the sample, they can still be found all over the world and are fairly evenly distributed across macroareas. Thus, forms clearly specializing in the relativization of the P participant are attested in 21 languages: in three Papunesian languages (Muna, Nias, and Wolio), three North American languages (West Greenlandic, Seri, and Wikchamni), three languages from South America (Kamaiurá, Mapudungun, and Tariana), three African languages (Fula, Ma'di, and Middle Egyptian), and nine languages spoken in Eurasia (Eastern Armenian, Finnish, Georgian, Japhug rGyalrong, Kalmyk, Lithuanian, Modern Standard Arabic, North Saami, and Russian). In the majority of these languages, passive participles exist together with at least one active participle (e.g. in Mapudungun and Middle Egyptian), or in a more complex paradigm that contains an active participle (e.g. in Ma'di and Seri). The only two exceptions are Nias, where the passive participle *ni-* is the only participial form, and Kalmyk, where the P-oriented resultative participle in *-ata* is attested alongside three contextually oriented forms. These two cases are discussed in more detail in Sections 7.2.1 and 7.6 respectively.

Among the 21 languages with passive participles, 5 (23.8%) are at least partly ergative, such as West Greenlandic (ergative case marking) or Nias (ergative case marking and split ergativity in verbal agreement based on TAM; see Brown 2005: 570). Thus, again, ergativity in main clause organization does not prevent a language from having P-oriented participles either.

The full list of languages with passive participles is provided in Table 5. Their worldwide distribution is shown in Figure 6.

Fig. 6: Languages with passive participles

Tab. 5: Languages with passive participles (% per macroarea)

Family	Language	Form(s)
Papunesia (3/7, 42.9%)		
Austronesian	Muna	PTCP.PASS *ni-*, NMZ *ka-*
	Nias	PTCP.PASS *ni-*
	Wolio	PTCP.PASS *i-*
North America (3/13, 23.1%)		
Eskimo-Aleut	West Greenlandic	PTCP.PASS *-saq*
Seri	Seri	NMZ.OBJ
Yokutsan	Wikchamni	VN.PASS {*-ʔaṅa/*}/{*-ʔ...aṅa/*}
South America (3/16, 18.8%)		
Araucanian	Mapudungun	PTCP.PASS *-el*
Arawakan	Tariana	NMZ.P *-nipe*
Tupian	Kamaiurá	NMZ.P *-ipyt*, NMZ.OBJ *-emi*
Africa (3/12, 25%)		
Afro-Asiatic	Middle Egyptian	PTCP.NS
Atlantic-Congo	Fula	PTCP.PST.PASS *-aa/-a*, PTCP.FUT.PASS *-etee/-ete*
Central Sudanic	Ma'di	SR.P *-lɛ́*
Eurasia (9/47, 19.1%)		
Afro-Asiatic	Modern Standard Arabic	PTCP.PASS
Indo-European	Eastern Armenian	PTCP.FUT *-ik'*
	Lithuanian	PTCP.PST.PASS *-t-*, PTCP.PRS.PASS *-m-*
	Russian	PTCP.PST.PASS *-n-/-t-*, PTCP.PRS.PASS *-em-/-im-*
Kartvelian	Georgian	PTCP.FUT *sa-V(-el)*
Mongolic	Kalmyk	PTCP.PASS *-ata*
Sino-Tibetan	Japhug rGyalrong	NMZ.P *kɤ-*
Uralic	Finnish	PTCP.PST.PASS *-tu*, PTCP.PRS.PASS *-tava*, PTCP.A *-ma*
	North Saami	PTCP.A *-n*

3.3.4 Agentive participles

As I mentioned in Section 3.3.1 above, alongside with participles that can relativize any subject regardless of transitivity, some languages use forms that can only relativize subjects of transitive clauses, i.e. A participants, as shown in Figure 7 below. I will refer to these forms as *agentive participles*.

Fig. 7: Orientation of agentive participles

In my sample, agentive participles are attested in only five languages, all of which are spoken in South America, namely Kamaiurá, Cocama, Matsés, Panare, and Urarina. An example from Cocama is provided below, compare the instance of A relativization by means of an agentive participle in (73a) with the instance of S relativization by means of an absolutive participle in (73b):

(73) Cocama (Tupian)
    a. *yawara*   [*tsa=mimira*   ***karura-tara***]   *yapana=uy*
        dog   1SG.F=woman.son   bite-NMZ.A   run=PST₁
        'The dog that bit my son escaped.' (Vallejos Yopán 2010: 585)
    b. *yawara*   [*ikuachi*   ***yapana-n***]   *karuta*   *tsa*   *mimira=uy*
        dog   yesterday   run-NMZ.S/P   bite   1SG.F   son=PST₁
        'The dog that yesterday escaped bit my son.' (Vallejos Yopán 2010: 593)

It should be noted, though, that the relevant participial form in Matsés (Pano-Tacanan) is not agentive in all contexts, but rather shows TAM-based split ergativity. In present or generic contexts, the suffix *-quid* is used to create forms which are oriented towards either S or A participant (i.e. active forms). On the other hand, in the recent past tense the same forms switch to ergative alignment, that is, they confine their orientation to A participants. Since this kind of split pattern in connection to participial orientation appears relevant for absolutive (S/P) participles in a larger number of languages, it will be discussed further in the next section. The resulting distribution in Matsés is presented in Table 6 below based on (Fleck 2003: 316):

Tab. 6: Participial markers for relativizing core participants in Matsés

Relativized participant	Present or generic	Recent past (inferential evidentiality)
A	-quid	-quid
S	-quid	-aid
P	-aid	-aid

In Matsés, ergative–absolutive alignment is relevant for other syntactic domains as well. In particular, case marking of nouns follows an ergative–absolutive pattern (Fleck 2003: 821). Similarly, Panare (Cariban) and Kamaiurá (Tupian) have also been shown to demonstrate certain ergative features in various parts of their grammar; see Payne and Payne (2013: 161, 255–257, 313) and Seki (2000: 191–192) for some discussion. For languages with agentive participles the share of at least partly ergative languages is, therefore, larger than overall in the sample (60%), but the absolute numbers are too small for any decisive conclusions.

Except for Matsés, where agentive orientation of the *-quid* participle is a result of a TAM-split, and Kamaiurá, which shows a threefold distinction (see Section 3.3.2), in the other three languages agentive participles exist in opposition to participles with S/P orientation, which will be discussed in more detail in the Section 3.3.5 below. For instance, in Urarina, the agentive nominalization *-era* is used to relativize A participants (74a), while the absolutive nominalization *-i* can relativize both S and P participants; see (74b) and (74c) respectively:

(74) Urarina (Urarina)
  a. [katɕa **rela-era**]   eene
     man   teach-NMZ.A woman
     'a woman who teaches people' (Olawsky 2006: 162)
  b. [kɨ **ne-rehete-kɨr-i**]   katɕa-ɨrɨ
     there be-HAB-NMZ.S/P   man-PL
     'the people who used to live here' (Olawsky 2006: 325)
  c. [ii   raj kiitɕa   **te-j**]   anofwa presta-ɨ
     2SG for 1SG.EMP give-NMZ.S/P knife   lend-IMP
     'Lend me the knife that I gave to you!' (Olawsky 2006: 325)

From an explanatory perspective, this means that such agentive participles could in principle lack semantic/pragmatic motivation in their own right, but rather "take over" the only core participant that cannot be relativized by the absolutive participle. If this is the case, we should rather try to uncover the motivation of the latter; see Section 3.8 for the relevant discussion.

Table 7 lists the languages of the core sample featuring agentive participles, and Figure 8 shows their location on the map.

Fig. 8: Languages with agentive participles

Tab. 7: Languages with agentive participles (% per macroarea)

Family	Language	Form(s)
South America (5/16, 31.3%)		
Cariban	Panare	PTCP.A -*jpo*
Pano-Tacanan	Matsés	NMZ.A/S -*quid* (not REC)
Tupian	Cocama	NMZ.A -*tara*
	Kamaiurá	NMZ.A -*tat*
Urarina	Urarina	NMZ.A -*era*

3.3.5 Absolutive participles

It is a well-known fact that participles traditionally labelled as "passive" can actually be oriented not just towards the direct object in a transitive construction, but also towards the only argument of an intransitive verb (see Haspelmath 1994). This phenomenon can be illustrated by examples from English, where past, or "passive", participles can be oriented both towards the object of a transitive verb, as in (75a)–(75b), and towards the single argument of some intransitive verbs, as in (75c)–(75d):

(75) English (Indo-European)
 a. *an abused child*
 b. *a murdered politician*
 c. *a rotten apple*
 d. *a fallen leaf*

Since this pairing of participants is parallel to that characteristic of absolutive coding in the languages with ergative–absolutive alignment, I refer to this type of participial orientation as *absolutive*; see Figure 9. Payne and Payne (2013: 107) also use this term to refer to this type of participles in Panare (Cariban).

Fig. 9: Orientation of absolutive participles

Many linguists have noticed that the formation of such forms is subject to semantic restrictions. In particular, past participles of this type tend to have certain constraints as regards the intransitive verbs they can be formed from. These constraints have been formulated in semantic as well as syntactic terms. According to Bresnan (1982: 30), for instance, past participles in English can only be formed from intransitive verbs when the subject of the intransitive verb has the semantic role theme, and not agent, and if it undergoes the change of state specified by the verb, as in *a fallen leaf*, *a collapsed lung*, *a lapsed Catholic*, or *a failed writer*. If, on the other hand, the subject of the intransitive verb is an agent, the formation of a corresponding participle is impossible, compare *a worked clerk, *a run athlete, or *a danced girl.

Haspelmath (1994: 159–161) regards these forms as *resultative* participles, since P and S_P participants can be usually characterized by a state resulting from the event in which they participated; see examples above. According to Haspelmath, resultative participles are semantically most natural, because they are typically oriented towards the patient, which is a semantic notion in its essence. Passive participles, on the other hand, are syntacticized to a considerable extent, since they exhibit orientation towards the direct object, a participant defined in purely syntactic terms. Based on a comparative analysis of Indo-European languages, Haspelmath claims that semantics-based resultative participles are primary to syntax-based passive participles. Pure passive participles are characteristic of Modern Russian (e.g. *ubi-t-yj* 'kill-PTCP.PST.PASS-M.NOM.SG'), and were attested in Latin (e.g. *scrip-t-us* 'write-PTCP.PST.PASS-M.NOM.SG'), but comparative evidence shows that this -*t*- passive form used to be a resultative participle in Proto-Indo-European. For instance, its Old Indic cognate -*tá* could be added to intransitive verbs to form resultative participles, e.g. Vedic *ga-tá-* 'gone', *mr-tá-* 'dead, lit. died', or Sanskrit *bhuk-ta-* 'having eaten', *pi-ta-* 'having drunk' (Haspelmath 1994: 161–162).

The orientation of resultative participles, however, is not always restricted to the patient. Haspelmath himself shows that in German the resultative participle can also characterize the agent. The crucial requirement in such cases is *telicity*, that is, an agentive verb can form a resultative participle only if it is telic; compare the grammatical construction in (76a) where the verb *tanzen* 'to dance' is used for directed motion, to the ungrammatical example (76b) where it refers to the manner of motion:

(76) German (Indo-European)
    a. *der* [*in einer Minute über den Hof* **getanzte**] *Junge*
       the in one minute across the courtyard dance.PTCP.PST boy
       'the boy who danced across the courtyard in one minute'
       (Haspelmath 1994: 160)
    b. **der* [*eine Minute lang* **getanzte**] *Junge*
       the one minute long dance.PTCP.PST boy
       'the boy who danced for one minute'
       (Haspelmath 1994: 160)

Indeed, the majority of participles with S/P orientation in my sample show very similar aspectual characteristics. All the Indo-European languages with participles of this type (Albanian, Eastern Armenian, Irish, German, Modern Greek, and Italian), and also Beng (Mande) and Panare (Cariban) have resultative absolutive participles.[17] Absolutive participles in Mochica (Mochica, Adelaar 2004) and Tarma Quechua (Quechua, Adelaar 2011) are reported to refer to "accomplished events", and relevant forms in Uralic languages (Erzya and Hungarian), Basque (Basque, Hualde and Ortiz de Urbina 2003), Georgian (Kartvelian, Hewitt 1995), and Tsafiki (Barbacoan, Dickinson 2002) are classified as "perfective".

A rare example of absolutive participial orientation that is not associated with perfectivity can be found in Koryak, where two absolutive participles form a future vs. non-future opposition. The future form in *-lqəl-* is not perfective, but it is still used to relativize both S participants (77a) and P participants (77b):

(77) Koryak (Chukotko-Kamchatkan)
  a. *əccaj-Ø* [*jaja-k* **ŋajqətva-jo-lqəl-Ø**] *pəce*
    aunt-ABS.SG house-LOC clean-NMZ-NOMFUT-ABS.SG first
    ajm-e-Ø
    go.to.fetch.water-PFV-3SG.S
    'The aunt who is supposed to clean at home has gone for water.'
    (Kurebito 2011: 28–29)
  b. *kalikal* [***akmec-co-lqəl-Ø***]
    book.ABS.SG buy-NMZ-NOMFUT-ABS.SG
    'the book which someone intends to buy'
    (Kurebito 2011: 29)

Non-perfective absolutive forms are also attested in two South American languages, Cocama (Tupian) and Urarina (Urarina).

The fact that absolutive participles tend to be resultative or perfective can be seen as parallel to a well-known connection between perfectivity and ergativity

---

17 Apparently, Kayardild (Tangkic) also has absolutive resultative participles, but their only relative uses reported in Evans (1995) are instances of P relativization, not S. However, when employed in independent sentences, the same forms demonstrate ergativity in their argument marking, i.e. they require nominative marking on S and P participants, which is a unique context in Kayardild (Evans 1995: 476–477). Because I do not have sufficient information on this question, I will not further discuss the orientation of resultative participles in Kayardild. Similarly, Shaul (1986) provides only examples of P relativization by means of the nominalization *-cugai* (labelled "future resultative" in Shaul 1986: 46) in Nevome (Uto-Aztecan), and does not discuss its orientation. This form, therefore, is excluded from the counts dealing with orientation.

(see DeLancey 1981, 1982), which is not uncommonly manifested in the alignment systems of various languages. It has been shown in numerous studies that this type of alignment in independent clauses can be historically derived from constructions involving participles or nominalizations (see DeLancey 1986 and Noonan 1997 for Sino-Tibetan, and Gildea 1998 for Cariban). This implies that it is the absolutive orientation of participles/nominalizations that needs to be explained in the first place in order to understand this phenomenon. I will propose some tentative explanations in Section 3.8.

Apart from the presence of basic absolutive forms outlined above, absolutive participial orientation can be prominent in a number of languages in some other ways. For instance, Northern Khanty has one negative participle that is absolutive, contrasting with two affirmative participles with wider relativizing capacity. The two affirmative participles can both relativize any participants up to obliques, and they only differ in their tense characteristics, one being used to refer to past and the other to non-past events. The negative participle *-li*, on the other hand, is neutral with respect to temporal and aspectual characteristics, but its orientation is restricted to intransitive subjects (78a), and transitive objects (78b):

(78) Northern Khanty (Uralic)
    a. [pe:jal-ti **xo:s-li**] ń a:wre:m il su:wil-ə-ti pit-ə-s
        swim-INF can-PTCP.NEG child down drown-EP-INF start-EP-PST.3SG
        'A child who could not swim started drowning.'
        (Nikolaeva 1999: 34)
    b. [**jo:nt-li**] je:rnas śuŋ-na xu:j-ə-l
        sew-PTCP.NEG dress corner-LOC lie-EP-NPST.3SG
        'A dress which someone did not finish sewing lies in the corner.'
        (Nikolaeva 1999: 34)

As I will show in Section 5.3.2, Northern Khanty is the only language where the orientation of the negative participle is more limited than the orientation of its affirmative counterparts. The paradigmatic preference towards absolutive orientation shown under negation could possibly reflect the fact that relativization of S and P participants is more common in negative contexts (which may lead to the grammaticalization of the pattern; see Bybee (2003) on the role of frequency), at least in Northern Khanty, but possibly also more widely. However, any further discussion of this matter would require a corpus-based analysis, which is beyond the scope of this study.

Absolutive orientation is also found in languages with very poor morphology, whose participial forms are at a very early stage of development. Ndyuka, a creole spoken in French Guiana and Suriname, has forms that are regularly derived from verbs via reduplication and can function as adnominal modifiers; compare the two sentences in (79):

(79) Ndyuka (Creole)
    a. *A   bai   wan   dagu*
       3SG   buy   a   dog
       'She bought a dog.' (Huttar and Huttar 1994: 537)
    b. ***Bai-bai***   *dagu   ná   abi   gwenti*
       buy-buy   dog   NEG   have   custom
       'Bought dogs never get used to you.' (Huttar and Huttar 1994: 537)

According to Huttar and Huttar (1994: 543), who refer to these forms as "participles", they can be derived both from transitive verbs as in the example above, and from intransitive verbs, thus behaving as absolute participles in other languages. These forms seem to be unable to take any dependents, and are therefore more like verbal adjectives than like participles (see Section 2.3.2 on the differences), but their orientation, nevertheless, is noteworthy in the context of the present discussion. A creole is a language that builds its grammar "from scratch". It can, therefore, be expected that it will first develop the most pragmatically valuable constructions.

Absolutive orientation can sometimes appear as a tendency rather than a strict rule. In Ket, for instance, action nominals used for non-finite relative clause formation are contextually oriented, that is, in principle, they can freely relativize S, P and A participants. If the corresponding verb is intransitive, it is inevitably the S participant that is relativized. However, if the verb is transitive, the default interpretation of the modified noun is as a P participant, as in (80a). An interpretation as an A participant is only possible if the head noun is highly agentive, as in (80b); the only way to make this really natural is to overtly express the P participant in the relative clause, as in (80c):

(80) Ket (Yeniseian)
    a. *tàrʲ   tīp*
       [*tàd*]   *tīb*
       hit.NMZ   dog
       'a beaten dog' (Nefedov 2012: 199)

b. *tàrʲ   kɛʔt*
   [*tàd*]   *keʔd*
   hit.NMZ   person
   'a beaten man'/'a man who is/was beating' (Nefedov 2012: 199)
c. *tīp   tàrʲ   kɛʔt*
   [*tīb   tàd*]   *keʔd*
   dog   hit.NMZ   person
   'a man who was beating his dog' (Nefedov 2012: 199)

In Hinuq, most participles (except for the locative participle), are contextually oriented, and they can relativize a wide range of participants, including locatives and possessors. The resultative participle in *-s* also has this type of wide relativizing capacity, but, according to Forker (2013: 570), in the majority of cases it is formed from intransitive verbs, or transtive verbs lacking an overt agent. Consequently, it is mostly used to relativize S and P participants, as in (81a) and (81b):

(81) Hinuq (Nakh-Daghestanian)
   a. *Ibrahim-ez   r-ik-o   haylu-s   rorbe   [hezzo-r*
      Ibrahim-DAT   V-see-PRS   she.OBL-GEN₁ leg.PL   back-LAT
      r-uti-š]
      NHPL-turn-PTCP.RES
      'Ibrahim sees their legs, which were turned around.' (Forker 2013: 570)
   b. *de   goł   hažilaw   ʔisa-s   uži   ʔali,   [Ø-u:-s   ʔazal*
      I   be   Isaew   Isa-GEN₁   son(I)   Ali   I-do-PTCP.RES 1000
      ʔačʼino   bišonno   qʼono   quno   ocʼeno   łono   eλa   λeba-ł
      nine   100   two   twenty   ten   three   ORD   year.OBL-CNT
      Čačan-λʼo   Erseni   aλ-a]
      Chechnya-SPR Erseni   village-IN
      'I am Isa Isaew's son Ali, born in the year 1953, in Chechnya, in the village of Erseni.' (Forker 2013: 570–571)

To summarize, not counting non-strict preferences described above, participles with absolutive orientation are attested in 19 languages in my sample (see Table 8 and Figure 10 below). Unlike passive participles, which are attested all over the world, absolutive participles are rather an areal phenomenon: they are more common in Europe and South America than elsewhere. In 15 languages, affirmative absolutive participles refer to accomplished events (i.e. they convey resultative or perfective meaning), while in three they can exhibit other aspectual properties. In seven languages, a single absolutive form is the only participle

(Albanian, Basque, Beng, Irish, Italian,[18] Mochica, and Modern Greek), in German and Hungarian it is opposed to an active participle, in Panare and Urarina to an agentive participle, in Koryak two absolutive participles form a paradigm of their own, while in the rest of the languages systems containing absolutive participles are more complex.

Fig. 10: Languages with absolutive participles

Out of 19 languages with absolutive participles, five (26.3%) show some degree of ergativity, ranging from Beng, where verb reduplication indicating participant plurality is controlled by S or P participants (see Paperno 2014: 41), to Koryak, which is consistently ergative in both argument marking and verbal agreement. This means that among languages with the S/P pattern in participial orientation, languages with the same pattern in basic clause structure are not more common than among languages with A/S- or P-oriented participles (see Sections 3.3.2 and 3.3.3 above), or in the sample in general. Importantly, nominative–accusative

---

18 In Italian, there are also forms in *-nte* traditionally referred to as "present participles", which demonstrate active orientation, e.g. *un quadro [raffigurante la Firenze di Dante]* 'a picture representing Dante's Florence'. I do not, however, consider these forms in this study, since they can only be derived from few verbs indicating properties or states, they often have idiosyncratic differences in meaning with the original verbs, and they only occur in relative clauses in the bureaucratic register (Maiden and Robustelli 2000: Sections 3.32, 7.23).

languages with absolutive participles (especially Cocama and Urarina, where absolutive orientation is not limited to perfective contexts) clearly contradict Dixon's (1979) and Kazenin's (1994) earlier observations that syntactic ergativity cannot co-exist with accusativity in morphology. This, however, is not a very strong contradiction, since relativization has been shown to be the domain that is most likely to be ergative in a language with split-ergative syntax (when compared to coordinate constructions and sentences with purposive clauses; see Kazenin 1994).

Tab. 8: Languages with absolutive participles (% per macroarea)

Family	Language	Form(s)
South America (6/16, 37.5%)		
Barbacoan	Tsafiki	PTCP.PFV -*ka*
Cariban	Panare	PTCP.PST -*sa'*
Mochica	Mochica	NMZ.STAT -*d.o*
Quechuan	Tarma Quechua	NMZ.STAT -*sha*
Tupian	Cocama	NMZ.S/P -*n*
Urarina	Urarina	NMZ.S/P -*i*
Africa (1/12, 8.3%)		
Mande	Beng	NMZ -*lɛ*
Eurasia (12/47, 25.5%)		
Basque	Basque	PTCP.PFV -*tu/(e-)V-i*
Chukotko-Kamchatkan	Koryak	NMZ -*lʕ-*, NMZ-NOMFUT -*jo-lqəl*
Indo-European	Albanian	PTCP -*rë/-r/-ur/-ë*
	Eastern Armenian	PTCP.RES -*ac*
	German	PTCP.PST
	Irish	PTCP.PST -*tha/-the*
	Italian	PTCP.PST -*t-*
	Modern Greek	PTCP.PST -*ménos*
Kartvelian	Georgian	PTCP.PST -*ul/-il/m-V-ar*, PTCP.PRIV *u-V(-el)*
Uralic	Erzya	PTCP.PFV -*z'*, PTCP.PST -*vt*
	Hungarian	PTCP.PST -*ott*
	Northern Khanty	PTCP.NEG -*li*

3.4 Orientation towards non-core participants

Although inherently oriented participles are most commonly oriented towards core participants (as in the active, passive, agentive and absolutive participles discussed above), there are also specialized participial forms for relativizing participants from the lower part of the Accessibility Hierarchy. In fact, in this case the relativized participants are best characterized not as representing a particular position on the Accessibility Hierarchy, but rather one or more semantic functions. For instance, Muna employs the marker *ka-V-ha* to relativize locatives, i.e. it has locative participles; see (82):

(82) Muna (Austronesian)
 naando fato-ghonu sikola [***ka-fo-fo-guru-ha-ku*** *wamba*
 be four-CL school NMZ-DETR-CAUS-learn-LOC-my language
 Inggirisi welo se-minggu]
 English in one-week
 'There were four schools where I taught English in one week.'
 (van den Berg 2013: 236)

Judging from the available data, forms like this can refer to any location irrespective of its precise role. It is the context that further specifies what is being relativized, as illustrated by the examples from Guarijío, where the form in *-ači* can relativize a location (83a), or a source (83b):

(83) Guarijío (Uto-Aztecan)
 a. *kahóni* [*no'ó katewe-ri-**ači** anío*]
  box 1SG.NS keep-PFV-NMZ.LOC ring
  'the box where I kept the ring' (Félix Armendáriz 2005: 97)
 b. *kahóni* [*no'ó mačipa-ri-**ači** anío*]
  box 1SG.NS take.out-PFV-NMZ.LOC ring
  'the box that I took the ring out of' (Félix Armendáriz 2005: 97)

Other non-finite verb forms that specialize in relativizing locatives include the local participle in *-a* in Hinuq (see example (88a) below), and the form in *-tupa* in Cocama (Tupian, Vallejos Yopán 2010: 595–598). Nevome (Uto-Aztecan, Shaul 1986: 46–48) appears to be able to use a whole set of locative nominalization markers for relative clause formation, *-cami* being used in present contexts, *-carhami* in habitual contexts, *-parhami* referring to the past, and *-aicami* to the future. Unfortunately, the data on the question is too scarce to present any consistent description of these constructions.

In addition to locative participles, some languages have verb forms whose relativization potential is limited to instruments, that is, instrumental participles. Probably the clearest example of this is the form in -*nanɨ* in the Apatani language; see (84):

(84) Apatani (Sino-Tibetan)
 [nɨka **panɨnanɨ**] ilyo mi mó bitɨ
 I.GEN cut.NMZ.INS sword ACC he bring.PST
 'He brought the sword with which I cut.' (Abraham 1985: 133)

Another Sino-Tibetan language that has instrumental participial relative clauses is Qiang. In some varieties, such as Ronghong or Qugu, the nominalizer -*s-/-sa*- is used for relativization of other non-core participants as well (see Huang 2008: 743), but at least in Muka Qiang instrumental relativization is the only possibility; see (85):

(85) Muka (Southern) Qiang (Sino-Tibetan)
 [zedə **se-sa**] tɕi-to balubase
 book write-NMZ.INS that-CL thing
 'the thing that is used to write with' (Huang 2008: 745)

In Ma'di, the -*dʒɔ́* form also functions primarily as an instrumental relativizer, although the relativized participant can be interpreted as the reason as well, as shown in (86a). According to Blackings and Fabb (2003: 203), the range of meanings of the noun modified by the -*dʒɔ́* form is similar to that of the complement of the postposition *sɨ* associated with source, as illustrated in (86b). It is interesting though, that this "instrumental" participle is extending its orientation beyond the possibilities of the postposition. For instance, it can be used to modify some nouns with a generic meaning, such as 'way' (86c), or 'time' (86d). A possible explanation might be that, unlike with the postposition in simple clauses, the context of a relative clause makes the interpretation easy and less ambiguous, and therefore, the participle is able to function in a wider range of contexts.

(86) Ma'di (Central Sudanic)
 a. ílí [ágɔ́ rì nɨ̄ **lī-dʒɔ́**] rì lɔ́tʃī rì ʔɨ̄
 knife man DEF PRON NPST.cut-SR.INS DEF sharp DEF FOC
 'The knife with/for which the man was cut was the sharp one.'
 (Blackings and Fabb 2003: 204)

b. ō-lī   ílí   nā   sɨ̀
   3-cut knife AFR   SRC
   'He cut it with/because of his/her knife.' (Blackings and Fabb 2003: 369)

c. ɔ̄vī̄   [āná-à   sī-dʒɔ́]   rì̀   bá   nì-bá   rá
   way   3SG-POSS NPST.build-SR.INS DEF people NPST.know-SR.S/A.PL AFF
   nā
   AFR   small
   'How she built it is known only to a few people.'
   (Blackings and Fabb 2003: 204)

d. sáà   [sī-dʒɔ́]   rì̀   bá   nì-bá   rá   nā
   time   NPST.build-SR.INS DEF people NPST.know-SR.S/A.PL AFF   AFR
   gà
   small
   'Only a few people know about the time it was built.'
   (Blackings and Fabb 2003: 205)

The uses illustrated in (86c) and (86d) actually bring the instrumental participle in Ma'di closer to another class of forms, namely those exhibiting contextual orientation within a range of possibilities limited to non-core or non-subject participants. I will discuss these forms in detail in Section 3.5.2. Similarly, the *-nun* nominalization in Tsafiki (Barbacoan) can relativize instrumental and locative participants (Dickinson 2002: 239).

It is important to mention that most of the forms in my sample that from a comparative perspective qualify as participles inherently oriented towards a particular peripheral participant (instrumental or locative) are actually considered participant nominalizations by the authors of the respective grammars (on the syncretism of participles and nominalizations see Section 2.4). This primarily reflects the fact that most of these forms commonly occur on their own, without head nouns, compare example (87) from Ma'di to (86) above:

(87) Ma'di (Central Sudanic)
mgbā-dʒɔ́   rì̀   dì̀   ʔī̄
[NPST.beat-SR.INS] DEF this FOC
'The one with which/for which it was beaten is this one.'
(Blackings and Fabb 2003: 204)

A notable exception in terms of labelling is Hinuq, where the relevant form is referred to as a "local participle". However, even there, according to Forker (2013:

257), these forms only occasionally appear with a modified noun, as in (88a), and primarily function in headless relative constructions, as in (88b):

(88) Hinuq (Nakh-Daghestanian)
  a. [eli   xalq'i   b-iči-ya]   **moč-a**   zoq'ʷe-s   goɬ,
     we.GEN₁   people   HPL-be-PTCP.LOC   place.OBL-IN   be-RES   be
     b-ʔeži   obšestwo rik'zi.b.u:-ho   zoq'ʷe-s   goɬ
     HPL-big   society   count.HPL-CVB.IPFV   be-RES   be
     'In the place where our people lived, there was a big society.'
     (Forker 2013: 253)
  b. zurmaqan   [buq   b-oλex-a-do]   q'iliqan   [buq
     zurna.player   sun(III)   III-appear-PTCP.LOC-DIR   drummer   sun(III)
     b-iλ'i-ya-do]   b-eze-n   b-iλ'i-š=eλ
     III-go-PTCP.LOC-DIR   HPL-look-CVB.NARR   HPL-go-PST=NARR
     'The zurna player went into the direction of the rising sun, the drummer went into the direction of the setting sun.'
     (Forker 2013: 258)

Judging from their use (reflected in the descriptive practices), inherently oriented forms used to relativize peripheral participants are, therefore, fairly nouny in their nature, whereas participles oriented towards core participants do not commonly exhibit this type of syncretism.

While locatives and instrumentals can have specialized participles, the possessor does not seem to have any participles specifically employed for its relativization. This is indeed very natural, since participles as verb forms are expected to be oriented towards clausal participants, while possessors are nominal dependents in their essence. All types of verbal dependents, on the other hand, can in principle be targets of inherent participial orientation. Table 9 and Figure 11 give information on participles oriented towards non-core participants attested in the languages of the sample.

Fig. 11: Languages with participles oriented towards non-core participants
(▲ – locative, ● – instrument, ■ – several participants)

Tab. 9: Languages with participles oriented towards non-core participants (number of languages per macroarea)

Family	Language	Participant(s)	Form(s)
Papunesia (1/7)			
Austronesian	Muna	Locative	NMZ-V-LOC *ka-V-ha*
North America (2/13)			
Uto-Aztecan	Guarijío	Locative	NMZ.LOC -*ači*
	Nevome	Locative	NMZ.LOC.PRS -*cami*, NMZ.LOC.HAB -*carhami*, NMZ.LOC.PST -*parhami*, NMZ.LOC.FUT -*aicami*
South America (2/16)			
Barbacoan	Tsafiki	Several	NMZ.INS/LOC -*nun*
Tupian	Cocama	Locative	NMZ.LOC -*tupa*
Africa (1/12)			
Central Sudanic	Ma'di	Several	SR.INS -*dʒ5*

Family	Language	Participant(s)	Form(s)
Eurasia (3/47)			
Nakh-Daghestanian	Hinuq	Locative	PTCP.LOC -*a*
Sino-Tibetan	Apatani	Instrument	NMZ.INS -*nanɨ*
	Ronghong Qiang	Instrument	NMZ.INS -*s*

3.5 Contextual orientation

As defined in Section 3.1, contextually oriented participles are forms that can relativize several different participants depending on the context. The main parameter according to which such forms can differ across languages is the range of participants they can relativize. In this section, I will distinguish between *full contextual orientation* (3.5.1) and *limited contextual orientation* (3.5.2). It is important to emphasize that the term "full contextual orientation" does not mean that a certain form has no restrictions whatsoever as to which participants it can relativize, but rather that it does not have such restrictions in the higher part of the Accessibility Hierarchy. In other words, forms demonstrating full contextual orientation are always able to relativize at least all of the core participants (A, S, and P). By contrast, forms demonstrating limited contextual orientation are unable to relativize some or all of the core participants, but otherwise they can still be oriented towards several different participants depending on the context. Further clarifications and examples will be provided in the respective sections.

3.5.1 Full contextual orientation

In most cases, the range of participants relativizable by a certain contextually oriented participial form can be represented as a continuous segment of the Accessibility Hierarchy starting from its left end:[19]

(89) Subject > Direct Object > Indirect Object > Oblique > Possessor

---

[19] In the version of the Accessibility Hierarchy used in this section I do not distinguish between transitive subjects (A) and intransitive subjects (S), since this opposition is mostly irrelevant for contextually oriented participles. It should also be noted that in some languages, participles can have wider relativization capacity than presented here, because the grammatical descriptions may simply lack relevant examples for some non-core participants, such as, for instance, locatives and possessors.

Since, according to the definition, contextually oriented participles have to be able to relativize at least all of the core participants (subject and direct object in this representation), there can be four major types of such forms with respect to their relativization capacity: (1) subjects and direct objects, (2) from subjects to indirect objects, (3) from subjects to obliques, and (4) from subjects to possessors. All of these types are attested among the languages of the sample, although they are not equally common.

Contextually oriented participles of the first type can be found in Chimariko, where dependent forms in -*rop*/-*rot*/-*lop*/-*lot* can relativize subjects and direct objects; see example (90a) for subject relativization, and (90b) for direct object relativization:[20]

(90) Chimariko (Chimariko)
 a. [*moʔa pʰuncar h-uwa-tku-rop*] *pʰaʔyi-nip*
    yesterday woman 3-go-DIR-DEP thus.say
    'That woman who came yesterday told me.' (Jany 2008: 42)
 b. [*čʰeʔnew y-ewu-rop*] *hačmukčʰa čʰ-awu-n*
    bread 1SG.A-give-DEP axe 1SG.P-give-ASP
    'For the bread I gave him, he gave me an axe.' (Jany 2008: 42)

Forms relativizing all of the core participants are also attested in Tundra Nenets (referred to as "participles" in Nikolaeva 2014), but, importantly, they co-exist in the language with forms relativizing other participants, namely indirect objects and various obliques; see Section 3.5.2.

Two other examples of the first type are negative participles in North Saami (Uralic) and Yimas. In the latter, negative non-finite relative forms in -*kakan* can be interpreted as relativizing either subjects or direct objects, hence the ambiguity illustrated in example (91):

(91) Yimas (Lower Sepik-Ramu)
 wakn na-mpu-ŋa-tkam-t [*namat*
 snake(CL5.SG) CL5.SG.T-3PL.A-1SG-show-PFV person(CL1.PL)

---

[20] It should be noted though, that Chimariko is an extinct language, for which only a limited amount of data is available. It is, therefore, possible, that the relativizing capacity of the forms in question used to be wider.

tu-kakan-Ø]
kill-NF.NEG-CL5.SG
'1. They showed me the snake that doesn't kill people.
2. They showed me the snake that people don't kill.' (Foley 1991: 407)

The second type can be illustrated by contextually oriented nominalization in Apatani (Sino-Tibetan), which is used to relativize subjects, direct objects, and datives, as shown earlier in Section 3.2, example (55). It is important to note in this connection that Apatani also has a separate nominalization specializing on instrumental relativization, as shown in example (84) above. At least one lower position on the Accessibility Hierarchy is, therefore, "taken" by a different form, so it is fairly natural that the contextually oriented participle does not spread down the Accessibility Hierarchy. The only other language in my sample that presumably demonstrates the same type of contextual orientation is Wappo (Yuki-Wappo, Thompson, Park, and Li 2006). However, restrictions on the range of relativizable participants are not explicitly discussed in the grammar of this language. Thus, it is possible to conclude that contextually oriented forms that are limited to subjects, direct objects and indirect objects are not very common either.

As is clear from the discussion above, most contextually oriented participles belong to the third type, that is, they can relativize a broad range of positions on the Accessibility Hierarchy. Illustrations of such forms have already been provided, as the examples in (2) for Kalmyk (Mongolic), or the examples in (53) for Lezgian (Nakh-Daghestanian). If we only take into account the internal relativizing capacity of participles (excluding their ability to relativize a possessor provided by resumptive pronouns; see Section 3.6.2), most of the forms in my sample are able to relativize all positions on the Accessibility Hierarchy down to the obliques. However, participants encoded as obliques are not equal as to how easily they can be relativized in different languages. In many languages, the limits for contextual orientation of participles are determined by properties of the verbs from which the participles are derived. For instance, Malchukov (2008: 218) reports for Even (Tungusic) that the participial gap strategy can only be employed if the relativized participant belongs to the valency of the verb, hence the impossibility of the locative relativization *d'ep-teng-u d'u* eat-PTCP.PST-POSS.1SG 'the house where I ate', or the instrument relativization *xör-deng-u kingne* go.away-PTCP.PST-POSS.1SG 'the skis on which I went away'. I will further refer to this restriction as the *valency rule*.

Nikolaeva (2014: 326) describes a similar tendency for Tundra Nenets, where it is possible to relativize the object of a postposition if the modifying verb is frequently collocated with the respective postpositional phrase. Under this rule, for example, the relativization of the postpositional phrase headed by the postposition *n'amna* 'about' is perfectly fine with the verb *yi-yader* 'to think' but unacceptable or very marginal with the verbs *xinoq-* 'to sing' or *tolaŋo-* 'to read'. With both types of verbs, a postpositional phrase headed by *n'amna* is totally acceptable in independent sentences, but while the oblique object is virtually obligatory with the verb 'to think', referring to singing or reading usually does not require specifying the content of the song or the reading material.

Contextual relativization is, therefore, commonly regulated by pragmatics. When the head noun is not overtly represented within the relative clause introduced by a contextually oriented participle, the relation between the relative clause and the head noun remains underspecified. For instance, the relative construction of the type [*cat$_S$ sit$_{PTCP}$*] *table* can mean 'the table on which the cat is sitting', 'the table at which the cat is sitting', 'the table under which the cat is sitting', etc. Accessibility to relativization in such cases commonly depends on how easy it is to reconstruct the relation between the verbal form and the relativized noun. As a result, it is often not possible to relativize any objects of postpositions with a specific meaning. However, simple locations and similar participants are comparatively easy to relativize.

Interestingly, this rule works to a certain extent even in the languages that mainly favour inherent orientation in their participial systems. Slight extensions of the orientation of passive participles also rely on the frequency of collocation and the recoverability of the relativized participant; see Section 3.3.3. As a result, the Finnish negative participle in *-maton*, for instance, is very similar in its orientation to the forms attested in Even or Tundra Nenets. Structurally, it is the counterpart of active and passive participles. However, apart from relativizing the core participants (see (92a), (92b) and (92c) for S, A and P relativization respectively), it can also relativize at least locatives (92d), and temporal adverbials (92e):

(92) Finnish (Uralic)
    a. [*koskaan*   *kuole-maton*]   *rakkaus*
        never   die-PTCP.NEG   love
        'love that never dies'
    b. [*loppututkinto-a*   *suoritta-maton*]   *hakija*
        final.degree-PTV   complete-PTCP.NEG   applicant
        'the applicant that did not complete the final degree'

c. [*kenen-kään   tietä-mätön*]   *määrä*
   who.GEN-POL   know-PTCP.NEG   amount
   'the amount that nobody knows'
d. [*lähes   istu-maton*]   *vuodesohva*
   almost   sit-PTCP.NEG   sofa
   'the sofa that almost was not sat on'
e. [*täysin   syö-mätön*]   *päivä*
   fully   eat-PTCP.NEG   day
   'the day when (someone) did not eat at all'

Example (92e) above from Finnish illustrates an interesting cross-linguistic tendency. Even in languages that follow the valency rule in relativization, temporal adverbials can often be relativized, although in many cases they clearly do not belong to the set of obligatory arguments. Malchukov (1995: 36) proposes to account for this exception by making the assumption that temporal noun phrases in these languages actually count as arguments. He also points out that this assumption is independently required for lexicological reasons, according to Plungian and Raxilina (1990).

The fourth type, again, is less common. As can be expected on the basis of the Accessibility Hierarchy, possessors are the most problematic participants for participial relativization. If a language uses internally headed participial clauses to relativize a possessor, usually no special means are needed to ensure its recoverability. Both the possessor and the possessum occur within the relative clause, and their relation is clearly indicated in the construction, as in example (93) from Nanga:

(93) Nanga (Dogon)
[*àrnà   nàŋá   sà:dì-sɛ̀*]   *bû:*
man.L   cow   die.without.slaughter-PTCP.PFV.L   DEF.AN.PL
'the men whose cow died (naturally)' (Heath 2008: 286–287)

On the other hand, if a language with externally headed relative clauses employs participles for relativizing possessors, this is usually realized with resumptive pronouns; see further in Section 3.6.2 for discussion. However, in certain languages, the participial gap strategy is also available for possessor relativization, as in example (94) from Korean (notice though that the resumptive pronoun *casinuy* is still possible in this context):

(94) Korean (Koreanic)
[(casin-uy) cha-ka kocangna-n] Peter
oneself-of car-NOM broke-REL Peter
'Peter whose own car broke down' (Shin 2003: 33)

In several languages in the sample, the participial gap strategy allows relativization of possessors in situations of inalienable possession, but not alienable possession. For instance, in Ingush, it is only possible to relativize the possessor of a kin term (95a), or the possessor of a body part (95b). Other type of possessors are not relativizable, as reflected in the ungrammaticality of (95c):

(95) Ingush (Nakh-Daghestanian)
 a. [___ voshaz suona axcha deitaa] sag
  GEN brother.ERG 1SG.DAT money D.give.PTCP.PST person
  'the person whose brother gave me money' (Nichols 2011: 592)
 b. [zhwalez ___ kyljgaa carjg tiexaa] sag
  dog.ERG GEN hand.DAT tooth bite.PTCP.PST person
  'the person whose hand the dog bit' (Nichols 2011: 592)
 c. *[suoga ___ gour jola] sag
  1SG.ALL GEN horse J.be.PTCP.PRS person
  'the person whose horse I've got' (Nichols 2011: 592)

The same constraint on the relativization of possessors is reported at least for Malayalam (Dravidian, Asher and Kumari 1997), and Lezgian (Nakh-Daghestanian, Haspelmath 1993). Pragmatically, this constraint makes perfect sense, since the main problem with the gap strategy in general concerns the recoverability of the relativized participant. In cases of inalienable possession, the relation between the possessor and the possessum is considerably more transparent and expected than in cases of alienable possession. This restriction can, therefore, be regarded as another modification of the valency rule discussed above.

To summarize, in my sample, four languages have participles allowing relativization up to direct objects, two languages up to indirect objects, 30 languages up to obliques, and 11 languages up to possessors. Tables 10 to 13 present languages that feature contextually oriented participles with different relativization capacity. The data is also presented on the map in Figure 12.

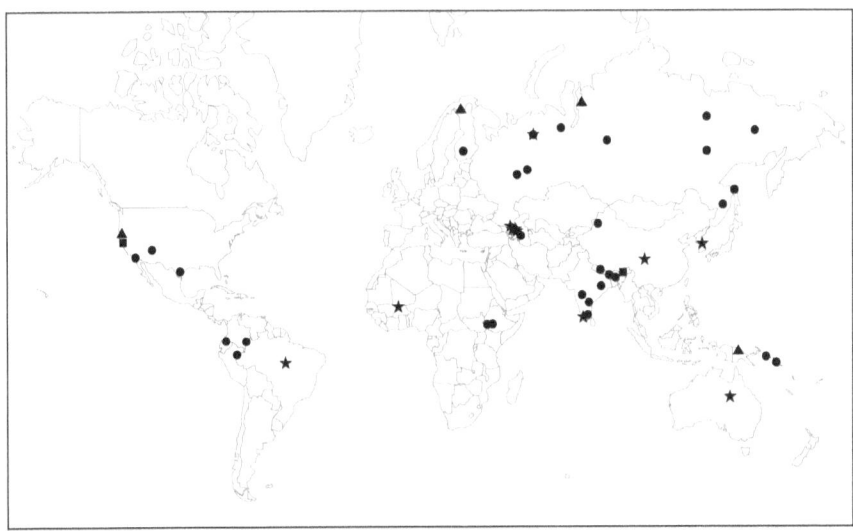

Fig. 12: Languages with contextually oriented participles: full contextual orientation
(Relativization up to: ▲ – P, ■ – IO, ● – OBL, ★ – POSS)

Tab. 10: Languages with contextually oriented participles: relativization up to P (number of languages per macroarea)

Family	Language	Form(s)
Papunesia (1/7)		
Lower Sepik-Ramu	Yimas	NF.NEG -*kakan*
North America (1/13)		
Chimariko	Chimariko	DEP -*rop*/-*rot*/-*lop*/-*lot*
Eurasia (2/47)		
Uralic	North Saami	PTCP.NEG -*keahtes*
	Tundra Nenets	PTCP.PFV -*miə*/-*me*, PTCP.IPFV -*n(ʼ)a*/-*t(ʼ)a*, PTCP.FUT -*mənta*, PTCP.NEG -*mədawe(y(ə))*

Tab. 11: Languages with contextually oriented participles: relativization up to IO (number of languages per macroarea)

Family	Language	Form(s)
North America (1/13)		
Yuki-Wappo	Wappo	DEP (system)
Eurasia (1/47)		
Sino-Tibetan	Apatani	NMZ -nɨ

Tab. 12: Languages with contextually oriented participles: relativization up to OBL (number of languages per macroarea)

Family	Language	Form(s)
Papunesia (2/7)		
Savosavo	Savosavo	REL -tu
South Bougainville	Motuna	PTCP -(wa)h
North America (3/13)		
Coahuilteco	Coahuilteco	SUB p-/pa-
Uto-Aztecan	Hopi	REL -qa
	Luiseño	REL (system)
South America (3/16)		
Nadahup	Hup	DEP -Vp
Pano-Tacanan	Matsés	NMZ (system)
Quechuan	Imbabura Quechua	NMZ.PST -shka, NMZ.PRS -j, NMZ.FUT -na
Africa (2/12)		
Afro-Asiatic	Kambaata	REL, PTCP.NEG -umb
Dizoid	Sheko	REL -àb, -àbe
Eurasia (20/47)		
Austroasiatic	Kharia	PTCP
Dravidian	Tamil	PTCP -a, PTCP.FUT -um
	Telugu	PTCP.PST -ina, PTCP.FUT -ee, PTCP.DUR -tunna, PTCP.NEG -ani

Family	Language	Form(s)
Indo-European	Apsheron Tat	PTCP -*de*/-*re*
	Marathi	PTCP (system)
Mongolic	Kalmyk	PTCP.PST -*sən*, PTCP.FUT -*xə*, PTCP.HAB -*dəg*
Nivkh	Nivkh	PTCP
Sino-Tibetan	Dhimal	NMZ -*ka*
	Garo	NMZ -*gipa*
	Manange	NMZ -*pʌ*
Tungusic	Even	PTCP.NFUT -*ri*/-*i*/-*si*/-*di*, PTCP.PRF -*ča*/-*če*, PTCP.PST -*daŋ*/-*deŋ*, PTCP.NEC -*nna*/-*nne*, PTCP.HYP -*d'iŋa*/-*d'iŋe*
	Nanai	PTCP.PST -*xan*/-*kin*/-*čin*, PTCP.NPST -*j*/-*ri*/-*di*/-*či*
Turkic	Yakut	PTCP.PST -*bït*, PTCP.PRS -*ar*/-*ïr*, PTCP.FUT -*ïax*, PTCP.NEG.PST -*batax*, PTCP.NEG.PRS -*bat*, PTCP.NEG.FUT -*(i)mïax*
Uralic	Beserman Udmurt	PTCP.PST -*m*
	Finnish	PTCP.NEG -*maton*
	Komi-Zyrian	PTCP.HAB -*an(a)*, PTCP.NEG -*təm*
	Meadow Mari	PTCP.FUT -*šaš*, PTCP.NEG -*dəme*
	Northern Khanty	PTCP.PST -*m*, PTCP.NPST -*ti*
Yeniseian	Ket	NMZ
Yukaghir	Kolyma Yukaghir	NMZ -*l*

Tab. 13: Languages with contextually oriented participles: relativization up to POSS (number of languages per macroarea)

Family	Language	Form(s)
Australia (1/5)		
Pama-Nyungan	Pitta Pitta	PST -*ka*
South America (1/16)		
Nuclear-Macro-Je	Mēbengokre	NMZ

Family	Language	Form(s)
Africa (1/12)		
Dogon	Nanga	PTCP.PFV -sɛ̂, PTCP.IPFV -mî
Eurasia (8/47)		
Dravidian	Malayalam	PTCP -a, PTCP.NEG -aatta
Koreanic	Korean	REL -n, REL.PRS -nɨn, REL.FUT -l
Nakh-Daghestanian	Hinuq	PTCP -o goɬa, PTCP.PST -(y)oru, PTCP.HAB -ƛ'os, (PTCP.RES -s)
	Ingush	PTCP.PST -aa/-na, PTCP.PRS -a, CVB.SIM -(a)zh
	Lezgian	PTCP -j
	Tanti Dargwa	PRET[PTCP]/ATTR -se, PRS[PTCP]/ATTR -se, PTCP.POT -an
Sino-Tibetan	Ronghong Qiang	NMZ.AN -m
Uralic	Komi-Zyrian	PTCP.PFV -əm(a)

3.5.2 Limited contextual orientation

As shown above, in most languages with contextually oriented participles, these forms can be used to relativize a particular number of positions on the Accessibility Hierarchy starting from its left end, i.e. from the subject. Some languages, however, use certain participles to relativize a range of positions starting from a lower point, such as the direct object or the indirect object. In fact, one form, the patientive nominalization in -aid in Matsés (Pano-Tacanan) is even used in non-A relativization rather than in non-subject relativization, but this only concerns recent past contexts (see Table 6 in Section 3.3.4 and related discussion for details).

Most of the languages with limited contextual orientation (13 out of 17) can relativize all positions on the Accessibility Hierarchy except for the subject; see Table 14 in the end of this section for an exhaustive list. An example of a form with non-subject contextual orientation is the participle in -me in Meadow Mari; see (96a) for direct object relativization, (96b) for indirect object relativization, and (96c) and (96d) for the relativization of locatives with different semantics:

(96) Meadow Mari (Uralic)
    a. [koka-m-ən   kalas-en **kod-əmo**]   legend-əʒe
       aunt-POSS.1SG-GEN tell-CVB leave-PTCP.NS legend-POSS.3SG
       'the legend told by my aunt'
       (Serdobolskaya and Paperno 2006: 5)
    b. [məj-ən kup   gə-tʃ'   **polʃ-əmo**]   ajdeme
       1SG-GEN swamp from-ABL help-PTCP.NS man
       'the man whom I helped to get out of the swamp'
       (Serdobolskaya and Paperno 2006: 5)
    c. [mə-lam kaj-aʃ **kyl-me**]   jal   peʃ toraʃte-ʒ-ak   ogəl
       1SG-DAT.1SG go-INF need-PTCP.NS village very far-POSS.3SG-EMP NEG.3SG
       'The village where I need to go is not too far.'
       (Serdobolskaya and Paperno 2006: 6)
    d. [oksa **kij-əme**] kvartire de-tʃ' kl'utʃ mə-lam   kyl-eʃ
       money lie-PTCP.NS apartment near-ABL key 1SG-DAT.1SG need-PRS.3SG
       'I need a key for the apartment where money is situated.'
       (Serdobolskaya and Paperno 2006: 6)

Languages with contextual orientation limited to non-core participants are much rarer. One of them, Tundra Nenets, has two sets of forms used for relativization. The first set (forms mentioned earlier in Section 3.5.1) can relativize subjects and direct objects, while the second set can relativize a wide range of peripheral participants, i.e. the positions of the Accessibility Hierarchy from the indirect object extending to the right. The forms in the second set are referred to by Nikolaeva (2014) as perfective action nominal, modal converb, and imperfective action nominal. The examples below illustrate their use for relativization of the indirect object (97a), the instrument (97b), the comitative adjunct (97c), and the time and locative adverbials; see (97d) and (97e) respectively:

(97) Tundra Nenets (Uralic)
    a. [kniga-m m'is-oqma(-m'i)] xasawa ŋac'ekem'i
       book-ACC give-NMZ.PFV-1SG man   child.1SG
       'the boy to whom I gave the book' (Nikolaeva 2014: 323)
    b. [ŋuda-m'i   məda-qma(-m'i)] xər°-m'i
       hand-ACC.1SG cut-NMZ.PFV-1SG knife-1SG
       'the knife with which I cut my hand' (Nikolaeva 2014: 324)
    c. [yil'e-s'°   / yil'es'ə-m'i]   n'enec'ə-m'i
       live-CVB.MOD / live.CVB.MOD-1SG person-1SG
       'the person with whom I live' (Nikolaeva 2014: 324)

d. [*toxodənə-°* *xǽ-s'°*] *yal'a-doh*
   study-CVB.MOD go-CVB.MOD day-3PL
   'the day for them to go to study' (Nikolaeva 2014: 324)
e. [*m'ūd°-naq* *m'i-ma*] *soti°*
   caravan-GEN.1PL move-NMZ.IPFV hill
   'the hill over which our caravan is moving' (Nikolaeva 2014: 325)

The same type of limited contextual orientation (from indirect object down the Accessibility Hierarchy) is also attested in Kamaiurá (Tupian) and Japhug rGyalrong (Sino-Tibetan). The only language in my sample that has specialized participial forms specialized in the relativization of a wide variety of obliques (and possessors of obliques) is Seri (Seri). According to Marlett (2012: 223), the form *ʔi-Ø-asi* (POSS.1-NMZ.OBL-drink) can mean '(the one) with which I drink', '(the place) where I drink', '(the way) how I drink', etc.

At first glance, these forms with limited contextual orientation may seem to contradict the formulation of the Accessibility Hierarchy, since they allow the relativization of lower positions (e.g. obliques) without being able to relativize higher positions (e.g. subjects). However, what Keenan and Comrie (1977) actually claim is that this rule should be true for a given relativization strategy rather than for any single form, and all the forms discussed in this section belong to participial paradigms where other non-finite forms are specialized in relativizing the higher part of the Accessibility Hierarchy. Therefore, all of these languages comply with the general rule. The only possible exception is Wan (Mande), where the attributive nominalization in *-ŋ*, which is the only nominalized form used for relativization, has limited contextual orientation starting from the direct object. Nevertheless, in this language all contexts where we could expect subject (S or A) relativization are covered by an agent nominalization, which cannot be used for adnominal modification (Tatiana Nikitina, p.c.). Keenan and Comrie's (1977) generalization thus holds in the case of Wan as well, at least to a certain extent.

As an aside, it is interesting to note that the limits of contextual orientation can be a pragmatic consequence of expressing a certain category within the participial form. In Matsés (Pano-Tacanan), TAM-coding participant nominalizations, which are one of the primary means for relativizing a very wide range of core and peripheral participants, can express two evidentiality values, viz. experiential and inferential. As reported in Fleck (2003: 306), the referent of the experiential participant nominalization (and, presumably, also the modified noun when the nominalization is used as a relative clause predicate) may be tangible or intangible, and witnessed with any of the five senses. With the inferential nominalizers, there is a further restriction that the participant being referred to (or, conceivably, modified) must have some persisting, detectable, resulting mark that allows the speaker to infer the event without having seen the actual event. This condition excludes some entities as potential referents of inferential nominalizations, such as visibly unaffected participants. As a result of the outlined condition, Matsés inferential nominalizations tend to exhibit limited contextual orientation of the non-A type, since agents are typically not affected by the situation they take part in. The difference between the two types of nominalization in Matsés is illustrated in (98), where examples (a) and (c) show experiential nominalizations, and examples (b) and (d) show inferential nominalizations.[21] For the inferential nominalizations in (b) and (d), the agentive interpretation is impossible, since neither killing nor running typically affect the appearance of agents in a significant way:

(98) Matsés (Pano-Tacanan; Fleck 2003: 306)
    a. *cues-boed*
       hit/kill-NMZ.PST.EXP
       'person/animal who did the hitting/killing'
       'dead person/animal'
       'wounded or unwounded person/animal'
       'wound'
       'weapon used'
    b. *cues-aid*
       hit/kill-NMZ.PST.INFR
       *'person/animal who did the killing'
       'dead person/animal'
       'wounded person/animal'
       'wound'
       'bloody weapon'
    c. *titinque-ondaid*
       run-NMZ.PST.EXP
       'person/animal who ran'
       'old footprints'
       'path (where speaker saw S running)'
    d. *titinque-nëdaid*
       run-NMZ.PST.INFR
       *'person/animal who ran'
       'old footprints'
       'path (with old footprints)'

This is, however, a very marginal case specific to a particular language and, therefore, it is not relevant for the general typology of participial forms.

The orientation of a given participle can also depend on the type of relative construction it is used in. In Imbabura Quechua (Quechuan), all nominalized predicates of externally headed relative clauses are purely contextually oriented, and the choice is determined by the tense of the relative clause. The suffix *-shka*

---

[21] For an example of an actual relative clause introduced by a TAM-coding participant nominalization see sentence (148) in Section 5.2.5.

is used for all kinds of past events, -*j* for the present, and -*na* for the future. By contrast, in internally headed relative clauses the relativizers refer to both the position being relativized and to the tense: subject in present contexts is relativized by -*j*, while non-subject in past contexts is relativized by -*shka*. Unfortunately, Cole (1985) does not provide any explanations for this phenomenon.

In sum, among the languages with participles showing limited contextual orientation, 13 relativize non-subject participants, three relativize non-core participants (not subjects and not direct objects), and one language relativizes all kinds of obliques. The list of these languages is given in Table 14.[22] Figure 13 presents their geographical distribution.

Fig. 13: Languages with contextually oriented participles: limited contextual orientation (● – non-subject, ▲ – IO and obliques, ■ – obliques only)

---

[22] The table only indicates relativizing capacity of the forms with respect to restrictions in the higher end of the Accessibility Hierarchy. For full information on the relativizing capacity of individual forms see Appendix 3a.

Tab. 14: Languages with participles demonstrating limited contextual orientation (number of languages per macroarea)

Family	Language	Orientation	Form(s)
North America (4/13)			
Cochimi-Yuman	Maricopa	Non-Subject	NMZ.NS
Seri	Seri	Obliques only	NMZ.OBL
Uto-Aztecan	Guarijío	Non-Subject	NMZ.P/OBL -*a*
	Tümpisa Shoshone	Non-Subject	PTCP.PST -*ppüh*, INF -*nna*
South America (5/16)			
Arawakan	Tariana	Non-Subject	NMZ.NS -*mi*
Chicham	Aguaruna	Non-Subject	REL.NS -*mau*
Pano-Tacanan	Matsés	Non-Subject	NMZ.INS -*te*/-*tequid*
Quechuan	Tarma Quechua	Non-Subject	NMZ.NFUT -*nqa*, NMZ.FUT -*na*
Tupian	Kamaiurá	IO and obliques	NMZ.OBL -*tap*
Africa (2/12)			
Mande	Wan	Non-Subject	NMZ.ATTR -*ŋ*
Ta-Ne-Omotic	Koorete	Non-Subject	PTCP.PFV.NS -*o*
Eurasia (6/47)			
Sino-Tibetan	Dolakha Newar	Non-Subject	NMZ.NS -*e*/-*a*
	Japhug rGyalrong	IO and obliques	NMZ.OBL *sɤ-*
Uralic	Beserman Udmurt	Non-Subject	PTCP.NPST -*n*
	Meadow Mari	Non-Subject	PTCP.NS -*me*
	Tundra Nenets	IO and obliques	NMZ.PFV -*(o)qm(')a*, NMZ.IPFV -*m(')a*, CVB.MOD -*s'a*/-*a*
Yukaghir	Kolyma Yukaghir	Non-Subject	ATTR.PASS -*me*

3.6 Orientation extension

In many languages, participial forms inherently oriented towards core participants can have regular ways of extending their orientation towards particular peripheral participants. It is important to bear in mind that in most such cases the original participial form itself does not change its orientation, because the extension is a result of specific morphological or syntactic changes in the construction.

Therefore, this topic is only indirectly related to the concept of orientation as an inherent property of participial forms. However, since possibilities for extension can be found all over the world, I will briefly consider them here. Three types of orientation extension attested in my sample are extension by means of specialized affixes (3.6.1), extension by means of resumptive pronouns (3.6.2), and extension based on pragmatics, where no additional material is used (3.6.3).

3.6.1 Extension by means of specialized affixes

This section provides an overview of cases where orientation extension involves the use of a specialized marker in the participial form. In most cases, these are valency-increasing affixes, which extend the orientation of participles from core arguments (or a specific core argument) to a range of peripheral participants.

The Austronesian language Muna, for example, uses a suffix to transform a passive participle into a participle oriented towards certain peripheral participants. The form marked by *ni-* is normally oriented towards the direct object, as in (99a). However, in combination with the marker *-ghoo*, the *ni-* participle becomes oriented towards a peripheral participant, instrumental in the case of (99b). When attached to independent predicates, the marker *-ghoo* seems to function as an applicative in that it allows the verbs to take peripheral participants, such as instruments (99c), recipients (99d), or reason (99e). Unfortunately, the description available for Muna does not provide any examples of relativization for other peripheral participants than instruments, but we could expect that the speakers would employ the suffix *-ghoo* in these contexts as well.

(99) Muna (Austronesian)
    a. *sau*   [*ni-bhogha-mu*]   *no-wolo-mo*
        wood   PTCP.PASS-chop-your   3SG.REAL-finish-PFV
        'The wood that you have chopped has been used up.'
        (van den Berg 2013: 234)
    b. *aitu-ha-e-mo*   *polulu*   [*ne-bhogha-ghoo-no*   *sau*]
        that-HA-it-PFV   axe   PTCP.PASS-chop-IO-his   wood
        'That is the axe with which he has chopped the wood.'
        (van den Berg 2013: 234)
    c. *ae-ghome-ghoo*   *sabo*
        1SG.REAL-wash-IO   soap
        'I wash with soap.'
        (van den Berg 2013: 176)

d. *ne-owa-ghoo   ama-ku   kenta*
   3SG.REAL-bring-IO father-my fish
   'She brought my father some fish.'
   (van den Berg 2013: 176)
e. *inodi   ini   a-rugi-ghoo-mo   ka-pudhi-no   dahu*
   I   this   1SG.REAL-lose-IO-PFV   NMZ-praise-POSS.LK dog
   'I suffered a loss because of the dog's praises.'
   (van den Berg 2013: 152)

A similar strategy with the causative affix *-bta-* is attested in Tundra Nenets (Nikolaeva 2014: 321). Another option this language has for extending the participial orientation is to use a periphrastic construction. Normally, perfective, imperfective, future and negative participles in Tundra Nenets are used to relativize only subjects and direct objects, as shown in (100a) and (100b) respectively.[23] However, in order to relativize lower positions of the Accessibility Hierarchy, speakers regularly use the periphrastic construction, where the lexical verb appears in the form of a modal converb (optionally bearing an essive case marker) accompanied by an auxiliary verb *me-* 'use' in the appropriate participial form. As discussed in Section 2.3.2, periphrastic constructions of this kind can be regarded as proper participles on a par with other analytic verb forms; see example (38) from Nanga. This strategy allows the relativization of peripheral participants, such as instrumentals (100c), and locatives (100d):

(100) Tundra Nenets (Uralic)
   a. [*Moskva-xəna yil'e-n'a*]   *nəni-m   xamc°ə-d°m*
      Moscow-LOC   live-PTCP.IPFV   guy-ACC   love-1SG
      'I am in love with a guy who lives in Moscow.' (Nikolaeva 2014: 318)
   b. [(*mən'°*)   *ŋəw°la-w°dawey°*]   *wen'ako-m'i*
      I   feed-PTCP.NEG   dog-1SG
      'the dog which I didn't feed' (Nikolaeva 2014: 319)
   c. [*ŋəmca-m   məda-ba-°   meq-mer°*]   *xərə-r°*
      meat-ACC   cut-DUR-MOD use-PTCP.PFV.2SG knife-2SG
      'the knife with which you had cut the meat' (Nikolaeva 2014: 320)
   d. [*yil'e-s°-(ŋe°)   meq-m°nta(-m'i)*] *m'aq-m'i*
      live-CVB.MOD-ESS   use-PTCP.FUT-1SG   tent-1SG
      'the tent in which I will live' (Nikolaeva 2014: 321)

---

23 Some speakers of Western dialects occasionally use these forms to relativize locative participants as well (Nikolaeva 2014: 320).

In Barasano, the participle -ri on its own can only be used to relativize subjects, as in (101a). However, with the non-subject nominalizing suffix -a, its orientation can be extended to direct objects (101b), and non-core participants (101c):

(101) Barasano (Tucanoan)
    a. *bõa-ri   bãs-o*
       work-PTCP   human-F.SG
       'a woman/girl worker (a working girl)'
       (Jones and Jones 1991: 144)
    b. *ba-ri-a-rã*
       eat-PTCP-NS-AN.PL
       'ones who are eaten'
       (Jones and Jones 1991: 144)
    c. *kahi   gate-ri-a-bedo*
       coca   toast-PTCP-NS-ring
       '(vine) ring with which one toasts (coca leaves)'
       (Jones and Jones 1991: 144)

In Kayardild, consequential nominalizations are inherently oriented towards syntactic subjects only, as illustrated in (102a). However, if an original direct object or a locative is promoted to the subject position by adding a middle suffix, the relativization of direct objects and peripheral participants becomes possible as well; see (102b) and (102c) respectively:

(102) Kayardild (Tangkic)
    a. [**wungi-n-ngarrba**] *dangka-a bala-a-j*
       steal-NMZ-CONS   man-NOM   shoot-MID-ACTUAL
       'The man who had stolen (the cattle) was shot.'
       (Evans 1995: 483)
    b. *nyingka kamburi-ja dathin-a dangka-a *[*yarbu-nyarrba*
       2SG.NOM speak-IMP   that-NOM   man-NOM   snake-CONS
       balangkali-ngarrba   **ba-yii-n-ngarrb**]!
       brown.snake-CONS   bite-MID-NMZ-CONS
       'You speak to that man who was bitten by a brown snake.'
       (Evans 1995: 481)
    c. *ngada   mungurru   dathin-ki   dulk-i*
       1SG.NOM know.NOM   that-MLOC place-MLOC

[*ngijin-marra-a-n-ngarrba-y*]
1SG.POSS-go-MID-NMZ-CONS-MLOC
'I know that familiar place.' (Lit. 'that place gone to by me')
(Evans 1995: 483)

All examples mentioned so far were of valency-increasing markers. There is one instance in the sample that uses a valency-decreasing marker, which extends orientation by just one core argument. As mentioned earlier (see Section 3.3.2), West Greenlandic bare participial markers can only be used to relativize intransitive subjects (*-soq*) and direct objects (*-saq*). The marker of the passive participle *-saq* can attach to verbs with valency-increasing derivational markers, such as *-ffigi-* 'have as place of' or *-ssut-* 'means/cause/reason for' in order to enable the relativization of participants other than P, as illustrated in (103). The S-oriented *-soq* participle, on the other hand, can attach to verbs with a detransitivizing (valency-decreasing) suffix to relativize original transitive subjects, as shown in example (63b).

(103) West Greenlandic (Eskimo-Aleut)
    a. *angut*   [*iser-figi-sa-ra*]
        man   go.in-have.as.place.of-PTCP.PASS-POSS.1SG.ABS
        'the man to whom I went in' (Fortescue 1984: 53–54)
    b. *savik*   [*toqut-si-ssuti-gi-sa-a*]
        knife   kill-HTR-means.for-have.as-PTCP.PASS-POSS.3SG.ABS
        'the knife with which he killed' (Fortescue 1984: 54)

Despite being attested in typologically very diverse languages, instances of extension of this type, which involve additional morphology on the verb form, are fairly uncommon. In the next section, I discuss a more common way of extending participial orientation.

3.6.2 Extension by means of resumptive elements

The second type of orientation extension does not involve any additional morphology in the participial form, but instead is signalled by obligatory resumptive pronouns in the relative clause. In such cases, orientation can be extended to almost any non-core participant of the clause, as discussed, for example, in Keenan and Comrie (1977: 92). In Modern Standard Arabic, for example, there are two inherently oriented participles, one with active orientation, and one with passive orientation. However, these participles can sometimes be used to relativize other participants. In such cases, the relativized participant is obligatorily represented in the relative clause by a resumptive element, and the choice between the active and the passive participial form is primarily motivated pragmatically. For instance, in example (104a) the active participle is used to relativize a direct object, in example (104b) the passive participle relativizes a complement of a postposition, and in example (104c) an active participle is used for possessor relativization:

(104) Modern Standard Arabic (Afro-Asiatic)
    a. *ʔas-sayārat-u*   [*s-sāriq-u-**hā***   *ʔaḥmad-u*]
       the-car(F).SG-NOM   the-steal.PTCP.ACT.M.SG-NOM-ACC.3.F.SG   Ahmad-NOM
       'the car that Ahmad stole'
       (Doron and Reintges 2005: 24)
    b. *ʔal-jihat-u*   [*l-manūṭ-u*   *bi-**hā***
       the-agency.F.SG-NOM   the-trust.PTCP.PASS.M.SG-NOM   in-F.SG
       xtiyār-u   *l-musāfir-īna*]
       CONSTR.choice(M).SG-NOM   the-traveller-M.PL.GEN
       'the agency with which the choice of travellers has been entrusted'
       (Badawi, Carter, and Gully 2004: 114, as cited in Doron and Reintges 2005: 23)
    c. *waṣal-at*   *il-marʔat-u*   [*l-jālis-u-una*
       arrive.PRF-3.F.SG   the-woman(F).SG-NOM   the-sit.PTCP.ACT.M.PL-NOM
       *ʔawlād-u=**hā***]
       children.M.PL-NOM=POSS.3.F.SG
       'The woman whose children are sitting arrived.'
       (Doron and Reintges 2005: 13)

The same type of extension is also attested in Krongo (Kadugli-Krongo), where resumptive pronouns allow the active participle to relativize various participants at least down to obliques, and in Middle Egyptian (Afro-Asiatic), where the passive participle extends its relativization capacity at least to indirect objects and certain locatives.

    This type of extension of orientation is also very common for contextually oriented participles that cannot relativize possessors without any additional markers; see example (105) for possessor relativization in Yakut, where the possessive marker *-e* is an obligatory part of the relative construction:

(105) Yakut (Turkic)
   Min   [kergen-**e**   kïrb-ï:r]   jaχtar-ï̈   kör-büt-üm.
   1SG   spouse-POSS.3SG   beat-PTCP.PRS   woman-ACC   see-PTCP.PST-POSS.1SG
   'I saw the woman whose husband beats her.' (Brigitte Pakendorf, p.c.)

In some languages, the use of resumptive pronouns with contextually oriented participles can allow these forms to relativize both possessors and other participants that are encoded by a similar construction, e.g. when postpositions behave syntactically as possessa. This type of situation was illustrated in examples (56b) and (56c) from Kalmyk, repeated in (106) for convenience:

(106) Kalmyk (Mongolic)
   a. [**dotrə-n**ʲ   määčə   kevt-sən]   avdər   orə-n   dor   bää-nä
      inside-POSS.3   ball   lie-PTCP.PST   chest   bed-EXT   under   be-PRS
      'The chest in which there is a ball is under the bed.'
      (Krapivina 2009a: 503)
   b. [**gerə-n**ʲ   šat-žə   od-sən]   övgə-n   Elstə
      house-POSS.3   burn-CVB.IPFV   leave-PTCP.PST   old.man-EXT   Elista
      bää-xär   jov-la
      be-CVB.PURP   go-REM
      'The old man whose house had burned down moved to Elista.'
      (Krapivina 2009a: 503)

In West Greenlandic (Eskimo-Aleut), active participles are also used for relativizing a possessor of the subject, while passive participles are used to relativize a possessor of the object; see Fortescue (1984: 53). The same situation is observed in Azeri (Turkic, Authier 2012: 229), and in Kamaiurá (Tupian, Seki 2000: 181–182), where the choice of participle for possessor relativization depends on the role of the possessum in the relative clause.

This rule does not only concern core participants. In Ma'di, the -*dʒɔ́* form is chiefly employed for the relativization of instruments and reasons, as illustrated in (107a). However, this same form can also be used to relativize a possessor of an instrument, or a possessor of something perceived as a reason; see (107b):

(107) Ma'di (Central Sudanic)
   a. àdʒú   [má-à   ˋdî̀-**dʒɔ́**]   rì̀   ʔí̀   ēgwè   dì
      spear   1SG-POSS   NPST.kill-SR.INS   DEF   FOC   lose   COMPL
      'The spear with which I killed it is lost./The spear for which I killed it is lost.' (Blackings and Fabb 2003: 206)

b. ágɔ́ [má-à àdʒú àní drí (sɨ̀) òdrú **`dī-dʒɔ́**] rì ʔɨ̄
  man 1SG-POSS spear 3SG POSS SRC buffalo NPST-kill-SR.INS DEF FOC
  'The man with whose spear I killed a buffalo./The man for whose spear I killed a buffalo.' (Blackings and Fabb 2003: 205)

It is, therefore, a fairly general cross-linguistic tendency that if participles in a language have a specific distribution regarding the types of possessors they can relativize, then it is the syntactic function of the possessum that determines the choice of the participle for possessor relativization. The only language in my sample that deviates from this tendency to a certain extent is Tundra Nenets. As already mentioned in Sections 3.5.1 and 3.5.2, the language has two sets of forms used for relativization. The forms of the first set (participles, according to Nikolaeva 2014) can relativize subjects and direct objects, while the others (action nominals and modal converb) can relativize a wide range of peripheral participants, i.e. the positions of the Accessibility Hierarchy extending from the indirect object to the right. In both cases, the strategy used is gapping, i.e. there are no elements in the relative clause referring to the modified noun. Both sets of forms, however, can also be used for possessor relativization using the resumptive strategy, when the modified noun is represented in the relative clause by a possessive suffix. The choice of the adnominal verb form in this case is determined by the syntactic function of the possessum in the relative clause. If the possessum occupies the subject position, the speakers use the first set of forms (participles), as in (108a), while in all other cases they employ the second set (action nominals or modal converb), as in (108b)–(108d):

(108) Tundra Nenets (Uralic)
  a. [xərº-da / xərº-nta məl'º-wiº] xasawa
    knife-3SG knife-GEN.3SG break-PTCP.PFV man
    'the man whose knife broke' (Nikolaeva 2014: 328)
  b. [yəxa-m-da mənes-oqma-m'i] n'enec'ə-m'i
    river-ACC-3SG see-NMZ.PFV-1SG person-1SG
    'the man whose river I saw' (Nikolaeva 2014: 328)
  c. [n'e n'a-xºnta kniga-m m'is-oqma(-m'i)] n'enec'ə-m'i
    woman companion-DAT.3SG book-ACC give-NMZ.PFV-1SG person-1SG
    'the man to whose younger sister I gave book' (Nikolaeva 2014: 328)
  d. [xər-xºnanta ŋuda-m'i məda-qma(-m'i)] n'enec'ə-m'i
    knife-LOC.3SG hand-ACC.1SG cut-NMZ.PFV-1SG person-1SG
    'the man with whose knife I cut my hand' (Nikolaeva 2014: 329)

Although in general Tundra Nenets follows the tendency outlined above, the language is unique in that the sets of relativized positions do not match completely. In the relativization of clausal participants, the border between the strategies on the Accessibility Hierarchy is between the direct object and the indirect object. On the other hand, when it comes to possessor relativization, the border is between the subject and the direct object. The mismatch is illustrated in (109) below.

(109) a. Clausal participant relativization:
  (SUBJ > DO) > (IO > OBL) > POSS
 b. Sub-clausal participant relativization:
  (SUBJ) > (DO > IO > OBL) > POSS

This matter is obviously very complex and definitely requires further language-internal investigation.

3.6.3 Pragmatic extension

In the final type of orientation extension, no additional material whatsoever is required. This is the case for extension to possessor relativization, attested, for instance, in Muna, where the forms commonly used for subject relativization (110a), can also relativize possessors (110b):

(110) Muna (Austronesian)
 a. *ae-faraluu* dahu [so **me-dhaga-ni-no** lambu]
  1SG.REAL-need dog FUT PTCP.ACT-guard-TR-PTCP.ACT house
  'I need a dog that will guard the house.'
  (van den Berg 2013: 232)
 b. *ampa-mo* kaawu kampufu-ndo [**mo-de-dea-no**
  merely-PFV only youngest-their PTCP.ACT-INT~red-PTCP.ACT
  wangka(-no)]
  tooth(-his)
  'It was only their youngest child whose teeth were red.'
  (van den Berg 2013: 234)

As is clear from the example above, the relativization strategy in both cases is exactly the same. The only difference is that the sentence illustrating possessor relativization can contain a possessive affix *-no* on the possessum, which could be regarded as a resumptive element indicating the relativized position. This possessive marker is optional in this case, however, and without it the sentence would also be fully grammatical, which distinguishes this example from those considered in the previous section.

The only important restriction in Muna is that active participles can only relativize a possessor of the participant which is itself a subject within the relative clause, e.g. *wangka* 'teeth' in example (110b). It would be impossible, for instance, to produce a sentence like 'It was only their youngest child whose teeth the dentist removed', with 'teeth' as a direct object. This restriction is also present in Maricopa, which also allows extended use of active participles. Furthermore, in Maricopa the use of this relativization strategy is limited to relative clause predicates denoting properties, such as, for instance, colours. The examples below show how one and the same relative clause can be used to relativize different participants, (111a) being an instance of subject relativization, and (111b) illustrating possessor relativization:

(111) Maricopa (Cochimi-Yuman)
 a. [*sny'ak* ***e'e*** *ku-hmaaly-sh*] *sily-k*
    woman hair REL-white-SUBJ fall-REAL
    'The woman's white hair is falling out.' (Gordon 1986: 259)
 b. [***sny'ak*** *e'e* *ku-hmaaly-sh*] *ny-wik-k*
    woman hair REL-white-SUBJ 3/1-help-REAL
    'The woman with the white hair helped me.' (Gordon 1986: 259)

Importantly, in both cases attested in the sample, the examples provided in the grammars only illustrate extension of orientation in the contexts of inalienable possession, more precisely, possession of body parts.[24] The authors do not explicitly discuss whether it is the only context in which the extension is possible, but it would make sense in terms of recoverability; see the discussion of a similar restriction for participles with full contextual orientation up to possessors in Section 3.5.1.

3.7 Resumptive pronouns in participial relative clauses

It is commonly assumed that in participial relative clauses the modified noun is usually not represented in any way, and therefore, they are all instances of gap

---

24 I am grateful to Jean-Christophe Verstraete for pointing this out.

relativization strategy; see, for instance, Lehmann (1984). However, as it has already become clear in the preceding sections, the modified noun is in many cases represented with various resumptive pronominal elements. In this section, I will provide a brief overview of the use of these elements in participial relative clauses, especially as concerns their degree of obligatoriness. As could be expected, their use mostly conforms to predictions made by the Accessibility Hierarchy (Keenan and Comrie 1977: 92), as well as related predictions like the idea that prenominal relatives use fewer resumptive elements (Keenan 1985: 148; Givón 2001: 185). Even so, there are a few remarkable exceptions.

First of all, resumptive elements vary considerably in their form. For example, they can be third-person pronouns (112), reflexive pronouns (113), indefinite pronouns (114), or pronominal possessive affixes (115):

(112) Tümpisa Shoshone (Uto-Aztecan)
[**U** **tukkwa** nümmin nuunaahappüha] ukkwa samapitta u
it under our.EX sit.PL.SUB.O that.O cedar.O it
punikka nüü
see I
'I see the cedar under which we were sitting.'
(Dayley 1989: 369)

(113) Tanti Dargwa (Nakh-Daghestanian)
[dali (**sun-ni-ž**) čut:u b=ič:-ib] durħaʕ
I.ERG REFL-OBL-DAT chudu N=give.PFV-PRET[PTCP] boy
'the boy whom I gave chudu'
(Sumbatova and Lander 2014: 193)

(114) Coahuilteco (Coahuilteco)
pi·nwakta· [Dios **pil'ta** a-pa-ta·nko] tuče··m
things God something 3-SUB-command DEM-CONC.2
'the things which God commands'
(Troike 2010: 4)

(115) Meadow Mari (Uralic)
[Oza-ž-əm saj-ən pal-əme] pört vokte-č' tudo
owner-POSS.3SG-ACC good-ADV know-PTCP.NS house near-ELA he
č'üč'kədən ert-a.
often go.by-PRS.3SG
'He often walks by the house whose owner he knows well.'
(Brykina and Aralova 2012: 483)

Secondly and more importantly, resumptive pronouns and other resumptive elements differ in their obligatoriness in participial relative clauses. As I have shown in Section 3.6.2, for some languages they serve as regular means to allow inherently and contextually oriented participles to relativize certain lower positions of the Accessibility Hierarchy (predominantly obliques for inherently oriented forms, and possessors for contextually oriented forms). Since this topic has already been discussed earlier, in this section I will chiefly focus on the resumptive pronouns that are not obligatory, but can optionally occur in specific contexts.

In Savosavo, the obligatoriness of overt reference to the modified noun within the relative clause increases down the Accessibility Hierarchy (Wegener 2012: 254–257). When the subject is relativized, no overt cross-referencing material is present in the relative clause, as in (116a). When the direct object is relativized, no overt object noun phrase can be used in the relative clause, although an object marking affix on transitive verb stems remains,[25] as in (116b). For locative-marked adjuncts, a coreferential locative-marked pronoun often occurs in the corresponding place in the relative clause, but its use is optional; compare (116c) and (116d). Finally, when a possessor is relativized, the genitive-marked pronoun denoting the possessor is obligatorily present in the relative clause, as in (116e):

(116) Savosavo (Savosavo)
    a. [lo   Ø   kabu   ba-tu]   lo   mapa=gha
        DET.PL   move.away   come-REL det.PL   person=PL
       'the people who came running away'
       (Wegener 2012: 254)
    b. [Ze-va   Ø   bo   k-au-tu]   ko   adaki=e   ko=na
       3PL-GEN.M   go   3SG.F.O-take-REL   DET.SG.F   woman=EMP   3SG.F=NOM
       'She (was) the woman whom they had gone (to and) taken.'
       (Wegener 2012: 253)
    c. [lo   no   tone   lo   **lo=la**   vasikaka-tu]
       DET.SG.M   2PL.GEN   brother   3SG.M.GEN   3.SG.M=LOC.M   be.ungenerous-REL
       [lo   ghau
       DET.SG.M   fishing.bamboo
       'that fishing bamboo your brother is so ungenerous about'
       (Wegener 2012: 256)

---

25 In independent sentences, the predicate does not show subject agreement, but objects are indexed by affixes added to the verb root; see Wegener (2012: 164).

d. [lo   ko-va   ∅   bo tei-tu]   lo   peleni
   DET.SG.M   3SG.F-GEN.M   go   want.to.do-REL   DET.SG.M plane
   'the plane she will go with'
   (Wegener 2012: 256)
e. [to   no-va   **to**-ma   mama   k-aka   savu-li-tu]
   DET.DU   2SG-GEN.M   3DU-GEN.SG.F   mother   3SG.F-to   tell-3SG.M.O-REL
   to   gnuba=lo
   DET.DU   child=DU
   'those (two) boys whose mother you told it to'
   (Wegener 2012: 257)

A very similar situation is found in Kambaata (Afro-Asiatic) and Sheko (Dizoid), although in these two languages the use of resumptive elements is available from the direct object onwards. In Tümpisa Shoshone (Uto-Aztecan), where both the past participle in -ppüh and the infinitive in -nna allow the relativization of direct objects, indirect objects, and objects of postpositions, the use of resumptive pronouns is possible in all the contexts, but obligatory only in the last case. Judging by the data provided in Jeanne (1978), in Hopi the use of a resumptive pronoun is possible in the context of subject relativization, as illustrated in (117a). It is also optional when a direct object is relativized (117b), but obligatory for the relativization of objects of postpositions (117c):

(117) Hopi (Uto-Aztecan)
   a. *niʔ*   *tiyoʔya-t*   [**(pam)**   *pakmimiy-qa-t*]   *hoona*
      I   boy-OBL   he   cry-REL-OBL   sent:home
      'I sent home the boy that is crying.'
      (Jeanne 1978: 193)
   b. *niʔ*   *tiyoʔya-t*   [*ʔita-ŋi*   **(pi-t)**   *naawakna-qa-t*]   *tiwiʔyta*
      I   boy-OBL   our-mother   him-OBL   like-REL-OBL   know
      'I know the boy that my mother likes.'
      (Jeanne 1978: 196)
   c. *niʔ*   *tiyoʔya-t*   [*ʔita-na*   **(pi-t)**   **ʔa-mim**   *timalaʔyta-qa-t*]
      I   boy-OBL   our-father   him-OBL   him-with   work-REL-OBL
      tiwiʔyta
      know
      'I know the boy who my father works with.'
      (Jeanne 1978: 196)

Finally, another type of resumptive pronoun use is reported for three Nakh-Daghestanian languages, Lezgian (Haspelmath 1993: 413), Hinuq (Forker 2013: 553) and Tanti Dargwa (Sumbatova and Lander 2014: 192–194). In these languages, the use of resumptive pronominal elements is not directly dependent on the syntactic role being relativized. Their use is regulated by pragmatics: a speaker is more likely to use a resumptive pronoun if the relativized participant is not easily recoverable from the context. The following examples illustrate the structural possibility of resumptive pronoun use in Tanti Dargwa (which is apparently the most flexible in this respect) when the roles relativized are intransitive subject (118a), transitive subject (118b), direct object (118c), indirect object (118d), instrument (118e), and location (118f):

(118) Tanti Dargwa (Nakh-Daghestanian)
    a. [(*sa<r>i*)   *dam-š:u*   *r=ač'-ib*]   *rurs:i*
       REFL\<F\>   I.OBL-AD(LAT)   F=come.PFV-PRET[PTCP]   girl
       'the girl who came to me'
       (Sumbatova and Lander 2014: 193)
    b. [(*sun-ni*)   *čut:u*   *b=erk:-un*]   *umra*
       REFL-ERG   chudu   N=eat.PFV-PRET[PTCP]   neighbour
       'the neighbour who ate chudu'
       (Sumbatova and Lander 2014: 193)
    c. [(*sa<b>i*)   *umra-li*   *b=erk:-un*]   *čut:u*
       REFL\<N\>   neighbour-ERG   N=eat.PFV-PRET[PTCP]   chudu
       'the chudu that the neighbour ate'
       (Sumbatova and Lander 2014: 193)
    d. [*dali*   *ču-ž*   *žuž*   *b=ič:-ib-se*]   *durħ-n-a-li*
       I.ERG   REFL.OBL.PL-DAT   book   N=give.PFV-PRET-ATTR   boy-PL-OBL.PL-ERG
       sa<b>i   *b=it-aq-aq-ib*
       REFL\<N\>   N=thither-get.lost.PFV-CAUS-PRET
       'The boys whom I had given the book lost it.'
       (Sumbatova and Lander 2014: 192)
    e. [*dali*   (*sun-ni-c:ele*)   *ʔaˤml-e*   *kaˤ-d=aˤq-ib-se*]   *q'iq'*
       I.ERG   REFL-OBL-COM   nail-PL   down-NPL=hit.PFV-PRET-ATTR   hammer
       'the hammer with which I hammered the nails'
       (Sumbatova and Lander 2014: 194)
    f. [*du*   (*sun-ni-š:u*)   *q'̥-aˤn-se*]   *qali*
       I   REFL-OBL-AD(LAT)   go.IPFV-PRS-ATTR   house
       'the house that I am walking to'
       (Sumbatova and Lander 2014: 193)

Naturally, the probability of occurrence of resumptive pronouns in these languages is higher when a participant from the lower part of the Accessibility Hierarchy is relativized, since it is exactly in these contexts that recoverability might be difficult; see Sumbatova and Lander (2014: 195). However, these cases are still typologically remarkable since they contradict the two typological generalizations mentioned at the outset of this section. First, they are instances of resumptive pronoun use in prenominal relative clauses, against Keenan (1985: 148) or Givón (2001: 185). Second, at least in some cases they do allow the use of resumptive elements even when the highest positions of the Accessibility Hierarchy are relativized, such as subjects and direct objects, against Keenan and Comrie (1977: 92).

Optional resumptive pronouns can be used with inherently oriented participles as well. For instance, in Ma'di, participial relative clauses introduced by the instrumental participle in -dʒɔ́ can optionally contain the word drū 'with it' referring to the relativized participant, as illustrated in (119):

(119) Ma'di (Central Sudanic)
àdʒú   [má-à   `dī-dʒɔ́   (**drū**)]   rī   ʔī   ēgwè   dì
spear 1SG-POSS NPST.kill-SR.INS with.it DEF FOC lose COMPL
'The spear with which I killed it is lost.'
(Blackings and Fabb 2003: 206)

This situation is extremely rare, however, for a combination of reasons. First, as mentioned above, resumptive pronouns are not very common in participial relative clauses in general. Second, even if they do occur, they tend to be used only when some lower positions of the Accessibility Hierarchy are relativized, and participles inherently oriented towards a peripheral participant are only attested in a handful of languages in my sample (see Section 3.4). In addition, the main function of resumptive pronouns is to point to the relativized participant in the cases where it is not totally clear which participant is relativized, while for participles inherently oriented towards one particular participant this problem does not appear to be relevant. Therefore, the situation attested in Ma'di should rather be considered an exception.

Mẽbengokre provides an illustration of another cross-linguistically unusual phenomenon, because it features what can be classified as resumptive pronouns in internally headed relative clauses. In regular relative clauses in Mẽbengokre, the modified noun occupies the place that it is supposed to occupy due to its role in the relative clause; see (120a), where the relativized recipient 'the relative of mine' occurs after the ergative subject. However, according to Salanova (2011), the relativized participant can sometimes be left-dislocated within the relative clause (reasons for left-dislocation in relative clauses are unclear from the description as it is available). As a consequence, a resumptive third-person pronoun appears in place of the dislocated constituent, as in (120b), where the pronoun *kum* refers to the white man:

(120) Mẽbengokre (Nuclear-Macro-Je)
    a. [*i-je* **i-nhõ bikwa mã** idji jarẽnh] nẽ bôx mã
       1-ERG 1-POSS relative to 3.name say.NMZ NFUT arrive about.to
       'The relative of mine to whom I gave a name is about to arrive.'
       (Salanova 2011: 58)
    b. [**kubẽ** *i-je* **ku-m** katõk nhãr] nẽ jã
       barbarian 1-ERG 3-DAT gun give.NMZ NFUT this
       'This is the white man to whome I gave the gun.'
       (Salanova 2011: 66)

The overall use of resumptive pronouns in the languages of the sample is summarized in Table 15 and Figure 14:

Fig. 14: Languages with resumptive pronouns in participial relative clauses

Tab. 15: Resumptive pronouns in participial relative clauses

Language	Form(s)	SUBJ	DO	IO	OBL	POSS
Contextually oriented participles						
Korean	All participles	no	no	no	no	possible
Nanga	All participles	no	no	no	no	possible (INAL)
Even	All participles	no	no	no	no	oblig.
Nanai	All participles	no	no	no	no	oblig.
Yakut	All participles	no	no	no	no	oblig.
Apsheron Tat	PTCP	no	no	no	no	oblig.
Motuna	PTCP	no	no	no	no	oblig.
Meadow Mari	PTCP.FUT, PTCP.NEG	no	no	no	no	oblig.
Meadow Mari	PTCP.NS	–	no	no	no	oblig.
Northern Khanty	PTCP.PST, PTCP.NPST	no	no	no	no	oblig.
Kolyma Yukaghir	ATTR.ACT -*je*, NMZ -*l*	no	no	no	no	oblig.
Kalmyk	PTCP.PST -*sən*, PTCP.FUT-*xə*, PTCP.HAB -*dəg*	no	no	no	possible/ oblig.	oblig.
Coahuilteco	SUB *p-/pa-*	no	no	possible	possible	–
Luiseño	REL (system)	no	no	possible	possible	–
Savosavo	REL -*tu*	no	no	possible/ oblig.	possible/ oblig.	oblig.
Kambaata	REL, PTCP.NEG -*umb*	no	possible	possible	possible	oblig.
Sheko	REL -*əb*, -*əbe*	no	possible	possible/ oblig.	oblig./ possible	oblig.
Hopi	REL -*qa*	possible	possible	possible	possible/ oblig.	?
Tümpisa Shoshone	PTCP.PST -*ppüh*, INF -*nna*	–	possible	possible	oblig.	–
Hinuq	PTCP -*o goɫa*, PTCP.PST -*(y)oru*, PTCP.HAB -*ƛ'os*	(possible)	(possible)	(possible)	possible	possible
Tanti Dargwa	All participles	possible	possible	possible	possible	possible

Language	Form(s)	SUBJ	DO	IO	OBL	POSS
Lezgian	PTCP -j	(possible)	(possible)	(possible)	possible	possible
Mẽbengokre	NMZ	?	possible	possible	possible	possible
Ronghong Qiang	NMZ.AN -m	?	?	possible	?	?
Inherently oriented participles						
Muna	PTCP.ACT mo-V-no	no	–	–	–	possible
Japhug rGyalrong	NMZ.S/A kɯ-	no	–	–	–	oblig.
Japhug rGyalrong	NMZ.P kɤ-	–	no	–	–	oblig.
West Greenlandic	PTCP.ACT -soq	no	–	–	–	oblig.
West Greenlandic	PTCP.PASS -saq	–	no	–	–	oblig.
Modern Standard Arabic	PTCP.ACT	no	oblig.	oblig.	oblig.	oblig.
Modern Standard Arabic	PTCP.PASS	–	no	oblig.	oblig.	oblig.
Kamaiurá	All participles	(no)	(no)	(no)	(no)	oblig.
Krongo	CONN ŋ-	no	oblig.	oblig.	oblig.	?
Middle Egyptian	PTCP.NS	–	no	oblig.	oblig.	?
Ma'di	All participles	no	no	no	(possible)	oblig.
Hinuq	PTCP.LOC -a	–	–	–	possible	–

3.8 Discussion

In the preceding sections, I have outlined the types of participial orientation attested in the languages of the sample. The important question now is: can we explain these types, or, in other words, can we propose functional motivations for their existence? I will address this topic in the present section.

As regards participles oriented towards core participants, in principle, one could assume that inherent orientation in a particular language could be in some way parallel to the alignment found in other domains in the language, such as basic clause organization. When confronted with the data in this chapter, however, this generalization does not work. The share of languages that show certain degree of ergativity in argument marking or verbal agreement is roughly the same for languages with active, passive and absolutive participles, and in the sample overall, ranging from 21.7% for active participles to 26.3% for absolutive participles. Agentive participles are an exception here (60%), but this may well be accidental, due to the small total number of such languages (5). A number of languages with (split) ergative alignment in main clauses have active and/or passive participles (e.g. Dolakha Newar or West Greenlandic), and many accusative languages have absolutive participles (e.g. Tarma Quechua or Erzya). The first type of combination could, of course, be expected, since many morphologically ergative languages are known to have accusative syntax, but the the second type goes against the common assumption that morphologically accusative languages cannot be syntactically ergative (for an overview of this topic, see, for example, McGregor 2009). In sum, there seems to be no indication that morphosyntactic alignment in main clauses determines patterning of core participants in participial orientation. This means that we have to look elsewhere to explain participial orientation: I will mainly look at preferred argument structure-style arguments, following Du Bois (1987).

As discussed in Section 3.3.1, I suggest that the inherent orientation of participles is best explained by the semantics and pragmatics of the constructions they appear in. In particular, this concerns active and absolutive participles, which show participant associations attested elsewhere in languages. S and A participants tend to pattern together because they are commonly human and controlling. Languages that use active participles, therefore, grammaticalize the possibility to characterize discourse participants with respect to activities they control.

Absolutive participial orientation seems to be best explained in pragmatic terms. Specifically, the explanation is related to the Absolutive Hypothesis introduced in Fox (1987). It has been shown in this and further studies that S and P relativization have a special discourse function of introducing new participants (for a similar observation concerning independent sentences see Du Bois 1987: 805); it is also most frequent in the corpora of various languages (Fox and Thompson 1990; Krapivina 2007; Schmidtke-Bode 2012). S and P are, therefore, the participants that are most easily relativized. As a result, a language can be expected to develop a specialized form for this function. An intermediate stage of this process can arguably be seen in Ket, where the action nominal can in principle relativize a fairly wide range of core and peripheral participants, but S and P relativization is strongly preferred; see Section 3.3.5 and examples in (80).

Agentive participles typically relativize participants that are prototypically volitional and actively initiate the events. These forms are, therefore, highly semantically charged, and despite being described in some grammars in syntactic terms (as relativizers of transitive subjects; see Vallejos Yopán 2016: 116–117 for Cocama), they can usually be seen as relativizers of agents in terms of semantic roles. This brings them close to participles oriented towards peripheral participants, such as locatives or instrumentals, whose relativizing capacity in many cases can only be formulated semantically. For instance, the locative nominalization in *ka-V-ha* in Muna (Austronesian) is not oriented towards a participant encoded in any particular way, but rather to any participant denoting a location. In a similar fashion, the instrumental nominalization in *-nanɨ* in Apatani (Sino-Tibetan) can be oriented towards any participant acting as an instrument, no matter what formal encoding it would receive in an independent clause.[26] A case where a participle is oriented towards a participant that would have a particular type of encoding if expressed overtly, is found in Ma'di (Central Sudanic); see Section 3.4 and relevant examples in (86). This, however, is extremely rare in my sample.

Notably, forms with agentive, locative and instrumental orientation are also similar in that all of them are commonly classified as participant nominalizations in individual languages. It seems, therefore, that reference rather than modification is primary function for many of them, and some have not yet grammaticalized as full-fledged relative forms; see Fleck (2003: 1019) on Matsés, and Section 4.3.4 for further discussion. In other words, what they show is not participial orientation per se, but an ability to refer to a participant with a specific semantic role or specific semantic properties. This is particularly evident in the case of the nominalization *-m* in Ronghong Qiang, whose relativizing capacity cannot even be formulated in morphological or syntactic terms. According to LaPolla and Huang (2003: 226–227), this form can in principle be used to relativize animate participants irrespective of their syntactic function. However, the requirement for the modified noun to be animate results in a preference for subject (agent) and indirect object (recipient) relativization, as reflected by the examples provided in the grammar.

Passive participles, on the other hand, are oriented towards direct objects (and not patients or themes), and thus rely on syntax rather than semantics; see Haspelmath (1994: 161–162). Interestingly, as Haspelmath shows, this is a recent development for many languages, which originally had semantically defined patient-oriented forms. A possible explanation for the syntacticization of passive participles might be that in some cases their resulting orientation is simply

---

[26] This tendency is also relevant for restrictions imposed on contextually oriented participles. For instance, Nefedov (2012: 215) reports for Ket (Yeniseian) that the action nominal used for nonfinite relativization can relativize an instrument, but other participants encoded in exactly the same way (e.g. comitatives) cannot be relativized using the same strategy. It is, therefore, clear that it is the semantic role that is important here, and not morphological marking.

of a residual type, since P is the only core participant left when S and A are already "reserved" by semantically grounded active participles. The other type of participles for which this explanation seems plausible are forms with limited contextual orientation. As I have shown in Section 3.5.2, in all languages that have such forms, they belong to a larger paradigm of non-finite forms used to relativize different participants. I suggest that an important reason why these forms are oriented in this particular way is that they need to "take over" the positions of the Accessibility Hierarchy that are unavailable for the other participial forms existing in the language. As mentioned earlier in Section 3.3.4, this explanation may be relevant for agentive participles as well, since they tend to co-exist with absolutive participles, but they also seem to have a clear semantic basis of their own.

Finally, the presence of participles with full contextual orientation in a language seems to be related to the way in which this language handles relativization in general, more precisely whether or not it has other types of relative clauses. The expectation is that languages with only inherently oriented forms are likely to have non-participial relative clauses as well, but if a language has contextually oriented participles, these typically suffice as the sole means of relativization.

Among the 100 languages of my sample, 53 have finite relative clauses alongside participial constructions; see examples (121) from English and (122) from Meadow Mari illustrating synonymous participial and finite relative clauses:

(121) English (Indo-European)
 a. *Have you met the girl* [*living next door*]?
 b. *Have you met the girl* [*who lives next door*]?
(122) Meadow Mari (Uralic)
 a. [*Tud-ən il-əme*] *pört jər šuko peledəš ul-o.*
 that-GEN live-PTCP.NS house near many flower be-PRS.3SG
 (Brykina and Aralova 2012: 477)
 b. *Pört jər,* [*ku-što tudo il-eš*], *šuko peledəš*
 house near which-INE he live-PRS.3SG flower many
 ul-o.
 be-PRS.3SG
 'Near the house in which he lives there is a lot of flowers.'
 (Aralova and Brykina 2012: 522)

In 38 of these languages, finite relative clauses are the primary relativization strategy, like in English, or at least as common as participial relative clauses. In the other 15 languages, finite relative clauses are secondary in the sense that they are either a recent innovation (this is common, for example, for many languages spoken in Russia, which developed the relative pronoun strategy under Russian influence), or mostly appear in syntactic contexts that are typically problematic for participial relative clauses, such as relativization of the lower part of the Accessibility Hierarchy.

Notably, as shown in Table 16 below, finite relative clauses are mostly characteristic of languages that only have inherently oriented participles (75.7% of these languages have finite relative clauses), while in languages that have contextually oriented participles finite relative clauses are rare or at least secondary. This probably reflects the fact that even relatively large paradigms of inherently oriented participles have a more limited relativization capacity when compared to (paradigms of) participles with contextual orientation.

Tab. 16: Finite relative clauses in languages with different participial types

	Overall	Finite RCs common (available)	% Languages with finite RCs
Contextual only	38	5 (15)	13.2% (39.5%)
Inherent only	37	28	75.7%
Both	24	5 (10)	20.1% (41.7%)

Although synchronically the connection between finite relative clauses and typical participial orientation is quite clear, it can hardly help to explain the emergence of contextually oriented participles. Conversely, according to some scarce evidence available, finite relative clauses can be responsible for a reduction of participial orientation. For example, both Finnish and Northern Khanty have participles originating from the old Uralic non-finite *-*m* formant (see Shagal 2018: 80), but in Finnish, where finite relative clauses appeared centuries ago due to contact with Indo-European languages, the respective form has passive orientation, while in Northern Khanty, where finite strategy appeared relatively recently, the -*m* participle preserves contextual orientation. I was not able to find any sources that would report the opposite development.

3.9 Summary and conclusions

In this chapter, I discussed the notion of participial orientation, examined participial orientation in the languages of the sample, and proposed tentative motivations for attested orientation types. In general, participles in the world's languages can be either inherently oriented, or contextually oriented. Among inherently oriented participles, active participles and absolutive participles imply two different types of patterning of core clause participants, while passive participles and agentive participles are oriented towards one particular core participant each. Some languages also feature forms oriented towards a certain peripheral participant, such as instrumental or locative. Contextually oriented participles cover two major types, i.e. forms with full contextual orientation and forms with limited contextual orientation. Table 17 below shows the number of languages that have participles of each particular type (each language is counted as many times as many different types of orientation it has). To widen the inherent relativizing capacity of participial forms, languages may employ different means, such as specialized suffixes and resumptive pronouns.

Tab. 17: Different types of participial orientation across languages

Type of orientation	Number of languages
Inherently oriented	
Active	46
Passive	21
Agentive	5
Absolutive	19
Instrumental	2
Locative	5
Several non-core participants	2
Contextually oriented	
Full: up to direct objects	4
Full: up to indirect objects	2
Full: up to obliques	30
Full: up to possessors	11
Limited: non-subject	13
Limited: indirect objects and obliques	3
Limited: obliques only	1

The observed orientation types differ in the types of motivations that can best explain their existence. I suggest that the S/A pattern characteristic of active participles is based primarily on semantic properties of the participants, such as humanness and control. Absolutive participles, on the other hand, are an efficient means of introducing new discourse participants, which are commonly S or P. Relatively uncommon forms with agentive, instrumental or locative orientation often "moonlight" as participles, while their main function is that of semantically defined participant nominalizations. Passive participles, which are the most syntacticized among inherently oriented forms, may show orientation of a residual type, as well as participles with limited contextual orientation, such as non-subject form. As for participles with full contextual orientation, they seem to occur mostly in languages which do not have other means of relativization, in particular finite relative clauses.

4 Desententialization and nominalization

4.1 Introduction

In the definition introduced in Chapter 2, one of the crucial features of a participle is that it has to demonstrate a certain morphosyntactic deviation from the prototypical predicate of an independent sentence in a given language. This is referred to as *deranking* as opposed to *balancing*; see Section 2.3.3. The next three chapters discuss the specific ways in which a participial clause and a participle itself can differ from an independent sentence and its prototypical predicate. In order to account systematically for the diversity in the manifestations of deranking, it is first necessary to establish a set of parameters for cross-linguistic comparison, which can then be used for analyzing participial forms in sample languages. The aim of the current chapter is, therefore, to provide an overview of how dependent clauses can deviate from the independent clause standard, and to select those deviations that are particularly relevant for the typology of participial relative clauses.

In the functional-typological literature, the discussion of structural, semantic and functional differences between main clauses and dependent clauses has been particularly vigorous in relation to the notion of finiteness. The traditional approach to finiteness originates from classical grammar, which made a binary distinction between verbal forms specified for person and number (*verba finita*), and verbal forms without any person-number marking (*verba infinita*); see, for instance, Koptjevskaja-Tamm (1999) or Nikolaeva (2007a: 1) for an overview. However, as noted by Arkadiev (2014a: 69), the Neogrammarians were already aware of the fact that the morphological dichotomy does not exactly align with syntactic positions in which morphologically finite and non-finite verbal forms occur (see Brugmann 1892: 842). Also, in some languages, verb forms in general are not marked for most of the parameters normally relevant to verbs (tense, aspect, mood, person), and the notion of finiteness is, therefore, not applicable (see Cristofaro 2003: 53 on Gulf Arabic).

In the typological literature of the last two decades, it has become a fairly mainstream view that finiteness should be regarded as a gradual and multifactorial rather than a binary phenomenon (see, however, Bisang 2001, 2007). Nevertheless, authors differ significantly in the exact criteria they take into account, in their willingness to provide functional explanations for the observed patterning of these criteria, and the consequences of their treatment of finiteness for typology. In the following sections, I will take a closer look at scalar approaches to finiteness (4.2),[27] and on that basis identify the parameters of variation that I will consider further in the study of participial relative clauses (4.3). Finally, Section 4.4 is a brief summary of the chapter.

4.2 Scalar approaches to finiteness

The goal of this section is to provide an overview of the most important typological approaches treating finiteness as a scalar phenomenon. I will start with Lehmann's (1988) scale of desententialization (4.2.1), followed by Cristofaro's (2003) work on the typology of subordination (4.2.2), Malchukov's (2004) Generalized Scale Model (4.2.3), and Nikolaeva (2013), who applies a canonical approach to the notion of finiteness (4.2.4). Of course, this is by no means an exhaustive list of relevant works, but I consider these studies to be most representative of the existing diversity, because they incorporate a considerable number of earlier works, and differ significantly among themselves in their explanations and general typological understanding of finiteness. Some other approaches will be referred to more briefly throughout the section. The section will round off with a brief summary of the approaches (4.2.5).

4.2.1 Lehmann's (1988) scale of desententialization

In his study of the typology of clause linkage, Lehmann (1988) suggests that a subordinate clause can be reduced to varying degrees, which he regards as a combination of two simultaneous processes. First, the clause loses its clausal properties, which means the components which allow reference to a specific state of affairs are dropped, and the state of affairs is commonly typified. This process can be referred to as *decategorization* of a dependent clause (Hopper and Thompson 1984; Malchukov 2004; van Lier 2009), because it involves the non-expression of behavioural potential associated with the primary – predicational – function of a clause, or as *deverbalization* (Croft 1991: 79), because the properties lost (e.g. TAM distinctions or person-number marking) are primarily associated with the verb as the prototypical nucleus of a clause. Secondly, the clause increasingly acquires nominal properties and, as a result, becomes a constituent of the matrix clause.

---

[27] It should be noted that in this chapter I will only discuss different approaches to finiteness to the extent that they are relevant to the point of the present study. For a comprehensive overview of the topic see, for instance, van Lier (2009: 79–98).

This process is known as *recategorization* (Bhat 1994; Malchukov 2004; van Lier 2009), since it is reflected in the expression of behavioural potential associated with the secondary – referential or modifying – function of a dependent clause, or as *nominalization* (Lehmann 1988; Malchukov 2004), since the most salient properties acquired as a result of this process (e.g. case or definiteness) pertain to nouns in the first place.

Lehmann refers to the phenomenon in its entirety as *desententialization*. It can, however, be divided into two separate processes depending on what aspect of a subordinate clause is affected by the changes. Lehmann distinguishes between the changes affecting the internal syntax of a subordinate clause (desententialization in the narrow sense) and the changes affecting its external distribution (nominalization in the broad sense, including adverbialization/adjectivization). I will discuss these in turn, mainly illustrating the phenomena with the examples provided by Lehmann himself.

Desententialization in the narrow sense (changes in the internal structure) implies the loss of various semantic components and categories with their grammatical correlates which normally make up a full-fledged sentence (Lehmann 1988: 193). The relevant parameters thus include illocutionary force, modality, tense and aspect, personal inflection, polarity, and the expression of dependents taken by the verbal predicate.

Illocutionary force is lost in the vast majority of subordinate clauses, because a sentence may typically have only one illocutionary force, and it is determined by its main clause. Formally, this can be manifested in the fact that certain markers related to illocutionary force may be unavailable in dependent clauses. Examples of such illocutionary elements provided by Lehmann (1988: 193) are the validator *-mi* in Quechua and the assertive particle *ne* in Latin.

Desententialization also often imposes restrictions on the domain of modality, which can be manifested as constraints on the choice of mood and/or the use of modal elements, or as loss of the whole category. For example, in Latin, finite subordinate clauses conveying orders can only have subjunctive forms as their predicates, like the form *dicant* in (123a). When, on the other hand, a subordinate clause is non-finite, the category of mood is irrelevant altogether, e.g. for the conjunct participle *pugnans* in the adverbial clause in (123b):

(123) Latin (Indo-European)
    a. *Telebo-is*   *iube-t*   [*sententia-m*   *ut*   **dica-nt**
        Teleboan-DAT.PL order.PRS-3SG opinion(F)-ACC.SG that say.SJV.PRS-3PL

su-am].
POSS.REFL-F.ACC.SG
'He orders the Teleboans to give their opinion.'
(Lehmann 1988: 184, my glosses)

b. *L. Petrosidi-us   aquilifer   ... pro   castr-is*
   L. Petrosidius-NOM.SG standard.bearer.NOM.SG in.front camp-ABL.PL
   [*fortissime **pugn-an-s**]   occid-itur.*
   strong.SUP fight-PTCP.PRS-M.NOM.SG knock.down-PRS.PASS.3SG
   'L. Petrosidius, the colour-bearer, is killed in front of the camp, fighting most bravely.'
   (Lehmann 1988: 184, my glosses)

Similarly, the expression of tense and aspect (considered together, since these categories are commonly hard to discern in individual languages) in dependent clauses can be restricted as a result of desententialization, or even blocked completely. For instance, the active conjunct participle in Latin illustrated in (123b) above allows only the opposition between simultaneous (present) form *pugnans* and subsequent (future) form *pugnaturus*, which is notably limited in comparison to the tense system in the indicative. In non-final serial verbs in Kobon tense and aspect markers are missing altogether and are understood to be those of the final verb; see (124):

(124) Kobon (Nuclear Trans New Guinea)
*Nipe   [wañib   si   **ud**]   ar-öp.*
3SG   string.bag illicitly take   go-PRF.3SG
'He stole the string bag.' (Davies 1981: 203)

In languages where predicates of independent clauses show person agreement, desententialization commonly leads to the loss of agreement. This can be seen from examples (123b) and (124) above, where the conjunct participle in Latin and the medial verb in Kobon do not bear any person marking, while predicates of main clauses do.

Desententialization can also affect the polarity of the subordinate clause. For Lehmann, this primarily means that a dependent clause desententialized to a certain extent cannot be independently negated (other manifestations of desententialization in the domain of negation will be discussed in Sections 4.3.2 and 5.3). For example, in Jakaltek, negative markers can occur in finite subordinate clauses, compare (125a) and (125b), but not in non-finite clauses like (125c), where negation is unavailable:

(125) Jakaltek (Mayan)
   a. ç-w-acoj   yiŋ   hin   c'ul   [chubil   ch-in   to-yi].
      PRS-ERG.1SG-carry in   POSS.1SG stomach   that   PRS-1SG go-AUGM
      'I am thinking of going.'
      (Craig 1977: 242, as cited in Lehmann 1988: 198)
   b. ç-w-acoj   yiŋ   hin   c'ul   [chubil   mach   ch-in
      PRS-ERG.1SG-carry in   POSS.1SG stomach   that   NEG   PRS-1SG
      to-yi].
      go-AUGM
      'I am thinking of not going.'
      (Craig 1977: 242, as cited in Lehmann 1988: 198)
   c. ç-w-acoj   yiŋ   hin   c'ul   [hin   to-yi].
      PRS-ERG.1SG-carry in   POSS.1SG stomach   POSS.1SG go-AUGM
      'I am thinking of going.'
      (Craig 1977: 242, as cited in Lehmann 1988: 198)

Finally, desententialization can have a variety of consequences for the expression of dependents of the subordinate predicate. The subject slot of the subordinate verb can either be converted into an oblique slot, commonly a possessor, as in example (125c), or it is entirely lost, as in example (123b). The encoding of dependents other than subject can change as well. For example, in English, depending on the degree of desententialization, the non-finite predicate of a complement clause can take a regular direct object and an adverbial modifier (126a), or it can switch from verbal to nominal government, i.e. encode the object with an *of*-phrase and take an adjectival modifier (126b) (see Lehmann 1988: 197):

(126) English (Indo-European)
   a. *She objected to [his constantly reading magazines].*
   b. *She objected to [his constant reading of magazines].*

The phenomena discussed so far affect the internal structure of the subordinate clause. However, as mentioned earlier, desententialization in the broad sense can also cause changes in its external distribution. In particular, desententialized clauses acquire the ability to combine with adpositions and case markers, and, according to Lehmann (1988: 198), the more a subordinate clause is nominalized, the more easily it combines with these items. For example, in English, *in* is the only primary preposition that can govern a *that*-clause (127a), while with a non-finite form a range of prepositions is much wider, as shown in (127b) and (127c).

In Quechua, complement clauses headed by nominalizations can take accusative case marking, as in (128):

(127) English (Indo-European)
    a. *The problem lies in [that these guidelines are largely ignored].*
    b. *The night ended with [me ignoring him].*
    c. *His criticism is based on [his ignoring this important distinction].*

(128) Imbabura Quechua (Quechuan)
    alku-ta   kri-ni   [aycha-ta   shuwa-ju-j-ta]
    dog-ACC believe-1 meat-ACC steal-PROG-NMZ.PRS-ACC
    'I believe the dog to be stealing the meat.' (Cole 1985: 35)

These examples illustrate how the process of nominalization of a subordinate clause leads to it acquiring distributional properties of a noun. Similarly, desententialized clauses acting as adnominal attributes can behave as adjectives with respect to their external syntax. Therefore, in some languages, like Russian or Lithuanian, participles introducing non-finite relative clauses agree with the modified noun in case, number, and gender. For further discussion of this type of agreement see Lehmann (1984: 187–188), and Sections 4.3.4 and 5.5 of this book.

Based on the observations outlined above, Lehmann proposes a desententialization continuum ranging from sententiality to nominality, and connecting a clause and a verbal noun as two extreme points:

(129) The scale of desententialization (Lehmann 1988: 200)

    sententiality   ◄─────────────────────►   nominality
    clause   non-finite construction   verbal noun
    no illocutionary force
      constraints on illocutionary elements
        constraints on/loss of modal elements and mood
          constraints on/loss of tense and aspect
            dispensability of complements
              loss of personal conjugation
                conversion of subject into oblique slot
                  no polarity
                    conversion of verbal into nominal government
                      dispensability of subject
                        constraints on complements
    combinable with adposition / agglutinative case affix / flexive case affix

Lehmann himself does not explicitly link desententialization to finiteness (he seems to follow the traditional definition of finiteness; see Lehmann 1988: 195), but his work has later been cited as highly relevant in this connection; see, for instance, Haspelmath (1995: 5) on the definition of non-finiteness applied to converbs, or Malchukov (2004: 11). For Haspelmath, for instance, the traditional concepts of finiteness and non-finiteness are just two extreme points on a scale of desententialization, and languages can be regarded as located at various intermediate points on this scale.

The order of clausal properties in the scale is supposed to represent the order in which they are lost in the process of desententialization. It is, however, based on Lehmann's general observations and examples from individual languages rather than on any kind of consistent cross-linguistic analysis (for a similar kind of observations see, for example, Comrie 1976b, Givón 2001: Chapter 19). The question that one might ask is if these observations hold when tested on a representative language sample. The next two sections present two wide-scale cross-linguistic studies that aimed at establishing the hierarchichal ordering patterns in desententialization, namely Cristofaro (2003) and Malchukov (2004).

4.2.2 Cristofaro's (2003) approach

Cristofaro (2003) is a broad typological study of subordination, which considers dependent clauses in a genetically and areally representative sample of 80 languages. One of the goals of her study is to identify implicational patterns in the cross-linguistic coding of complement, adverbial and relative subordination relations as manifested in dependent clauses of the respective types. In order to do that, Cristofaro identifies an inventory of morphosyntactic phenomena relevant for the encoding of subordination, and investigates their various logically possible combinations.

The two major parameters that Cristofaro (2003) takes into account are (1) the form of the verb (dependent clause predicate), and (2) the coding of participants. The form of the verb is actually a complex parameter that includes three smaller domains, namely, (a) the expression of the tense, aspect and mood distinctions, (b) person agreement, and (c) the use of case marking and adpositions. Changes with respect to parameters (a) and (b) can usually be regarded as evidence that a dependent verb totally or partially lacks some verbal properties, while the ability to take case marking and/or adpositions signals that the verb has certain nominal features.

For the expression of TAM distinctions and person agreement the variation as analyzed by Cristofaro is threefold: the respective values can be expressed in the same way as in independent clauses, they can be expressed in a different way, or not expressed at all. Case marking, on the other hand, can simply be either available or unavailable. As regards the coding of participants, two deviations are most widely attested: (a) verb arguments may not be expressed in dependent clauses, and (b) verb arguments are expressed as possessors instead of receiving their regular marking. The implicational correlations discovered by Cristofaro in the languages of her sample are listed in (130):

(130) Implicational correlations between deranking phenomena in Cristofaro (2003: 277–284)
   1a. Distinctions in aspect not expressed → Distinctions in tense not expressed
   1b. Person agreement not expressed → T/A/M not expressed ∨ T/A/M special forms
   Person agreement special forms → T/A/M not expressed ∨ T/A/M special forms
   1c. Case marking/adpositions → T/A/M not expressed ∨ T/A/M special forms
   Case marking/adpositions → Person agreement not expressed
   2a. Arguments not expressed → T/A/M not expressed
   Arguments not expressed → Person agreement not expressed
   2b. Arguments expressed as possessors → T/A/M not expressed ∨ T/A/M special forms
   Arguments expressed as possessors → Person agreement not expressed ∨ Person agreement special forms
   Arguments expressed as possessors → Case marking/adpositions

Cristofaro proposes two major functional principles as possible explanations for these implicational correlations.[28] The first principle relates to the conceptualization of dependent states of affairs, which Cristofaro argues are closer to nouns

---

[28] Correlation (1a) is accounted for in terms of the principle of relevance, as discussed by Bybee (1985); see Cristofaro (2003: 277–278). According to Bybee, the universally preferred order of bound morphemes expressing verbal categories reflects the degree of relevance of each category for the interpretation of the verbal stem. Aspect is shown to occur cross-linguistically closer to the stem, because it affects the semantics of the verb, while tense and mood, expressed further away from the stem, do not affect the internal constituency of the situation. As a more relevant

(which prototypically encode things) rather than verbs (which prototypically encode processes) in their cognitive profile (see also Langacker 1987a, 1987b). According to Cristofaro (2003: 284), this is particularly relevant to explain why a lack of person agreement distinctions (or expression of person agreement with special forms, mainly using possessive markers), case marking/adpositions on the dependent verb, and the coding of arguments as possessors all entail a lack of temporal, aspectual or modal distinctions, or the expression of these distinctions by means of special forms.[29] The proposed explanation is that all the grammatical nominal properties listed above reflect conceptualization of the dependent state of affairs as a thing, which, in turn, requires that it be no longer conceptualized as a process. At the grammatical level, the latter requirement is reflected by a lack of TAM distinctions.

The same principle can be used to account for the fact that case marking/adpositions on the dependent verb and the coding of arguments as possessors entail a lack of person agreement distinctions. In this case, person agreement is not regarded as a category contributing to the conceptualization of the dependent state of affairs. Crucially, it is a verbal property, and the conceptualization of the dependent state of affairs as a thing (reflected in the acquisition of nominal properties) blocks its expression on the subordinate predicate.

As I will show in Chapter 5, both the loss of verbal properties and the acquisition of nominal properties are typical for participial relative clauses as considered in this study. It should be noted, though, that it is not entirely clear from Cristofaro's explanation how exactly the conceptualization of a state of affairs as a thing pertains to dependent clauses used for adnominal modification, that is, in the prototypical function of an adjective rather than a noun.

The correlations involving the impossibility for the verb to take overtly expressed arguments are, according to Cristofaro (2003: 286–288), best accounted for in terms of a second functional principle, namely, the principle of syntagmatic economy. The explanation is as follows. A number of subordination relations, such as modals, phasals, and purpose relations, entail or favour sharing of participants, which is economically reflected by a lack of overtly expressed arguments. The same relation types are also shown to involve predetermination of the time reference, aspect and mood value of the dependent state of affairs, which, again, is economically reflected by a lack of TAM distinctions. Thus, with these

---

category, aspect, therefore, is more frequently overtly encoded on dependent clause predicates, and remains unexpressed only if the less relevant distinctions are not expressed either.

29 It should be noted that these implications confirm Lehmann's (1988) observations reflected in the scale of desententialization; see Section 4.2.1.

relation types, economy motivates both a lack of overtly expressed arguments, and a lack of TAM distinctions. On the other hand, subordination relations like perception, reality condition or simultaneity, economically entail predetermination of TAM, but not a sharing of participants. There are, however, no subordination relations in which participants are predetermined and TAM values are not. This asymmetry is exactly what is reflected in the implicational correlation pattern.

Importantly, the implicational correlation between a lack of overtly expressed arguments and a lack of TAM distinctions has a number of exceptions, and almost all of them are provided by relative relations. According to Cristofaro (2003: 288), this is due to the fact that in this case a lack of TAM distinctions and a lack of overtly expressed arguments are motivated in terms of distinct principles. The lack of TAM distinctions is motivated in terms of the cognitive status of the dependent state of affairs (see above), while the lack of overtly expressed arguments is not motivated in terms of any particular semantic or cognitive feature of relative relations. In most cases, it is simply one of the possible means of indicating the role of the relativized item, the gap strategy; see Section 4.3.5 for further discussion.

This analysis of relative clauses is, in fact, a good illustration of why Cristofaro's (2003) work is especially relevant for the current study. Importantly, apart from establishing cross-constructional implicational patterns in subordination encoding, Cristofaro also provides a detailed analysis of different types of subordination relations, including relative structures (Cristofaro 2003: Chapter 7). Her book, therefore, provides an overview of the deranking phenomena specific for relative clauses, as well as their distribution across different relative constructions, and it proposes certain functional-typological explanations of the observed tendencies. Cristofaro's most important findings and observations on these matters will be discussed in more detail in what follows.

4.2.3 Malchukov's (2004) Generalized Scale Model

Malchukov (2004) is a typological study of transcategorial processes, primarily nominalization and verbalization. The two processes are shown to exhibit similar tendencies with respect to the loss/acquisition of properties. In this overview, I will only focus on nominalization as more relevant to the current study. Specifically, Malchukov aims to develop a principled account of the order in which verbal features are lost and nominal categories are acquired. He starts with two hierarchies, both of which are based on numerous earlier proposals introduced in earlier typological studies from a variety of theoretical frameworks.

An idea crucial for Malchukov's study is that grammatical categories are organized in layers. In the functional-typological paradigm, this idea is primarily represented in Role and Reference Grammar (Foley and Van Valin 1984; Van Valin and LaPolla 1997) and Functional Grammar (Hengeveld 1989; Dik 1997); see Narrog (2009: 33–36) for an overview of different approaches to layering. Layered structure can pertain both to the clause and to the noun phrase, and it can comprise verbal/clausal and nominal categories respectively. Morphosyntactic expressions of categories (bound morphemes) are referred to as *operators*, while lexical expressions (e.g. particles or adverbs) that convey meanings belonging to the same domain are termed *satellites*. Both operators and satellites have certain layers in their scope. The innermost layer of the clause structure is the predicate with its arguments, and the core of the noun phrase structure is the noun itself. The predicate and the noun are successively expanded by operators and satellites, starting from more internal categories and proceeding towards more external.

Malchukov's (2004) hierarchy of verbal features is based primarily on Bybee (1985), Noonan (1985) and Croft (1991), as well as on some work in the framework of Functional Grammar (e.g. Dik 1991, 1997; Hengeveld 1992).[30] The resulting hierarchy is presented in (131) on the next page.[31]

The sign "⊂" should be read as "entails the loss of". For nominalizations, the generalization is that the loss of a certain feature in a nominalization construction entails the loss of any feature occupying a lower (more external) position on the hierarchy, e.g. if a structure cannot express tense, this also entails that it cannot have illocutionary force markers, etc. In other words, the features are lost starting from the outermost layer.

---

[30] I will not discuss all the separate hierarchies in any detail here. An overview of relevant literature can be found in Malchukov (2004: 13–25).
[31] Following van Lier (2009), I adopt the visual representations of the hierarchies from Nikitina's (2007) review of Malchukov's book.

(131) Verbal hierarchy (Malchukov 2004: 20)
VERB stem
↓
voice/valency, direct object, object agreement
⊂
aspectual operators, adverbial satellites with aspectual value (manner adverbs)
⊂
tense and mood operators and corresponding satellites (temporal/modal adverbs)
⊂
subject agreement, clausal subject
⊂
illocutionary force markers

Malchukov's nominal hierarchy stems from the hierarchy of nominal inflectional categories proposed by Lehmann and Moravcsik (2000: 753), and from the layered structure of the noun phrase discussed by Rijkhoff (1992) and Van Valin and LaPolla (1997); see (132):

(132) Nominal hierarchy (Malchukov 2004: 47)
NOUN stem
↓
classifying/qualitative operators/satellites: singulative/collective markers, noun classifiers, nominal class markers, adjectives
⊂
quantitative operators/satellites: number markers, numerals
⊂
locative/possessive phrases
⊂
determiners
⊂
case markers/adpositions

Since in the process of nominalization verbal features are lost while nominal features are acquired, the generalization concerning the nominal hierarchy in this case works in the opposite direction: it is the expression of a certain feature in a nominalization that implies the expression of any feature occupying a lower (more external) position on the hierarchy, e.g. if a nominalization receives number marking it must be able to take case markers, etc. Malchukov (2004: 25–26) further suggests that the generalizations based on both hierarchies have a functional motivation: external categories on the hierarchies are more readily affected by transcategorial operations than the inner ones, because external operators (e.g. determiners) reflect the syntactic and/or pragmatic function of a given lexical item more directly than internal operators.

The major innovation proposed in Malchukov's work when compared to earlier typological studies is the Generalized Scale Model (Malchukov 2004: 57), which combines the verbal hierarchy and the nominal hierarchy (by attaching the lower part of the nominal hierarchy to the upper part of the verbal hierarchy) and establishes constraints on possible "mappings" between them. Malchukov supplements the scale with several *blocking effects*, which are essentially based on the fact that some nominal and some verbal categories are functionally too similar to be compatible. That is, in some cases a language has to make choice between taking recourse to nominal or verbal encoding for a particular function. *Subject-blocking effect*, for instance, is responsible for the fact that a verbal argument cannot be expressed in a verbal and a nominal way at the same time, hence ungrammaticality of structures of the type **I saw John's he going*. The combination of the hierarchical scale with the blocking effects yields three major types of nominalizations, which crucially differ in their ratio of verbal and nominal properties (see Malchukov 2004: 66–69).

In addition to the factors outlined above, Malchukov emphasizes the importance of language-specific structural factors for the outcome of transcategorial operations. For instance, in Limbu (Sino-Tibetan) aspect markers are lost in nominalizations/participles, while tense marking is retained (see van Driem 1987). Malchukov (2004: 40) suggests explaining this by the fact that aspect markers in Limbu are external to tense, and therefore are structurally more likely to be lost. Also, some categories can be expressed cumulatively in certain languages, such as subject and object agreement (Maricopa), or verbal agreement and voice (Modern Greek); see Malchukov (2004: 111–114). As a result, these categories can be either both retained or both lost in the process of nominalization. A further consequence of the latter observation is that languages from different morphological types can differ with respect to the graduality of transcategorial changes they exhibit: agglutinative languages, where one form normally performs one function, therefore, allow for more gradual deverbalization than fusional languages.

To summarize, Malchukov's proposal is to apply a competing motivations approach to the typology of nominalization. The hierarchy constraints, as well as blocking effects, are, in essence, functionally motivated. On the other hand, a number of structural factors can interfere with the hierarchy constraints. Other factors at play include economy (which disfavours the expression of categories recoverable in a given context), and diachronic processes, which may also influence the outcome of transcategorial operations. Malchukov (2004: 131) explicitly mentions that even though the Generalized Scale Model is not restricted to any particular lexical categories (e.g. nouns or verbs), it presupposes the existence of feature hierarchies for the lexical category in question. The model, therefore, cannot be directly applied to participles ("verbal adjectives"), since no feature hierarchies are available specifically for them. Nevertheless, the model can provide some important insights for the study of participial relative clauses, at least because many of them are introduced by forms that are best classified as belonging to the category of nouns in individual languages; see Section 2.4 for discussion.

4.2.4 Nikolaeva's (2013) canonical approach

It has often been noted by typologists that various criteria for desententialization or nominalization as discussed in the previous sections do not necessarily match. This is actually one of the motivations for a scalar approach to finiteness in the first place. However, Nikolaeva (2013: 117–118) provides several examples which not only challenge a binary approach to finiteness, but also contradict the proposed functional hierarchies and implications discussed in the previous sections. For instance, Cuzco Quechua nominalizations, according to Lefebvre and Muysken (1988), express verbal agreement but not tense, in spite of the fact that the former is generally regarded as a more external category than the latter. Another example cited by Nikolaeva comes from Ledgeway (1998), who shows that within Romance languages alone one can find all possible combinations of tense and agreement features on dependent verbs, including agreement on inflected Portuguese infinitives and Old Neapolitan gerunds and participles.

Based on these observations, Nikolaeva concludes that the functional pressures proposed earlier only work as very general tendencies, whereas the parameters crucially implicated in the definition of finiteness do not appear to form exceptionless implicational relations, and are better viewed as a set of discrete unrelated properties. She therefore proposes to treat (non-)finiteness in the vein of canonical typology (Corbett 2005; Brown et al. 2013), an approach developed to address variation in phenomena which do not easily fit into binary standards. Canonical typology takes the criteria used to define particular categories or phenomena in order to create a multidimensional space in which language-specific instances can be placed. Each instance can, consequently, demonstrate greater or lesser proximity to a canonical ideal.[32] The list of criteria that Nikolaeva considers relevant for canonical (non-)finiteness is presented in (133). The sign ">" should be read as "more canonical then":

(133) Criteria for canonical (non-)finiteness according to Nikolaeva (2013):
MORPHOLOGY
C-1: tense marking > no tense marking
C-2: subject agreement > no subject agreement
C-3: mood and/or illocutionary force marking > no such marking
C-4: politeness marking > no politeness marking
C-5: evidential marking > no evidential marking
C-6: no switch-reference marking > switch-reference marking
C-7: nominative subject > non-nominative subject
SYNTAX
C-8: independent clause > dependent clause
C-9: subject licensing > no subject
C-10: morphosyntactic expression of information structure > no such expression
SEMANTICS
C-11: assertion > no assertion
C-12: independent temporal anchoring > no independent temporal anchoring
C-13: information structuring > no information structuring

A distinctive feature of Nikolaeva's approach is that among the criteria considered crucial for (non-)finiteness she mentions not only structural properties of the form and its behavioural potential, but also the semantics of the construction. Semantics, of course, has also been taken into account in other scalar approaches to (non-)finiteness and related domains, but it was mostly used as an explanatory factor for certain observed structural or behavioural properties. Nikolaeva, on the other hand, puts semantics on a par with morphology and syntax. This is in congruence with Sells (2007), who suggests three ways in which the term "finite" can be used: (a) finiteness as a property of a verbal form, (b) finiteness as a clausal

---

[32] As can be clearly seen from (133), the criteria are not mutually independent (for instance, C-10: morphosyntactic expression of information structure, and C-13: information structuring), and the list, therefore, is not immediately suitable for any kind of quantitative measure of the proximity to the canonical ideal of finiteness.

attribute, and (c) semantic finiteness related to assertion or some such property of an utterance. All the semantic criteria are conditions on the independent interpretation of a clause. The relation between morphological finiteness and assertion has been suggested in numerous typologically oriented studies; see Klein (1994, 1998), Nikolaeva (2007b), and Kalinina (1998, 2001) with special reference to participles. The evidence includes, for example, the use of morphologically non-finite forms in dependent rather than independent clauses, and the lack of certain prototypically finite distinctions in imperatives, optatives, and other non-assertive speech acts. The canon of finiteness is also linked to the presence of independent (deictic) temporal anchoring, whereas in non-finite clauses the temporal and logophoric centres must be determined anaphorically. Finally, according to Nikolaeva, the canonically finite clause must be pragmatically structured, i.e. in terms of an asserted and a presupposed part, which is a property commonly lost in many types of embeddings.

Unfortunately, semantic criteria of this type can hardly be discussed in a large-scale cross-linguistic survey, chiefly due to the lack of adequate information for many languages. Another criterion discussed by Nikolaeva is, however, of more practical relevance to the current study, namely C-5 concerning evidentiality. This category and its markers are not discussed separately in the other studies outlined in this chapter, while it can in fact play an important role in the desententialization of participial relative clauses. This issue will be further addressed in Section 4.3.1. Another criterion belonging to the same category, namely politeness (C-4), appears as one of the crucial indicators of finiteness in Bisang's (2007) approach. In my data, however, it did not prove to be relevant for any of the languages in the sample.

4.2.5 Conclusions on the scalar approaches to finiteness

The current section has provided an overview of four approaches to finiteness and desententialization which I consider most relevant for my study. All of them take into account different parameters concerning the deviation of the non-finite/desententialized clause from the independent clause standard, they account differently for the combination of these parameters, and, where applicable, they suggest different explanations.

In this study, I do not aim to consistently test any of the proposed hierarchies or scales (Lehmann 1988; Cristofaro 2003; Malchukov 2004), nor do I intend to systematically assess all of the participial forms in the sample with respect to their proximity to the canonical ideal of finiteness (Nikolaeva 2013). For a significant share of languages examined in the study, the information on many relevant criteria is simply not available in the descriptions. Instead, the studies just outlined will serve two main purposes. First, I will use the range of features included in the hierarchies as a basis for the set of parameters to be considered in this study. Their choice is presented in the following section, along with some clarifications on each of the parameters. Second, different theoretical perspectives assumed in the studies highlight problematic issues, and provide valuable insights for the analysis. I will thus use some of the relevant findings and theoretical accounts to explain desententialization patterns in participial relative clauses.

4.3 Parameters considered in this study

As I mentioned in the introduction to the present chapter, the parameters discussed in the previous section have mostly been investigated in the context of subordination in general, i.e. covering complement, adverbial and relative constructions, which resulted in enormous diversity among the structures that were examined. In this study, I would like to apply these parameters exclusively to participial relative clauses, a significantly narrower domain, which, as I will show further, has certain distinctive features that are not characteristic of other types of deranked dependent clauses. Because of this, and also in order to ensure the meaningfulness of cross-linguistic comparison, I will only focus here on a subset of parameters, which (a) can be operationalized in a large-scale typological study, and (b) are most relevant to participial relative clauses. As mentioned in Section 4.2.4, the first requirement primarily rules out semantic parameters, such as the presence of assertion or independent temporal anchoring, because of the lack of relevant data. The second requirement implies paying particular attention to the prototypical function of participles, i.e. that of adnominal modification, and adjusting the subset of parameters accordingly. For example, switch-reference marking turns out to be irrelevant, since it mostly operates in adverbial clauses and clausal chains. The ability to take nominal morphology (e.g. case marking), by contrast, is relevant but can be replaced by the parameter of ability to agree with the modified noun, because this is the primary function of nominal morphology on relative clause predicates.

As a result, the list of parameters to be considered in this study comprises five morphosyntactic manifestations of participial desententialization or nominalization, which I will discuss one by one in the following sections. These are: restrictions on TAM (4.3.1), peculiarities in the domain of negation (4.3.2), verbal subject agreement (4.3.3), nominal agreement with the modified noun (4.3.4), and deviations in argument expression (4.3.5). First, I will comment on the place and role of each particular parameter in the hierarchies and other studies of subordination, as well as on the components of complex parameters, which can be further decomposed. Second, I will explain why each parameter is relevant for participles, and in what way. Finally, I will provide necessary clarifications concerning the application of the parameters to the languages of the sample.

4.3.1 TAM expression

The domain of tense, aspect and modality (TAM) comprises such a large range of phenomena that a number of clarifications are necessary before I can proceed to analyzing the data. The first and the most obvious thing to note is that this domain is clearly not an elementary one, with three subdomains that can be hard to untangle in individual languages, as well as cross-linguistically; see Comrie (1976a, 1985), Hopper (1982), Dahl (1985), Palmer (1986), Bybee, Perkins, and Pagliuca (1994), and many others (see also Uusikoski 2016 for a recent overview). In this section, I will, however, start out by discussing tense, aspect and modality separately (in the order corresponding to various hierarchies of verbal features, e.g. Bybee 1985), and then provide a justification for considering the domain on the whole in the study of participial relative clauses.

Aspect is concerned with the internal temporal constituency of the situation (Comrie 1976a: 5), that is, how the situation extends over time. The two major types traditionally distinguished are lexical aspect (Aktionsart), which is inherent to the verbal stem and not marked formally, and grammatical aspect, a grammatical category with specific formal encoding. In a way, both types are relevant for the typology of participles. Lexical aspect, for instance, can indirectly set constraints on the formation of certain participial forms: as I showed in Section 3.3.5, absolutive participles in many languages are resultative and, thus, can only be derived from telic verbs. Malchukov (1995: 17) also reports that the non-future participle in Even (Tungusic) conveys a meaning of priority if derived from telic verbs, and a meaning of simultaneity when derived from atelic verbs. Grammatical aspect, on the other hand, e.g. the perfective/imperfective distinction, as well as quantitative aspect, such as iterative, is more relevant for the topic of the current and following chapters, namely desententialization. Aspect has been shown by numerous authors (e.g. Bybee 1985) to be one of the categories that are both semantically and structurally most closely related to the verb stem (or most internal in layered models; see, for example, Malchukov's hierarchy presented in Section 4.2.3). Accordingly, it is almost never lost completely in participial forms. At the same time, it does demonstrate a lot of peculiarities in desententialized forms, as I will show further in Section 5.2.

Tense is usually understood as a category that relates the time of the situation referred to to some other time (Comrie 1976a: 1–2). If it is the moment of speaking that is taken as a reference point, the tense is referred to as *absolute*. However, in complex sentences, languages often relate the time of the situation expressed in the dependent clause to the time of the situation expressed in the main clause (which is itself related to the moment of speaking). This is known as *relative* time reference. For certain types of subordinate relations, the temporal relation between the situations expressed in the dependent clause and the main clause is basically fixed. For instance, complement clauses introduced by perception verbs typically imply a meaning of simultaneity (relative present), e.g. *I saw him playing in the garden*, whereas adverbial purpose clauses only make sense if the situation expressed in the dependent clause is understood as (potentially) following the situation in the main clause (relative future), e.g. *He came here to bring me this book*. These constructions, therefore, obligatorily feature a particular type of relative tense meaning. In their work on nominalizations, Comrie and Thompson (2007: 347) note that the interpretation of the tense category as relative rather than absolute tense is very common generally with non-finite verb forms.

On the other hand, relative relations are special, as noted by Cristofaro (2003: 198), because unlike some other subordination relations, they have no implications about the time reference (or aspect value) of the two situations. The speaker can arbitrarily select two situations simply on the grounds that they share a participant. The tense of a participle can therefore easily be either relative or absolute. In fact, for many languages it is very hard to determine whether a relative clause predicate has relative or absolute time reference. Grammars rarely specify this in their descriptions (a rare exception is, for instance, Bergsland's (1997: 281) description of Aleut (Eskimo-Aleut), which states clearly that participial tense markers refer to the matrix clause rather than to the moment of speech; see also Nikolaeva (2014: 316) on Tundra Nenets). Moreover, in some languages the situation can be very complicated, and the participial tense cannot be classified either as absolute or as relative, as shown in Shagal (2011) for Russian. Because of these issues, when analyzing the data I will not aim to consistently distinguish between relative and absolute tense in participles, unless it is especially relevant for a certain language.

The domain of *modality* can be decomposed into several levels, which are represented (starting from the outermost) in the hierarchy proposed by Malchukov (2004: 18), with reference to Van Valin and LaPolla (1997), Dik (1997), van der Auwera and Plungian (1998), Cinque (1999), and Nuyts (2000); see (134):

(134) illocutionary > evidential > epistemic > root modality

As the outermost ones among all verbal operators (see Malchukov's verbal hierarchy or Lehmann's desententialization scale), illocutionary force markers, such as validators in Quechua or various assertive particles in other languages, are the first to be lost in the process of desententialization. No languages in my sample allow for participial relative clauses containing any markers of this type, so this layer is not particularly relevant for the current discussion. Epistemic modality (the coding of the degree of commitment to the statement expressed by the speaker), and evidentiality (the coding of the source of information) can also be shown to belong to a fairly external level cross-linguistically. The only language in my sample where evidential distinctions can be regularly expressed within a participial relative clause is Matsés (Pano-Tacanan), which will be discussed further in Section 5.2.5. Thus, the only modal layer that is commonly attested and therefore cross-linguistically relevant for the typology of participial relative clauses is root modality, also referred to as deontic modality, which pertains to the external circumstances that make the actuation of the situation necessary or allowed (see Cristofaro 2003: 60).

As I mentioned in the beginning of the section, in many cases it can be hard to draw a distinction between the expression of tense, aspect and modality in a particular language. A widely recognized example of this problem is future tense, which in many languages has modal as well as tense values, and can therefore be considered as much a mood as a tense (Lyons 1968: 275–281; Comrie 1976a: 2). The distinction between tense and modality seems, therefore, especially subtle (if existing at all) for the forms labelled as future participles in various languages. Haspelmath (1994: 162–163) shows that future/necessitative/potential meaning is common for passive participles, and this is indeed the case, for instance, for the Eastern Armenian participle in *-ik'* (Dum-Tragut 2009: 207–208), or Georgian participle in *sa-V(-el)* (Hewitt 1995: 432–433). However, it is attested with other types of orientation as well. For example, in Meadow Mari (Uralic), the participle in *-šaš* is contextually oriented, and has a meaning of future or deontic modality (Brykina and Aralova 2012: 483). These phenomena can presumably be explained by pragmatic inefficiency of characterizing a participant by referring to an event that has not yet taken place, but is still regarded as factual. That is, however, exactly what pure future participles are supposed to do. Because of this, in many languages, participles expressing future meaning are also used to describe modified nouns with regard to possible or necessary situations.[33]

Another possible connection within the TAM domain relates to the interaction between aspect and relative tense. The three generally possible values of relative tense are priority, simultaneity, and posteriority (past, present, and future relative tense respectively). However, as noted above, future participles with non-modal meaning are cross-linguistically fairly uncommon, so the meaning of posteriority is also very rarely attested in participial relative clauses. Most temporal contrasts are therefore between relative past and relative present. A very central and typologically common distinction in the aspectual zone is that between perfective and imperfective. As defined by Comrie (1976a: 16), perfectivity indicates the view of a situation as a single whole, without distinguishing the various separate phases that make up that situation, while the imperfective pays essential attention to the internal structure of the situation. This opposition, though seemingly formulated in purely aspectual terms, actually shows significant interaction with temporal properties of situations, in that perfective verb forms are usually taken to refer to past events, whereas imperfective aspect is known to intertwine with the present tense (see Dahl and Velupillai 2013). In participial relative clauses, this connection reaches a point where the two categories are almost impossible to discern. A number of languages basically distinguish between two types of participles, those referring to accomplished events preceding the situation expressed in the main clause (perfective/relative past), and those referring to ongoing situations simultaneous to the situation expressed in the main clause (imperfective/relative present). Tellingly, in the descriptions of individual languages such participles can be labelled either as past/present, as, for instance, in Beserman Udmurt (Uralic, Brykina and Aralova 2012), or as perfective/imperfective, as, for instance, in Tsafiki (Barbacoan, Dickinson 2002).

Taking into account the points made in this section, in this study I will regard TAM as a single, though complex, parameter. I will distinguish between tense, aspect and modality meanings expressed by participles whenever possible, but it is also very important to bear in mind that this distinction in many cases cannot and, therefore, should not be made. In Section 5.2, I will show that this is, in fact, often reflected in the way meanings in the TAM domain are encoded in participial forms and what paradigmatic relations they form. I will also discuss the ways in

---

33 In addition to modality, the meaning of future can also alternate within a participial form with a certain aspect value, e.g. in the future-habitual participle in *-ee* in Telugu (Dravidian).

which the hierarchies proposed for the TAM domain are manifested in the behaviour of individual participles and in the structure of participial paradigms.

4.3.2 Negation

One further parameter relevant for the distinction between finite and non-finite structures is negation. So far, typological work on negation has mostly focused on standard negation, i.e. the basic way(s) a language has for negating declarative verbal main clauses (Miestamo 2003, 2005). There has been no systematic cross-linguistic investigation of negation in subordinate clauses, although it has been observed that languages can use different kinds of negative strategies in these contexts. For instance, a recent study of negation in Uralic languages shows that especially in non-finite subordinate clauses, standard negative strategies are often blocked, and special non-finite forms may be used to fill these functions (Miestamo, Tamm, and Wagner-Nagy 2015: 21–22).

Negation as a parameter for desentWe ntialization or nominalization has not been widely discussed in cross-linguistic studies; see Section 4.2 for an overview. Lehmann (1988: 197–198) does suggest that at some stage of strong desententialization the polarity of the subordinate clause is affected. However, he only provides an example from Jakaltek (Mayan), where a non-finite complement clause simply cannot be independently negated, and does not discuss any other deviations from main clause negation. Malchukov (2004: 18) mentions negation when discussing the relative ordering of verbal categories in the hierarchy proposed by Bybee (1985), as well as in those developed within Functional Grammar and Role and Reference Grammar (Foley and Van Valin 1984; Dik 1991, 1997; Hengeveld 1992; Van Valin and LaPolla 1997). He comments that the position of negation in such hierarchies is highly problematic, since negation operators may differ in scope and pertain to different semantic layers. Because of this, while admitting the relevance of negation for the phenomenon of nominalization, Malchukov disregards it almost completely in his study.

In the domain of subordination, negation has been primarily studied in the context of complement clauses. The most prominent phenomenon here is Neg-Raising (or Neg-Transport), which was introduced to account for the near equivalence of sentences like *I don't think that she came* and *I think that she didn't come*, which feature negation in the main and the complement clause respectively; see, for example, Fillmore (1963), Ross (1973), Bartsch (1973), and Horn (1978) for early accounts. Other subordination relations received much less attention in this respect, so the interaction of negation with the desentencialization of relative clauses has not yet been investigated in typological literature. In Section 5.3, I will provide an overview of negation strategies employed in participial relative clauses, with particular attention to those demonstrating deviations from the standard negation in respective languages.

4.3.3 Subject agreement

As discussed in the introduction to the current chapter (4.1), the presence of person and number marking in a verb form has for centuries been regarded as the standard way of distinguishing between finite and non-finite verbs. This is, of course, understandable from an Indo-European perspective, but it also makes perfect sense from the point of view of various hierarchies of verbal features. Both Cristofaro's (2003) and Malchukov's (2004) studies show that verbal agreement with the subject is among the first features to be lost in the process of desententialization/nominalization.[34] Thus, for languages featuring subject agreement in independent sentences, it is a very likely and notable signal of deranking.

It is important to emphasize that in this section (and, correspondingly, in Section 5.4) I am only concerned with subject agreement of the verbal type, i.e. identical or very close to that attested in independent sentences. The expression of subject by means of possessive affixes on the participial form, which is typical of dependent clauses in many languages, is regarded as a part of the broader phenomenon of expressing subject as a possessor, and is, therefore, discussed in the chapter on participant encoding; see in particular Section 6.2.1.

In Malchukov's (2004) version of the hierarchy of verbal properties, verbal subject agreement is mentioned together with the ability of the dependent clause predicate to have a clausal subject; see Section 4.2.3. Interestingly, according to my data, verbal agreement with the subject can be lost even if the subject of the dependent clause retains its sentential form. For instance, in Kalmyk, although

---

[34] In his study, Malchukov considers object agreement along with subject agreement, and argues that the former pertains more directly to verbal valency and, therefore, has a narrower scope (hence its higher position in the hierarchy). In my sample, there are no languages that would either confirm or contradict this claim. One language for which this observation might be relevant is Mapudungun (Araucanian), where, according to Zúñiga (2000: 20), non-finite forms employed in relative clause formation either do not take agreement markers referring to arguments, or allow for the expression of one participant less than finite verbs. However, there seems to be no information regarding the particular argument appearing on non-finite verb forms. Therefore, I will only discuss subject and not object agreement in this study.

the subject of a participial relative clause can occur in the nominative case in certain contexts, the dependent predicate never receives any agreement markers, as shown in (135a). On the other hand, the predicate of an independent sentence agrees with the nominative subject, irrespective of whether it appears in the finite form or the same participial form as in the relative clause, as shown in (135b):

(135) Kalmyk (Mongolic)
    a. [*dotrə-n^j*   **bi**   **kevt-xə**]   *avdər*   *širä-n*   *öör*
       inside-POSS.3   1SG.NOM   lie-PTCP.FUT   chest   table-GEN   near
       zogs-ža-na
       stand-PROG-PRS
       'The chest in which I will be lying is next to the table.'
    b. **bi**   *avdər*   *dotər*   **kevt-žä-nä-v**   /   **kevt-xə-v**
       1SG.NOM   chest   inside   lie-PROG-PRS-1SG   /   lie-PTCP.FUT-1SG
       'I am lying in the chest/I will be lying in the chest.'

In general, as I will show in Section 6.2, participial relative clauses following the main clause pattern in subject encoding are not at all uncommon. As for verbal subject agreement, in conformity with the documented cross-linguistic tendencies, I was able to find very few languages where participles show subject agreement in the same way as independent predicates but can be classified as deranked otherwise (e.g. due to changes in the TAM domain). The (potential) exceptions, as well as the general pattern, are discussed in some detail in Section 5.4.

4.3.4 Nominal agreement with the modified noun

Nominal agreement of non-finite relative clause predicates with the modified nouns has received very little attention in the previous typological studies of subordination. The main reason is that adjectival agreement is only relevant for the contexts of adnominal modification, while most relevant cross-linguistic studies focused on the domain of subordination/nominalization in general, and aimed at cross-constructional comparison (Lehmann 1988; Cristofaro 2003; Malchukov 2004).

As I have shown in Section 2.4, participle/nominalization syncretism is an extremely widespread phenomenon, and in many cases it is not possible to identify the primary function of a particular form within a language. However, among the languages showing nominal agreement between non-finite relative clause predicates and modified nouns, we can identify two types whose agreement patterns differ precisely because of the categorial status of participles (verbal adjectives vs. verbal nouns). First, there are languages that have typical adjectival agreement (in number, gender, and possibly case) as a way to show the connection between a highly adjectival participle and a noun, for instance, Russian or Lithuanian; see example (166) in Section 5.5.1. In languages of the second type, the non-finite relative clause predicate and the modified noun are, in fact, just two nominal elements appearing in apposition. In such structures, a clause headed by a verbal noun functions as a relative clause, which is syntactically manifested in case (and possibly number) agreement with the modified noun. The second case seems to be especially common in South American languages; see, for instance, Fleck (2003: 1019) on Matsés (Pano-Tacanan) illustrated by example (173) in Section 5.5.2. Gamble (1978: 126) proposes the description of this type for Wikchamni (Yokutsan). According to his analysis, appositional clauses are subordinate clauses containing a nominalized verb, usually an agentive, or passive verbal noun, and are juxtaposed to a main clause noun. Interestingly, for some languages of the second type, the existence of case marking on the participle (action/participant nominalization) is reported to be a sign of a very week grammaticalization of the relative construction. In such languages (e.g. in Desano, Tucanoan), it seems, it is exactly the lack of "agreement" in case that actually signals that we are dealing with a real relative clause (see Miller 1999: 149). A detailed account for such cases would, however, require deep syntactic analysis of the respective constructions, for which we do not have enough data in the grammars. Therefore, in Section 5.5, which is concerned with the patterns of nominal agreement between participles and the nouns they modify, I will consider all instances of cross-referencing of nominal features of the modified noun on the adnominal modifier attested in the sample, irrespective of the individual motivations.

4.3.5 Participant expression

As pointed out by Cristofaro (2003: 201), relative clauses have an important peculiarity with respect to participant expression when compared to other types of dependent clauses: by definition, they obligatorily share a participant with the main clause. Various options for the representation of the shared participant within the relative clause are usually referred to as different *relativizing strategies* (see Comrie and Kuteva 2013a, 2013b). As I have shown in Section 2.3.1, in participial relative clauses the relativized participant can be absent (*gap strategy*), represented by a resumptive pronoun (*pronoun-retention strategy*), or undergo no changes whatsoever if the language in question has internally headed relative clauses (*non-reduction strategy*). The way the relativized participant is expressed does not, however, have a direct connection to the deranking of the relative clause (although prototypical instances of participial relative clauses are said to employ a gap strategy; see Lehmann 1984: 49–58). Thus, in the discussion of participant encoding in participial relative clauses in Chapter 6, I will focus on the encoding of participants other than the relativized one, that is, A participants in case of P relativization, P participants in case of A relativization, S/A participants in case of locative relativization, etc. I will consider separately three main types of participants, namely subjects (6.2), direct objects (6.3), and non-core participants (6.4).

An important remark is in order here, regarding the notion of subject in participial relative clauses. The term "subject" in general has been amply discussed in linguistic literature, and can be understood differently by different authors following different approaches. In this study, I basically use this term to refer to the A participant of a clause that has undergone relativization if the clause is transitive, e.g. *nay-ka* 'I' in the Korean example of P relativization in (136a), or to the S participant of an intransitive relativized clause, e.g. *Peter-ka* 'Peter' in the example of locative relativization in (136b):

(136) Korean (Koreanic)
    a. [***nay-ka*** sa-l]   cha-nun   hankwukcey-i-ta
        I-NOM   buy-REL.FUT car-TOP   Korean.made-is-END
        'The car which **I** am going to buy is Korean-made.' (← **I** am going to buy a car) (Shin 2003: 27)
    b. [***Peter-ka***   ilha-nun]   siktang
        Peter-NOM   work-REL.PRS restaurant
        'The restaurant where **Peter** works.' (← **Peter** works in a restaurant) (Shin 2003: 33)

Classifying the subjects of Korean participial relative clauses as such is fairly uncontroversial, since they bear nominative marking and otherwise behave as regular subjects of independent sentences. In other languages, however, there are some problematic cases. The major type of these concern relativization by means of forms inherently oriented towards P participants, that is, passive participles. As I showed earlier in Section 3.3.3, cross-linguistically these forms often have properties of prototypical passives, including the pragmatic demotion of the A participant. Moreover, we have seen that at least in some languages the patient of the underlying situation behaves syntactically as the subject of the participial relative clause. For instance, in Modern Standard Arabic, it triggers verbal agreement in gender and number on the relative clause predicate (see example (66) and the accompanying discussion in Section 3.3.3). In such cases, it is clearly improper to refer to the A participant as the subject of the relativized clause. At the very least, this would be confusing, even if we intend *semantic subject* as understood, for instance, by Mel'čuk (1988: 167). On the other hand, agents in passive relative clauses ultimately do correspond to A participants, with which they share certain semantic properties, such as volition. Therefore, it makes sense to consider their encoding together with underlying A participants in other types of relative constructions. Because of this, in what follows I will discuss all instances of A/S participant expression in participial relative clauses together. However, as explained in Section 3.3.3, I refrain from using the term *subject* in unclear cases. In particular, for A participants in relative clauses introduced by passive participles, I use the term *agent* instead.

As is the case with many other observations on non-finite verb forms, most of the generalizations formulated about non-standard participant encoding concern different types of nominalizations rather than participles or converbs. For instance, Comrie (1976b) noted that the subject is more likely to receive possessive marking than other verbal arguments. As Malchukov (2004: 10) puts it, both A/S and P participants may retain sentential encoding, or both may be genitivized, but if only one argument is genitivized, it will be A/S, while P retains its sentential marking. Koptjevskaja-Tamm (1993) introduced a more elaborate typology of action nominalizations defining several cross-linguistic patterns in argument marking. Argument encoding in participial relative clauses, however, has not been studied in its own right. According to Cristofaro's (2003: 207–208) observations, the coding of arguments as possessors is quite rare in relative clauses, and is not subject to any constraints other than that the argument coded as a possessor should not be the relativized one. As I will show in Chapter 6, however, if one only takes into consideration languages with otherwise deranked relative clauses, this type of participant encoding is not at all uncommon. Moreover, it is possible to establish certain tendencies as to which participants are more likely to be encoded as possessors; see Section 6.5.

In principle, "the conversion of verbal into nominal government" as mentioned by Lehmann (1988), can affect not only argument encoding, but also the choice of modifiers. Comrie and Thompson (2007: 344), for instance, illustrate this with an example from English. In the independent sentence *The enemy de-*

stroyed the city rapidly the finite verb is modified by the adverb *rapidly*. The corresponding nominalized construction *the enemy's rapid destruction of the city*, on the other hand, features the adjective *rapid*, which attributively modifies the derived verbal noun. In my sample, however, I have not observed any changes in the expression of modifiers in participial relative clauses.[35] Therefore, the discussion in Chapter 6 will only be concerned with the peculiarities of participant expression.

4.4 Summary and conclusions

In this chapter, I started out by providing an overview of the most representative scalar approaches to desententialization/nominalization. The sections in the second part of this chapter then further introduced various ways of desententializing the predicate that are relevant for participial relative clauses. It should be emphasized that these criteria should not be considered as the markers that signal desententialization in each particular instance of participial relativization. Instead, they represent various ways in which participial relative clauses can differ from independent clauses within a language.

As I have shown in this chapter, all of the approaches recognize two main domains in which the difference between dependent and independent forms may lie, the verb form itself and the encoding of various clausal participants. I will further discuss these two domains based on the actual language data collected for this study in two separate chapters following this one. Chapter 5 will focus on the deviations related to the participle as a verb form, while Chapter 6 is concerned with argument encoding in participial relative clauses.

---

[35] This can be regarded as a reflection of the fact that participles have less in common with underived nouns than various types of nominalizations; see Section 8.2 for some further discussion.

5 Morphological desententialization of participial relative clauses

5.1 Introduction

In the previous chapter, I have shown that an important aspect of desententialization/nominalization in participial relative clauses is the loss of certain verbal properties characteristic of independent clause predicates. This chapter provides an overview of such phenomena attested in the languages of the sample.

It is important to note, though, that each of the following sections only deals with part of the language sample investigated in this study. This is the case for two main reasons. Firstly, for some languages, no data is available regarding particular phenomena. For example, a description can focus on the range of participants a participial form can relativize, but provide no, or only very little, information on the temporal properties of this form. Secondly and more importantly, for some languages certain parameters of desententialization are simply irrelevant. For instance, Cofán exhibits very little verbal inflection in general, and does not mark tense overtly in either main or subordinate clauses (see Fischer and van Lier 2011). The (non-)expression of tense, therefore, cannot serve as a desententialization criterion in this language. Similarly, many languages do not feature any verbal agreement with the subject, or nominal agreement with the modified noun, so the former obviously cannot be lost, and the latter cannot be acquired.

5.2 TAM expression

As I explained in Section 4.3.1, in this study I consider the TAM domain as a single, though complex, parameter for desententialization. Its varied manifestations will be discussed in the current section. In Section 5.2.1, I will introduce two major ways in which the restrictions on TAM are manifested in the languages of the sample. I will then discuss each of these ways in more detail, and provide several specific examples of restrictions in Sections 5.2.2 and 5.2.3. In Section 5.2.4, I will consider those participial forms that are most restricted with respect to TAM meanings and do not allow for any contrasts whatsoever. In Section 5.2.5, I will summarize the tendencies observed in TAM restrictions exhibited by participles in the languages of the sample, especially with regard to predictions made by various hierarchies of verbal features discussed in the previous chapter. Finally, in Section 5.2.6 I will discuss the role of structural factors in the expression of TAM meanings in participial forms.

5.2.1 Two types of participial markers

Before discussing restrictions for participles in the TAM domain, it is necessary to introduce a relevant distinction between two types of participial markers. Markers of the first type simply indicate the participial status of the form, and do not themselves express any aspectual, temporal, or modal contrasts. I will refer to these markers as –TAM participial markers. An example can be found in Malayalam, where a –TAM participial form in -*a* is itself neutral in terms of TAM values, but can take a considerable number of regular aspectual (e.g. perfective or progressive), temporal (e.g. past), and modal (e.g. debitive) affixes, as shown in (137):[36]

(137) Malayalam (Dravidian)
    a. [*paṭhiccirikkeeṇṭiyirunna*]   *kaaryyaŋŋaḷ*
       learn.DEB.PFV$_1$.PST.PTCP   thing.PL
       'things that (one) should have learnt' (Asher and Kumari 1997: 327)
    b. [*paṭhikkappeṭṭukoṇṭirunniṭṭuntaayirunna*]   *paaṭṭə*
       learn.PASS.PROG.PFV$_2$.PST.PTCP   song
       'the song that had been being learnt' (Asher and Kumari 1997: 326)

Participial markers of the second type, +TAM participial markers, not only derive a participle from the verb stem, but also convey some information on the TAM meaning of the resulting form. As a consequence, these participles can form their own TAM paradigm. In Nanga, for example, such a paradigm consists of a perfective participle in -*sɛ̀* (138a), and an imperfective participle in -*mì* (138b):

(138) Nanga (Dogon)
    a. *nàŋà*   [*ǐː^n*   *èmè-sɛ̀*]   *né*
       cow.L   1SG.SUBJ   milk-PTCP.PFV   DEF
       'the cow that I milked' (Heath 2008: 273)
    b. *nàŋà*   [*ǐː^n*   *émé-mì*]
       cow.L   1SG.SUBJ   milk-PTCP.IPFV
       'a cow/cows that I (will) milk' (Heath 2008: 275)

---

[36] The extensive assimilatory processes characteristic of Malayalam commonly make it impossible to establish exact morpheme boundaries in complex verb forms, but the participles presented in (137) do indeed feature all the affixes indicated in the glosses, in an order corresponding to the order of glossing abbreviations.

In the core sample, I was able to identify the type of all participial markers for 97 languages (insufficient information on the TAM of participles was available for Apatani, Tsafiki, and Wikchamni). The two options are almost equally common: in 44 languages, all participial markers are +TAM, in 41 languages all markers are –TAM, while 12 languages have markers of both types (see Appendix 3b for details). One of the languages with a mixed system is Tamil (Dravidian, Lehmann 1993: 284), which has two participial markers. One of them, -*a*, a –TAM marker, can attach to verb stems with regular past or present tense affixes to form past and present participles respectively. The second one, -*um*, a +TAM marker, is used to form the future participle, and can therefore be regarded as both a future tense marker and a participial morpheme at the same time. Mixed systems are often attested in languages which have a specialized negative participle alongside several affirmative forms. In this case, affirmative participles are +TAM, but in the single negative participle all TAM contrasts are neutralized, which results in a –TAM negative form; see Section 5.3.2. This type of paradigm is found in four Uralic languages (Finnish, Komi-Zyrian, North Saami, Northern Khanty), and one Dravidian (Telugu).

Importantly, +TAM markers with tense or modal values can still take markers belonging to the same domain, for instance expressing various aspectual distinctions; see Nanai examples in (139), where past participles take repetitive, inchoative, and resultative markers:

(139) Nanai (Tungusic)
    a. [*mi   niru-**gu-lu**-xəm-bi*]   *daŋsa*
       1SG   write-REP-INCH-PTCP.PST-POSS.1SG   book
       'the book that I started writing again'
    b. [*dərə-či   lakto-**ča**-xan*]   *xaosa*
       table-DIR   stick-RES-PTCP.PST   paper
       'the paper that stuck to the table'

In the core sample, there are 14 languages in which +TAM participles can, in principle, take additional TAM markers, although in some of them these possibilities are limited and more rarely realized; see Appendix 3b. In Korean, +TAM participial forms differ in their ability to take certain additional TAM affixes. The past/present relative form in -*n* can take the retrospective tense suffix, and the past tense suffix; the future/presumptive relative form in -*l* takes the past tense suffix, or, in rare cases, also the future tense suffix; the present tense relative form in -*nin* does not take additional tense morphology (Lee 1994; Shin 2003).

On the other hand, in some languages, –TAM particles do not take any TAM morphology whatsoever, and their meaning with respect to this domain is commonly inferred from the context (for more on such particles see Section 5.2.4).

5.2.2 Restrictions for –TAM participles

In this section, I will consider those forms in which participial markers themselves do not bear any TAM meaning, but certain TAM meanings can be expressed with other means (forms without any further TAM marking at all will be discussed in Section 5.2.4). Approximately half of the languages with –TAM participles allow for that (it is hardly possible to provide the exact number, since the data on this question is very limited). Theoretically, restrictions in these forms can work in two major ways: either the language imposes constraints only on particular values of a given feature (e.g. future markers are prohibited), or it blocks the expression of the feature altogether (e.g. aspect and tense meanings are allowed within a participial form, but modal meanings are not). In practice, almost all of the sample languages appear to belong to the first type.

An example of a language showing the first type of restriction is Nivkh, where participial relative clauses allow for a fairly wide range of aspectual, temporal and modal markers (see Gruzdeva 1998: 49–50), but do not allow the so-called indicative marker -ḍ (-ṭ, -d); compare the relative and the main clause in (140).

(140) Nivkh (Nivkh)
 ətək [tʼam lu] dəf-toχ vi-ḍ
 father shaman sing.PTCP house-DAT go-IND
 'Father went into the house where the shaman sang.'
 (Nedjalkov and Otaina 2013: 276)

In Malayalam (Dravidian, Asher and Kumari 1997: 304–314), modal marking in participial forms is restricted to the debitive, as illustrated in (137) above, while many other modal forms are available in independent clauses. Sino-Tibetan languages commonly allow for some aspectual marking by means of separate morphemes, whereas some other meanings cannot be expressed, e.g. Garo (Burling 2004), or Japhug rGyalrong (Jacques 2016). It seems, therefore, that for desententialization of participial relative clauses the level of particular meanings is more relevant than that of categories as a whole. This is, in fact, a further argument in favour of considering the TAM domain on the whole. In addition to the semantics of certain markers, structural factors can also play a role in the constraints on

TAM expression in participles; this issue will be further commented upon in Section 5.2.6.

For −TAM participles, deviations from the main clause standard can also be manifested structurally, that is, in the fact that a language expresses the same TAM meanings in participial relative clauses as it does in independent sentences, but with a different set of affixes. This situation is found in Guarijío subject relative clauses. The regular perfective marker *-re-* used in independent clause predicates corresponds to the past tense *-ka-* in participial forms, as shown in (141a) and (141b) respectively, while present/habitual expressed by *-ni-/-na-* in independent clauses is morphologically unmarked in participial relative clauses; see (141c) and (141d):

(141) Guarijío (Uto-Aztecan)
    a. *tihoé   tapaná   umá-si-**re***
        man   yesterday run-go-PFV
        'The man ran away yesterday.' (Félix Armendáriz 2005: 91)
    b. *tihoé*   [*tapaná*   *umá-si-**ka**-me*]
        man   yesterday run-go-PST-NMZ.S/A
        'the man who ran away yesterday' (Félix Armendáriz 2005: 91)
    c. *owítiame   umá-**ni**   ehpé*
        woman   run-PRS   now
        'The woman is running now.' (Félix Armendáriz 2005: 91)
    d. *owítiame*   [*umá-**Ø**-me*   *ehpé*]
        woman   run-PRS-NMZ.S/A now
        'the woman who is running now' (Félix Armendáriz 2005: 91)

Similarly, Seki (2000: 179) reports that in Kamaiurá (Tupian), nominalizers employed for relative clause formation take specialized tense markers associated with nouns, e.g. nominal past, rather than regular verbal TAM markers.

5.2.3 Restrictions within a paradigm of +TAM participles

So far, I have mostly examined properties of individual participial forms. However, when it comes to +TAM participles, it is crucial to consider whole paradigms, because this is often the only possible way to capture the deviation from the situation in independent clauses. In other words, in languages featuring +TAM participles, constraints on TAM expression are commonly manifested in the fact that participial markers allow fewer TAM contrasts than finite verb forms.

For instance, in Nanai (Tungusic), there are two distinct participial forms, the past participle and the non-past participle. Unlike participles, indicative verb forms in Nanai exhibit a tripartite tense paradigm, distinguishing also between present and future tense, as shown in Table 18 based on Avrorin (1961: 101–114):

Tab. 18: Indicative and participial forms in Nanai

Tense	Indicative verbs	Participles
Past	ǯobo-ka-Ø work-PST-3SG	ǯobo-xa-ni work-PTCP.PST-POSS.3SG
Present	ǯobo-ra-Ø work-PRS-3SG	ǯobo-j-ni work-PTCP.NPST-POSS.3SG
Future	ǯobo-ǯa-ra work-FUT-3SG	

A very similar situation is found in Russian, where the standard language features only present and past participles, while all three tenses, including future, are available in the finite paradigm.

A recurrent type of paradigm reduction is found in cases where +TAM participles only retain the paradigm of tenses expressed synthetically in a given language (the exact range of meanings expressed by the participle can, of course, differ from that expressed by the finite form). German, for example, only distinguishes between present and past participles, while four more tense forms are commonly regarded as such for main clauses, namely future, perfect, pluperfect, and future perfect. It is perhaps worth noting that in languages with this type of restriction (mostly Indo-European), many periphrastic tense forms actually consist of an auxiliary and a participle (see Ambrazas 2006: 237–238 for Lithuanian).

The existence of constraints within the paradigm of participles does not necessarily imply that certain meanings cannot be expressed in non-finite relative clauses. Languages tend to develop various ways to compensate for the lack of specialized participial tense forms. For instance, in Kalmyk, a specialized present tense marker -*na* is only available in independent sentences. In relative clauses, the only available paradigmatic options are the past participle in -*sən* denoting the events preceding the situation expressed in the main clause, and the future participle in -*xə* denoting the events following the situation expressed in the main clause; see examples (142a) and (142b). In spite of the absence of a specialized present form, the language does have a regular way of encoding relative present tense, that is, simultaneity with the situation in the main clause. For this purpose,

Kalmyk uses the marker -ža- normally used for expressing progressive aspect. This marker can be inserted into any of the two participial forms to convey the meaning of relative present tense. The resulting forms are used in free variation, as shown in (142c):

(142) Kalmyk (Mongolic)
    a. *Očər* [*söö-də* **xää-sən**]   *naadʁa*   *örü-n*
        Ochir   night-DAT   look.for-PTCP.PST   toy   morning-EXT
        ol-žə   *avə-v*
        find-CVB.IPFV   take-PST
        'In the morning, Ochir found the toy that he **was looking for** at night.'
        (Krapivina 2009a: 515)
    b. [*Badma-n*   **xää-xə**]   *bičg-igə*   *bi*
        Badma-GEN   look.for-PTCP.FUT   letter-ACC   I.NOM
        bult-ul-ža-na-v
        hide-CAUS-PROG-PRS-1SG
        'I am hiding the letter that Badma **will be looking for**.'
        (Krapivina 2009a: 513)
    c. [*Bajrta-n*   **xää-žä-sən**   / **xää-žä-xə**]
        Bayrta-GEN   look.for-PROG-PTCP.PST   / look.for-PROG-PTCP.FUT
        miis-in   *kičg-igə*   *Ajsa*   *il-žä-nä*
        cat-GEN   puppy-ACC   Aysa   caress-PROG-PRS
        'Aysa is caressing the kitten that Bayrta **is looking for**.'

It is noteworthy that in several languages of the sample, the markers in the reduced +TAM participial paradigm express the meanings from different subdomains of TAM. For instance, Tanti Dargwa (Nakh-Daghestanian, Sumbatova and Lander 2014: 122–125) distinguishes between preterite, present, and potential participles, i.e. two temporal forms and one modal. Even (Tungusic, Malchukov 1995: 17) exhibits a rich paradigm of five participial forms, that is, non-future participle, past participle, necessitative participle, hypothetical participle, and perfect participle. The language, therefore, picks two out of three tense values from the finite paradigm (excluding future), adds two modal meanings, and also a perfect participle, whose main function is to mark perfective aspect and anteriority. This, again, shows that there is a close connection between the different TAM subdomains in participial relative clauses.

5.2.4 No TAM contrasts

Finally, in a considerable number of languages (around 20), participial predicates of relative clauses cannot overtly express any TAM contrast at all.[37] In principle, participles in these languages can also be classified as +TAM or –TAM, but in some cases it can be fairly hard to draw a strict boundary. A participial form that does not allow any TAM markers can either be highly versatile in its temporal and aspectual characteristics, or it can possess some inherent temporal and/or aspectual properties even though they are not overtly expressed by any marker. Forms of the first type are close to –TAM participial forms, whereas form of the second type resemble the +TAM participles discussed above. However, when an assumed +TAM participle does not belong to any paradigm, its TAM meaning is typically more vague. This is why I discuss all the single participles together in the present section.

A participle of the first type, that is a single –TAM participle, is attested, for instance, in Motuna, where the participial verb forms consist exclusively of the verb stem and the derivational participial suffix -*wah*/-*ah* (Onishi 1994: 490). The TAM meaning in such relative clauses is inferred from the context; see (143):

(143) Motuna (South Bougainville)
  ... *hoo* [*huuru* **poruk-ah**] *kurano ti-ki   poruk-oi-juu*
  ART.M pig   put-PTCP   basket there-ERG be.put-MID.3S-CONT.DS
  '... while the basket with the (meat of a) pig in it was (placed) there.'
  (Onishi 1994: 527)

Languages with a single –TAM participle can still show some limitations on their TAM characteristics. Quite in line with the restrictions on modality expression discussed in the previous sections, the participle in -*de*/-*re* in Apsheron Tat (Authier 2012: 232–233) can have past or non-past reference depending on the context, as illustrated in (144a) and (144b), but it is not available in any non-factual contexts:

---

[37] In this section, I will only discuss forms that are the only participles in given languages. Participles allowing for no TAM contrast can, in principle, constitute a paradigm, but in this case it is based on participial orientation, or some other criterion. I will discuss the criteria underlying participial systems in Chapter 7.

(144) Apsheron Tat (Indo-European)
    a. [***rous-de***]   seg   dendu   ne-bzeren
       bark-PTCP   dog   tooth   NEG-EVT.strike.3
       'A dog **who barks** does not bite.' (Authier 2012: 233)
    b. [***rous-de***]   seg   kuf-de   bü
       bark-PTCP   dog   beat-PTCP   be.PST.3
       'The dog **who barked** was beaten.' (Authier 2012: 233)

Languages with a single –TAM participial form can also have temporal characteristics that are inferred from the semantic context. In Ket, non-finite relative clauses are introduced by action nominals, which do not have any intrinsic temporal or aspectual meaning. According to Nefedov (2012: 200), they do, however, show the following strong tendency: in subject relatives, action nominals usually receive a "present tense" reading, whereas for object relatives the time reference is usually "past"; compare (145a) and (145b) below. The temporal meaning of these forms is, therefore, conditional on their orientation, reflecting the general present-active vs. past-passive asymmetry described for participles by Haspelmath (1994). When other participants are relativized, the orientation does not seem to play a role any longer. In this case, temporal characteristics are presumably determined by the inherent properties of the verb from which it is derived: telic verbs are more likely to receive relative past tense interpretation (anteriority), while atelic verbs commonly prefer the relative present tense meaning (simultaneity), as shown in (145c) and (145d):[38]

(145) Ket (Yeniseian)
    a. *nanbɛt*   *qīm*
       [*nan-bed*]   *qīm*
       bread-make.NMZ   woman
       'a bread-making woman' (Nefedov 2012: 200)
    b. *tudə*   *iʲbet*   *sʲik*
       tu-de   [*il-bed*]   *sʲuk*
       this-INAN   small-make.NMZ   trough
       'this broken trough' (Nefedov 2012: 214)

---

[38] The same distribution is, in fact, reported by Malchukov (1995: 17) for the non-future participle in *-ri/-i/-si/-di* in Even (Tungusic), a form with a broad range of possible temporal meanings, compare *em-ri* '(one) who came' and *girka-ri* '(one) who walks'.

c. *qɔˀj   ɛj   attos*
   [qoˀj   ej]   attos
   bear   kill.NMZ   spear
   'the spear the bear was killed with' (Nefedov 2012: 215)

d. *dʌˀq   quˀs*
   [dɤˀq]   quˀs
   live.NMZ   tent
   'a birch-bark tent where someone lives' (Nefedov 2012: 216)

If a language makes use of a single participle that does have a specific TAM value (i.e. a +TAM form), the natural question is: what kind of value can this be? According to Haspelmath (1994: 164), "we do not expect to find progressive participles or hesternal past participles or immediate future participles". However, as I have shown earlier, in some languages such meanings are totally acceptable for participles, in particular for −TAM forms; see example (137) from Malayalam. On the other hand, the "exotic" TAM meanings mentioned by Haspelmath do not indeed occur as elementary markers in systems of +TAM participles, and especially in the systems consisting of a single form. Instead, +TAM single participles mainly fall into two major groups, habitual participles and resultative participles.[39]

Examples of clearly habitual single participles can be found in Yimas (Lower Sepik-Ramu; see Foley 1991: 404 and example (161a) in Section 5.3.2), and in Garrwa; see (146):

(146) Garrwa (Garrwan)
    *nayinda   juka   ngaki   [kudukudu-nyi   kaku-nyi   **wadamba-warr**]*
    this.NOM   boy.NOM   I.POSS.NOM   many-DAT   fish-DAT   feed-NMZ.CHAR
    'This is my boy who eats many fish.'
    (Furby and Furby 1977: 94, glosses and transcription by Mushin 2012: 202)

Interestingly, as reported by Nefedov (2012: 201), Ket action nominals demonstrating versatile temporal characteristics, when oriented towards the subject, do not only refer to the present rather than past, but they also convey a more generic

---

39 Haspelmath (1994: 164) also mentions eventualities (irrealis non-stative events which are nevertheless time-stable enough to characterize a thing) as a possible type of situations expressed by participles and verbal adjectives, e.g. *edible, learnable*, etc. This type of meaning is indeed observed among +TAM participles, but it is mostly attested for passive and absolutive participles within wider systems.

or habitual meaning than their finite counterparts. Therefore, in the function of active participles these forms are close in their behaviour to other single habitual participles.

Examples of single (productive) resultative participles can be found in abundance in European languages, such as Albanian (Buchholz and Fiedler 1987; Alexander Rusakov, p.c.), Irish (Ó Baoill 2009; Jane D'Altuin, p.c.), or Italian (Maiden and Robustelli 2000); see example (147) from Italian:

(147) Italian (Indo-European)
 la città [*distrutta* da Achille]
 DEF.F.SG city(F).SG destroy.PTCP.PST by Achilles(M).SG
 'the city destroyed by Achilles' (Francesca Di Garbo, p.c.)

In accordance with Haspelmath's (1994) observations, and in line with the Ket situation described above, single habitual participles in my sample are always oriented towards the A(/S) participant, while single resultative participles are oriented towards the P/S participant. This kind of asymmetry, therefore, does not need any paradigmatic relations within a language, but rather exists on its own.

5.2.5 Hierarchical tendencies in TAM constraints

In this section, I will investigate the TAM features lost by participial relative clauses due to desententialization, in connection with the hierarchies discussed in Malchukov (2004) and summarized in Section 4.2.3 in the previous chapter. Because of the considerable differences in TAM expression in participles across languages, I do not aim to propose a full account of the phenomenon of desententialization. Instead, this section brings together a set of observations on hierarchical tendencies in the expression of TAM meanings in participial relative clauses. These tendencies can be manifested in two ways: whether a specific category is likely to be present in participles at all, and if so, which values it is likely to have. The second way is particularly relevant for the category of tense, so I will discuss it in more detail in what follows.

As predicted by Malchukov's hierarchy (see Section 4.2.3), evidentiality is a category in the TAM domain whose expression is rarely available in participial relative clauses. Grammatical evidentiality distinctions are, in fact, lost in most languages where they exist in independent sentences, e.g. in Kayardild (Tangkic), Lezgian (Nakh-Daghestanian), Maricopa (Cochimi-Yuman), and many others. A noteworthy exception in this respect is Matsés (Pano-Tacanan),[40] where TAM-coding participant nominalizations commonly used to form relative clauses referring to the past, distinguish between three tenses (recent past, distant past, and remote past) and two evidentiality values (inferential and experiential); see Fleck (2003: 305).[41] In parallel to the distinction observed in main clauses, experiential nominalization implies that encoded event was witnessed by the speaker, while inferential nominalization is used for events which have not been witnessed, but rather inferred; for more information on this see Section 3.6.2 and, in particular, example (98). The sentence in (148) below illustrates a relative clause introduced by an experiential nominalization, where the act of asking must have occurred in a face-to-face interaction:

(148) Matsés (Pano-Tacanan)
në   [mimbi   daëdca-ta   ca-boed]   tote
here   2ERG   weave-IMP   say-NMZ.PST.EXP   woven.carrying.strap
que-quin   tote   mene-quid
say-while:S/A>A   woven.carrying.strap   give-HAB
'Saying, "Here! The woven carrying strap that you asked (me) to weave," they [women] give the woven carrying strap [to their brother, boyfriend, or husband].' (Fleck 2003: 1018)

The possibility of expressing modal distinctions within the participial form also tends to be lost fairly easily as a result of deranking. I discuss primarily deontic (root) modality here, since no indisputable instances of epistemic modality expression were discovered in the sample (see, however, the discussion of Russian

---

40 Adelaar (2011) provides several examples from Tarma Quechua (Quechuan), where the stative nominalizer -*sha* commonly used to form relative clause predicates, takes the affirmative evidential marker -*m*. None of the examples, however, represent a relative clause, but rather conditional and temporal constructions. It is, thus, unclear if Tarma Quechua allows for evidential markers in participial relative clauses. Similarly, in Panare (Cariban), the form in -*jpë* is claimed to be a past inferential participle (Payne and Payne 2013: 324), as opposed to the past participle in -*sa'* with no evidential meaning, but this form was not included in the sample, since no clear evidence is available confirming its use in relative clauses.

41 As shown in Fleck (2003: 319–321), all nominalizations in Matsés capable of functioning as relative clause predicates in the language, include the element -*ed* (or one of its numerous allomorphs), which presumably used to be a generic participant nominalizer. Nevertheless, for multiple morphophonological and morphosyntactic reasons, Fleck claims that this element should no longer be considered as synchronically segmentable.

below). Languages with certain temporal and aspectual contrasts but no modality within the participial paradigm include, for instance, Koorete (Ta-Ne-Omotic, Hayward 1982), or Kolyma Yukaghir (Yukaghir, Maslova 2003). In languages that do allow the systematic expression of a certain modal meaning (e.g. potentiality or necessity), it usually belongs to the same paradigm as temporal markers; see Section 5.2.3 above (as well as the analysis of tense below) for discussion.

If a language does not allow for the standard (finite) way of expressing modality in participial relative clauses, it can resort to some other way, for example, using a periphrastic construction. Tundra Nenets, for instance, does not allow any modal markers to be incorporated into regular participial forms as illustrated in (149a). However, periphrastic expression of modality is possible. Dependent modal situations can be described by periphrastic combinations of the purposive converb and the imperfective participle of the semantically light verb *me-* 'to take'; see (149b), and compare to a similar meaning conveyed in the main clause (149c):

(149) Tundra Nenets (Uralic)
    a. [*xada-wənta*]   *tem'i*
       kill-PTCP.FUT   reindeer.1SG
       'the reindeer which I will kill'
       (Nikolaeva 2014: 316)
    b. [*xada-wənc'°*   *me-na*]   *tem'i*
       kill-PURP   take-PTCP.IPFV   reindeer.1SG
       'the reindeer which I have to/would/should/must kill'
       (Nikolaeva 2014: 316)
    c. *pidər°*   *ti-m*   *xada-bc'u-n°*
       you   reindeer-ACC   kill-NEC-2SG
       '(I agree,) you should kill a reindeer.'
       (Nikolaeva 2014: 91)

Russian participles present a very interesting case with respect to the place of modality in the hierarchy of desententialization. Although they are otherwise highly desententialized and nominalized according to other criteria (e.g. a reduced tense paradigm, full adjectival agreement with the modified noun, and lack of verbal agreement with the subject), they allow for the expression of subjunctive mood in a relative clause, in a way that corresponds to its expression in independent sentences, namely by a combination of the subjunctive particle *by* and the form bearing a past tense marker, as shown in (150):

(150) Russian (Indo-European)
   a. *Šag-i   Leny,   [dnëm   **po-gas-š-ie**   **by***
      step-NOM.PL Lena-GEN.SG day-INS.SG PFV-fade-PTCP.PST.ACT-NOM.PL   SJV
      v   šum-e   ulicy],   ...   razdava-l-i-s'   sejčas
      in   noise-PREP.SG street-GEN.SG   sound-PST-PL-REFL   now
      bespoščadn-ymi   šlepk-ami.
      merciless-INS.PL   flap-INS.PL
      'Lena's steps, which would have faded in the street noise in the daytime, sounded now as merciless flaps.' (Saj 2016: 369)
   b. *Šag-i   Leny   dnëm   **po-gas-l-i**   **by***
      step-NOM.PL Lena-GEN.SG day-INS.SG   PFV-fade-PST-PL   SJV
      v   šum-e   ulicy.
      in   noise-PREP.SG   street-GEN.SG
      'Lena's steps would have faded in the street noise in the daytime.'

As Saj (2016) shows, in some contexts the overt expression of subjunctive mood in participial relative clauses is optional, but in the situation illustrated above, where the "real" event in the main clause (Lena's steps sounding as merciless flaps) is opposed to another event, which could otherwise have happened (Lena's steps fading in the street noise), the subjunctive particle cannot be omitted. Such sentences are considered ungrammatical by prescriptive grammarians, but they do occur in natural texts.

Apart from the loss of categories, it is also possible for particular values within a category to be lost. This is particularly relevant to the domain of tense, where some values are more likely to be lost in participles than others. The temporal meaning that is most likely to be lost in participial relative clauses is future. For one thing, future interacts to a large extent with modality (see Section 4.3.1 above for discussion). As a result, some forms which can in principle convey future meaning are widely used for expressing potentiality or necessity. But this is clearly not the only factor. Future participles in general appear to be cross-linguistically rare when compared to participles with other temporal properties (see Vlaxov 2010: 10–16 for an overview). Languages that have specialized future forms in the finite paradigm sometimes do not distinguish between present and future in the participial paradigm; see the case of Nanai (Tungusic) discussed in Section 5.2.3, Even (Tungusic, Malchukov 1995: 15–17), Ingush (Nakh-Daghestanian, Nichols 2011: 243), or Northern Khanty (Uralic, Nikolaeva 1999: 26, 33). In Russian, future participles have a peculiar status with respect to the standard language. There is a morphologically transparent way to form future active perfective participles: by adding a present participle suffix *-ušč-/-ašč-* to a perfective verb stem; see example (151a), which is parallel to the way the finite perfective future is formed in Russian (151b):

(151) Russian (Indo-European)
 a. *Imenno et-o mest-o dolžn-o sta-t'*
  exactly this-N.NOM.SG place(N)-NOM.SG must-N.SG become-INF
  osnovn-ym mest-om palomničestv-a futbol'-n-yx
  main-N.INS.SG place(N)-INS.SG pilgrimage(N)-GEN.SG football-ADJR-GEN.PL
  bolel'ščik-ov, [**pried-ušč-ix** *na turnir-Ø*].
  fan-GEN.PL come.PFV-PTCP.PRS.ACT-GEN.PL on tournament(M)-ACC.SG
  'It is this place that must become the main place of pilgrimage for the football fans who will come to the tournament.' (found by Google)
 b. *Bolel'ščik-i* **pried-ut** *na igr-u.*
  fan-NOM.PL come.PFV-PRS.3PL on game(F)-ACC.SG
  'The fans will come to the game.'

These forms are attested in written texts and spontaneous speech, but they are considered ungrammatical in prescriptive grammars. As suggested by corpus data, Russian speakers tend to resort to these forms when the primary relativization strategy employing the relative pronoun *kotoryj* is impossible to process for syntactic reasons. Except in cases of pied-piping, the relative pronoun has to appear at the left edge of the clause, directly following the modified noun. If, on the other hand, the speaker starts the relative clause with a temporal adverbial, which is not subject to pied-piping, the future participle becomes the only alternative allowing to complete the clause; see example (152) and Kirjanov and Shagal (2011) for further discussion:

(152) Russian (Indo-European)
 Togda ja sčita-l sebja velik-im
 then I.NOM consider-PST.M.SG REFL.ACC great-M.INS.SG
 pisatel-em, [*rano ili pozdno* ᴼᴷ**na-piš-ušč-im** /
 writer(M)-INS.SG early or late PRF-write-PTCP.PRS.ACT-M.INS.SG
 ***kotor-yj na-piš-et** genial'n-oe proizvedeni-e*].
 which-M.NOM.SG PRF-write-PRS.3SG brilliant-N.ACC.SG work(N)-ACC.SG
 'Then I considered myself a great writer, who will sooner or later create a brilliant work.' (Kirjanov and Shagal 2011: 96)

Future participles can also show further peculiarities within the system. For instance, in Section 5.2.3, I have already mentioned the case of Tamil, where the future participle in *-um* is the only +TAM form, whereas other temporal meanings are expressed by specialized affixes attached to the –TAM form in *-a*.

While there is considerable evidence that the future is most easily lost in participial relative clauses in comparison with independent clauses, so far we do not have enough data to say which tense value is most easily retained. There is, however, one case suggesting that the present might be the best candidate. In one of the sample languages, Martuthunira, the only existing participial form in *-nyila* is used in relative clauses with a present meaning or a meaning of simultaneity, while in all other cases regular finite forms are used as relative clause predicates; see examples in (153). In this case, the present tense behaves as the value most suitable for a deranked form if compared to independent verbs.

(153) Martuthunira (Pama-Nyungan)
    a. *Ngayu   ngurnu   murla-a wantha-rralha ngulangu, murtiwala-la*
       1SG.NOM that.ACC meat-ACC place-PST   there   car-LOC
      [***karri-nyila-la***   *pal.yarra-la*].
      stand-REL.PRS-LOC   plain-LOC
      'I put that meat there, in the car which is standing on the flat.'
      (Dench 1994: 244)
    b. *Ngayu   **yanga-lalha-rru**   ngurnu   pawulu-u *[*muyi-i*
       1SG.NOM chase-PST-now   that.ACC child-ACC dog-ACC
      thani-lalha-a].
      hit-PST-ACC
      'I chased that kid who hit the dog.'
      (Dench 1994: 241)

Finally, aspect is the category which is most likely to be retained in desententialized participial relative clauses. Among the languages which do not have temporal and modal distinctions in participles but still allow for certain aspectual marking are at least Guarijío (Uto-Aztecan), and Malayalam (Dravidian), where this situation is characteristic of the negative participial form in *-aatta* (Asher and Kumari 1997: 327).

5.2.6 Structural factors influencing TAM expression

As can be seen from the discussion above, participial relative clauses in the languages of the sample generally confirm existing functional generalizations about desententialization. At the same time, quite in line with Malchukov's (2004) observations, there are also structural factors that can play a role here. For instance, in Maba, the past tense marker is widely attested in participial relative clauses, as illustrated in (154a), while the future tense cannot be overtly expressed. This looks similar to certain desententialization effects discussed above, e.g. those observed in the participial systems of Nanai or Russian. However, in this case the unavailability of future meaning should not be explained by any semantic or functional constraints, according to the description provided in Weiss (2009). Instead, it should be attributed to the fact that the relevant meaning in independent sentences is conveyed by constructions with clitics, not affixes, as shown in (154b):

(154) Maba (Maban)
    a. *kàŋ*   *máʃi-g*   [*kùndán*   *kèdémí:*   *n-ánár-á*]=*gù*
        human   man-SG   yesterday   egg   PTCP-bring-PST=SG.DEF
        t-ár-à
        3SG-come-PST
        'The man who brought eggs yesterday has come.' (Weiss 2009: 320)
    b. *m-ú-g*   *kàŋ*   *sû:=gín*   *á-ká=tè*
        1SG-sister-SG   COM   market=LOC   1SG-go=FUT
        'I will go to the market with my sister.' (Weiss 2009: 297)

Similarly, Russian does not allow for the formation of imperfective future active participles. Future in imperfective contexts is periphrastic in Russian, formed using the auxiliary 'to be' with a future meaning, as shown in (155a). This type of periphrastic construction is, consequently, the only potential means for forming imperfective future participles; see (155b):

(155) Russian (Indo-European)
    a. *Učenik*   **bud-et**   *čita-t'*   *knig-u.*
        student(M).NOM.SG   be.FUT-3SG   read-INF   book(F)-ACC.SG
        'the student will be reading a book'
    b. *učenik*   [**bud-ušč-ij**]   *čita-t'*
        student(M).NOM.SG   be.FUT-PTCP.PRS.ACT-M.NOM.SG   read-INF
        knig-u
        book(F)-ACC.SG
        'the student who will be reading a book'

Even though occasionally attested in informal texts, these forms are extremely rare and marginal. Theoretically, it may still be possible that the formation of imperfective future participles is dispreferred for some pragmatic reasons, but I assume that the nature of this constraint is structural.

One more example of this kind comes from Mẽbengokre. According to Salanova (2011: 52), the left periphery of matrix clauses in this language is constituted by a focus position, which can contain at most one dislocated phrase, a delimiting particle that indicates tense (future vs. non-future) or mood (realis vs. irrealis), and a position reserved for nominative subjects. None of these positions, however, are available in internally headed relative clauses, compare (156a) and (156b). Again, therefore, the restriction affecting TAM expression in (156b) is formulated in structural terms, and is based on the position of the TAM particles within a clause rather than on their semantics. This view is supported by the fact that very similar meanings can be conveyed in relative clauses by a series of special postverbal markers, mostly directional postpositions; see (156c) and (156d):

(156) Mẽbengokre (Nuclear-Macro-Je)
    a. *kukryt* **nẽ** *ba arỹm ku-bĩ*
        tapir(FOC) NFUT 1.NOM already 3.ACC-kill.V
        'I killed *tapir*.' (Salanova 2011: 52)
    b. (**kukryt*) (***nẽ**) (**ije*) [*arỹm ije bĩn*]
        tapir(FOC) NFUT 1.ERG already 1.ERG kill.NMZ
        'the one I killed' (Salanova 2011: 52)
    c. [*kute kà nhipêx* **mã**] *jã*
        3ERG canoe make.NMZ to this
        'the canoe he's about to make' (Salanova 2011: 52)
    d. [*kute kà nhipêx* **'ỹr**] *jã*
        3ERG canoe make.NMZ up.to this
        'the canoe he almost made' (Salanova 2011: 53)

As I have already mentioned in Section 4.2.3 on Malchukov's Generalized Scale Model, structural factors in desententialization commonly go hand in hand with the tendencies reflected in the functional hierarchies. For instance, certain modal meanings can be unavailable in participial relative clauses for structural reasons, because they are expressed periphrastically or otherwise further away from the verbal stem. This, in turn, can be explained functionally, with reference to the relevance of the meaning in question for the semantics of the verb (see Bybee

1985). Consequently, in many languages it can be simply impossible to distinguish between the influence of semantic and pragmatic factors on the one hand, and structural factors on the other hand.

5.3 Expression of negation

This section investigates various ways in which participial relative clauses can differ from the independent clause standard in the domain of negation. The data on non-finite negation in descriptive grammars is typically very scarce, so the observations presented in this section are based on 64 languages (2/3 of the core sample). Approximately half of those seem to use standard negation with participles (see Appendix 3b). Three types of deviations attested in the languages of the sample include the use of non-finite or nominal negation markers (5.3.1), specialized negative participial forms (5.3.2), as well as the impossibility to express negation in a participial structure (5.3.3).

5.3.1 Non-finite or nominal negation

The first type of deviation actually relates to the fact that the predicate of a participial relative clause either belongs to the class of non-finite forms or is treated as a regular noun or adjective. Among other things, this can be reflected in the use of specialized non-finite or nominal negation. This type is attested in 16 languages. For instance, while finite forms in Lezgian are negated with the suffix -č (157a), participles follow the non-finite pattern, which they share with other non-finite as well as non-indicative forms; see (157b) for a synthetic form and (157c) for a periphrastic construction:

(157) Lezgian (Nakh-Daghestanian)
    a. *gu-zwa* / *gu-zwa-č*
       give-IPFV / give-IPFV-NEG
       'he gives' / 'he does not give'
       (Haspelmath 1993: 133)
    b. *fi-zwa-j* / **te-fi-zwa-j**
       go-IPFV-PTCP / NEG-go-IPFV-PTCP
       'the one that goes' / 'the one that does not go'
       (Haspelmath 1993: 127)
    c. *Caw=tahar aburu-n* [*kas agaq' **t-iji-da-j**]* [*caw-a*
       Caw-tahar 3PL-GEN man reach(PER) NEG-do-FUT-PTCP sky-INESS

  awa-j] q̃ele ja.
  be.in-PTCP fortress COP
  'The Caw-tahar is their fortress in the sky which people do not reach.'
  (Haspelmath 1993: 134)

From a formal point of view, non-finite negation of participial forms comes in a variety of options, including particles (Kalmyk *esə*, Muna *pata*), proclitics (Ingush *cy=*), suffixes (Garo *-gija*, Beserman Udmurt *-te*, Wappo *-lah*, Mapudungun *-no/-nu*), and periphrastic constructions (Tundra Nenets).

 The other option for participial negation is to use a marker which the language otherwise employs for negating nouns or adjectives. This situation can be illustrated by an example from Modern Standard Arabic; compare (158a) and (158b) where the marker *ghayr* is used for negating active and passive participles, and (158c) for its use with an adjective:

(158) Modern Standard Arabic (Afro-Asiatic)
  a. *nās-un* [***ghayr-u*** *qāri'-īna*]
    people-NOM NEG-NOM.CONSTR read.PTCP.ACT-PL.GEN
    'non-reading people' (Aleksandr Letuchiy, p.c.)
  b. *ḥurūf-un* [***ghayr-u*** *maktūb-at-in*]
    letter.PL-NOM NEG-NOM.CONSTR write.PTCP.PASS-F-GEN
    'unwritten letters' (Aleksandr Letuchiy, p.c.)
  c. *al-bilād-u* ***ghayr-u*** *l-'islamiyy-at-i*
    DEF-country.PL-NOM NEG-NOM.CONSTR DEF-Islamic-F-GEN
    'the non-Islamic countries' (Ryding 2005: 649)

The Finnish negative participle in *-maton* illustrated in (159a) below is also related to the regular suffix of nominal negation *-ton*.[42] Finite clauses, on the other hand, are negated with the negative auxiliary followed by a connegative form, as shown in (159b):

(159) Finnish (Uralic)
  a. *On-ko* *kysee-ssä* *se* [*kenen-kään* ***näke-mätön-Ø***]
    be.PRS.3SG-Q issue.SG-INESS this who.GEN-POL see-PTCP.NEG-NOM.SG

---

[42] The negative participle has, however, developed a number of idiosyncratic properties due to which it does not appear reasonable to regard *-maton* as a composite marker in this study.

[*pöydä-n   alta   anne-ttu-Ø*]   *raha-Ø?*
   table.SG-GEN below.ABL give-PTCP.PST.PASS-NOM.SG money-NOM.SG
   'Is it about this money not seen by anybody, which was given from under the table?' (found by Google)
b. *Kuka-an   ei   näe   raha-a.*
   who.NOM-POL NEG.3SG   see.CNG   money-PTV
   'Nobody sees the money.'

Outside of relative clauses the negative suffix *-ton* is used in various instances of nominal negation, for instance, for deriving adjectives with privative meaning from nouns; compare *asunto-Ø* apartment-NOM.SG – *asunno-ton-Ø* apartment-NEG-NOM.SG 'one without an apartment'.[43]

In at least two languages, both ways to negate participial relative clauses are attested, and in both cases the distribution of negation strategies seems to correspond to the degree of nominalization of the respective forms. According to Brykina and Aralova (2012), in Beserman Udmurt (Uralic), the present participle in *-š'* and the non-past participle in *-n* are negated by a regular adjectival negative marker *-tem* ("a derivative suffix with caritive meaning" according to Edygarova 2015: 278), while the past participle in *-m* is negated with the specialized participial negative marker *-te*. It is noteworthy that both the present and the non-past participles are commonly used in habitual contexts or to denote a permanent property of the modified noun, while the past participle usually refers to a completed action preceding the situation expressed in the main clause. The past participles, therefore, appear to be more verbal in their meaning, so it seems natural that they take a less nominal form of negation than other participial forms.

In Muna (Austronesian), the two non-finite verb forms used (interchangeably) for direct object relativization differ in their negation markers. The passive participle in *ni-* takes the non-finite negation marker (160a), which is also characteristic of so-called reason clauses (160b), while relative clauses introduced by the nominalization in *ka-* feature the nominal negator *suano*, which is used for constituent negation and thus attaches to noun phrases (160c). Unfortunately, since relative clauses introduced by the nominalization in *-ka* are rarely negated at all, the only available examples that illustrate this negation marker are of the

---

[43] Privative adpositions and affixes are commonly used in Papunesian languages to negate relative clauses nominalized to a certain extent, e.g. in Ama (Left May, Årsjö 1999), or in Iatmul (Ndu, Jendraschek 2012). In neither of these two languages, however, do nominalized relative clauses qualify as participial according to the definition formulated in this study. Therefore, they will not be discussed further here.

type provided in (160d), where the nominalization functions as a noun, not as an adnominal modifier. Interestingly, the difference in degree of verbality between these two structures is not only reflected in the choice of the negative marker. In addition, passive participles allow the use of the preposition *so* as a future marker, thus allowing some kind of temporal distinction, as illustrated in (160e), while nominalizations do not allow this marker.

(160) Muna (Austronesian)
    a. *garaa giu* **pata** *s<um>aha-no maitu miina*
       SURPR something NEG legal.PTCP.ACT-PTCP.ACT that not
      na-ti-perapi
      3SG.IRR-ACC-enjoy
      'Something unlawful cannot be enjoyed.'
      (van den Berg 2013: 211)
    b. **pata**-*ho ka-mai-ha-no rampano no-saki ana-no*
      NEG-yet NMZ-come-REAS-his because 3SG.REAL-sick child-his
      'The reason he has not come yet is that his child is ill.'
      (van den Berg 2013: 212)
    c. **suano** *kaawu inodi, do-bhari*
      not just I 1PL.REAL-many
      'not just me, there were many of us'
      (van den Berg 2013: 212)
    d. **suano** *ka-ghosa-no pikore*
      not NMZ-strong-POSS.LK pikore.bird
      'It was not the pikore's strength.'
      (van den Berg 2013: 212)
    e. *ae-faraluu dahu* [**so** *me-dhaga-ni-no lambu*]
      1SG.REAL-need dog FUT PTCP.ACT-guard-TR-PTCP.ACT house
      'I need a dog that will guard the house.'
      (van den Berg 2013: 232)

5.3.2 Specialized negative participles

The second type comprises languages where the negative meaning in participial relative clauses is conveyed by a separate participial form or a set of forms, i.e. specialized negative participles. In such cases, the negative participial marker is not diachronically related to any other negative morpheme in the language, or it has developed enough idiosyncratic properties to be regarded as a separate unit.

The relation between affirmative and negative participial forms in these languages can be of two major types. In the first type, each negative participle can function as a counterpart for a specific affirmative participle. In the second type, a language can employ a single form for negating all participles irrespective of their distinctive features, or a limited set of negative participial forms when compared to affirmative.[44] The first type can be regarded as a symmetric system of participial forms, while the second one is an asymmetric system as discussed in Miestamo (2005) for standard negation.

Two languages in my sample, Yakut (Turkic) and Marathi (Indo-European), show symmetric participial systems with several negative participles. The participial system in Yakut, for instance, consists of three affirmative participles with different temporal meanings, and three corresponding negative forms, as represented in Table 19 below based on Ubrjatova (1982: 227–240):[45]

Tab. 19: Participial system in Yakut

TAM	Affirmative	Negative
Past	-bït	-bataχ
Present	-ar/-ïr	-bat
Future	-ïaχ	-(ï)mïaχ

---

44 The only case in my sample where negative contexts show more distinctions in the TAM domain when compared to the affirmative ones is Ma'di (Central Sudanic). In this language, non-finite relative forms do not exhibit any overt tense expression in affirmative contexts, and are free with respect to temporal interpretation. In negative contexts, on the other hand, these forms take the regular negative markers kō and kōrù, which are employed in non-past and past contexts respectively (Blackings and Fabb 2003: 473), therefore allowing for differentiation between non-past and past relative clauses. This situation reflects the properties of the Ma'di negative markers rather than subordinate forms, however, and thus will not be discussed in detail here.

45 As is clear from the table, the markers of negative participles in Yakut differ in their level of derivational transparency. The future negative marker -(ï)mïaχ, which is most transparent, is simply a combination of the regular verbal negative marker and the participial suffix. Still, the resulting system can be regarded as symmetric, since every affirmative participle has its own negative counterpart.

The rest of symmetric participial systems consist of only two participial forms, an affirmative and a negative. The three languages of this type are Kambaata (Afro-Asiatic), Malayalam (Dravidian), and Yimas (Lower Sepik-Ramu). None of these systems, however, is truly symmetric with respect to the morphological properties of participial forms and their syntactic behaviour. For instance, in Yimas, the affirmative non-finite form is only used for subject relativization (161a), while the negative non-finite form can relativize any core participant (161b):

(161) Yimas (Lower Sepik-Ramu)
    a. *namarawt*   [*tamana*   ***ti-r-awt***]   *na-mal*
       person.CL1.SG   sickness.CL9.SG   feel-NF-M.SG   3SG.S-die
       'The person who was always sick died.' (Foley 1991: 404)
    b. *wakn*   *na-mpu-ŋa-tkam-t*   [*namat*
       snake.CL5.SG   CL5.SG.T-3PL.A-1SG.R-show-PFV   person.CL1.PL
       tu-kakan-Ø]
       kill-NF.NEG-CL5.SG
       'They showed me the snake that doesn't kill people.'/
       'They showed me the snake that people don't kill.' (Foley 1991: 407)

In Kambaata, the negative participle formed by the marker *-umb* shows agreement in gender and case with the nominal head (while affirmative participles do not) and neutralizes the aspectual distinction perfective vs. imperfective, which is present in the paradigm of its affirmative counterparts; compare (162a) and (162b) below:[46]

(162) Kambaata (Afro-Asiatic)
    a. [*cíil-at*   ***it-tumb-úta***]   *inchch-áta*
       baby.girl-F.NOM   eat-3F.PTCP.NEG-F.ACC   food-F.ACC
       'the food that the baby girl does not eat' (Treis 2008: 171)
    b. [*bux-íchch-u*   ***it-anó***]   *bar-í*   *móoq-ut*
       poor-SG-M.NOM   eat-3M.IPFV.REL   day-M.ACC   spoon-F.NOM
       ba'-áa'a
       disappear-3F.IPFV
       'On the day on which a poor man has some food to eat his spoon cannot be found.' (Treis 2008: 180)

---

[46] Interestingly, the asymmetry in Kambaata is only attested in the participial system. Negation in main clauses does not trigger any aspectual neutralization.

A similar neutralization is found in Malayalam (Dravidian), where forms with the affirmative participial suffix -*a* can take tense markers, while forms with the negative participial suffix -*aatta* cannot (Asher and Kumari 1997: 327).

If we do not take into account the difference between languages that express TAM meanings within participial markers and separately (see Section 5.2.1 on these two options), the situation in Malayalam is, in fact, very close to the situation observed in the languages with asymmetric participial systems. For example, in Telugu (Dravidian), a language fairly closely related to Malayalam, the affirmative paradigm of participles includes a past participle in -*ina*, a future-habitual participle in -*ee*, and a durative participle in -*tunna*. The single negative participle in -*ani* can be used to negate any of the affirmative forms, and its exact temporal meaning is understood from the context (Krishnamurti and Gwynn 1985: 242). A system with three affirmative participles and one negative participle is attested in Georgian as well, although the negative form *u-V(-el)* has absolutive orientation and can only be used to negate the absolutive perfective participle -*ul*/-*il*/*m-V-ar* and the passive future participle *sa-V(-el)* (Hewitt 1995: 433). All of the Uralic languages with a specialized negative participle also fall into this category, namely Finnish, Meadow Mari, Komi-Zyrian, North Saami, Tundra Nenets, and Northern Khanty.

Matsés (Pano-Tacanan) is the only language in my sample that has an asymmetric participial system with more than one negative form. As shown in Section 5.2.5, the participial system in Matsés is extremely elaborate, with three inherently oriented participles and a number of contextually oriented forms that differ in their temporal and evidential characteristics (see also Section 7.6). The significantly restricted set of negative relative clause predicates consists of only three forms, namely the negative habitual S/A nominalizer in -*esa*, the negative habitual P/INS nominalizer in -*temaid*, and the negative perfect P/INS nominalizer in -*acmaid* (Fleck 2003: 307).

As can be seen from the examples above, if negative participial relative clauses are subject to certain restrictions in negative contexts (that is, if they are not universal negators), their meanings and syntactic properties are not random. If the range of temporal and aspectual characteristics is reduced, the habitual interpretation is more common than others. For Kambaata, Treis (2008: 172) even states explicitly that the negative participle is used to express "constant, habitual, or repeated not V-ing". In the only language where the range of participants that can be relativized by the negative form is smaller than that of the affirmative participles it can negate, the orientation of the negative is absolutive. This is the case of the negative participle in -*li* in Northern Khanty; see Section 3.3.5 for details. In the more complex negative participial system attested in Matsés, both factors come into play. As shown above, both S/A and P/INS orientation is available for habitual contexts, but in addition there is also a perfect participle specializing in non-subject relativization. The observed distribution can be regarded as another instance of a more general interconnection between TAM and participial orientation that will be discussed further in Chapter 7.

Finally, in several languages the situation is in a way intermediate between a symmetric and an asymmetric system. In Aguaruna (Chicham), there are two affirmative participial forms, the subject relative form in -*u* and the non-subject relative form in -*mau*, and one negative, formed by the marker -*tʃau*. Even though, according to Overall (2007), synchronically the three participial markers should be regarded as separate affixes, diachronically both the non-subject relative form and the negative relative form are clearly derived from the subject relative form in -*u*. As a result, the negative participle in -*tʃau* is in a symmetric relation with the subject relative form, while the non-subject relative form does not have a negative counterpart whatsoever. Similarly, in Kamaiurá (Tupian), the negative form in -*uma'e* can only negate S-oriented participles, and in Tundra Nenets (Uralic), the participle in -*mədawe(y(ə))* only acts as a negative counterpart for participles oriented towards core participants. The rest of the participial forms in these languages cannot be negated using specialized forms. Other languages where participial relative clauses cannot be negated are discussed in the following section.

Altogether, specialized negative participles are attested in 15 languages of the core sample, and they are presented in Table 20. For more information on their affirmative counterparts see Appendix 3b.

Tab. 20: Negative participles in the languages of the sample

Language	Form	Relativizing capacity	Compared to the affirmative paradigm	+TAM/ –TAM	+TAM/–TAM affirmative forms
Aguaruna	REL.NEG	S/A	less	–	–
Finnish	PTCP.NEG	S/A/P	more	–	+
Georgian	PTCP.PRIV	S/P	less	+	both
Kamaiurá	NMZ.NEG.S	S	less	–	–
Kambaata	PTCP.NEG	up to OBL	same	–	–
Komi-Zyrian	PTCP.NEG	up to OBL	same	–	+
Malayalam	PTCP.NEG	up to POSS	same	–	–
Matsés	NMZ.NEG. S/A.HAB	S/A	less	+	both

Language	Form	Relativizing capacity	Compared to the affirmative paradigm	+TAM/−TAM	+TAM/−TAM affirmative forms
Matsés	NMZ.NEG. P/INS.PFV	P/INS	less	+	both
Matsés	NMZ.NEG. P/INS.HAB	P/INS	less	+	both
Meadow Mari	PTCP.NEG	up to OBL	same	−	both
North Saami	PTCP.NEG	S/A/P	same	−	+
Northern Khanty	PTCP.NEG	S/P	less	−	+
Telugu	PTCP.NEG	up to OBL	same	−	+
Tundra Nenets	PTCP.NEG	S/A/P	less	+	+
Yakut	PTCP.NEG.PST	up to OBL	same	+	+
Yakut	PTCP.NEG.PRS	up to OBL	same	+	+
Yakut	PTCP.NEG.FUT	up to OBL	same	+	+
Yimas	NF.NEG	S/A/P	more	+	+

5.3.3 No participial negation available

The impossibility of negating a participial relative clause is very rarely mentioned explicitly in grammars. The only four languages in my sample whose descriptions make it clear are Imbabura Quechua (Quechuan, Cole 1985), Kayardild (Tangkic, Evans 1995), Fula (Atlantic-Congo, Arnott 1970), and Nias (Austronesian, Brown 2001). If the negative meaning has to be expressed in a relative clause, these languages commonly use a finite relative construction with standard negation and internal main clause syntax.

The situation in Nias is, however, somewhat different. Relative clauses formed by passive participles marked with *ni-* are not negated directly. Instead, a headless relative clause with a *ni-* participle as its predicate occurs inside another relative clause, introduced by a relative marker *si=*, regularly used for subject relativization. The *si=* relativizer attaches to the negative marker *löna*, and the resulting structure is as follows:

(163) Nias (Austronesian)
 Andrehe'e   nohi   [si=löna   [ni-lau   nono
 DIST   coconut.tree:MUT   REL=NEG   PTCP.PASS-climb   child:MUT

matua]].
male

'That is the coconut tree the boy did not climb.' (Lit. 'That is the coconut tree which is not the one climbed by the boy.') (Brown 2001: 422)

Presumably, the four languages mentioned in this section are hardly the only cases where negation markers are not compatible with participial forms. Most probably, many authors simply do not discuss this constraint, just like they often do not discuss other "negative" facts about languages, such as the lack of a certain grammatical category. The real scale of this phenomenon, therefore, awaits further investigation.

5.4 Subject agreement

As I explained earlier in Section 4.3.3, in this section I only consider instances of verbal subject agreement, while the use of possessive markers referring to the subject will be discussed in Chapter 6. As can be expected based on the relevant implicational hierarchies, almost all of the languages in the sample that have subject agreement in independent sentences, do not show any trace of this in participial relative clauses. This is the case, for instance, in the Indo-European languages of the sample, in Koorete (Ta-Ne-Omotic), Mapudungun (Araucanian), Quechuan languages, and several others. There are, however, several languages that do show some agreement with the subject, and do not use possessive markers. In what follows, I will provide an overview of these cases.

Some languages use a different paradigm of person-number markers in participial relative clauses from the one used in independent sentences. For instance, in Krongo (Kadugli-Krongo, Reh 1985: 167–168), the set of person-number affixes used in non-finite relative clauses is reserved for expressing subjects in nominalized and other types of dependent clauses, as well as subjects of hortative and optative forms. In Aguaruna (Chicham, Overall 2007: 420–421), the subject relative form in *-u* takes the so-called subordinate-clause person marking, which is not used in main clauses. In both cases the set of affixes is also different from the forms employed to indicate possession.

In Hinuq, both finite verbs and relative participles use the same set of prefixes to show agreement with their absolutive argument, either intransitive subject, as in (164a)–(164b), or direct object, as in (164c)–(164d). Notably, when the absolutive participant is relativized and is, therefore, overtly expressed only in the main clause, the participle still shows agreement with it (164e)–(164f), which in this case looks similar to adjectival agreement as illustrated in (164g). However, examples like (164b) and (164d) clearly show that the prefix on relative participles refers to the absolutive argument rather than the modified noun, which means that participles in Hinuq do preserve verbal agreement.

(164) Hinuq (Nakh-Daghestanian)
 a. *aže-yi-ƛ'o* *ƛ'ere* *coy* **b**-*iči-š* *goł*
   tree(IV)-OBL-SPR on eagle(III) III-sit-RES be
   'The eagle is sitting on the tree.'
   (Forker 2013: 558)
 b. [*coy* (*ƛ'ere*) **b**-*iči-yo* *goła*] *aže* *čeq-i* *goł*
   eagle(III) (on) III-sit-CVB.IPFV be.PTCP tree(IV) forest-IN be
   'The tree where the eagle is sitting stands in the forest.'
   (Forker 2013: 558)
 c. *de=tow* *y-oc'-iš* *aže*
   I.ERG=EMP IV-cut-PST tree(IV)
   'I myself cut the tree.'
   (Forker 2013: 689)
 d. [*obu-y* *aže* *y-occo* *goła*] *og* *xexza-y*
   father-ERG tree(IV) IV-cut.CVB.IPFV be.PTCP ax(V) child.OBL.PL-ERG
   r-uqi-š
   V-hide-PST
   'The children hid the ax with which the father cut the tree.'
   (Forker 2013: 556)
 e. [*bołiƛ'o* **b**-*iƛ'i-yo* *goła*] **essni**, *xu=n*
   hunting HPL-go-CVB.IPFV be.PTCP **brother.PL** meat(V)=and
   r-aq'er-no *b-aq'e-n*
   V-bring-CVB HPL-come-UWPST
   'The brothers, who had gone hunting, came and brought meat.'
   (Forker 2013: 551)
 f. *hagze-s* [*r-u:-ho* *goła*] **biša** *anƛ'-ma*
   they.OBL-GEN₁ V-do-CVB.IPFV be.PTCP **food(V)** week.OBL-IN
   ƛex^{w}e-n
   remain-UWPST
   'Their food that they had prepared remained for one week.'
   (Forker 2013: 552)
 g. **b**-*eg^{w}ey* *k'et'u* / *y-eg^{w}ey* *t'ek* / *r-eg^{w}ey* *t'oq*
   III-small cat(III) / IV-small book(IV) / V-small knife(V)
   'small cat'/'small book'/'small knife' (Forker 2013: 464)

Another language in which verbal agreement is in a way disguised as adjectival agreement is Modern Standard Arabic. Most adjectives in Modern Standard Arabic agree with the noun they modify in definiteness, gender, case, and number, as in (165a). The example in (165b) shows an active participle in subject relativization demonstrating the identical agreement pattern. However, when another participant is relativized using the same form (and a resumptive pronoun), the participle only agrees with the modified noun in definiteness and case, while the number and gender values are taken from the subject of the relative clause. This agreement "mismatch" is illustrated by the example of possessor relativization in (165c), where the participle *l-jālis-a* 'sitting' receives definite and accusative marking due to the nominal agreement with the modified noun *l-marʔat-a* 'woman', but at the same time it is masculine and singular due to the verbal agreement with the word *zawj-u=hā* 'her husband', the subject of the participial relative clause:

(165) Modern Standard Arabic (Afro-Asiatic)
    a. *xilāl-a*   *l-sanat-**ayni***   *l-māḍiy-**at-ayni***
        during-ACC   DEF-year(F)-GEN.DU   DEF-last-F-GEN.DU
        'during the last two years' (Ryding 2005: 243)
    b. *bi-l-muʃkilat-**ayni***   [*s-sābiq-**at-ayni***]
        with-DEF-problem(F)-GEN.DU   DEF-precede-PTCP.ACT.F-GEN.DU
        'with the two previous problems'
        (Badawi, Carter, and Gully 2004: 103, as cited in Doron and Reintges 2005: 11)
    c. *qābal-tu*   *l-marʔat-a*   [*l-**jālis**-a*
        meet.PRF-1SG DEF-woman.F.SG-ACC DEF-sit.PTCP.ACT.M.SG-ACC
        ***zawj**-u=hā*]
        husband(M).SG-NOM=POSS.3F.SG
        'I met the woman whose husband is sitting.'
        (Doron and Reintges 2005: 13)

Based on these examples, it is reasonable to assume that the "full" agreement of the participle with the modified noun in (165b) is actually due to the fact that the modified noun is the relativized subject of the dependent clause. The participle, therefore, receives both number and gender values, and definiteness and case values from the same participant, but for different reasons. This kind of double (verbal and nominal) agreement on a single participial form is also attested for negative participles in Kambaata (Afro-Asiatic). According to Treis (2008: 171), these forms demonstrate person, gender and number agreement with the subject of the relative clause, and case and gender agreement with the modified noun. Affirmative participles in Kambaata only agree with the relative clause subject; see examples (162a) and (162b) provided in the previous section.

5.5 Nominal agreement with the modified noun

The previous sections have focused on the loss of verbal properties in participial forms, when compared to main clauses. As mentioned in Section 4.2.1, however, participial forms often also acquire typically nominal properties. One of these is the ability to agree with the modified noun with respect to various nominal categories, which, depending on a particular language, may include number, case, gender, noun class and definiteness. The present section describes two major types of nominal agreement between participles and modified nouns that can be identified cross-linguistically. Section 5.5.1 deals with obligatory agreement, whereas Section 5.5.2 discusses agreement conditional on certain properties of the relative construction.

5.5.1 Obligatory agreement

Participial predicates of relative clauses can agree with modified nouns in a variety of nominal categories. For instance, in Lithuanian, participles used for adnominal modification show agreement in gender, case and number; see (166):

(166) Lithuanian (Indo-European)
    a. *Mėgėj-ų*   *komand-os,*   *ne-turė-dam-os*   *kur*   *žais-ti,*
        amateur-GEN.PL team-NOM.PL NEG-have-CVB-PL.F where play-INF
        noriai   *dalyvav-o*   [*mūs-ų*   *rengi-a-m-**uose***]
        willingly participate-PST.3 we-GEN arrange-PRS-PTCP.PRS.PASS-**LOC.PL.M**
        turnyr-uose
        tournament(M)-LOC.PL
        'Amateur teams, having no places where they could play [basketball], willingly participated in the tournaments we were organizing.'
        (Arkadiev 2014a: 86)
    b. [*Už-si-rakin-dav-us-**iai***   *kambar-y*]   **Edit-ai**
        PREV-REFL-lock-HAB-PTCP.PST.ACT-**DAT.SG.F** room-LOC.SG **Edita(F)-DAT.SG**

> po to tek-dav-o atkentė-ti
> after that get-HAB-PST.3 suffer-INF
> 'Edita, who used to lock herself in the room, would have to suffer afterwards.' (Arkadiev 2014b: 9)

The same agreement pattern is also found in many other Indo-European languages, the only difference being the range of nominal categories available for agreement. In Russian, German and Modern Greek, the ending of the participle depends on the gender, case and number of the modified noun, whereas participles in Italian and Marathi only agree in gender and number. In Albanian, the participle itself is uninflected, and agreement with the head noun in case, number and gender is shown on the prepositive article pertaining to the participial form (Buchholz and Fiedler 1987: 173–175; Alexander Rusakov, p.c.).

A subtype of gender agreement is agreement in noun class (the term traditionally used for languages with rich gender systems that make four or more distinctions; see Corbett 1991, 2013, Di Garbo 2014). Among the languages of the sample, agreement in noun class is attested in Fula (Atlantic-Congo), Yimas (Lower Sepik-Ramu), and Wambaya, an example from which is provided in (167):

(167) Wambaya (Mirndi)
  Janji   ng-a   daguma   [dawi-j-**barli**].
  dog:CL1(ACC) 1SG.A-PST hit(NFUT)   bite-TH-NMZ.A:CL1(ACC)
  'I hit that biting dog.' (Given as a translation for 'I hit the dog that bit me.') (Nordlinger 1998: 105)

Finally, in Modern Standard Arabic, definiteness is also a category with respect to which participles agree with the modified nouns, as shown in examples (165b) and (165c) in the previous section. In addition, the instances of non-subject participial relativization in Modern Standard Arabic illustrate the fact that nominal categories of the head noun can be represented in the attributive participle only partially, i.e. with partial instead of full nominal agreement; see Section 5.4 for the relevant discussion.

Like the distinction between +TAM and –TAM participial markers, languages differ in whether agreement of participles with the modified nouns is external to the participial marker or fused with it. In other words, participial markers can be genderless or gendered. In all cases considered above, the participial marker can in principle be segmented from the agreement morphology (even though the segmentation can be hindered by morphophonological processes, as in Wambaya). By contrast, three languages in the sample have portmanteau participial markers that at the same time express a certain gender value; see example (168) from Krongo:

(168) Krongo (Kadugli-Krongo)
    a. *n-ŭllà*   *àʔàŋ*   *kà-**káaw***   [***ŋ**-àttàdì-ttí*   *kànίŋ*]
       1/2-IPFV.love   I   LOC-**person(M)**   CONN.M-PFV.lean-1SG   LOC.he
       'I like the man that I lean on.' (Reh 1985: 257)
    b. *n-àdéelà*   ***tìnkìryá***   [***n**-ófù-n-tíní*   *kí-tì*]
       N-IPFV.be.good   **bed(N)**   CONN.N-IPFV.rest-TR-3SG   LOC-it
       'The bed on which he/she rests is good/beautiful.' (Reh 1985: 257)

In the second language, Sheko, the marker *-àbe* (*-àbe*) is used when the modified noun is feminine singular, whereas for all other kinds of modified nouns (masculine singular, feminine or masculine plural) the marker *-àb* (*-àb*) is employed; compare (169b) and (169a). The same opposition is also observed in other domains where gender distinctions are relevant, e.g. in demonstratives and nominalizers (Hellenthal 2010: 136).

(169) Sheko (Dizoid)
    a. [*gōnà*   *íʃ-ka*   *dààn-tə*   *há=ày-**àbe***]
       yesterday   3F.SG-with   together-SS   3M.SG=dance-REL.F.SG
       ***bààrǹ**-əra*   *ha=see-kì*
       maiden(F).DEF(SG)-ACC   2SG=see-exist.Q
       'Do you see the girl with whom he danced yesterday?'
       (Hellenthal 2010: 350)
    b. [*sāāy-ǹ-s*   *ás-kì̀*   *màtk-**àb***]   ***də̀d-ǹ-s***
       fable-DEF-M   3M.SG-DAT   tell.PASS-REL   **child-DEF-M**
       'the boy to whom the story was told'
       (Hellenthal 2010: 344)

Apparently, the expression of both participial status and gender in a single marker may in some cases reflect a relatively early stage of its grammaticalization. According to Hellenthal (2010: 344), the origin of the feminine participial marker in Sheko is fairly transparent: its second syllable is related to the word *bây ~ bé* 'mother'.[47] Interestingly, the same element seems even less grammati-

---

[47] It is not clear from Hellenthal's description whether it is the first syllable (or the first vowel) in the relative morpheme that actually indicates the participial status of the form. Therefore, I

calized when used as a nominalizer. In this case, it has the form -*bé* and is opposed to the masculine nominalizer -*bāāb* 'father'; cf. (170a) and (170b). The same elements can also function as nouns meaning 'mother, woman' and 'father, man' respectively, as in examples (170c) and (170d):

(170) Sheko (Dizoid)
    a. *bēɾn*   *t'ár-ǹ-s*   *kāts-m̄-**be***
        tomorrow   injera-DEF-M   cook-IRR-**mother**
        'the one (F) who will bake injera tomorrow' (Hellenthal 2010: 345)
    b. *tàmār*   *ìy-tà*   *tág-m̄-**bààb***   *kì=â*
        education   house-LOC   go-IRR-**father**   exist=3M.SG.Q
        'Is there someone who will go to school?' (Hellenthal 2010: 345)
    c. *ēkī*   ***be-ì-s***
        money   **mother-F-PL**
        'rich women' (Hellenthal 2010: 182)
    d. *ēkī*   ***bààb-ù-s***
        money   **father-M-PL**
        'rich women' (Hellenthal 2010: 182)

As an aside, it can be noted that agreement patterns in participial relative clauses tend to vary significantly within particular language families and smaller genealogical units. For instance, among Tungusic languages, Nanai does not have any agreement at all, Uilta only shows occasional case agreement in the accusative, whereas Evenki in its standard variety shows full agreement of the participle with the modified noun, but lacks case agreement in the easternmost dialects (Shagal 2016). As for Berber languages, in the Riffian variety the participle contains no gender-number distinctions, in Tashelhiyt only number agreement exists, while in Touareg both gender and number of the modified noun are reflected in the participle (see Kossmann 2007: 440 and further references there). There is also considerable variation among Indo-European and Uralic languages. This tendency suggests that nominal agreement of participles is not a very time-stable feature, and it may be acquired and lost relatively simply. This issue, however, requires further diachronic work before any decisive generalizations can be put forward.

Altogether, participles show obligatory nominal agreement with modified nouns in 31 languages from the core sample. Importantly, in all of these languages, which also have a category of adjectives, adjectives show the same type

---

follow the analysis proposed in the grammar, and consider it a single marker that has two gender agreement options.

of agreement. In other words, in terms of agreement, participles behave as a subclass of adjectives. Conditional agreement discussed in the next section is, however, a different phenomenon, which is to a large extent specific to participial forms introducing relative clauses.

5.5.2 Conditional agreement

Agreement of a relative participle with the modified noun can be conditional on specific syntactic factors, like adjacency or ordering principles. For example, in Beserman Udmurt, the regular position of a participle or a participial relative clause is before the modified noun; in this position, the participle does not show agreement either in case or in number, as illustrated in (171a) and (171b). When, on the other hand, the participial relative clause is for some reasons used postnominally, agreement in case and number is obligatory, as in (171c):

(171) Beserman Udmurt (Uralic)
    a. *Mon jarat-iš'ko* [***turna-m***]   *turân-lâš'*   *zân-z-e.*
       I   love-PRS   mow-PTCP.PST   grass-GEN₂   smell-POSS.3-ACC
       'I love the smell of mowed grass.' (Brykina and Aralova 2012: 509)
    b. *Andrej*   *lâkt-i-z*   *polka dorâ,*   *kud-a-z*
       Andrey   come-PRET-3   shelf near.ILL   which-INESS/ILL-POSS.3
       sâl-o   [***lâʒ'-em-te***]   *so-jen]*   *kn'iga-os.*
       stand-PRS.3PL   read-PTCP.PST-NEG   that-INS   book-PL
       'Andrey came up to the shelf where the books that he had not read were (standing).' (Brykina and Aralova 2012: 510)
    c. *Stud'ent-**jos-lâ**,*   [***lâkt-em-jos-lâ***]   *dor-a-z],*
       student-PL-DAT   come-PTCP.PST-PL-DAT   time-INESS/ILL-POSS.3
       puk-t-âl-i-z-â   *vit'.*
       put-TR-ITER-PRET-3-PL   five
       'The students that came on time were given "fives" (A grades).'
       (Brykina and Aralova 2012: 515)

An identical rule applies to some other Uralic languages, such as Meadow Mari and Komi-Zyrian (see Brykina and Aralova 2012).

    A similar situation is observed in Imbabura Quechua. When a participial relative clause appears in its regular prenominal position, it is only the modified noun that takes case marking, while case marking on the non-finite relative clause predicate is prohibited, as shown in (172a). The language, however, also allows for the relative constructions in which the modifying clause appears to the right of the head, and need not even be contiguous with it, as shown in (172b) (with the same meaning). In this situation, case marking is obligatory on both the modified noun and the participle:

(172) Imbabura Quechua (Quechuan; Cole 1985: 51–52)
    a. *juya-ni* [*Juan-wan tushu-shka ka-shka(*-ta)*] *kwitsa-ta*
        love-1 Juan-with dance-NMZ.PST be-NMZ.PST(*-ACC) girl-ACC
        'I love the girl who had danced with Juan.'
    b. *kwitsa-ta juya-ni* [*Juan-wan tushu-shka ka-shka-ta*]
        girl-ACC love-1 Juan-with dance-NMZ.PST be-NMZ.PST-ACC

Based on a set of syntactic tests, Cole (1985: 50–53) shows that the observed difference in case-marking patterns is due to the fact that in (172a) the relative clause and the modified noun form a single constituent, while in (172b) they are two separate constituents of the main clause. A more accurate translation of the second sentence would, therefore, be something like 'I love the girl, the one who had danced with Juan'.

Almost the same principle works in Matsés. When the nominalized relative clause and the modified noun occur in non-adjacent positions, they must both carry case marking, as illustrated in (173a). When, however, they are adjacent, either both of them can be case-marked, as in (173b), or just whichever comes second; see (173c) and (173d):

(52) Matsés (Pano-Tacanan; Fleck 2003: 1023)
    a. *chido-n cues-o-sh-i* [*umbi muaua-boed-n*]
        woman-ERG hit-PST-3-1O 1ERG lie.to/about-NMZ.PST.EXP-ERG
        'The woman that I lied to hit me.'
    b. [*umbi muaua-boed-n*] *chido-n cues-o-sh-i*
        1ERG lie.to/about-NMZ.PST.EXP-ERG woman-ERG hit-PST-3-1O
    c. *chido* [*umbi muaua-boed-n*] *cues-o-sh-i*
        woman 1ERG lie.to/about-NMZ.PST.EXP-ERG hit-PST-3-1O
    d. [*umbi muaua-boed*] *chido-n cues-o-sh-i*
        1ERG lie.to/about-NMZ.PST.EXP woman-ERG hit-PST-3-1O

The relative order of the modified noun and the nominalized clause is not restricted and does not affect these patterns, nor is the status of a noun phrase as "head noun" relevant. The observed variation may be seen as evidence that the connection between the non-finite relative clause and the modified noun in

Matsés is even looser than that in Imbabura Quechua. Fleck (2003: 1025–1026) argues that the nominalized clause and the modified noun in Matsés, in fact, never behave as a single syntactic constituent. Nevertheless, the construction still complies with the functional definition of a relative clause adopted in this study (see Section 2.3.1), since the nominalized clause is interpreted as attributively modifying the noun.

To summarize this section, language-internal conditional agreement in general tends to depend on the position of the participial relative clause with respect to the head: whether it is adjacent to the head noun or not, or whether it precedes or follows the head noun. Whenever the participial relative clause occurs in an uncommon position (postnominal in Uralic languages and non-adjacent in Imbabura Quechua or Matsés), it is more likely to receive agreement marking. This can presumably be regarded as a means to avoid ambiguity which arises when the relation between the relative clause and the modified noun cannot be easily inferred from word order. In this case, the overt agreement marking on the participle unequivocally signals that the participle and the noun share the semantic referent.

5.6 Summary and conclusions

In this chapter, I have discussed how participial relative clauses deviate from the main clause standard in the morphosyntactic domain. I have shown that their desententialization is commonly manifested in peculiarities in TAM marking, such as restrictions on the expression of certain TAM values by separate affixes (–TAM participles), or within a paradigm (+TAM participles). Many participles differ from independent sentences in the way they express negation, or in the fact that negation is prohibited in participial relative clauses altogether. Verbal subject agreement is generally among the first signs of desententialization, although some languages do allow this type of agreement, at least to a limited extent. In many languages, participles acquire nominal agreement, which can be regarded as a manifestation of the word class change (verb > adjective). However, this can be conditional on certain features of the structure, among which word order is especially common.

6 Participant expression in participial relative clauses

6.1 Introduction

As shown in Chapter 4, the desententialization/nominalization of non-finite dependent clauses is often manifested in non-standard marking of certain participants, or in restrictions on their use. In one case in my sample, the deviation from the independent clause standard even affects the alignment of the dependent clause in general, rather than the marking of a single participant. According to Salanova (2011), in Mẽbengokre, main clauses have accusative alignment (174a), while in non-finite relative clauses the alignment is ergative (174b):[48]

(174) Mẽbengokre (Nuclear-Macro-Je)
    a. *ba*   *hadju*   *kate*
       1NOM radio   break.V
       'I broke the radio.' (Salanova 2011: 53)
    b. [*ije*   *hadju*   *ka'êk*]
       1ERG   radio   break.NMZ
       'the radio that I broke' (Salanova 2011: 54)

However, in all other cases considered in this study, the changes in encoding concern separate participants of a participial relative clause. In Section 6.2, I present all the deviations in the expression of subjects (S/A) in participial relative clauses. Section 6.3 provides the same kind of information regarding direct objects (P). All the non-core participants that can receive special marking in non-finite relative clauses are covered in Section 6.4. In Section 6.5, I summarize the main observed tendencies and suggest motivations that could explain these tendencies. The data on argument expression in the languages of the core sample is presented in Appendix 3c.

---

[48] Other languages showing ergativity split based on the main vs. subordinate opposition are, for example, Jakaltek (Mayan), with ergative alignment in main clauses and accusative alignment in certain types of subordinate clauses (see Craig 1977: 115–117), and Xokleng (Nuclear Macro-Je), with accusative alignment in active main clauses and ergative alignment in subordinate clauses (see Urban 1985). As shown in Gildea (1992, 1998) on the basis of Cariban languages, many of which have a similar pattern, ergative alignment in subordinate clauses can be a source of ergativity in main clauses.

6.2 Subject encoding

Since participial relative clauses commonly preserve full clausal structure, in many languages (39 in the core sample) they allow for regular subject expression. This is the case, for instance, in all the Dravidian and Nakh-Daghestanian languages in my sample; see example (175) from Ingush:

(175) Ingush (Nakh-Daghestanian)
    a. ***Muusaaz***   *sy*   *axcha*   *hwa-dalar*
        Musa.ERG   1SG.GEN   money   DX-D.give.WPST
        'Musa returned my money.'
        (Nichols 2011: 354)
    b. [***Muusaaz***   *suoga*   *hwa-danna*]   *axcha*
        Musa.ERG   1SG.ALL   DX-D.give.PTCP.PST   money
        'the money Musa loaned me'
        (Nichols 2011: 587)

However, in many cases, languages do show differences in subject encoding. In the following sections, I discuss the types of deviation from the independent clause standard in the languages of the sample. First, I will consider subjects encoded as possessors (6.2.1) and various non-core participants (6.2.2). Next, I will deal with languages that show variation in subject encoding in participial relative clauses (6.2.3). Finally, I will briefly cover the cases where subject expression is lacking altogether (6.2.4).

6.2.1 Subject as a possessor

The most common deviation in participial relative clauses is encoding of the subject as a possessor, which is found in 32 languages and 106 participial forms in my sample. Possessive marking can appear in a variety of forms. For instance, in Kharia, the subject of a non-finite relative clause simply receives genitive marking, as in (176). In Luiseño, the nominalized dependent predicate features a possessive marker referring to the agent, as in (177). In Kolyma Yukaghir, the subject is expressed by possessive marking on the modified noun outside the relative clause, as in (178). Finally, the combination of the last two strategies is attested in Tundra Nenets, where possessive marking can optionally be present both on the relative clause predicate and the head noun, as in (179):

(176) Kharia (Austroasiatic)
[iɲ=aʔ   yo~yo]   lebu
1SG=GEN   see~PTCP person
'the person I saw/see/will see' (Peterson 2011: 413)

(177) Luiseño (Uto-Aztecan)
Nawítmal [ʔéxŋi   ʔu-qáni-pi]   pilék yawáywiš
girl   tomorrow   your-meet-REL.FUT   very   pretty
'The girl you're going to meet tomorrow is very pretty.' (Davis 1973: 237)

(178) Kolyma Yukaghir (Yukaghir)
[odu-pe   modo-l]   jalhil-**pe-gi**   čomōd'e   jalhil   ō-l'el
Yukaghir-PL   live-NMZ lake-PL-POSS   big.ATTR.ACT lake   COP-INFR(3SG)
'The lake where the Yukaghirs lived was a large lake.' (Maslova 2003: 421)

(179) Tundra Nenets (Uralic)
[wolʔtampǝ-**wemtº**]   xoba-**mtº**
dislike-PTCP.PFV.ACC.POSS.2SG   skin-ACC.POSS.2SG
'the skin (ACC) that you disliked' (Nikolaeva 2014: 315)

A single language can also show different strategies for subordinate subject encoding. In Kolyma Yukaghir, this distinction is one of the differences between so-called "attributive relative clauses" and "nominal relative clauses" (see Maslova 2003: 329). In attributive relative clauses, which represent the primary relativization strategy in the language, the A/S participant is encoded as the possessor of the modified noun. In nominal relative clauses, the A/S participant is encoded as the possessor of the nominal predicate. As mentioned in Maslova (2003: 329), however, these two situations are, in a way, two instances of one single rule: the A/S participant is marked as the possessor of the noun heading the whole construction. If the predicate of a relative clause is nominal in its nature, it is treated as a possessee itself, while if it is adjectival, the modified noun is regarded as the head noun of the whole construction instead.[49]

In addition, in a number of languages, it is not possible to determine whether the subject of a non-finite relative clause should be regarded as a possessor or not, since in some of them possession is expressed through mere juxtaposition.

---

[49] As shown in Pakendorf (2012) on the data from the languages of North Asia, even languages that at the first glance may seem very similar with respect to their relative clause structure, can show considerable divergence, in particular regarding the types of possessive marking in relative constructions. The differences can be the result of structural analogy of relative clauses with other types of constructions, such as complement clauses or possessive constructions. However, encoding of possession is relevant in all such cases, so I consider all of them together in this study.

For example, in Cocama, the agent in a clause relativizing a direct object (180a) does not receive any special marking and appears in exactly the same form as in an independent sentence (180b). However, the form in -*n*, the predicate of the relative clause, behaves as noun in many respects, and a sequence of two nouns (or a pronoun and a noun) is likely to be interpreted as [Npossessor Npossessed]; see (180c):

(180) Cocama (Tupian)
    a. *tsa   mimira   [**yawara**   karuta-n]   yapana=uy*
       1SG.F woman.son dog   bite-NMZ.S/P run=PST₁
       'My son that the dog bit escaped.'
       (Vallejos Yopán 2010: 590)
    b. ***yawara**   mui   karuta-ari*
       dog   snake   bite-PROG
       'The dog is bitting the snake.'
       (Vallejos Yopán 2010: 469)
    c. *rikua   **tapira**   **rimariru**   iriw=uy*
       reason   tapir   grandson   return=PST₁
       'And that's why the tapir's grandson returned.'
       (Vallejos Yopán 2010: 275)

As a result, it is not possible to identify whether the agent in the participial relative clause in Cocama is a possessor of the nominalized verb form, or a regular subject. Both nominative arguments and possessors are also zero-marked in Cofán (Cofán, Fischer and van Lier 2011: 223), which neutralizes the difference between the most typical verbal and nominal subject expression.

Quite naturally, if a language employs possessive marking for the subject of a participial relative clause, it may be able to use reflexive possessive marking for a relative clause subject coreferential with the subject of the main clause. Malchukov (2008: 216–217) reports this type of expression for Tungusic languages (Even, Nanai, Evenki); see examples in (181) from Nanai, where the non-coreferential subject requires the 3rd person possessive marker -*ni* on the participle, while the coreferential subject is represented by the reflexive possessive marker -*bi*:

(181) Nanai (Tungusic)
    a. *mi   daŋsa-sal-ba   [ama   aŋo-xa-**ni**]   taaxe-du*
       1SG book-PL-ACC   father make-PTCP.PST-POSS.3SG shelf-DAT

nəə-ktə-xəm-bi
put-PLR-PTCP.PST-POSS.1SG
'I put books on the shelf that my father had made.'
b. *Polokto* [*čimi waa-xam-**bi**] sogdata-wa arčokam-ba
Polokto morning kill-PTCP.PST-POSS.REFL.SG fish-ACC girl-ACC
sea-wan-ki-ni
eat-CAUS-PTCP.PST-POSS.3SG
'Polokto fed the girl with the fish that he caught in the morning.'

Dayley (1989: 360–362) provides similar examples of direct object relativization in Tümpisa Shoshone (Uto-Aztecan), where the subject of the relative clause is expressed as a regular possessor if it is not coreferential with the subject of the main clause, but a reflexive possessive pronoun is used if the subjects of the two clauses are coreferential. Unfortunately, it is hardly possible to assess how widespread this phenomenon is, since the topic is very rarely discussed in language descriptions.

One more remark is in order in this section. Some languages in which the subject of a participial relative clause is regularly encoded as a possessor have accusative subject marking in non-finite complement clauses that use the same nominalized forms. This is illustrated in examples (182a) and (182b) from Kalmyk, where the form in -*sən* occurs with a genitive subject in a relative clause and with an accusative subject in a complement clause:

(182) Kalmyk (Mongolic)
    a. [*čini uu-čk-sən*] *cä jir sän bilä*
        2SG.GEN drink-COMPL-PTCP.PST tea very good be.REM
        'The tea that you drank up was very good.'
    b. [***čamagə** cä uu-čk-s-i-n^j*] *med-sən*
        2SG.ACC tea drink-COMPL-PTCP.PST-ACC-POSS.3 know-PTCP.PST
        uga-v
        NEG.COP-1SG
        'I did not know that you had drunk up the tea.'
        (Serdobolskaya 2009: 597)

Accusative subject marking in such contexts is commonly explained by raising of the dependent clause subject (see Serdobolskaya 2009). Since raising implies that the subordinate clause is an argument of the main clause predicate, and relative clauses are not arguments but adnominal modifiers, the phenomenon of raising is not relevant for relativization. Consequently, accusative subjects are almost never attested in participial relative clauses. Probably the closest to accusative subject encoding can be found in Wappo, where the subject of a non-finite relative clause does not receive any marking and therefore should, according to Thompson, Park, and Li (2006: 117), be regarded as an accusative; compare the form of the 1st person singular subject in the relative clause and the main clause below:

(183) Wappo (Yuki-Wappo)
[i   k'ew   naw-ta]   (ce)   **ah**   hak'-še?
1SG   man   see-PST:DEP   DEM   1SG:NOM   like-DUR
'I like the man I saw.' (Thompson, Park, and Li 2006: 117)

This example is, however, the only one attested in my sample, and it does not have any overt accusative marking, so it is possible to conclude that accusative is definitely not among the prominent strategies of subject encoding in participial relative clauses.

6.2.2 Subject as a non-core participant

The subject of a participial relative clause can also be encoded as a non-core participant, for instance, as a noun phrase in an oblique case, or as an adpositional phrase. The two options are illustrated below by an example from West Greenlandic with an ablative subject (184), and an example from Hungarian, where the agent is introduced by the postposition *által* (185):

(184) West Greenlandic (Eskimo-Aleut)
nanoq   [**Piita-mit**   toqu-taq-Ø]
bear.ABS   Peter-ABL   kill-PTCP.PASS-ABS
'the bear killed by Peter' (Fortescue 1984: 53)

(185) Hungarian (Uralic)
az   [**Anna**   által   tegnap   olvas-ott]   könyv
DEF   Anna   by   yesterday   read-PTCP.PST   book
'the book read by Anna yesterday' (Kenesei, Vago, and Fenyvesi 1998: 46)

This type of subject expression is commonly the only possibility for inherently oriented passive or absolutive participles, in particular in Indo-European languages. Among the Indo-European languages of the sample, Russian employs instrumental case to express the agent in a participial relative clause, while Albanian, German, Modern Greek and Italian use prepositions. Other forms with this strategy are, for example, the Kalmyk passive participle in -*ata* (instrumental agent, Krapivina 2009a: 520), the Kamaiurá passive participle in -*ipyt* (dative agent, Seki 2000: 179), and the Panare absolutive participle in -*sa'* (dative agent, Payne and Payne 2013: 321–324).

Interestingly, almost all of these languages seem to have a participle-based passive construction used in independent sentences, which employs the same agent encoding, like English *This book is written by my grandfather*. Apart from Indo-European languages like German or Italian, which are commonly cited as an example of this phenomenon (see Haspelmath 1990, or Siewierska 1984: 126), such constructions are also attested at least in Kalmyk (Krapivina 2009a: 518–520) and Panare; see (186):

(186) Panare (Cariban)
    a. *Moma tityasa wainki'* [*ch-achukë-sa'* **ta'nimën úya**
        EXIST one anteater TR-squeeze.out-PTCP.PST vehicle DAT
        chima ta].
        road in
        'There was an anteater squashed (killed) by vehicle(s) on the road.'
        (Payne and Payne 2013: 322)
    b. *Y-an-sa'* *mën mankowa* ***ana-úya***.
        3-get-PTCP.PST SPEC poison 1EX-DAT
        'The poison was gotten by us.'
        (Payne and Payne 2013: 161)

In languages with contextually oriented participles, the subject of a participial relative clause also can sometimes be encoded as a non-core participant; consider examples of an instrumental agent in Komi-Zyrian (187), and a locative agent in Northern Khanty (188):

(187) Komi-Zyrian (Uralic)
    [*Menam* **pač'-lən** *vur-əm*] *dərəm zev bur*
    I.GEN₁ grandmother-INS sew-PTCP.PFV shirt very good
    'The shirt that my grandmother sewed is very good.'
    (Brykina and Aralova 2012: 504)

(188) Northern Khanty (Uralic)
 [*loŋkər-na* xir-ə-m]   o:ŋxi   xośa   muwle:r   u:-l
 mouse-LOC dig-EP-PTCP.PST hole at snake be-NPST.3SG
 'In the hole dug by the mouse lives a snake.'
 (Nikolaeva 1999: 76)

However, in these cases, this is never the only possible way to express the subject of this particular participle, but it alternates with some other options. The rules regulating this variation are discussed in the following section.

6.2.3 Language-internal variation in subject encoding

As mentioned in the previous section, some languages use more than one strategy for expressing the subject of a single participial form. In some cases, the rules regulating the choice are not fully described in the grammar, or the options exist in free variation. For example, there is hardly any data on the distribution of possessive and ablative subjects in participial relative clauses in West Greenlandic (Eskimo-Aleut), or possessive and locative subjects in Northern Khanty (Uralic). Similarly, several ways to express the subject of a non-finite relative clause in Georgian (Kartvelian) seem to be used interchangeably with very few restrictions, according to Hewitt (1995: 539). Nevertheless, in some languages, the variation does follow some fairly strict principles.[50]

In Muna, the encoding of the agent in the constructions with direct object relativization depends on whether the relative clause predicate has any other dependents or not. If the agent is the only participant overtly expressed within the relative clause, it is encoded as a possessor, as in (189a). If, however, there is an indirect object marker on the relative clause predicate, the possessive suffix is interpreted as referring to the indirect object, and therefore the agent can only be expressed by means of a prepositional phrase with the locative marker *ne* (189b), which is also used for animate recipients (189c), and sources (189d):

---

[50] It should be noted that in all the cases outlined further, differential subject marking is only present in dependent clauses, while independent clause subjects are always encoded in the same way. As I will show in Section 6.3.3, the mechanism is different for direct objects. It is commonly not the emergence of differential object marking, but the change in the rules regulating the variation that signals the desententialization of the participial clause.

(189) Muna (Austronesian)
    a. *sura*   [*ka-pakatu-**ku***]
        letter   NMZ-send-my
        'the letter that I sent' (van den Berg 2013: 235)
    b. *sura*   [*ka-pakatu-ghoo-ku*   ***ne***   ***ina-ku***]
        letter   NMZ-send-IO-my   LOC   mother-my
        'the letter that was sent to me by my mother' (van den Berg 2013: 235)
    c. *no-bisara-mo*   ***ne***   ***robhine-no***
        3SG.REAL-speak-PFV   LOC   wife-his
        'He said to his wife.' (van den Berg 2013: 139)
    d. *a-fetingke-e*   ***ne***   ***Ali***
        1SG.REAL-hear-it   LOC   Ali
        'I heard it from Ali.' (van den Berg 2013: 140)

In Kalmyk, the choice of subject expression in a participial relative clause is determined by the relativization strategy employed. If the relativized participant is not in any way represented in the relative clause, the subject receives genitive marking, while in a relative clause with a resumptive element -*nʲ*, the subject appears in the nominative. This rule is illustrated in (190) by two instances of the postpositional phrase relativization, the only position of the Accessibility Hierarchy where both strategies are available in Kalmyk:

(190) Kalmyk (Mongolic)
    a. *kuuxənʲ-də*   [***miis-in***   *suu-xə*]   *stul*   *av-ad*   *irə-Ø*
        kitchen-DAT   cat-GEN   sit-PTCP.FUT   chair   take-CVB.ANT   come-IMP
    b. *kuuxənʲ-də*   [*deer-nʲ*   ***mis***   *suu-xə*]   *stul*   *av-ad*
        kitchen-DAT   surface-POSS.3   cat   sit-PTCP.FUT   chair   take-CVB.ANT
        irə-Ø
        come-IMP
        'Bring the chair on which the cat will be sitting to the kitchen.'

While each of these two principles is only attested once in my sample, there is another tendency in subject marking variation, which seems relevant for a slightly wider range of typologically distinct languages. Specifically, the choice of strategy for subject encoding can also depend on the position of the subject in question on the Animacy Hierarchy (Silverstein 1976) presented as follows:

(191) 1st person > 2nd person > 3rd person > proper names > humans > non-humans animates > inanimates

For instance, in Meadow Mari (Uralic), the subject of contextually oriented participles can be expressed by a possessive affix on the head noun, or as a genitive, nominative, or instrumental participant. The range of possibilities is different for personal pronouns, other pronouns, proper names, noun phrases denoting humans, noun phrases denoting other animate participants, and noun phrases denoting inanimate participants, as represented in Table 21 from Brykina and Aralova (2012: 488).

Tab. 21: Subject encoding in participial relative clauses in Meadow Mari

Expression	Personal pronoun	Other pronoun	Proper name	Human NP	Animate NP	Inanimate NP
Possessive affix	+	–	–	–	–	–
Genitive	+	+	+	+	+	+
Nominative	–	–	–	no data	+	+
Instrumental (postposition)	–	–	–	–	–	+

Among the Uralic languages, a very similar situation is found in Komi-Zyrian, with a slightly wider range of options available for each type of participant (Brykina and Aralova 2012: 503), and in Beserman Udmurt relative clauses formed by -*m* participles (Brykina and Aralova 2012: 515). In participial relative clauses in Kayardild (Tangkic), pronominal subjects are expressed as possessors, noun phrases denoting humans receive ablative marking, and other noun phrases appear in either consequential or origin case (Evans 1995: 470).

Other languages show a simpler version of this system. For instance, in Eastern Armenian (Indo-European), the split is only binary: subjects expressed by nouns receive dative marking, while pronouns appear in genitive or in the form of 1st and 2nd person possessive markers (Dum-Tragut 2009: 209).[51] In Guarijío (Uto-Aztecan), pronominal subjects of participial relative clauses are expressed

---

[51] If the future participle or the resultative participle take a passive suffix, their subject can also be encoded by the postposition *kołmic'*, or by the ablative or instrumental case (depending on the properties of the verb and the subject itself); see Dum-Tragut (2009: 510). This, however, reflects the behaviour of the passive rather than the participles, and is, therefore, outside the scope of this study.

by a special set of pronouns which are otherwise used for encoding non-core participants of independent clauses and possessors, while nominal subjects appear in the same form as in independent clauses (Félix Armendáriz 2005: 93).

On the whole, the tendencies presented above can be summarized in the following rule: If a language shows variation with respect to subject expression in participial relative clauses, subjects occupying higher positions on the Animacy Hierarchy are more likely to be expressed as possessors, while subjects occupying lower positions on the Animacy Hierarchy tend to be expressed either as non-core participants, or in the same way as in independent sentences.

6.2.4 Subject expression unavailable

In some languages which allow for non-subject participial relativization, the agent of the situation denoted by the participle cannot be expressed at all. This constraint, however, does not seem to be related to the desentard ialization of the dependent clause. In almost all cases attested in my sample, a complete or partial restriction on agent encoding is characteristic of inherently oriented passive participles (Finnish past and non-past passive participles in *-tu* and *-tava*, Irish participle in *-tha/-the*, Beng participle in *-lɛ*), or participles strongly preferring passive/absolutive orientation (resultative participle *-s* in Hinuq). This suggests that the restriction is more likely to be conditioned by the passive meaning, and for all except for the Finnish *-tava* participle also by the resultative meaning, both of which commonly induce agent demotion in the clause (see Section 3.3.3 on passive participles).

6.3 Direct object encoding

When compared to subjects of non-finite relative clauses, direct objects much more rarely demonstrate peculiarities in their encoding. In my sample, 204 of the participial forms and 92 languages allow for direct object expression identical to that of independent sentences. Nevertheless, certain deviations can be identified, and I will discuss them in the following sections. The expression of direct objects as possessors and non-core participants is considered in Sections 6.3.1 and 6.3.2 respectively. Section 6.3.3 is devoted to languages showing variation in direct object marking with differential object marking in main clauses, which in some cases changes in participial relative clauses.

6.3.1 Direct object as a possessor

Even though it is much less common for the direct objects of participial relative clauses to be expressed as possessors than for their subjects, possessive marking is still the most frequent non-standard way to encode objects. An example in (192) with the direct object in the genitive case comes from Georgian:

(192) Georgian (Kartvelian)
[*a+m šarvl-is   še-m-k'er-v-el-i*]   kal-i
these trousers-GEN PREV-PTCP.ACT-sew-TS-PTCP.ACT-AGR woman-NOM
'the woman who sewed these trousers' (Hewitt 1995: 539)

In Wan, attributive nominalization in *-ŋ* expresses the agent in the relative clause as an inalienable possessor, as illustrated in (193a). However, in case the nominalization is associated with two arguments (one corresponding to the verb's object and the other to its subject), the subject, an external argument, is realized as an alienable possessor, while the inalienable possessor position is taken up by the direct object, as in (193b):

(193) Wan (Mande)
  a. [*à*   *zò-ŋ*]   *gbè*
     3SG   come-NMZ.ATTR   manner
     'the manner of his arrival' (Nikitina 2009: 25)
  b. [*àà*   *pɔ́*   *lɔ́-ŋ*]   *gbè*
     3SG.ALN thing   eat-NMZ.ATTR   manner
     'the manner of his eating' (Nikitina 2009: 26)

In the same way as agents, direct objects can also be expressed by possessive suffixes. In Japhug rGyalrong, the participle in *kɯ-* relativizing the A participant takes an obligatory possessive prefix representing P if no overt noun phrase corresponding to P is present, and when no other prefix is added to the participle; see (194):

(194) Japhug rGyalrong (Sino-Tibetan)
[*ɯ-kɯ-sat*]
POSS.3SG-NMZ.S/A-kill
'the one who kills him' (Jacques 2016: 7)

According to Abraham (1985: 131), in another Sino-Tibetan language, Apatani, the P participant of a nominalized relative clause receives the genitive marker in addition to the accusative marker that it has to take as a direct object. Compare the direct objects in the main and dependent clauses in (195):

(195) Apatani (Sino-Tibetan)
 ṅo [sɨ mi ka panɨbo] myu mi kapato
 1SG cattle ACC GEN cut.NMZ man ACC see.PST
 'I saw the man who killed the cattle.' (Abraham 1985: 131)

This example is, however, fairly problematic, since double case marking does not seem to be attested in any other constructions in the language. Sun (2003: 465) suggests that genitive marking in this case belongs not to the P participant, but rather to the A participant (*myu* 'man'), which is deleted from the relative clause to become the modified noun, as shown in (196a). The genitive marker is exactly the encoding that the A participant receives in Apatani when the P participant is relativized with the same nominalized form in -*nɨ(bo)*,[52] as shown in (196b):

(196) Apatani (Sino-Tibetan)
 a. ṅo [sɨ-mi **Ø-ka** panɨbo] myu-mi kapato
 1SG cattle-OBJ Ø-GEN kill.NMZ.A person-OBJ see.PFV
 'I saw the person who killed the cattle.'
 (Abraham 1985: 131, as cited in Sun 2003: 465)
 b. [**kago-ka** tunɨ] my
 Kago-GEN kick.NMZ man
 'the man whom Kago kicked'
 (Abraham 1985: 131, as cited in Sun 2003: 465)

The data available on subordination in Apatani is, unfortunately, too scarce to provide any cogent arguments in favour of any of the two analyses, so I will not draw any conclusions here.

---

52 According to Abraham (1985: 131), -*bo* is added to the nominalized embedded verb "when the range of reference is restricted (i.e., when a noun is specified)".

6.3.2 Direct object as a non-core participant

The only clear example in my sample where the direct object in a participial relative clause is expressed as a non-core participant is the Australian language Garrwa, which employs dative marking in this context; see (197):

(197) Garrwa (Garrwan)
nayinda   juka   ngaki   [kudukudu-nyi **kaku-nyi** wadamba-warr]
this.NOM boy.NOM I.POSS.NOM many-DAT   fish-DAT   feed-NMZ.CHAR
'This is my boy who eats many fish.'
(Furby and Furby 1977: 94, glosses and transcription by Mushin 2012: 202)

Interestingly, a dative dependent for what would be a direct object in a regular main clause is found not just in Garrwa (Mushin 2012: 201), but also in Wambaya (Nordlinger 1998: 105), another Australian language. In Wambaya, however, this is only possible when the nominalization functions as a main clause predicate, and in the descriptions of Garrwa there are just a couple of examples of this construction with no detailed clarification. It should be noted though, that this pattern can be regarded as a part of the broader phenomenon of encoding core participants by dative case in subordinate clauses in Australia. According to Nordlinger (2002: 5), Warlpiri (Pama-Nyungan) encodes the subject of the subordinate clause with a dative instead of the ergative, and Jiwarli (Pama-Nyungan) employs dative instead of absolutive for the object of the non-finite dependent predicate. Although the data on this question is fairly limited, there clearly is a tendency for Australian non-finite predicates to take dative dependents expressing core arguments of the clause; see also Dench and Evans (1988) and Dench (2009) for Nyamal (Pama-Nyungan). Thus, this may be relevant to a larger number of participial relative clauses than included in the current sample.

6.3.3 Language-internal variation in object encoding

Several languages in the sample show variation in object encoding in participial relative clauses. Unlike languages with differential subject marking in dependent clauses (Section 6.2.3), most of these languages show differential object marking in independent clauses as well. For example, in Eastern Armenian (Indo-European), both in independent clauses and in participial relative clauses, direct objects denoting humans receive dative marking, while non-human direct objects appear in the unmarked nominative form (Dum-Tragut 2009: 1, 511). As a result, deviations in direct object expression in participial relative clauses in such cases are manifested not in the emergence of variation, but rather in a change of rules regulating the choice of marking strategy.

For instance, in the Kolyma Yukaghir finite clauses, 1st and 2nd person direct objects are always encoded as accusatives or instrumentals, while for 3rd person direct objects this marking is only used when the A participant is a 3rd person as well. In all other cases, namely if the A participant of a finite clause is a 1st or 2nd person, the 3rd person direct object appears in the unmarked nominative form. In non-finite relative clauses, the distribution of possible marking strategies is the same, except for the fact that the situation when both A and P 3rd person participants are unmarked is also available. According to Maslova (2003: 331–336), in this case, it is not the person of the A participant that regulates differential object marking, but instead it correlates with the relative prominence of the core participants outside the given clause, i.e. in some higher-level text unit. The P participant in such contexts only receives accusative marking if it is a more or equally prominent entity on the episode and text level if compared to the A participant; see (198a). If, on the other hand, the A participant is more prominent (or "global", in Maslova's terminology) than the P participant, then the latter appears in the unmarked form; see (198b):

(198) Kolyma Yukaghir (Yukaghir)
    a. [***tude-gele***   joq-to-l]   ani-pe   čobul   pugedend'e-ŋin
        he-ACC   arrive-CAUS-NMZ fish-PL   sea   king-DAT
        mol-l'el-ŋi
        say-INFR-3PL.INTR
        'The fishes that had brought him said to the sea king: ...'
        (Maslova 2003: 336)
    b. ediŋ   [met   ***marqil'***   leg-u-l]   alme   juø-k!
        this   my   girl   eat-EP-NMZ shaman   see-IMP.2SG
        'Look for the shaman who has eaten my girl!'
        (Maslova 2003: 334)

Consequently, what changes here is not the marking of the P participant (or the range of marking options), but rather the rules regulating differential object marking in non-finite relative clauses if compared to independent sentences.

In Apsheron Tat, the direct object in a participial relative clause can receive accusative marking, as in (199a), like a regular definite direct object in a main clause. On the other hand, when describing participial constructions in this language, Authier (2012: 233–234) specifically points out the existence of attributive idiomatic expressions where the direct object appears unmarked; see (199b):[53]

(199) Apsheron Tat (Indo-European)
    a. [*şir-e*   *xar-de*]   *nozu*   *ez-i*   *xune*   *nisdü*
        milk-ACC   eat-PTCP   cat   ABL-PROX   house   NEG.COP3
        'The cat who has drunk the milk is not from this house.'
        (Authier 2012: 234)
    b. *Molla*   *yeto*   [*xob-e*   **şir**   *de-re*]   *go*   *doş-de-s*
        Molla   one   good-ATTR   milk   give-PTCP   cow   have-PRF-3
        'Mulla has a cow giving good milk.'
        (Authier 2012: 234)

As a special type of deviation in differential object marking, in languages allowing for the incorporation of a direct object in the verbal predicate, direct objects can behave differently in participial relative clauses than in other clause types. For example, in Imbabura Quechua, where direct object incorporation (manifested in a lack of case marking and in obligatory position right before the verb form) is only available in nominalized clauses, it is more common in participial relative clauses than in other types of non-finite clauses (Cole 1985: 48, 69). This is true in spite of the fact that incorporation in participial relative clauses often leads to ambiguity with regard to the grammatical role of the relativized noun phrase. For instance, the incorporated version of (200) is structurally ambiguous. It may be understood as 'the woman who bought a cow' (*warmi* 'woman' interpreted as subject and *wagra* 'cow' as incorporated object), or 'the woman which the cow bought' (*wagra* 'cow' interpreted as subject, and *warmi* 'woman' as a direct object):

(200) Imbabura Quechua (Quechuan)
     [***wagra(-ta)***   *randi-shka*]   *warmi*
     cow(-ACC)   buy-NMZ.PST   woman
     'the woman who bought a cow/the woman which the cow bought'
     (Cole 1985: 48)

---

[53] It is not clear from the available sources whether these expressions are also found in main clauses.

Similarly, in Ket (Yeniseian, Nefedov 2012: 200–201), direct objects in relative clauses formed by action nominals can be incorporated in the verb form (a pattern that does not occur in finite clauses), thus forming compound lexicalized units. This is apparently due to the fact that non-finite relative clauses usually convey a more generic or habitual meaning than their finite counterparts, which leads to perception of the direct object as indefinite or non-specific. Very few authors of grammatical descriptions make such claims explicitly, but based on the examples generally provided in grammars it seems that this tendency might be relevant for many languages, and it can be expected to be reflected in the types of argument marking other than incorporation as well.

The only language in the sample where differential object marking is only present in dependent clauses is Meadow Mari (Uralic). In Mari languages, the direct object of a finite independent clause always receives accusative marking, while non-finite clauses show differential object marking (accusative vs. zero-marking). Among the factors regulating the variation are specificity of the direct object, its semantics (whether the object is perceived as an uncountable entity), and its communicative status in the discourse; see Toldova and Serdobolskaya (2002), Serdobolskaya and Toldova (2017), Shagal and Volkova (2018).

6.4 Encoding of non-core participants

Even though it is most common for subjects and certain direct objects to change their encoding in dependent clauses, in some languages non-core participants of participial relative clauses can also be expressed in a non-standard way. In all such cases attested in my sample (except for a very specific construction in Wan discussed below), the resulting type of expression is a possessive construction. For instance, in Muna, nominalizations used for direct object relativization allow for non-standard indirect object encoding with possessive suffixes. For example, the 2nd person indirect object in the relative clause in (201a) is expressed as a possessor, while in independent clauses it is regularly encoded by means of an indirect object suffix, as illustrated in (201b):

(201) Muna (Austronesian)
    a. *bheta* [*ka-waa-ghoo-**mu*** *ne* *robhine* *aitu*]
       sarong NMZ-give-IO-your LOC woman that
       'The sarong that was given to you by that woman.'
       (van den Berg 2013: 236)

b. *a-gh<um>oro-**angko**   dua   na-se-wua*
   1SG.IRR-throw.you-you also FUT-one-fruit
   'I will also throw you another piece of fruit.' (van den Berg 2013: 179)

In Georgian, not only direct objects of active participles can receive genitive case marking, as illustrated in (192) above, but also other participants marked by dative in independent sentences, compare the participial use of the verb meaning 'behold, view' in (202a) and its occurrence in an independent clause in (202b):

(202) Georgian (Kartvelian)
   a. *[mo+sa(+)ub(+)r-is   še-m-q'ur-e]*
      interlocutor-GEN   PREV-PTCP.ACT-behold-PTCP.ACT(NOM)
      'gazing upon the interlocutor'
      (Hewitt 1995: 539)
   b. *gul-gril-ad   še-(Ø-)h-q'ur-eb   sa+zog+ad+o+eb-is*
      heart-cool-ADV   PREV-(you-)it-view-TS(PRS)   society-GEN
      azr-s
      opinion-DAT
      'you look upon the opinion of society with a cool heart'
      (Hewitt 1995: 539)

As mentioned in Section 6.3.1, in Wan, two participants can be expressed within a non-finite relative clause, the first as an inalienable possessor, and the second as an alienable possessor. It is important though, that it is not specific participants that can be expressed in a possessive construction, but rather any two participants at maximum. The example (203) illustrates a location expressed as an inalienable possessor of the action nominalization in -*wa*, which cannot be used for adnominal modification, but uses exactly the same syntax as the attributive nominalization in -*ŋ*. The nominalized clause in (203b) is in square brackets:

(203) Wan (Mande)
   a. *è   gā   kɔ̄ŋ   cɔ̄̃ŋ   gó*
      3SG went village distant in
      'She went to a distant village.'
      (Nikitina 2009: 26)
   b. *lē   [kɔ̄ŋ   cɔ̄̃ŋ   gà-wà]   lá   lé   éé   nɛ̀̃   é   lèŋ*
      woman village distant go-NMZ   show PROG REFL.ALN child DEF to
      'The woman is showing her child how to go to a distant village.'
      (Nikitina 2009: 26)

If, however, this type of expression does not allow for unambiguous interpretation of the construction, Wan uses another type of oblique argument realization, namely postpositional phrases adjoined to the entire sentence. Thus, in (204) below, the postpositional phrase *gbā̃nḗ mū yā* 'with dogs' appears after the main verb, although it is associated with the attributive nominalization *wìté-ŋ* 'hunt', the predicate of the relative clause:

(204) Wan (Mande)
 yāá [*wìté-ŋ*] *gbè lá lé* **gbā̃nḗ mū yā** *é*
 3SG+COP hunt-NMZ.ATTR manner show PROG dog PL with REFL
 gbè lèŋ
 son to
 'He is showing to his son the way of hunting with dogs.'
 (Nikitina 2009: 26)

The small number of cases of non-standard encoding of peripheral participants in my sample is in line with Comrie and Thompson's (2007: 355) observation on action nominals. They note that while subjects and direct objects are interesting with respect to their encoding, other kinds of objects (marked objects) provide, in general, less interesting material, since they usually occur in the same form with both verb and action nominal.

A final way in which participial relative clauses can deviate from the independent clause standard in the marking of non-core participants are restrictions on their occurrence. For example, in Kalmyk, the resultative participle in *-ata*, which can serve not only as a predicate of a relative clause (205a), but also as a predicate of an independent clause (205b),[54] can take instruments and temporal adverbials in the latter case, while in the former case only temporal adverbials are commonly allowed by speakers:

(205) Kalmyk (Mongolic)
 a. [**kezänä** (??***sük-är*)** *al-ata*] *taka jamaran ner-tä*
    long.ago axe-INS kill-PTCP.PASS hen which name-ASSOC be.REM
    'What was the name of the hen killed long ago (with an axe)?'
 b. *taka* **kezänä sük-är** *al-ata*
    hen long.ago axe-INS kill-PTCP.PASS
    'The hen was killed long ago with an axe'.

---

[54] This type of multifunctionality is fairly common in the languages of the proposed Altaic family, as shown, for example, in Kalinina (2001).

In Kayardild (Tangkic), resultative nominalizations in *-thirri-n-* do not allow any dependents in non-finite relative clauses apart from demoted subjects and instruments (Evans 1995: 470). Resultative and habitual participles in Hinuq (Nakh-Daghestanian) can in principle take all kinds of adverbials, but do so very rarely (Forker 2013: 570). In these cases, however, it is hardly possible to determine whether these restrictions are due to the desententialization of the relative clause, or due to the aspectual characteristics of the participial form. Unfortunately, in general, very little data is available on the matter in descriptive grammars, and many languages seem to show tendencies rather than strict rules in this domain. At the moment, therefore, we can only provide some scattered observations instead of a consistent cross-linguistic survey of this phenomenon.

6.5 Summary and conclusions

In this chapter, I have examined various ways in which participant expression in participial relative clauses deviates from independent clauses. In subject expression, the most common non-standard strategy is encoding the subject as a possessor, which can be found in 32 languages of my sample. In 20 languages, the subject can be encoded as a non-core participant, receiving some type of oblique case marking (instrumental, dative, ablative, locative, consequential, origin), or marking with an adposition. In some cases (at least five languages), the expression of the agent in a participial relative clause is blocked altogether or highly dispreferred. As for direct objects, in most languages of the sample (92 languages), these regularly receive standard marking in participial relative clauses. Rare deviations include encoding direct objects as possessors (three languages) or datives (one language), and changes in the rules regulating differential object marking (five languages). In the three languages allowing for non-standard expression of peripheral participants, they can also be encoded as possessors, while Wan, in addition, employs a special construction for expressing non-core arguments of the attributive nominalization outside the relative clause (more details on argument marking in individual languages can be found in Appendix 3c). I suggest that these deviations can mainly be explained by two types of factors, structural (syntactic) and semantic.

Syntax comes into play when subjects, direct objects, and other participants receive possessive marking. Due to desententialization/nominalization, the predicates of non-finite relative clauses change word class and acquire certain nominal features. As a result, they naturally switch their verbal government to nominal government and start taking the kind of dependents characteristic for nominals, i.e. possessors and other genitives. It is noteworthy that this rule does not only concern languages in which predicates of participial relative clauses actually belong to the class of nouns (e.g. Kayardild or West Greenlandic, where a separate class of adjectives does not exist whatsoever), but also some languages with well-formed adjectives, where participles belong to this class (e.g. Lithuanian or Georgian). This fact shows that nominalization in the context of participial deranking should indeed be regarded as a broad phenomenon including adjectivization; see Section 4.2.1 for discussion. It is also important to note that direct objects and peripheral clause participants do not have their own rules requiring possessive expression. In all cases in my sample where the direct object or some other argument can be expressed as a possessor, the subject of the same participial form always can be expressed as a possessor as well. This observation is in line with the generalization formulated in Comrie (1976b) that the subject is the first candidate to receive possessive (genitive) encoding among the verbal arguments.

Another case where structural factors appear to be relevant is the expression of agents as non-core participants. As I have shown in Section 6.2.2, this kind of marking is mostly attested in participial relative clauses formed by passive participles. For many of these forms, the label "passive" does not only refer to their orientation towards the P participant, but also to the fact that they perform the prototypical functions of passive, including agent demotion (on different types of passive participles, see Section 3.3.3). Consequently, the agent is encoded as a peripheral argument in the relative clause. This can be seen as a cross-constructional phenomenon, that is, passive participles preserve a similar meaning and clause structure irrespective of the context they appear in. A complete prohibition of subject expression has apparently very similar reasons, since it is also attested mostly with the participles which specialize exclusively or predominantly on direct object relativization; see Section 6.2.4.

On the other hand, changes in the differential marking of direct objects in participial relative clauses are best explained by the semantics of the whole construction. Non-finite relative clauses (especially those with the A participant relativized) commonly convey a generic or habitual meaning, which results in the direct objects being incorporated into the verb or expressed with no overt marking in these clauses.

7 Participial systems

7.1 Introduction

At different points in the analysis so far, it has become clear that participles can often most fruitfully be investigated in the context of the broader participial system found in a specific language. For instance, in some languages, TAM-related deviations from the independent clause standard only become visible if we compare the full participial paradigm and the full finite paradigm, as discussed in Sections 5.2.1 and 5.2.3. By comparing the properties of affirmative and negative participles within individual languages, we can show that negative forms are cross-linguistically consistently more nominal in their nature than affirmative forms; see Section 5.3.2. Still, full paradigms of participles, however, have never been studied cross-linguistically as systems. The goal of this chapter is to provide a basic overview of the participial systems attested in the languages of the sample, and to discuss certain cross-linguistic tendencies related to this matter. The topic itself is very extensive and requires a lot more data and further expert analysis, so this chapter should only be regarded as a first attempt to approach it. Also, in order to focus on the oppositions within a more homogeneous class of forms, in this chapter I limit the discussion to paradigms of affirmative participles. The place of negative participles in participial systems has been addressed in Section 5.3.2.

I will consider in turn various types of participial systems based on different criteria, starting from the least complicated, and proceeding towards the most complicated. Clearly, the least complicated system is one containing a single participial form. I will briefly discuss this type in Section 7.2. In Section 7.3, I will discuss systems for which participial orientation is the defining criterion for classification. Participial systems based on TAM distinctions will be considered in Section 7.4. A combination of the two criteria as a basis for a participial system will be the topic of Section 7.5. Section 7.6 will provide an overview of several more complex participial systems attested in the sample, which do not fit into any of the previous categories. In Section 7.7, I will briefly present several additional criteria relevant for participial systems in particular languages. Finally, in Section 7.8, I will summarize the findings and discuss some typological generalizations regarding participial systems in the world's languages.

7.2 Single participle

In this section, I will consider forms that can be classified as the only participle in their respective languages. The TAM properties of single participles have already been discussed to a certain extent in Section 5.2.4. Here I will, therefore, focus on the orientation of such forms, starting with inherently oriented forms (7.2.1), and then proceeding to contextually oriented ones (7.2.2).

7.2.1 Inherently oriented participle

Three types of single inherently oriented forms are attested in the languages of the sample, namely active participles, absolutive participles, and a passive participle (the full list of these languages is provided in Table 31 in Section 7.8). In European languages, active forms always occur in opposition to either passive forms (e.g. in Russian, Lithuanian, Finnish, and North Saami), or absolutive forms (e.g. in English, German, or Hungarian); see Section 7.5. In some other languages, such as Dolakha Newar (Sino-Tibetan) or Maricopa (Cochimi-Yuman), the opposition is rather between subject and non-subject participles; see Section 7.3. However, there are also languages where active participles exist without a counterpart. In my sample, there are nine languages with a single active participle, and they are found primarily in Africa (Krongo, Maba, and Rif Berber) and Australia (Garrwa, Martuthunira, and Wambaya), but also in Papunesia (Kobon and Yimas), and South America (Cofán).[55] For instance, in Kobon, the -*ep* form is the only possible predicate of a deranked relative clause, and still, its use is restricted to subject relativization, as shown in example (206):

(206) Kobon (Nuclear Trans New Guinea)
 Yad Hab Haułamö [siŋib ñig **ñiŋ-eb**] bɨ.
 1SG Hab Haułamö greens water eat-NMZ/ADJR man
 'I am a man from Hab Haułamö who drinks cabbage water.'
 (Davies 1981: 31)

In my sample, seven languages have an absolutive participle as a single participial form. Absolutive participles, as I have shown in Section 3.3.5, in general are

---

[55] It seems that Santiam Kalapuya (Kalapuyan) also has a single active participle, but too little data is available to be sure that it cannot relativize any lower positions on the Accessibility Hierarchy.

often resultative, but this is a tendency rather than a strict rule, as shown by an analysis of the whole sample. By contrast, among single absolutive participles, all of the relevant forms show strong tendency to be resultative and to characterize the modified noun with respect to the state following from an accomplished event; see examples (207) from Beng and (208) from Mochica:

(207) Beng (Mande)
    a. *ŋ-ó*   [*zrȉŋ*   **kásíé-lɛ́**]   *lú.*
        1SG-STAT   corn   fry-NMZ   buy
        'I'll buy some fried corn.' (Serdobolskaya and Paperno 2006: 6)
    b. [*ŋ*   *gā*   **wī-lè**]   *ó*   *ŋ*   *sɛ̰*
        1SG   foot   swell-NMZ   3SG:PST   1SG   ache
        'My swollen foot ached.' (Serdobolskaya and Paperno 2006: 6)

(208) Mochica (Mochica)
     œnta-zta   *f(e)*   *queix*   [*Limac*   **tœ-d.ô**]   *ñofœn*
     not-NEG   be   return   Lima   go-NMZ.STAT   man
     'The man who went to Lima has not yet returned.'
     (Altieri 1939: 19, as cited in Adelaar 2004: 341)

Apart from Beng and Mochica, all other languages in my sample whose participial system is limited to a single absolutive participle are spoken in Europe,[56] namely Albanian, Irish, Modern Greek, Italian and Basque. Interestingly, Basque, the only non-Indo-European language in this set, is claimed by Hualde and Ortiz de Urbina (2003: 197) to have borrowed its absolutive participle in *-tu* from Latin.

The one language in my sample whose only participial form is passive is Nias; see example (209a). For relativizing other positions on the Accessibility Hierarchy, the language employs a finite strategy where the relative clause is introduced by the particle *si=*. This form differs from the participial clause in the ability to take TAM markers (e.g. perfective *ma=*) and personal agreement markers, as shown in (209b):

(209) Nias (Austronesian)
    a. *Tebai*   *lö'ö*   *la-doro*   *fakake*   [**ni-o-guna-'ö**]
        can't   NEG   3PL.REAL-carry   tools   PTCP.PASS-HAVE-use-TR
        'They have to carry any tools they'll need.' (Brown 2001: 420)

---

[56] However, according to Valentin Vydrin (p.c.), absolutive participial orientation seems to be common in other Mande languages than Beng, so some of them can behave similarly to Beng in this respect.

b. *Niha* [*si=ma=u-ßaßalö*   *kefe*] || *sibaya-gu*
person REL=PRF=1SG.REAL-borrow   money   uncle-1SG.POSS
'The person I borrowed money from is my uncle.' (Brown 2001: 417)

In a way, the existence of a single passive participle can be seen as contradicting the generalization by Keenan and Comrie (1977), who claim that each relativizing strategy has to apply to a continuous segment of the Accessibility Hierarchy starting from the left end. The *ni-* participle in Nias is the only representative of a non-finite strategy, and it can relativize direct objects, but it is unable to relativize subjects, which are higher in the Hierarchy. Moreover, Nias does not have any passive constructions otherwise, which challenges the analysis of the relativized participant as the subject of a previously passivized clause (a possibility discussed earlier in Section 3.3.3). Any decent explanation of this phenomenon would, however, require a profound investigation of Nias data, including all other possible relativization strategies in the language, which is not possible based on the available data.

It should be noted that since the relativization capacity of a single inherently oriented participle is limited to just one participant, languages of this type tend to have other relativization strategies to relativize at least some other participants; see also Section 3.8 on the connection between participial orientation and availability of finite relative clauses. For instance, Standard Average European languages typically employ relative pronouns (see, for instance, example (3a) from Russian), which allow to relativize all the positions on the Accessibility Hierarchy. The question of how the two strategies compete within a language is an interesting research topic in its own right, but one that is too broad to include in the scope of the current study.

7.2.2 Contextually oriented participle

A considerable number of languages in the sample (20 in total, listed in Table 32 in Section 7.8) have only one participle that is contextually oriented, that is, it can relativize different participants depending on the context. In fact, the relevant –TAM forms as defined in Section 5.2.1, can, by means of various TAM markers, create oppositions very similar to those attested in TAM-based participial systems (see Section 7.4). However, since there is still only one participial marker in these languages, I will discuss them here.

Almost all of the single contextually oriented forms demonstrate full orientation in the sense discussed in Section 3.5.1, that is, they can relativize a specific range of participants starting from the leftmost position on the Accessibility Hierarchy. Since these participles are the only participial forms in the respective languages, they can also commonly occur in different TAM contexts. In the majority of forms in question, the exact TAM meaning can either be conveyed by separate TAM markers, as shown in (210) from Lezgian, or inferred from the context; see examples from Apsheron Tat in (211) presented earlier in (144) and repeated here for convenience:

(210) Lezgian (Nakh-Daghestanian)
    a. *A   xwanaxwa.di-z   [q̇e   za   koncert.d-a ja-**da**-j]*
       that   friend-DAT   today I:ERG concert-INESS play-FUT-PTCP
      daldam   xutax-iz   k'an-zawa.
       drum   take.away-INF want-IPFV
      'That friend wants to take away the drum that I will play today at the concert.'
      (Haspelmath 1993: 155)
    b. *Dide.di   sufra   ek'ä-na,   axpa   ada-l   [hele*
       mother.ERG cloth   spread-AOR then   it-SRESS still
      *rga-**zma**-j]   samovar ecig-na.*
       boil-IPFV.CONT-PTCP samovar put-AOR
      'Mother spread out a cloth, and then she put a samovar on it that was still boiling.'
      (Haspelmath 1993: 156)
    c. *[Q'aradi-z awat-**aj**]   q̇izil   q'alu   že-da-c.*
       mud-DAT fall-PTCP.AOR gold   dirty   become-FUT-NEG
      'Gold which has fallen into the mud does not become dirty.'
      (Haspelmath 1993: 156)

(211) Apsheron Tat (Indo-European)
    a. [***rous-de***] *seg   dendu   ne-bzeren*
       bark-PTCP   dog   tooth   NEG-EVT.strike.3
      'A dog who barks does not bite.' (Authier 2012: 233)
    b. [***rous-de***] *seg   kuf-de   bü*
       bark-PTCP   dog   beat-PTCP be.PST.3
      'The dog who barked was beaten.' (Authier 2012: 233)

The first option, with TAM meanings expressed by separate markers, is attested, in addition to Lezgian, also in Garo (Sino-Tibetan), Hup (Nadahup), Kambaata (Afro-Asiatic), Malayalam (Dravidian), Mẽbengokre (Nuclear-Macro-Je), Nivkh (Nivkh), and Sheko (Dizoid). In all of these languages TAM expression can, of course, be subject to certain restrictions related to the process of desententialization discussed in detail in Section 5.2. The second option, with TAM interpretation primarily based on the context, is characteristic of participial relative clauses in Apsheron Tat (Indo-European), Chimariko (Chimariko), Coahuilteco (Coahuilteco), Ket (Yeniseian), Kharia (Austroasiatic), Manange (Sino-Tibetan), Motuna (South Bougainville), and Savosavo (Savosavo). No information on this question is available for Dhimal (Sino-Tibetan) and Hopi (Uto-Aztecan).[57]

Importantly, among single contextually oriented participles, there are almost no forms that are fixed in their temporal orientation, i.e. all of them can occur in different TAM contexts. The only possible counterexample is Pitta Pitta (Pama-Nyungan), where the participial marker -*ka* is only attested in past contexts (Blake 1979: 216–219). This marker, however, is diachronically related to the regular past tense marker, so this restriction probably reflects historical processes within the language. The observed tendency, apparently, follows from the fact that for many languages contextually oriented participles are the only (or primary) means of relativization in general (see Section 3.8 for a brief discussion of competition between relativization strategies). Therefore, they need to be versatile to allow the language to produce a wider variety of relative structures.

The only language with a single participial form demonstrating limited contextual orientation is Wan (Mande). Like the Nias participle in *ni-*, which is passive, the Wan attributive nominalization in *-ŋ* seems to contradict the Accessibility Hierarchy, since it freely relativizes participants from the lower part of the Hierarchy, but is not capable of subject (A/S) relativization. However, as discussed in Section 3.5.2, this phenomenon can be easily explained by the fact that Wan has an agent nominalization which is used to refer to A/S participants but cannot be employed for adnominal modification (Tatiana Nikitina, p.c.). This is not, therefore, a full-fledged participial form, but it covers the contexts of A/S relativization and prevents the attributive nominalization from occurring in this function.

---

57 In addition to these two major options, the orientation of certain participles can also be conditional on the temporal context. For instance, according to Yoshioka (2012: 90), in Eastern Burushaski (Burushaski), the only attested participle in *-um*, which has perfective meaning with no aspectual marking and imperfective meaning when attaching an imperfective suffix, changes its orientation depending on the aspect of the form: it has a passive reading when perfective, and an active reading when imperfective. This can be regarded as an instance of the common TAM-orientation asymmetry mentioned in Section 3.3.5. However, this case is not treated in detail in this book due to the lack of data. For instance, judging by examples provided in Klimov and Èdel'man (1970: 93–94), the particle in Burushaski can also be used to relativize locatives and possessors, so it may actually be contextually rather than inherently oriented.

7.3 Orientation-based systems

In this section, I will discuss systems based exclusively on the contrasts in orientation between the members of the participial paradigm (systems that additionally take into account TAM of the forms, such as Russian, German or Finnish, will be considered in Section 7.5). Such systems are found in 18 languages in the sample and listed in Table 33 in Section 7.8.

It is important to remember that the participial system found in a given language does not necessarily represent the relativizing capacity of the language in general. Many of the languages discussed in this study, have alternative relativization strategies, which may differ in the range of participants they can relativize. This is expecially common for languages with compact systems of inherently oriented participles specializing on core participant relativization, e.g. active vs. passive, or active vs. absolutive. For instance, languages of the Standard Average European type (see Haspelmath 2001), both Indo-European (e.g. Russian, German, Italian) and non-Indo-European (e.g. Finnish or Hungarian), widely employ relative pronouns as a means of relativization; see examples in (212) from English and Section 3.8 for some discussion:

(212) English (Indo-European)
 a. *The girl [**who** lives in this apartment] bakes the best cookies.*
    (Subject relativization)
 b. *The girl [**with whom** I used to study] now lives in Paris.*
    (Comitative relativization)
 c. *The girl [**whose** dog stole my door mat] refused to pay for it.*
    (Possessor relativization)

Moreover, even languages with contextually oriented participles that can relativize a broad range of core and peripheral participants, can also use balanced relative clauses. Dravidian languages, for example, widely use correlative structures (Asher and Kumari 1997: 52–53), while many Siberian languages that have been in close contact with Russian tend to develop the European type of relative clauses (Comrie 1998: 77–78). The distribution of distinct relativizing strategies within a specific language can be conditioned by a number of pragmatic and stylistic factors, apart from their relativizing capacity. This topic is, however, outside the scope of the current study, since I am only concerned with participial systems and their properties here.

In purely orientation-based systems, we find four recurrent types of oppositions: (1) active vs. passive, (2) absolutive vs. agentive, (3) subject vs. non-subect, and (4) threefold (mostly active vs. passive vs. oblique). In addition, two Sino-

Tibetan languages, Apatani and Ronghong Qiang, have unique orientation-based participial paradigms. I will deal with all of these cases in turn.

Languages with the first type of opposition include Middle Egyptian (Afro-Asiatic), Wolio (Austronesian), Wikchamni (Yokutsan), and Mapudungun (Araucanian). An unusual type of active-passive system, which has already been discussed earlier, is attested in West Greenlandic (Eskimo-Aleut). The active participle in *-soq* allows relativiziation of intransitive subjects (213a), whereas the passive participle in *-saq* is used for direct object relativization (213b):

(213) West Greenlandic (Eskimo-Aleut)
    a. *arnaq* [***suli-soq***]
       woman   work-PTCP.ACT.3SG
       'the/a woman who is working' (van der Voort 1991: 17)
    b. *angut* [*ippassaq* ***naapi-ta-ra***]   *sianiip-poq*
       man   yesterday meet-PTCP.PASS-POSS.1SG.ABS be.stupid-IND.3SG
       'The man I met yesterday is stupid.' (van der Voort 1991: 20)

Interestingly, West Greenlandic seems to have had a specialized participle *-si/-tsi/-(r)ti/-seq/-teq* for relativizing transitive subjects as well, but this suffix is no longer productive (van der Voort 1991: 18), thus leaving West Greenlandic only with the means to relativize S and P participants.[58] This can be regarded as another illustration of the relevance of absolutive orientation for participial relativization (see Section 3.3.5), even though in this case it is the whole system that shows absolutive pattern, and not a single participle.

Two languages in my sample show a strict absolutive–agentive opposition in their participial paradigms, namely, Panare (Cariban, Payne and Payne 2013), and Urarina (Urarina, Olawsky 2006). The system in Urarina is illustrated in (74) in Section 3.3.4. Similarly, the agentive participle in *-jpo* in Panare can only relativize A participants (214a), whereas the past participle in *-sa'* is suitable for both S and P relativization, as shown in (214b) and (214c) respectively:

---

58 A similar diachronic development is reported for Tat (Indo-European). In Old Persian, from which, according to Authier (2012: 232), Tat inherited its only participial form in *-de/-re*, the corresponding participle was absolutive, and another participle, in *-ân*, was employed for the relativization of an agent. Tat, however, lost the form in *-ân* altogether. As argued by Authier, the loss of a means to relativize transitive subjects then led to the expansion of the relativization capacity of the remaining form in *-de/-re*, which switched to contextual orientation, possibly also due to the influence of East Caucasian languages widely employing contextually oriented participles.

(214) Panare (Cariban)
   a. *Yu tu-mu'na'-yaj   apoj   [aro y-utu-**jpo**   y-ïpïj   kuya]*.
      1SG 1SG-deceive-PPERF man   rice TR-give-PTCP.A 3-wife   DAT
      'I deceived the man who gave rice to his wife.'
      (Payne and Payne 2013: 46)
   b. *Ñi-yaj   Toma   asonwa   kanawa   [kïmï-**sa'**]*.
      see-PPERF   Tom   three   canoe   rot-PTCP.PST
      'Tom saw three rotten canoes.'
      (Payne and Payne 2013: 281)
   c. *Kara-pe-putu   [y-apopë-**sa'**]   t-aparentya   amën   amen*.
      good-ADF.NEW-AUG   TR-record-PTCP.PST   GNO-learn   you   now
      'You may learn very well now what has been recorded (i.e., on a casette tape).' (Payne and Payne 2013: 125)

The last type of binary system is based on an opposition between the subject and all other participants. It is attested in Aguaruna (Chicham), Dolakha Newar (Sino-Tibetan), and Maricopa (Cochimi-Yuman). For example, in Dolakha Newar, the nominalization in *-gu* is used to relativize subjects (215a), while the nominalization in *-a* appears in all other contexts, such as direct object relativization (215b), or locative relativization (215c):

(215) Dolakha Newar (Sino-Tibetan)
   a. *[pali   depān   **coŋ-gu**]   kok*
      roof   on   stay-NMZ.SUBJ crow
      'the crow that is on the roof' (Genetti 2007: 312)
   b. *[jin   **phoŋ-a**]   misā*
      1SG.ERG ask.for-NMZ.NS woman
      'the woman whom I asked for (in marriage)' (Genetti 2007: 313)
   c. *[thamun   je   **yeŋ-a**]   ṭhãĩ*
      2HON.ERG work do-NMZ.NS   place
      'the place where you work' (Genetti 2007: 313)

Regarding the diachronic development of such systems, Genetti (2007: 406–407) suggests that in Dolakha Newar, there used to be a 1st/2nd person nominalizer and a 3rd person nominalizer. The former was reanalyzed as the non-subject nominalizer, and the latter as the subject nominalizer. Indeed, 1st and 2nd person pronouns do not usually occur as heads of relative clauses, since the identity of the 1st and 2nd person is recoverable from the discourse context. Subject relative clauses with 1st and 2nd person subjects, therefore, do not make much sense, which allows for the reanalysis of the 3rd person nominalizer to a marker of subject relative clauses. The original 1st/2nd person nominalizer, consequently, takes up non-subject relativization.[59] The subject vs. non-subject binary distinction can also, to a certain extent, be observed in the languages where passive participles allow for occasional orientation extension, e.g. Russian *obitaemyj ostrov* 'the island where someone lives', or Finnish *asuttu saari* with the same meaning; see Section 3.3.3.

The fourth type is represented by six languages from different geographical macroareas, which show a threefold distinction in their orientation-based participial systems. Kamaiurá (Tupian) uses different means for relativizing each of the core participants, A, S and P, as discussed in Section 3.3.2 and shown in example (64). Japhug rGyalrong (Sino-Tibetan) and Seri (Seri) distinguish between an active participle, a passive participle, and an oblique participle that is used for relativizing all the other participants available for relativization in a given language. On the other hand, Ma'di (Central Sudanic), Cocama (Tupian), and Guarijío (Uto-Aztecan) have three inherently oriented participles. In addition to active and passive participles, Ma'di has a form in -*dʒɔ́* used to relativize instruments and purposes, Cocama has a locative nominalization in -*tupa*, and Guarijío has a locative nominalization in -*ači*.

Finally, Apatani and Ronghong Qiang have unusual participial paradigms not attested elsewhere. Both languages have an instrumental nominalization/participle, which, according to Genetti et al. (2008), is not uncommon for Sino-Tibetan languages; see example (84) for Apatani, and example (85) for Qiang in Section 3.4. In addition, Apatani has a form with full contextual orientation up to indirect objects; see example (55) in Section 3.2. As with the case of subject vs. non-subject opposition, this results in a participial paradigm covering a substantial part of the Accessibility Hierarchy. This system, however, is peculiar in that an inherently oriented form is used for the lower part of this segment. In Ronghong Qiang, the second participial form also has a fairly flexible orientation, but this orientation is formulated in semantic rather than morphosyntactic terms: as discussed in Section 3.8, the -*m* nominalization in Qiang is oriented towards animate participants. Unlike in Apatani, the complete set of forms used for relativization in Ronghong Qiang includes one more form, the genitive marker -*tɕ* used primarily for relativizing undergoers (LaPolla and Huang 2003: 225–226). This marker, however, is not considered in this study, since it belongs primarily

---

59 This scenario is supported by the fact that Sino-Tibetan nominalizations are multifunctional and appear in complement clauses as well, otherwise the 1st/2nd person relativizer/nominalizer would not have emerged in the first place.

to the domain of nominal morphology and does not qualify as a participial marker.

7.4 TAM-based systems

When a language has several participial forms with the same orientation, the participial system is in most cases based on TAM distinctions demonstrated by the forms. This section provides an overview of the languages of this type found in my sample. It is important to emphasize, once again, that I only consider affirmative participial paradigms here, while negative participles and their properties have already been discussed in Section 5.3.2. In my sample, there are 15 languages with TAM-based participial paradigms. They are listed in Table 34 in Section 7.8.

Quite naturally, if a language has several participial forms oriented towards the same (or almost the same) range of participants, these forms are usually contextually oriented, since this is the type of orientation that allows a participle to function in the widest possible range of contexts. As shown in Section 5.2.3, in many such cases the TAM system is reduced in comparison with the system of finite forms. In my sample, one language, Nanga (Dogon), has a twofold distinction between perfective and imperfective participles, two languages, Nanai (Tungusic) and Northern Khanty (Uralic), distinguish between past and non-past, and one more, Tamil (Dravidian), has an opposition between future and non-future (Lehmann 1993: 284).[60] Most other languages have a tripartite system. Interestingly, only two of them, Yakut (Turkic) and Imbabura Quechua (Quechuan) distinguish between past, present and future. The rest tend to "mix" temporal, aspectual and modal meanings, as well as absolute and relative tense, in their participial systems. Telugu (Dravidian) has a past participle, a future-habitual participle, and a durative participle. Korean (Koreanic) has a present relative form, a present/past relative form, and a future/presumptive relative form. The distinction is between preterite, present, and potential in Tanti Dargwa, and between past, present and simultaneous in Ingush (both Nakh-Daghestanian). Even (Tungusic) has five participial forms with different temporal and modal meanings; see Section 5.2.3. Finally, Luiseño (Uto-Aztecan), Marathi (Indo-European) and Wappo (Yuki-Wappo) have complicated TAM-based systems of contextually oriented forms (although in Marathi and Wappo it is not entirely clear if they

---

60 In the case of Tamil, there is, in fact, also a cross-linguistically relatively rare opposition between a +TAM form and a –TAM form within one language; see Section 5.2.1.

should be considered as separate forms, or as instances of a single derivational process, which in this case could be regarded as a peculiar –TAM marker).

The only language in the sample that has a TAM-based system that is not contextually oriented is Koryak, which distinguishes between non-future nominalization (216a), and future nominalization (216b):

(216) Koryak (Chukotko-Kamchatkan, Kurebito 2011: 22–23)[61]
    a. *kalikal,*   [ʕamin   ajyəve   qajəkmiŋ-a   jəlŋ-ə-**lʕ**-ə-n]
        book.ABS.SG   INTRJ   yesterday   boy-INS/ERG   read-EP-NMZ-EP-ABS.SG
        'the book which the boy read yesterday'
    b. *kalikal,*   [ʕamin   mitiw   yəmnan   akmec-**co-lqəl**-Ø]
        book.ABS.SG   INTRJ   tomorrow   I.ERG   buy-NMZ-NOMFUT-ABS.SG
        'the book which I will buy tomorrow'

Both Koryak forms, as I have shown in Section 3.3.5, demonstrate absolutive orientation. Information on the functioning of participles in Koryak is, however, very limited, so any discussion of the motivation of such an exceptional system remains beyond the scope of this study.

7.5 Orientation and TAM-based systems

Orientation and TAM characteristics are clearly the most relevant criteria for the organization of participial systems in languages throughout the world. As I have shown in the preceding sections, each of these two parameters can function on its own, but it is also quite common for languages to have participial systems based on both orientation and TAM simultaneously. Systems of this kind will be examined in the current section. I will start with symmetric participial systems, where orientation and TAM are independent from each other (7.5.1), and then proceed to asymmetric participial systems, where the two parameters are interrelated (7.5.2). The list of languages with orientation and TAM-oriented systems is provided in Table 35 in Section 7.8.

---

61 In these examples, participial relative clauses start with an element that Kurebito (2011) glosses as "interjection", while it appears to have a function very similar to complementizers in other languages. If this was the only type of participial clauses available in Koryak, they would not be classified as participial according to the definition given in Section 2.3. However, relativization by means of non-finite forms is possible in Koryak without the "interjection", so these examples can still be used as an illustration.

7.5.1 Symmetric systems

An example of a symmetric participial system is Standard Russian (Indo-European), where the participial paradigm is built on a binary opposition in orientation (active vs. passive) and a binary opposition in tense (present vs. past), as presented in Table 22:

Tab. 22: Participial system in Standard Russian

	Active	Passive
Past	-vš-	-n-/-t-
Present	-ušč-/-ašč-	-em-/-im-

A similar system is also found in Lithuanian (Indo-European, Ambrazas 2006: 326–346), the only difference being the number of tenses. Lithuanian has preterite, present, future (derived from the present), and habitual (derived from the past) participles, both for active and for passive (though see below), which is parallel to the system of finite synthetic verb forms. Fula (Atlantic-Congo, Arnott 1970: 373–374) has a system of six participles, with two tenses (past and future) and three voices (active, middle, and passive).

Interestingly, among these three systems, only the one in Fula is fully symmetric (or so it seems, since fairly little information on participles in Fula is available). In addition to the four forms attested in Standard Russian (see Table 22 above), speakers commonly produce at least future active participles, which were discussed earlier in Section 5.2.5; see example (151a). Future passive participles, on the other hand, are almost never attested. The participial paradigm in Lithuanian lacks a passive habitual participle, and, as a result, the language has only seven participial forms instead of expected eight. These minor deficiencies even in the most symmetric participial systems, as well as the fact that all the other orientation and TAM-based systems are asymmetric, can be regarded as indicative of the fact that participial orientation and TAM characteristics of participles are not fully independent parameters. This thesis will be further illustrated in the next section, and later discussed in more detail in Section 7.8.

7.5.2 Asymmetric systems

First, as shown in Haspelmath (1994), participial systems with active and passive forms tend to be asymmetric. The forms that are most likely to exist in natural languages are present active participles and past passive participles; see Table 23 for an example of the simplest participial system of this kind in Modern Standard Arabic (Haspelmath 1994: 156):

Tab. 23: Participial system in Modern Standard Arabic

	Active	**Passive**
Past		*maktūbu* write.PTCP.PASS
Present	*kātibu* write.PTCP.ACT	

Relatively simple asymmetric systems of a similar kind are also attested in German, Hungarian, Eastern Armenian, Erzya, North Saami, Georgian, and Tarma Quechua. In all of these languages, active participles are typically present or habitual, while passive or resultative forms are past, perfective, or resultative. In addition to these two types of participles, Tsafiki (Barbacoan) has a form with instrumental/locative orientation, but the basic asymmetry is the same there as well. In Kayardild (Tangkic), which also has two inherently oriented forms that differ in TAM meaning, the active participle has a relative past meaning, but the second form, in line with the general tendency, is resultative and can relativize at least P participants, but presumably also S (see footnote 17 in Section 3.3.5). These observations further strengthen the idea discussed in Sections 3.3.5, 3.8, and 5.2.4, that passive/absolutive resultative participles tend to be important for typologically diverse languages. Judging from the available data, this asymmetric pattern may also be present in Wikchamni (Yokutsan), where the agentive verbal noun tends to refer to habitual actions, while the passive verbal noun usually refers to past events (Gamble 1978: 70–72). The data, however, is too limited to confidently classify this system as asymmetric.

Another type of asymmetry is attested in Tümpisa Shoshone (Uto-Aztecan), which also has both TAM and orientation splits within the participial system. In the TAM domain, it shows an opposition between past/perfective and present/simultaneous, and the opposition in orientation is subject vs. non-subject.

However, instead of expected four forms, Tümpisa Shoshone only has three, lacking a form for subject relativization in past/perfective contexts; see Table 24 based on Dayley (1989: 358):

Tab. 24: Participial system in Tümpisa Shoshone

	Subject	Non-Subject
Past/Perfective		-ppüh
Present/Simultaneous	-tün	-nna

Koorete (Ta-Ne-Omotic) also shows an opposition between subject and non-subject participial forms, but instead of an empty cell in the paradigm, it has the opposition in orientation neutralized for one of the TAM values. Participles in Koorete can be perfective and imperfective. The perfective participial paradigm consists of two forms. The form in -*a* is employed for relativizing S and A participants (active orientation), while the form in -*o* is claimed to be used in all other cases (Hayward provides examples of P relativization and locative relativization, so apparently this is an instance of limited contextual orientation). The single imperfective participial form in -*e*, on the other hand, can relativize both subject and non-subject participants (the examples given in the grammar actually illustrate only S and P relativization, but the author reports no restrictions, so it can be assumed that the imperfective form has full contextual orientation; I do not, however, consider this form when providing the relevant counts). The system is presented in Table 22 based on Hayward (1982: 254–257):

Tab. 25: Participial system in Koorete

	Subject	Non-Subject
Perfective	-a	-o
Imperfective		-e

A similar situation is found in Meadow Mari (Uralic, Brykina and Aralova 2012), which has an active participle which can be used to relativize the subject of either transitive or intransitive verb, a multifunctional participle which allows the relativization of several lower positions of the Accessibility Hierarchy starting from the direct object, and a contextually oriented participle with full orientation. In examples below, the *-əše* participial form is used for subject relativization (217a), whereas the form realized as *-əmo*, *-mo* or *-me* depending on the morphophonemic context can relativize, for instance, the direct object (217b), the indirect object (217c), the locative argument (217d), and the possessor (217e):

(217) Meadow Mari (Uralic)
    a. *Me [korn-əm sajən **pal-əše**] šoför de-ne mutlan-ena.*
       we way-ACC well know-PTCP.ACT driver near-INESS talk-PRS.1PL
       'We are talking to the driver who knows the way well.'
       (Brykina and Aralova 2012: 480)
    b. *[Təj-ən **kuč'-əmo**] kugu kol-et peš tamle.*
       you(SG)-GEN catch-PTCP.NS big fish-POSS.2SG very delicious
       'The big fish that you caught is very delicious.'
       (Brykina and Aralova 2012: 485)
    c. *[Təj-ən tunem-mašte **polš-əmo**] rvez-et de-ne kaj-em*
       you(SG)-GEN study-VN.INESS help-PTCP.NS boy-POSS.2SG near-INESS go-PRS.1SG
       'I am walking with the boy whom you have helped in his studies.'
       (Brykina and Aralova 2012: 481)
    d. *[Saša-n **košt-mo**] pölem – məj-ən pört-em.*
       Sasha-GEN enter-PTCP.NS room I-GEN house-POSS.1SG
       'The room into which Sasha entered is my home.'
       (Brykina and Aralova 2012: 487)
    e. *[Saša-n ukš-əm püč'k-ən **nal-me**] pušeŋge košk-en.*
       Sasha-GEN branch-ACC break-CVB take-PTCP.NS tree dry.up-PRET
       'The tree whose branch Sasha broke has dried up.'
       (Brykina and Aralova 2012: 483)

The first two forms are fairly free in their TAM characteristics, and can refer to all kinds of situations in past or present contexts. The use of the third participle with wider orientation, by contrast, is restricted to future contexts. The participial system of Meadow Mari is summarized in Table 26:

Tab. 26: Participial system in Meadow Mari

	Subject	Non-Subject
Non-Future	-še	-me
Future	-šaš	

Some other Uralic languages show a very similar type of system, in particular Beserman Udmurt and Komi-Zyrian; see Appendices 3a and 3b. In Tundra Nenets, the future participle stands out as well, although in a different way: while being oriented towards core participants, it does not have a counterpart for the lower part of the Accessibility Hierarchy, unlike the past and present forms, as shown in Table 27:[62]

Tab. 27: Participial system in Tundra Nenets

	Core participants	Non-Core participants
Past	-miə/-me	-(o)qm(')a
Present	-n(')a/-t(')a	-m(')a and -s'ə/-ə
Future	-mənta	

In Finnish, the system also has a minor asymmetry: it is primarily based on two binary oppositions (active vs. passive, present vs. past), but has an additional P-oriented form that, unlike the other two passive participles, requires the agent to be expressed; see Section 3.3.3 and example (68).

7.6 Complex orientation + TAM systems

In this section, I will provide an overview of four complex participial systems in which several parameters are at play that do not interact with each other in a clearly structured and symmetric way. All four systems have both inherently and

---

[62] Setting aside the exact relativizing capacity of the forms, the participial paradigm in Tundra Nenets is very similar to the system in Russian discussed in Section 7.5.1. I analysed the latter as symmetric due to the problematic status of the future participles in the standard language (see Section 5.2.5), but in fact, spoken Russian shows a type of asymmetry that is very similar to the one in Tundra Nenets.

contextually oriented participles, and two of them also have both –TAM and +TAM participles.

In the first three of these languages, there is one type of orientation that stands out in the paradigm. Kalmyk, for example, has three contextually oriented participial forms which differ in their temporal and aspectual characteristics, and one form with inherent orientation, namely the resultative passive participle in *-ata*, as shown in Table 28. This once again supports the idea that resultative participles have a special status; see Section 5.2.4 for some discussion.

Tab. 28: Participial system in Kalmyk

	Contextually oriented	Inherently oriented
Past	*-sən*	
Future	*-xə*	
Habitual	*-dəg*	
Resultative		*-ata*

The sentences below illustrate the use of the contextually oriented past participle in *-sən* for indirect object relativization (218a), instrument relativization (218b), and direct object relativization (218c). Naturally, since participles with full contextual orientation are able to relativize P participants, in resultative contexts both the *-sən* participle and the *-ata* participle can be used; see (218d). Unfortunately, no data is available on the distribution of the forms in this case.

(218) Kalmyk (Mongolic)
    a. [mini kičəg ög-sən] küük-üd nan-də en cecg-igə ögə-v
       I.GEN puppy give-PTCP.PST girl-PL I-DAT this flower-ACC give-PST
       'The girls whom I gave a puppy gave me this flower.'
       (Krapivina 2009a: 498–501, 519)
    b. [mini alʲmə zur-sən] šir širä deerə kevt-nä
       I.GEN apple draw-PTCP.PST paint table surface lie-PRS
       'The paint with which I drew the apple is on the table.'
       (Krapivina 2009a: 500)
    c. [mini al-sən] ükər dala üsə ög-dəg bilä
       I.GEN kill-PTCP.PST cow much milk give-PTCP.HAB be.REM
       'The cow that I killed used to give a lot of milk.'
       (Krapivina 2009a: 501)

d. *Badma* [*xojr zu-n   ǯil   ardə ke-sən   /ke-ʁätä*
   Badma two hundred-EXT year back make-PTCP.PST /make-PTCP.PASS
   širä   xamxər-čkə-v
   table   break-COMPL-PST
   'Badma has broken the table that was made two hundred years ago!'
   (Krapivina 2009a: 519)

In the other two languages, the orientation that behaves differently in a paradigm is locative. In Hinuq (Nakh-Daghestanian), the system is similar to Kalmyk in that it also has several contextually oriented forms (general, past, habitual, and resultative), and one inherently oriented form, locative participle in -*a*. The difference, however, is in the temporal characteristics of the locative participle, which can have any time reference depending on the context. In other words, it is both the only inherently oriented participle in the system, and the only –TAM form. In Nevome (Uto-Aztecan), the locative orientation stands out in a different way. The paradigm consists of a habitual participle with presumably active orientation, a future resultative participle with presumably passive orientation (too little data is available to determine the exact orientation of these forms), and four locative participles with different TAM characteristics; see Appendix 3b.

A very complicated participial system can be found in Matsés (Pano-Tacanan). First, the language has two sets of relativizers/nominalizers which differ in the factors that regulate their distribution. The first set of suffixes derives contextually oriented verb forms that can refer to virtually any participant, and the choice of the actual form is defined by tense/evidentiality distinctions. The second set of suffixes, which is more common in discourse, derives verb forms that do not show any tense distinctions, but are used depending on the relativized participant, i.e. they demonstrate inherent orientation. The temporal reference of the relative clause, however, does play a role in this case as well, since it determines the exact orientation of inherently oriented verb forms. For instance, the suffix -*quid*, which is used to refer to all types of subjects in present or generic contexts and can thereby be classified as an active participle, shows ergative orientation when used to encode the events in the recent past (unfortunately, the only available grammar of Matsés does not provide any good sentential examples to illustrate this ergativity split). The suffix -*aid* is only used to relativize direct objects and affected peripheral participants (APP) in present or generic contexts, while in recent past it can relativize anything except for transitive subjects. All information on the participial system of Matsés is summarized in Table 29 taken from Fleck (2003: 316):

Tab. 29: Participial system in Matsés

	Remote past		Distant past		Recent past		Present/ Generic	Future
	Observ.	Infer.	Observ.	Infer.	Observ.	Infer.		
A						-quid	-quid	-quid
S								
P	-ampid	-denned	-nëdaid	-ondaid	-boed	-aid	-aid	
INS							-te	-te
APP							-aid	

Another language with a participial system that seems particularly complex is Tariana (Arawakan), but unfortunately, the information on the distribution of the participial forms is very limited (though see Appendices 3a and 3b for some details).

7.7 Other criteria for classification

Finally, it should be mentioned that in certain cases neither participial orientation nor TAM meaning can fully account for the distribution of participial forms in a given language. For instance, Kolyma Yukaghir has two contextually oriented forms that are commonly used for relative clause formation, the active attributive form in *-je* and the action nominal in *-l*. The range of participants that can be relativized by these forms is almost the same, and both of them inflect for tense in the same fashion, so none of these two parameters is crucial for the choice of the form. On the other hand, when the head of a relative clause is indefinite, only the *-je* form can be used. First, this is reflected in the fact that only the head nouns modified by this form can be accompanied by the numeral determiner *irkin* 'one' indicating indefiniteness; see (219a). Second, even when this determiner is not present, the relative clause whose head's indefiniteness is inferred from the previous context, can only have the *-je* form as its predicate; see (219b):

(219) Kolyma Yukaghir (Yukaghir)
    a. *irkin ʃoromə jaqdat'ə-lə* **irkin** [*omnii modo-jə*] *meestə-ŋin*
       one person horse-INS one people live-ATTR.ACT place-DAT
      kebe-s'.
      go.away-IND.INTR.3
      'One man went by horse to a place where the people lived.'
      (Nikolaeva 1997: 21, as cited in Nagasaki 2014: 91)

b. *met   tudaa   [amdə-j]   ʃoromə   əl=juɵ-je   n'ə=qajin.*
   1SG   before   die-ATTR.ACT   person   NEG=see-IND.INTR.1SG   NEG=when
   'I never saw dead person before.'
   (Nikolaeva 1997: 55, as cited in Nagasaki 2014: 91)

By contrast, relative clauses expressing propositions familiar to the hearer and having definite noun phrases as their heads can employ both non-finite forms as their predicates. Thus, the *-l* form appears to be restricted to relative clauses with definite head nouns, while the *-je* form has no restrictions regarding the pragmatic status of the relativized participant. Presumably, this kind of pragmatic motivation can reflect one of the first steps in the development of the regular participial orientation, since different participants are not typically equal in their definiteness status. This issue, however, needs further language-internal investigation before any claims can be made regarding a possible diachronic development.

In the Muna language (Austronesian), direct object relative clauses can be formed with two different types of deranked verb forms, which do not seem to show any semantic or functional difference (van den Berg 2013: 235). The first form is a passive participle in *ni-*, and the second is a nominalization marked by the prefix *ka-*. Both types of relative clauses are clearly deranked, since they have very limited capacity for expressing tense, and they encode agents as possessors (van den Berg 2013: 230–238). The only parameter with respect to which the two types clearly differ is the degree of nominalization/deranking, the latter form being more nominalized; see Section 5.3.1 for discussion. This distinction, however, is clearly fully language specific, and should be explained by certain diachronic processes rather than by any functional motivations.

Barasano (Tucanoan, Jones and Jones 1991) seems to have two types of markers that can qualify as participles as defined in this study. These forms differ with respect to a number of parameters. Markers of the first type (referred to as nominalizers) contain some information on TAM of the resulting form, allow for additional TAM markers, and reflect gender and number of the participant or the relativized noun (for animates); see (220a)–(220b). The marker of the second type (referred to as a participial marker) does not have any TAM meaning of its own, does not allow for additional TAM markers, and takes classifiers to refer to the head noun; see (220c):

(220) Barasano (Tucanoan)
    a. *bue-go*
       study-NMZ.PRS/PST.F.SG
       'female student' (Jones and Jones 1991: 43)
    b. *bue-ka-ko*
       study-PSTFAR-NMZ.PROX.F.SG
       'past female student' (Jones and Jones 1991: 43)
    c. *hũɨ*   [õ   kãhi-ri-kɨ]   ãbo-a-ha   yɨ
       hammock there hang-PTCP-hammock want-PRS-NON3 1SG
       'I want that hammock which is hanging there.'
       (Jones and Jones 1991: 150)

In addition, the participle in Barasano is inherently subject-oriented (although it allows for orientation extension by means of an affix; see Section 3.6.1 on this option), while nominalizations can relativize at least all of the core participants (Jones and Jones 1991: 146–149; the exact relativizing capacity of Barasano nominalizations is, unfortunately, unknown). In other words, it is impossible to formulate a single criterion distinguishing between these two types of forms in Barasano, so they are better seen as different means of relativization rather than a system of forms based on clear oppositions.

7.8 Summary and conclusions

In the present chapter, I have discussed possible criteria for the organization of participial paradigms, and proposed a preliminary classification of the systems attested in the languages of the sample. As I have shown, participial systems are most commonly based on orientation (7.3), TAM properties of the forms (7.4), or on both of these criteria simultaneously (7.5 and 7.6). I have also provided an overview of participles that do not form an opposition with any other participial forms (7.2). Data on all the participial systems in the languages of the sample is summarized in Tables from 31 to 36 in the end of this section, and the geographical distribution of systems is presented on the map in Figure 15.

    The data presented in the chapter allows for two important generalizations regarding the organization of participial systems in the languages of the sample. The first one concerns the applicability of the Accessibility Hierarchy to separate participles and participial systems. Based on the investigation of relative clauses in a sample of 80 languages, Cristofaro (2003) formulates the following generalization:

(221) If deranked verb forms (in particular, forms showing no TAM or person agreement distinctions, or forms with case marking or adpositions) are used for a role less accessible to relativization, then they are used for the roles more accessible to relativization. (Cristofaro 2003: 208)

This generalization obviously does not hold if applied to individual participles. The most obvious counterexamples are various forms inherently oriented towards certain peripheral participants, such as instrumentals and locatives; see Section 3.4 for more information. The generalization does work, however, if considered in connection with participial systems. It can, therefore be reformulated in the following way to better account for the observed diversity:

(222) If a language has a participial form inherently oriented towards a certain participant, then it tends to have participial forms inherently oriented towards all the participants more accessible to relativization.[63]

This generalization can be seen as complementing Keenan and Comrie's (1977) claim regarding the availability of a certain relativization strategy for a continuous segment of the Accessibility Hierarchy. It confirms the original observation, while at the same time highlighting the peculiarity of participial forms among the range of various relativization strategies.[64]

The second important generalization stems from the fact that almost all participial systems considered in this study are asymmetric if they are based on both orientation and TAM characteristics of participial forms. Based on this, we can conclude that these two parameters are not independent from each other but rather tightly intertwined. Importantly, it is exactly these two parameters that are definitional for participles as a comparative concept, as discussed in Section 2.3. Functionally, participles are forms specializing in relativization, so the range of participants that an individual form can relativize is one of its crucial properties. Formally, participles must show morphosyntactic deviation from the finite prototype, which is commonly manifested in TAM expression. The fact that the values of these parameters are interdependent can be seen as strengthening the status of participles as a cross-linguistically valid category.

---

[63] I am grateful to Alexander Piperski for raising discussion of this issue at the XII Conference on Typology and Grammar for Young Scholars (Saint Petersburg, 19–21 November 2015).
[64] The only notable exception to this generalization is Hinuq (Nakh-Daghestanian), which has four contextually oriented participles and a locative participle, but the latter also stands out in the paradigm otherwise; see Sections 3.4 and 7.6.

I have also shown throughout the study that particular combinations of orientation and TAM are especially common, both among forms that belong to more or less complex participial paradigms, and forms that are single participles in the respective languages. Active participles often refer to habitual events, and absolutive participles are mostly perfective or resultative, while the reverse combinations of features are rarely attested; see Sections 3.3.5, 7.2.1, and 7.5.2. This observation is in line with earlier studies on interrelation between morphosyntactic alignment and TAM, which claimed a connection between ergativity and perfectivity, such as DeLancey (1981, 1990). These studies were later criticized for proposing far-fetched functional explanations where a diachronic account has more explanatory power (see Cristofaro 2012). However, since participles are a well-known source of ergativity in independent clauses (see DeLancey 1986, Noonan 1997, and Gildea 1998, among others), such explanations focusing specifically on participles are probably the best way to approach this issue in functional terms. I do not aim to speculate on the possible motivations behind the asymmetry in question, but in this book I hope to have shown that it is on many levels fundamental for participles in a typological perspective.

Fig. 15: Participial systems in the languages of the core sample (● – single inherently oriented form, ✚ – single contextually oriented form, ◆ – orientation-based, ■ – TAM-based, ★ – orientation and TAM-based, ▲ – other oppositions)

Tab. 30: Different types of participial systems across languages

Type of system	Subtype of system	Languages
Single participle	Active	9
	Passive	1
	Absolutive	7
	Full contextual orientation	19
	Limited contextual orientation	1
Orientation-based	Active vs. Passive	5
	Absolutive vs. Agentive	2
	Subject vs. Non-Subject	3
	Threefold	6
	Other	2
TAM-based	Twofold	5
	Threefold	6
	More values	4
Orientation and TAM-based	Symmetric	3
	Asymmetric	17
	Complex	4
Other criteria for classification		3
Unclassified (little data)		3

Tab. 31: Languages with a single inherently oriented participle

Subtype	Macroarea	Family	Language
Active participle	Australia	Garrwan	Garrwa
		Mirndi	Wambaya
		Pama-Nyungan	Martuthunira
	Papunesia	Lower Sepik-Ramu	Yimas
		Nuclear Trans New Guinea	Kobon
	South America	Cofán	Cofán
	Africa	Afro-Asiatic	Rif Berber
		Kadugli-Krongo	Krongo
		Maban	Maba

Subtype	Macroarea	Family	Language
Passive participle	Papunesia	Austronesian	Nias
Absolutive participle	South America	Mochica	Mochica
	Africa	Mande	Beng
	Eurasia	Basque	Basque
		Indo-European	Albanian
			Irish
			Italian
			Modern Greek

Tab. 32: Languages with a single contextually oriented participle

Subtype	Macroarea	Family	Language
Full contextual orientation	Australia	Pama-Nyungan	Pitta Pitta
	Papunesia	Savosavo	Savosavo
		South Bougainville	Motuna
	North America	Chimariko	Chimariko
		Coahuilteco	Coahuilteco
		Uto-Aztecan	Hopi
	South America	Nadahup	Hup
		Nuclear-Macro-Je	Mẽbengokre
	Africa	Afro-Asiatic	Kambaata
		Dizoid	Sheko
	Eurasia	Austroasiatic	Kharia
		Dravidian	Malayalam
		Indo-European	Apsheron Tat
		Nakh-Daghestanian	Lezgian
		Nivkh	Nivkh
		Sino-Tibetan	Dhimal
			Garo
			Manange
		Yeniseian	Ket
Limited contextual orientation	Africa	Mande	Wan

Tab. 33: Languages with an orientation-based system

Subtype	Macroarea	Family	Language
Active vs. Passive	Papunesia	Austronesian	Wolio
	North America	Eskimo-Aleut	West Greenlandic
		Yokutsan	Wikchamni
	South America	Araucanian	Mapudungun
	Africa	Afro-Asiatic	Middle Egyptian
Absolutive vs. Agentive	South America	Cariban	Panare
		Urarina	Urarina
Subject vs. Non-Subject	North America	Cochimi-Yuman	Maricopa
	South America	Chicham	Aguaruna
	Eurasia	Sino-Tibetan	Dolakha Newar
Threefold	North America	Seri	Seri
		Uto-Aztecan	Guarijío
	South America	Tupian	Cocama
			Kamaiurá
	Africa	Central Sudanic	Ma'di
	Eurasia	Sino-Tibetan	Japhug rGyalrong
Other	Eurasia	Sino-Tibetan	Apatani
			Ronghong Qiang

Tab. 34: Languages with a TAM-based system

Subtype	Macroarea	Family	Language
Twofold	Africa	Dogon	Nanga
	Eurasia	Chukotko-Kamchatkan	Koryak
		Dravidian	Tamil
		Tungusic	Nanai
		Uralic	Northern Khanty

Subtype	Macroarea	Family	Language
Threefold	South America	Quechuan	Imbabura Quechua
	Eurasia	Dravidian	Telugu
		Koreanic	Korean
		Nakh-Daghestanian	Tanti Dargwa
			Ingush
		Turkic	Yakut
More values	North America	Uto-Aztecan	Luiseño
		Yuki-Wappo	Wappo
	Eurasia	Indo-European	Marathi
		Tungusic	Even

Tab. 35: Languages with an orientation and TAM-based system

Subtype	Macroarea	Family	Language
Symmetric	Africa	Atlantic-Congo	Fula
	Eurasia	Indo-European	Lithuanian
			Russian
Asymmetric (including complex)	Australia	Tangkic	Kayardild
	North America	Uto-Aztecan	Nevome
			Tümpisa Shoshone
	South America	Barbacoan	Tsafiki
		Pano-Tacanan	Matsés
		Quechuan	Tarma Quechua
	Africa	Ta-Ne-Omotic	Koorete
	Eurasia	Afro-Asiatic	Modern Standard Arabic
		Indo-European	Eastern Armenian
			German
		Kartvelian	Georgian
		Mongolic	Kalmyk
		Nakh-Daghestanian	Hinuq
		Uralic	Beserman Udmurt
			Erzya
			Finnish

Subtype	Macroarea	Family	Language
Asymmetric	Eurasia	Uralic	Hungarian
			Komi-Zyrian
			Meadow Mari
			North Saami
			Tundra Nenets

Tab. 36: Languages with other oppositions and unclassified languages

Subtype	Macroarea	Family	Language
Other oppositions	Papunesia	Austronesian	Muna
	South America	Tucanoan	Barasano
	Eurasia	Yukaghir	Kolyma Yukaghir
Unclassified	North America	Kalapuyan	Santiam Kalapuya
	South America	Arawakan	Tariana
	Eurasia	Burushaski	Burushaski

8 Conclusions and further prospects

8.1 Summary of the findings

This book aimed at filling a gap in the literature on non-finite verb forms and relativization. One of its primary goals was to introduce participles as a cross-linguistically valid and consistent category to typological studies and studies of individual languages. In order to do this, it was necessary to identify exactly how participles differ from similar typological concepts, such as nominalizations, converbs, infinitives, etc. These aspects have been discussed in different chapters throughout the book.

I started in Chapter 2 by formulating a definition of participle that allows for fruitful cross-linguistic comparison. The definition is based on several classic comparative concepts, relative clause, verb form and deranking, and can, therefore, be applied to verb forms in any language irrespective of its typological characteristics. Based on the proposed definition, I compiled a representative sample of 100 languages that have the relevant forms. Participles and participial systems in these languages were examined with respect to a number of parameters in further chapters.

Chapter 3 elaborated on the concept of participial orientation, which has never been a subject of a wide-scale cross-linguistic investigation, but appears to be useful in describing participial forms in individual languages. Participles in the world's languages can either be inherently oriented towards a particular core or peripheral participant, or they can change their orientation depending on the context. I showed that the most prominent types of both inherently and contextually oriented participles (active, absolutive, and contextually oriented with full relativizing capacity) are primarily motivated by pragmatic factors, and that the structure of the participial paradigm can trigger the development of other types of participial orientation (e.g. passive participles, or participles with limited contextual orientation). I also discussed various means that participles use to widen their relativizing capacity, and demonstrated that the use of resumptive elements in participial relative clauses is a much more widespread phenomenon than has been assumed in typological literature to date.

Chapters 4–6 were devoted to differences between participles and predicates of independent sentences. Following the major theoretical approaches to subordination and desententialization outlined in Chapter 4, I focused on two main domains of difference, namely the verb form and the encoding of various clausal participants.

In Chapter 5, I discussed deviations from the main clause standard in the morphosyntactic domain. Most commonly, participial relative clauses show various peculiarities in TAM marking, such as restrictions on the expression of certain TAM values by separate affixes (–TAM participles), or within a paradigm (+TAM participles). Participles also tend to differ from independent clause predicates in the domain of polarity. Negative meaning in participial relative clauses can be conveyed by nominal negation markers or specialized negative participles, and in some cases its expression is not possible at all. Verbal subject agreement is almost never allowed in participial relative clauses. On the other hand, in many languages, participles acquire nominal agreement, which is crucial in the prototypical participial function of adnominal modification. Importantly, I also showed that the expression of various morphosyntactic features in the participles of the sample confirms earlier hierarchies of verbal and nominal features involved in desententialization/nominalization (which were formulated on a more general level, often for subordinate structures more generally).

Chapter 6 focused on deviations in participant expression. The participant that is most likely to change its marking in participial relative clauses is the subject (S/A), but some languages employ non-standard ways of encoding other participants as well. The most common non-standard coding strategy is possessive, which is very natural considering that most participles are highly nominalized. Based on the analysis of the sample, I discussed main types of factors that can motivate the attested deviations. Syntax is mainly responsible for the encoding of various arguments of participles as adnominal dependents (due to the change of the word class). Cross-constructional analogy motivates the expression of agents as non-core participants in relative clauses, since many participial forms, in addition to their relativizing functions, perform the prototypical functions of passive, including agent demotion. As a result, the agent is encoded as a peripheral argument in the relative clause. Generic or habitual meaning characteristic of participial relative clauses in many languages can, in turn, motivate changes in the differential marking of direct objects in participial relative clauses.

In Chapter 7, all of the parameters considered earlier were studied together in a survey of participial systems. As I showed, participial systems in languages with more than one form can be based on orientation, TAM distinctions, or the intersection of the two. Two generalizations were formulated concerning the organization of participial systems. First, if a language has a participial form inherently oriented towards a certain participant, then it tends to have participial forms inherently oriented towards all the participants more accessible to relativization. This can be regarded as an extension of Keenan and Comrie's (1977) Accessibility Hierarchy specifically for participles. Second, based on the fact that almost all participial systems considered in this study are asymmetric if they are based on both orientation and TAM characteristics of participial forms, I concluded that these parameters are clearly interrelated, which reflects the mixed nature of the participle as a hybrid (verbal-adjectival) category.

The findings reported in the chapters of the book show significant diversity in the morphology of participles, their syntactic behaviour, and the oppositions they form in the system of the language. I hope to have shown, however, that despite their versatility and multifunctionality, participles exhibit enough properties distinguishing them from other non-finite structures and related phenomena to be recognized as a cross-linguistically relevant category and studied in their own right.

8.2 Further prospects

As the first systematic cross-linguistic analysis of participles and participial relative clauses, this study naturally invites further research on a broad range of issues. First, as I mentioned in the introduction (Section 1.3), there is currently a growing interest in typology in studying the geographical distribution of linguistic phenomena and using this to explain the attested patterns of diversity. When collecting the data for the current study, I aimed to include languages from all over the world by using a sample stratified at the level of genus, and I paid particular attention to less studied geographical areas, such as Papunesia or the Americas. However, since my main goal was simply to find as many languages featuring participial forms as possible, I did not strictly follow the procedures that are required in statistically oriented studies (cf. Dryer 1989, Rijkhoff and Bakker 1998, Bickel 2008, and others). Thus, any observations I could make on the geographical distribution of participles are impressionistic. The next step, therefore, would be a quantitative study of the distribution of participles and participial relative clauses, focusing on establishing and explaining areal skewings of forms, structures, and their particular features. Various types of oppositions discovered in this book can serve as a basis for variables considered in this type of quantitative investigation. The study could also be further complemented by examining the correlations of participial types in given languages with some other typological parameters. For example, the type of participles preferred by a language seems to correlate with its preferred word order. As shown in Table 37, a language that has only contextually oriented participles is very likely to be verb-final (34 out of 38 languages, 89.5%). On the other hand, if a language with the VO constituent order has participles, in most cases they are inherently oriented (20 out of 24 languages, 83.3%).

Tab. 37: Constituent order in languages with different participial types

	OV	VO	No dominant order
Contextual only	34	1	3
Inherent only	9	20	10
Both	17	3	2

In addition, as shown in Table 38, languages with only contextually oriented participles tend to use them in prenominal relative clauses, while languages with only inherently oriented participles often use them postnominally. All of these tendencies clearly call for further investigation and explanation.

Tab. 38: Position of participial relative clauses in languages with different participial types

	Prenominal	Postnominal	Other
Contextual only	28	6	4
Inherent only	12	23	4
Both	14	4	4

Since some participles show an unusual relativization pattern (S/P association, syntactic ergativity in a broad sense), one could look for connections with other instances of ergative alignment in the respective languages. In this book, I have shown that there is no connection between participial orientation and morphosyntactic alignment in independent sentences (see Sections 3.3.1 and 3.8). It remains an open question, however, which other domains can be connected to properties of participles and/or participial systems. One noteworthy domain in this respect is switch-reference. Overall and Vuillermet (2015) show that the indigenous languages of Western Amazonia are rich in typologically rare switch-reference systems. In particular, these systems can treat S participants in the same way as P participants but differently from A participants, which is parallel to absolutive–ergative morphosyntactic alignment. At the same time, the only three languages with absolutive–agentive patterning in their participial systems found in my sample, Urarina, Cocama and Panare (see Sections 7.3 and 7.5.1), are spoken roughly in the same region (Peru and Southern Venezuela). Cocama, in addition, shows an absolutive pattern in purpose constructions: only S and P participants of the main clause can control the implicit argument of the purpose clause. Example (223a) illustrates the case of S=A coreference, and example (223b) the case of P=A coreference as opposed to A=A, which is impossible:

(223) Cocama (Tupian)
    a. *tsumi   uri=ui   [nai   mutsanaka-tara]*
       shaman come=PST grandmother cure-PURP
       'The shaman came to cure grandmother.'
       (Vallejos Yopán 2016: 496)
    b. *rana   erura   tsumi   [nai   mutsanaka-tara]*
       3PL.MS bring shaman grandmother cure-PURP
       'They bring the shaman in order (for him) to cure grandmother.'
       *'They bring the shaman so that they cure grandmother.'
       (Vallejos Yopán 2016: 496)

Cocama is, therefore, an interesting and typologically rare example of a language that fairly consistently shows ergative pattern in clause combining (see Vallejos Yopán 2016: 494 for a summary), while lacking any signs of ergative alignment within the (independent) clause.

Another approach to participles that could be followed up in more detail concerns their position on the verb–noun cline. It is an acknowledged fact among linguists that participles (and adjectives) possess both verbal and nominal properties, and are basically hybrid categories (Ross 1972; Hopper and Thompson 1984). The verb–noun cline can, thus, be represented as a continuum with verb and noun as extreme points, and participle and adjective somewhere in between. In his article on participles, Haspelmath (1994: 171–172) proposes a special case of this general scale, namely the scale representing the relative positions of five types of forms with respect to five relevant parameters; see (224):

(224) Scale of participant nominalizations (Haspelmath 1994: 171)

finite verb	relative participle	oriented participle	verbal adjective	participant noun

(A) more verbal ⟵⎯⎯⎯⎯⎯⎯⎯⎯⎯⎯⟶ more nominal
(B) more inflectional ⟵⎯⎯⎯⎯⎯⎯⎯⎯⎯⎯⟶ more derivational
(C) more relational ⟵⎯⎯⎯⎯⎯⎯⎯⎯⎯⎯⟶ more absolute
(D) less inherent orientation ⟵⎯⎯⎯⟶ more inherent orientation
(E) less time-stable ⟵⎯⎯⎯⎯⎯⎯⎯⎯⎯⎯⟶ more time-stable

As mentioned above, the intermediate status of participles in general is not a recent discovery. However, in this scale, Haspelmath, in fact, makes a statement that is of great importance for the overall typology of participles: he suggests that contextually oriented participles (or relative participles in his terms) are *intrinsically* less nominal than inherently oriented participles. Indeed, this claim seems to hold for the convenience sample considered in Haspelmath's article. Some supporting observations can be made based on my sample as well, especially concerning two of the clines, (A) more verbal vs. more nominal, and (E) more time-stable vs. less time-stable. As regards cline (A), encoding subjects in accordance with the independent clause model (e.g. nominative) is more common for contextually oriented participles than for inherently oriented forms, which allows one to see the former as more verbal (see Appendix 3c). On the other hand, inherently oriented participles often show nominal agreement with the nouns they modify, while for contextually oriented forms this is fairly rare (see Appendix 3b). In this sense, inherently oriented participles can be seen as more nominal. In addition, contextually oriented participles tend to have –TAM markers, while markers of inherently oriented participles are typically +TAM (see Appendix 3b). In other words, contextually oriented participles tend to be less time-stable, while inherently oriented participles tend to be more time-stable, as predicted by cline (E).

Although these preliminary observations do provide some support in favour of Haspelmath's (1994) scale, it still needs to be tested in more detail, and the main problem here is to develop an appropriate methodology. Indeed, many typologists have noted that detailed cross-linguistic comparison of different verb forms in different languages with respect to the degree of nominalization or (non-)finiteness they exhibit is not very fruitful, since the morphosyntactic properties relevant to the phenomena in question (e.g. expression of TAM distinctions, compatibility with nominal morphology, encoding of participants and modifiers, etc.), differ tremendously across languages; see, for instance, Cristofaro (2003), or Nikolaeva (2013). On the other hand, participial relative clauses are considerably more homogeneous if compared to all kinds of subordinate forms and structures in general, which may facilitate a systematic cross-linguistic analysis.

Yet another question concerns the degree of nominalization of participles when compared to other non-finite verb forms, in particular event and participant nominalizations. If we think of adjectives as occupying a middle position on the verb–noun cline, participles (≈ verbal adjectives) can be expected to be more verbal than nominalizations (≈ verbal nouns). Some facts do point in this direction. For example, in the 70-language sample investigated by Koptjevskaja-Tamm (1993), in 17 out of 70 languages (24.3%) event nominalizations can express the subject in the same way as independent verbal predicates. In my sample, this type of subject expression is available in 40 out of 91 languages with non-active participles (44.0%). In this sense, participles are closer to verbs than event nominalizations.

The methodological problem outlined earlier is, however, even more crucial here: we are comparing different forms in different languages, selected on the basis of different criteria. In order to avoid dealing with forms and structures that are too diverse, one solution would be to compare the degree of desententialization/nominalization of individual non-finite forms within one language depending on the constructions they are used in, which is quite in line with the suggestions by Dryer (1997), Croft (2001), and Cristofaro (2007), as well as with Creissels' (2009) constructional approach to finiteness. For many languages this is possible, because the forms that fit into the typological definition of participle adopted in this study (see Section 2.3) are highly multifunctional. In particular, they can take on not just the prototypical adjectival function of adnominal modification, but also a referring function typical of nouns (see Section 2.4). The prediction is, thus, that one and the same form will show more signs of nominalization when used nominally than the same form functioning as an adnominal modifier. Some data in support of this prediction is provided at least by van den Berg (2013) for Muna; see Section 5.3.1 and examples in (160). This method, however, is only applicable to a very small set of languages. In particular, it is not suitable for those languages where the use of participles is limited to adnominal contexts, and for those languages where non-finite forms behave in the same way in relative and complement clauses). Applying it, therefore, creates the risk of the final language sample being too limited for conclusive cross-linguistic generalizations.

The current study focused on the typological classification of participles based on the synchronic data provided by descriptive grammars. However, for a deeper understanding of participles and their nature, it is very important to also examine, where this is possible, the diachronic development of participial constructions and participial paradigms, since looking at the historical processes has been proved to be a fruitful way to explain certain cross-linguistic tendencies; see, for example, Cristofaro (2012, 2014, 2017). In the linguistic literature, very little has been written so far about the origin of participles as a word class. Hendery (2012: 172) suggests that at least some deranked relative clauses may have originated as deverbal adjectives whose verbal nature allowed the addition of arguments and adjuncts, expanding them into full (though deranked) clauses. This scenario is also discussed by Haspelmath (1994) and Harris and Campbell (1995), but evidence for this type of development is still fragmentary.

A stronger focus on diachrony as advocated here also implies the study of genealogically related languages that show considerable variation in the types of participles and participial constructions. The Uralic and Indo-European language families are the most promising groups in this respect. Since in most languages within one family it is usually possible to identify cognates among participial markers, the observed variation is clearly a result of diachronic development. However, it is not always clear in which direction the changes proceeded, or what the factors triggering them may have been. Areal typology is, therefore, also very important in the study of participles. For example, Uralic languages with extensive variation in the domain of participial orientation clearly follow areal tendencies in the distribution of participial types. In particular, western Uralic languages (e.g. Finnish and Hungarian), which for centuries have been influenced by Slavic, Germanic and Baltic varieties, have inherently oriented participles characteristic of Standard Average European languages. On the other hand, in eastern Uralic languages (e.g. Tundra Nenets and Northern Khanty), which historically form a linguistic area with northern Eurasian languages, such as Turkic and Yeniseian, most participles are contextually oriented; see Shagal (2018). Importantly, the languages in question do not borrow any segmental material (affixes). Instead, what is transmitted via contact is the syntactic behaviour of participles (their functions and rules of use). In other words, we are dealing with *pattern borrowing* rather than *matter borrowing* (see Matras and Sakel 2007). Although contact phenomena in participial constructions and relative clauses in general have been mentioned in the literature (see, for instance, Comrie 1998, Shagal 2016), no explanations for the observed pattern diffusion have been proposed. Unveiling the specific mechanisms underlying the formation of various relative clause structures and participial paradigms can provide valuable insights for the overall typology of participles, and help us understand the role of different factors in the development of subordinate structures more generally.

Appendix 1. Languages investigated in the study

Appendices 1a to 1c present languages investigated in this study. In all of the appendices, top-level language families are listed according to Glottolog 4.0 (Hammarström, Forkel, and Haspelmath 2019). Language isolates and languages with unknown genealogical affiliation are considered as families consisting of a single language. The information on genera, as well as on the countries where specific languages are (or were) spoken, comes either from WALS (Dryer and Haspelmath 2013) or from grammatical descriptions of the respective languages. The names of languages come from WALS, in some cases with a specification of the variety considered in the study, e.g. Tanti Dargwa (a variety of Dargwa spoken in the village of Tanti, Russia). If a language has a different primary name in Glottolog 4.0, this name is provided in brackets. The last column contains all the sources of data on individual languages used in this study.

Appendix 1a. Languages of the core sample

Family	Genus	Language	Country	Source
Australia				
Garrwan	Garrwan	Garrwa	Australia	Furby and Furby (1977), Mushin (2012)
Mirndi	Wambayan	Wambaya	Australia	Nordlinger (1998)
Pama-Nyungan	Central Pama-Nyungan	Pitta Pitta	Australia	Blake (1979)
Pama-Nyungan	Western Pama-Nyungan	Martuthunira	Australia	Dench (1994)
Tangkic	Tangkic	Kayardild	Australia	Evans (1995)
Papunesia				
Austronesian	Celebic	Muna	Indonesia	van den Berg (2013)
Austronesian	Celebic	Wolio	Indonesia	Anceaux (1952), Foley (1980)
Austronesian	Northwest Sumatra-Barrier Islands	Nias	Indonesia	Brown (2001, 2005)
Lower Sepik-Ramu	Lower Sepik	Yimas	Papua New Guinea	Foley (1991)

Appendix 1a. Languages of the core sample

Family	Genus	Language	Country	Source
Nuclear Trans New Guinea	Madang	Kobon	Papua New Guinea	Davies (1981)
Savosavo	Savosavo	Savosavo	Solomon Islands	Wegener (2012)
South Bougainville	East Bougainville	Motuna (Siwai)	Papua New Guinea	Onishi (1994)
North America				
Chimariko	Chimariko	Chimariko	United States	Jany (2008, 2009)
Coahuilteco	Coahuiltecan	Coahuilteco	United States	Troike (1996, 2010)
Cochimi-Yuman	Yuman	Maricopa	United States	Gordon (1980, 1986)
Eskimo-Aleut	Eskimo	West Greenlandic (Kalaallisut)	Greenland	Fortescue (1984), van der Voort (1991)
Kalapuyan	Kalapuyan	Santiam Kalapuya	United States	Banks (2007)
Seri	Seri	Seri	Mexico	Marlett (2012)
Uto-Aztecan	California Uto-Aztecan	Luiseño	United States	Davis (1973)
Uto-Aztecan	Hopi	Hopi	United States	Jeanne (1978)
Uto-Aztecan	Numic	Tümpisa Shoshone (Panamint)	United States	Dayley (1989)
Uto-Aztecan	Tarahumaran	Guarijío (Huarijio)	Mexico	Félix Armendáriz (2005)
Uto-Aztecan	Tepiman	Nevome (Pima Bajo)	Mexico	Shaul (1986)
Yokutsan	Yokuts	Wikchamni	United States	Gamble (1978)
Yuki-Wappo	Wappo	Wappo	United States	Li and Thompson (1978), Thompson, Park, and Li (2006)
South America				
Araucanian	Araucanian	Mapudungun	Chile	Zúñiga (2000), Smeets (2008), Golluscio (2012)
Arawakan	Inland Northern Arawakan	Tariana	Brazil	Aikhenvald (2003)
Barbacoan	Barbacoan	Tsafiki	Ecuador	Dickinson (2002)
Cariban	Cariban	Panare	Venezuela	Payne and Payne (2013)

Appendix 1. Languages investigated in the study

Family	Genus	Language	Country	Source
Chicham	Jivaroan	Aguaruna	Peru	Overall (2007)
Cofán	Cofán	Cofán	Colombia, Ecuador	Fischer and van Lier (2011)
Mochica	Chimúan	Mochica	Peru	Adelaar (2004), Altieri (1939)
Nadahup	Nadahup	Hup	Brazil, Colombia	Epps (2008, 2012)
Nuclear-Macro-Je	Ge-Kaingang	Mẽbengokre (Kayapó)	Brazil	Salanova (2011)
Pano-Tacanan	Panoan	Matsés	Brazil, Peru	Fleck (2003)
Quechuan	Quechuan	Imbabura Quechua (Imbabura Highland Quichua)	Ecuador	Cole (1985)
Quechuan	Quechuan	Tarma Quechua (North Junín Quechua)	Peru	Adelaar (2011)
Tucanoan	Tucanoan	Barasano	Colombia	Jones and Jones (1991)
Tupian	Tupí-Guaraní	Cocama (Cocama-Cocamilla)	Peru	Vallejos Yopán (2010, 2016)
Tupian	Tupí-Guaraní	Kamaiurá (Kamayurá)	Brazil	Seki (1990, 2000)
Urarina	Urarina	Urarina	Peru	Olawsky (2006)
Africa				
Afro-Asiatic	Berber	Rif Berber	Algeria, Morocco	Kossmann (2000, 2003, 2007), Kossmann, p.c.
Afro-Asiatic	Egyptian-Coptic	Middle Egyptian	Egypt	Depuydt (1996), Kramer (2003), Haspelmath (2015)
Afro-Asiatic	Highland East Cushitic	Kambaata	Ethiopia	Treis (2008)
Atlantic-Congo	Northern Atlantic	Fula	Cameroon	Arnott (1970)
Central Sudanic	Moru-Ma'di	Ma'di	Sudan, Uganda	Blackings and Fabb (2003)
Dizoid	North Omotic	Sheko	Ethiopia	Hellenthal (2010)
Dogon	Dogon	Nanga	Mali	Heath (2008)
Kadugli-Krongo	Kadugli	Krongo	Sudan	Reh (1985)

Appendix 1a. Languages of the core sample — 255

Family	Genus	Language	Country	Source
Maban	Maban	Maba	Chad	Weiss (2009)
Mande	Eastern Mande	Beng	Côte d'Ivoire	Paperno (2014)
Mande	Eastern Mande	Wan	Côte d'Ivoire	Nikitina (2009)
Ta-Ne-Omotic	North Omotic	Koorete	Ethiopia	Hayward (1982)
Eurasia				
Afro-Asiatic	Semitic	Modern Standard Arabic	multiple countries	Hazout (2001), Badawi, Carter, and Gully (2004), Ryding (2005), Doron and Reintges (2005)
Austroasiatic	Munda	Kharia	India	Peterson (2011)
Basque	Basque	Basque	France, Spain	Hualde and Ortiz de Urbina (2003)
Burushaski	Burushaski	Burushaski	Pakistan	Klimov and Èdel'man (1970), Berger (1998), Yoshioka (2012)
Chukotko-Kamchatkan	Northern Chukotko-Kamchatkan	Koryak	Russia	Zhukova (1972), Kurebito (2011)
Dravidian	South-Central Dravidian	Telugu	India	Krishnamurti and Gwynn (1985)
Dravidian	Southern Dravidian	Malayalam	India	Asher and Kumari (1997)
Dravidian	Southern Dravidian	Tamil	India, Sri Lanka	Keenan and Comrie (1977), Lehmann (1993)
Indo-European	Albanian	Albanian	Albania	Newmark, Hubbard, and Prifti (1982), Buchholz and Fiedler (1987), Makartsev, p.c., Rusakov, p.c.
Indo-European	Armenian	Eastern Armenian	Armenia	Dum-Tragut (2009)
Indo-European	Baltic	Lithuanian	Lithuania	Ambrazas (2006), Arkadiev (2014a)
Indo-European	Celtic	Irish	Ireland	Xalipov (1997), Ó Baoill (2009), d'Altuin, p.c.
Indo-European	Germanic	German	Austria, Germany, Switzerland	Haspelmath (1994), personal knowledge

Appendix 1. Languages investigated in the study

Family	Genus	Language	Country	Source
Indo-European	Greek	Modern Greek	Greece	Mackridge (1985), Anagnostopoulou (2003), Hämeen-Anttila, p.c., Korhonen, p.c.
Indo-European	Indic	Marathi	India	Pandharipande (1997), Dhongde and Wali (2009)
Indo-European	Iranian	Apsheron Tat	Azerbaijan	Grjunberg (1966), Authier (2012)
Indo-European	Romance	Italian	Italy, Switzerland	Maiden and Robustelli (2000), Di Garbo, p.c.
Indo-European	Slavic	Russian	Russia	personal knowledge
Kartvelian	Kartvelian	Georgian	Georgia	Harris (1981), Hewitt (1995)
Koreanic	Korean	Korean	North Korea, South Korea	Lee (1994), Shin (2003), Kim, p.c.
Mongolic	Mongolic	Kalmyk	Russia	Bläsing (2003), Krapivina (2009a), personal field notes
Nakh-Daghestanian	Avar-Andic-Tsezic	Hinuq	Russia	Forker (2013)
Nakh-Daghestanian	Lak-Dargwa	Tanti Dargwa	Russia	Sumbatova and Lander (2014)
Nakh-Daghestanian	Lezgic	Lezgian	Azerbaijan, Russia	Haspelmath (1993)
Nakh-Daghestanian	Nakh	Ingush	Russia	Nichols (2011)
Nivkh	Nivkh	Nivkh	Russia	Gruzdeva (1998), Mattissen (2003), Nedjalkov and Otaina (2013), personal field notes
Sino-Tibetan	Bodic	Manange	Nepal	Hildebrandt (2004), Genetti et al. (2008)
Sino-Tibetan	Bodo-Garo	Garo	India	Burling (2004)
Sino-Tibetan	Dhimalic	Dhimal	Nepal	King (2009)
Sino-Tibetan	Mahakiranti	Dolakha Newar (Eastern Newari)	Nepal	Genetti (2007)
Sino-Tibetan	Qiangic	Ronghong Qiang	China	LaPolla with Huang (2003), Huang (2008)
Sino-Tibetan	rGyalrong	Japhug rGyalrong (Japhug)	China	Jacques (2013, 2016)
Sino-Tibetan	Tani	Apatani	India	Abraham (1985), Sun (2003)
Tungusic	Tungusic	Even	Russia	Malchukov (1995, 2008)

Family	Genus	Language	Country	Source
Tungusic	Tungusic	Nanai	Russia	Avrorin (1961), personal field notes
Turkic	Turkic	Yakut (Sakha)	Russia	Ubrjatova (1982), Pakendorf, p.c.
Uralic	Finnic	Finnish	Finland	personal knowledge
Uralic	Mari	Meadow Mari	Russia	Brykina and Aralova (2012)
Uralic	Mordvin	Erzya	Russia	Bartens (1999), Hamari and Aasmäe (2015), Rueter, p.c.
Uralic	Permic	Beserman Udmurt	Russia	Brykina and Aralova (2012), Edygarova (2015)
Uralic	Permic	Komi-Zyrian	Russia	Brykina and Aralova (2012)
Uralic	Saami	North Saami	Finland, Norway, Sweden	Ylikoski (2009)
Uralic	Samoyedic	Tundra Nenets	Russia	Nikolaeva (2014)
Uralic	Ugric	Hungarian	Hungary	Kenesei, Vago, and Fenyvesi (1998), Kiss (2015)
Uralic	Ugric	Northern Khanty	Russia	Nikolaeva (1999)
Yeniseian	Yeniseian	Ket	Russia	Georg (2007), Nefedov (2012)
Yukaghir	Yukaghir	Kolyma Yukaghir	Russia	Nikolaeva (1997), Maslova (2003), Nagasaki (2014)

Appendix 1b. Languages with little information on presumably participial forms

Family	Genus	Language	Country	Source
Afro-Asiatic	Beja	Beja	Eritrea, Sudan	Hudson (1974)
Afro-Asiatic	Biu-Mandara	Margi (Marghi Central)	Nigeria	Hoffmann (1963)
Atlantic-Congo	Nupoid	Gwari (Gbagyi)	Nigeria	Hyman and Magaji (1970)
Austronesian	Paiwan	Paiwan	Taiwan	Egli (1990)
Boran	Boran	Bora	Colombia, Peru	Thiesen and Weber (2012)
Cariban	Cariban	Apalaí	Brazil	Koehn and Koehn (1986)
Central Sudanic	Bongo-Bagirmi	Mbay	Chad	Fortier (1971)

Appendix 1. Languages investigated in the study

Family	Genus	Language	Country	Source
Central Sudanic	Lendu	Ngiti	Democratic Republic of Congo	Kutsch Lojenga (1994)
Central Sudanic	Mangbetu	Mangbetu	Democratic Republic of Congo	Tucker and Bryan (1966)
Central Sudanic	Moru-Ma'di	Lugbara	Democratic Republic of Congo, Uganda	Tucker and Bryan (1966)
Cuitlatec	Cuitlatec	Cuitlatec	Mexico	Escalante (1962)
Dravidian	Central Dravidian	Kolami (Northwestern Kolami)	India	Emeneau (1955)
Dravidian	Northern Dravidian	Brahui	Pakistan	Andronov (1980), Elfenbein (1998)
Eskimo-Aleut	Aleut	Aleut	United States	Bergsland (1997)
Karok	Karok	Karok	United States	Bright (1957)
Kresh-Aja	Kresh	Kresh (Gbaya)	South Sudan	Santandrea (1976)
Kunama	Kunama	Kunama	Ethiopia, Eritrea	Bender (1996), Böhm (1984)
Maban	Maban	Masalit	Chad, Sudan	Edgar (1989)
Mayan	Mayan	Mam	Guatemala	England (1983)
Misumalpan	Misumalpan	Miskito (Mískito)	Nicaragua	Salamanca (1988)
Mosetén-Chimané	Mosetenan	Mosetén (Mosetén-Chimané)	Bolivia	Sakel (2004)
Natchez	Natchez	Natchez	United States	Kimball (2005)
Nubian	Nubian	Dongolese Nubian (Kenuzi-Dongola)	Sudan	Armbruster (1960)
Nyimang	Nyimang	Nyimang (Ama)	Sudan	Stevenson (1981)
Otomanguean	Pamean	Northern Pame	Mexico	Berthiaume (2012)
Palaihnihan	Palaihnihan	Achumawi	United States	de Angulo and Freeland (1930)
Pirahã	Mura	Pirahã	Brazil	Everett (1986)

Family	Genus	Language	Country	Source
Puquina	Puquina	Puquina	Bolivia, Peru	Adelaar and van de Kerke (2009)
Saharan	Western Saharan	Kanuri (Central Kanuri)	Nigeria, Chad, Niger, Sudan	Lukas (1937)
South Omotic	South Omotic	Aari	Ethiopia	Hayward (1990)
South Omotic	South Omotic	Dime	Ethiopia	Fleming (1990)
Taiap	Gapun	Taiap	Papua New Guinea	Kulick and Stroud (1992)
Tarascan	Tarascan	Purépecha (Purepecha)	Mexico	Foster (1969)
Tonkawa	Tonkawa	Tonkawa	United States	Wier (2014)
Wakashan	Northern Wakashan	Kwakw'ala (Kwak'wala)	Canada	Boas (1947)

Appendix 1c. Languages without participles

Family	Genus	Language	Country	Source
Abkhaz-Adyge	Northwest Caucasian	Abkhaz (Abkhazian)	Georgia	Hewitt (1979)
Afro-Asiatic	Biu-Mandara	Malgwa (Wandala)	Cameroon, Nigeria	Frajzyngier (2012)
Afro-Asiatic	East Chadic	Kera	Chad	Ebert (1979)
Afro-Asiatic	Masa	Masa (Masana)	Chad, Cameroon	Melis (1999)
Afro-Asiatic	Southern Cushitic	Burunge	Tanzania	Kiessling (1994)
Afro-Asiatic	Southern Cushitic	Iraqw	Tanzania	Mous (1992)
Afro-Asiatic	West Chadic	Miya	Nigeria	Schuh (1998)
Ainu	Ainu	Hokkaido Ainu	Japan	Bugaeva (2017)
Algic	Wiyot	Wiyot	United States	Teeter (1964)
Algic	Yurok	Yurok	United States	Robins (1958)
Andoque	Andoke	Andoke (Andoque)	Colombia	Landaburu (1979)
Angan	Angan	Menya	Papua New Guinea	Whitehead (2004)
Arawakan	Bolivia-Parana	Baure	Bolivia	Danielsen (2011)

Family	Genus	Language	Country	Source
Arawakan	Central Arawakan	Waurá	Brazil	Derbyshire (1986)
Arawakan	Pre-Andine Arawakan	Ashéninka Perené	Peru	Mihas (2010)
Arawakan	Purus	Apurinã	Brazil	Facundes (2000)
Arawakan	Yanesha'	Amuesha (Yanesha')	Peru	Wise (1986)
Arawan	Arauan	Jarawara (Madi)	Brazil	Dixon (2004b), Vogel (2009)
Arawan	Arauan	Paumarí	Brazil	Chapman and Derbyshire (1991)
Athabaskan-Eyak-Tlingit	Athapaskan	Chipewyan	Canada	Wilhelm (2014)
Athabaskan-Eyak-Tlingit	Tlingit	Tlingit	United States	Crippen (2012)
Atlantic-Congo	Adamawa	Samba Leko	Nigeria, Cameroon	Fabre (2003)
Atlantic-Congo	Bantoid	Makua (Makhuwa)	Mozambique	van der Wal (2010)
Atlantic-Congo	Cross River	Ogbronuagum	Nigeria	Kari (2000)
Atlantic-Congo	Defoid	Yoruba	Nigeria, Benin	Ajíbóyè (2005)
Atlantic-Congo	Edoid	Degema	Nigeria	Kari (1997)
Atlantic-Congo	Gbaya-Manza-Ngbaka	Gbeya Bossangoa (Gbaya Bossangoa)	Central African Republic	Samarin (1966)
Atlantic-Congo	Gur	Koromfe (Koromfé)	Burkina Faso, Mali	Rennison (1997)
Atlantic-Congo	Idomoid	Igede	Nigeria	Bergman (1981)
Atlantic-Congo	Igboid	Igbo	Nigeria	Emenanjo (1987)
Atlantic-Congo	Kru	Vata (Lakota Dida)	Côte d'Ivoire	Koopman (1984)
Atlantic-Congo	Kainji	Duka (Hun-Saare)	Nigeria	Bendor-Samuel and Cressman (1973)
Atlantic-Congo	Kwa	Ewe	Togo, Ghana	Ameka (1991)
Atlantic-Congo	Kwa	Fongbe (Fon)	Benin	Lefebvre and Brousseau (2002)

Appendix 1c. Languages without participles — 261

Family	Genus	Language	Country	Source
Atlantic-Congo	Mel	Kisi	Sierra Leone, Guinea, Liberia	Childs (1995)
Atlantic-Congo	Platoid	Fyem (Fyam)	Nigeria	Nettle (1998)
Atlantic-Congo	Ubangi	Sango	Central African Republic	Thornell (1997)
Austroasiatic	Aslian	Jahai (Jehai)	Malaysia	Burenhult (2005)
Austroasiatic	Bahnaric	Chrau	Vietnam	Thomas (1971)
Austroasiatic	Katuic	Pacoh	Vietnam	Jenny, Weber, and Weymuth (2014)
Austroasiatic	Khasian	Khasi	India	Jenny, Weber, and Weymuth (2014)
Austroasiatic	Khmer	Khmer (Central Khmer)	Cambodia	Jenny, Weber, and Weymuth (2014)
Austroasiatic	Monic	Mon	Thailand, Myanmar	Jenny, Weber, and Weymuth (2014)
Austroasiatic	Nicobarese	Nancowry (Central Nicobarese)	India	Jenny, Weber, and Weymuth (2014)
Austroasiatic	Palaung-Khmuic	Palaung	Myanmar	Mak (2012)
Austroasiatic	Viet-Muong	Vietnamese	Vietnam	Jenny, Weber, and Weymuth (2014)
Austro-Asiatic	Pearic	Kasong (Suoy)	Thailand	Sunee (2003)
Austronesian	Atayalic	Mayrinax Atayal	Taiwan	Huang (1995)
Austronesian	Atayalic	Seediq	Taiwan	Tsukida (2005)
Austronesian	Barito	Malagasy (Plateau Malagasy)	Madagascar	Keenan (1972)
Austronesian	Batanic	Ivatan (Itbayat)	Philippines	Reid (1966)
Austronesian	Central Luzon	Kapampangan (Pampanga)	Philippines	Mirikitani (1972)
Austronesian	Central Malayo-Polynesian	Kambera	Indonesia	Klamer (1998)
Austronesian	Chamorro	Chamorro	Guam	Topping (1973)
Austronesian	East Formosan	Amis	Taiwan	Wu (2006)

Appendix 1. Languages investigated in the study

Family	Genus	Language	Country	Source
Austronesian	Greater Central Philippine	Tagalog	Philippines	Foley (1980)
Austronesian	Javanese	Javanese	Indonesia	Ogloblin (2005)
Austronesian	Lampungic	Lampung (Lampung Api)	Indonesia	Walker (1976)
Austronesian	Minahasan	Tondano	Indonesia	Sneddon (1975)
Austronesian	North Borneo	Tatana'	Malaysia	Dunn and Peck (1988)
Austronesian	Northern Luzon	Ilocano (Iloko)	Philippines	Foley (1980)
Austronesian	Northwest Sumatra-Barrier Islands	Karo Batak	Indonesia	Woollams (2005)
Austronesian	Oceanic	Fijian	Fiji	Foley (1980)
Austronesian	Oceanic	Tolai (Kuanua)	Papua New Guinea	Foley (1980)
Austronesian	Palauan	Palauan	Palau	Josephs (1975), Foley (1980)
Austronesian	Rejang	Rejang	Indonesia	McGinn (1982)
Austronesian	Sama-Bajaw	Bajau (Indonesian Bajau)	Philippines	Jun (2005)
Austronesian	Sangiric	Toratán (Ratahan)	Indonesia	Himmelmann and Wolf (1999)
Austronesian	South Halmahera-West New Guinea	Taba (East Makian)	Indonesia	Bowden (2005)
Austronesian	South Sulawesi	Makassar (Makasar)	Indonesia	Jukes (2005)
Austronesian	Tsou	Tsou	Taiwan	Zeitoun (2005)
Austronesian	Western Plains Austronesian	Thao	Taiwan	Wang (2004)
Austronesian	Yapese	Yapese	Micronesia	Jensen (1977)
Bangime	Bangime	Bangime	Mali	Hantgan (2013)
Berta	Berta	Berta	Ethiopia, Sudan	Triulzi, Dafallah, and Bender (1976)
Betoi-Jirara	Betoi	Betoi (Betoi-Jirara)	Colombia, Venezuela	Zamponi (2003)
Bilua	Bilua	Bilua	Solomon Islands	Obata (2003)

Appendix 1c. Languages without participles — 263

Family	Genus	Language	Country	Source
Border	Border	Imonda	Papua New Guinea	Seiler (1985)
Bororoan	Bororoan	Bororo	Brazil	Crowell (1979)
Bosavi	Bosavi	Edolo	Papua New Guinea	Gossner (1994)
Bunaban	Bunuban	Gooniyandi	Australia	McGregor (1990)
Chapacuran	Chapacura-Wanham	Wari'	Brazil	Everett and Kern (1997)
Chibchan	Arhuacic	Ika (Arhuaco)	Colombia	Frank (1985)
Chibchan	Guaymiic	Ngäbere	Panama	Alphonse (1956), Quesada Pacheco (2008)
Chibchan	Paya	Pech	Honduras	Holt (1999)
Chibchan	Rama	Rama	Nicaragua	Grinevald (1990)
Chibchan	Talamanca	Teribe	Panama, Costa Rica	Quesada (2000)
Chimakuan	Chimakuan	Quileute	United States	Andrade (1933)
Chitimacha	Chitimacha	Chitimacha	United States	Granberry (2004)
Chonan	Chon Proper	Selknam (Selk'nam)	Argentina	Rojas Berscia (2014)
Chukotko-Kamchatkan	Southern Chukotko-Kamchatkan	Itelmen (West Itelmen)	Russia	Volodin (1976)
Chumashan	Chumash	Ineseño Chumash (Ineseño)	United States	Applegate (1972)
Dagan	Dagan	Daga	Papua New Guinea	Murane (1974)
Dajuic	Daju	Sila (Dar Sila Daju)	Chad	Boyeldieu (2008)
East Bird's Head	East Bird's Head	Sougb	Indonesia	Reesink (2002)
Eastern Daly	Eastern Daly	Matngele (Madngele)	Australia	Zandvoort (1999)
Eastern Jebel	Eastern Jebel	Ingessana (Gaam)	Sudan	Bender (1989)
Eastern Trans-Fly	Western Fly	Meryam Mir (Meriam)	Australia	Piper (1989)
Esselen	Esselen	Esselen	United States	Shaul (1995)
Furan	Fur	Fur	Sudan	Beaton (1968), Jakobi (1990)

Appendix 1. Languages investigated in the study

Family	Genus	Language	Country	Source
Gaagudju	Gaagudju	Gaagudju	Australia	Harvey (2002)
Geelvink Bay	East Geelvink Bay	Bauzi	Indonesia	Briley (1997)
Goilalan	Goilalan	Kunimaipa	Papua New Guinea	Geary (1977)
Greater Kwerba	Kwerba	Kwerba	Indonesia	de Vries and de Vries (1997)
Guahiboan	Guahiban	Sikuani (Guahibo)	Colombia	Queixalós (2011)
Guaicuruan	South Guaicuruan	Toba	Argentina	Carpio and Censabella (2012)
Gumuz	Gumuz	Gumuz (Northern Gumuz)	Ethiopia, Sudan	Ahland (2012)
Gunwinyguan	Gunwinygic	Bininj Gun-Wok (Bininj Kun-Wok)	Australia	Evans (2003)
Gunwinyguan	Ngalakan	Ngalakan (Ngalakgan)	Australia	Merlan (1983)
Gunwinyguan	Ngandi	Ngandi	Australia	Heath (1978)
Gunwinyguan	Rembarnga	Rembarnga (Rembarrnga)	Australia	McKay (1975)
Gunwinyguan	Warayic	Waray (Warray)	Australia	Harvey (1986)
Haida	Haida	Haida	Canada, United States	Enrico (2003)
Hatam-Mansim	Hatam	Hatam	Indonesia	Reesink (1999)
Heibanic	Heiban	Moro	Sudan	Black and Black (1971)
Hmong-Mien	Hmong-Mien	Hmong Njua	China	Purnell (1972)
Huavean	Huavean	San Francisco del Mar Huave	United States	Kim (2008)
Ijoid	Ijoid	Ijo (Izon)	Nigeria	Williamson (1965)
Inanwatan	South Bird's Head	Inanwatan (Suabo)	Indonesia	de Vries (1996)
Iroquoian	Northern Iroquoian	Oneida	United States	Abbott (2000)
Iroquoian	Southern Iroquoian	Cherokee	United States	Lindsey and Scancarelli (1985)

Appendix 1c. Languages without participles

Family	Genus	Language	Country	Source
Itonama	Itonama	Itonama	Bolivia	Crevels (2010)
Iwaidjan Proper	Iwaidjan	Maung (Mawng)	Australia	Singer (2006)
Japonic	Japanese	Japanese	Japan	Comrie (1998)
Jarawa-Onge	South Andamanese	Jarawa	India	Kumar (2012)
Jarrakan	Jarrakan	Miriwung	Australia	Kofod (1978)
Katla-Tima	Katla-Tima	Katla	Sudan	Tucker and Bryan (1966)
Katukinan	Katukinan	Canamarí (Katukína-Kanamarí)	Brazil	Queixalós (2010)
Keresan	Keresan	Acoma (Western Keres)	United States	Maring (1967)
Khoe-Kwadi	Khoe-Kwadi	Khoekhoe (Nama)	Namibia	Hagman (1973)
Kiowa-Tanoan	Kiowa-Tanoan	Kiowa	United States	Watkins (1984)
Koman	Koman	Uduk	Sudan	Don Killian (p.c.)
Kresh-Aja	Kresh	Aja	Central African Republic, South Sudan	Santandrea (1976)
Kuliak	Kuliak	Ik	Uganda	Serzisko (1989)
Kuot	Kuot	Kuot	Papua New Guinea	Lindström (2002)
Kutenai	Kutenai	Kutenai	Canada, United States	Morgan (1991)
Kwaza	Kwaza	Kwaza	Brazil	van der Voort (2004)
Kwomtari-Nai	Kwomtari	Nai	Papua New Guinea	Hamlin (1998)
Kxa	Ju-Kung	Ju|'hoan (South-Eastern Ju)	Angola, Namibia, Botswana	Dickens (1991)
Lakes Plain	Lakes Plain	Iau	Indonesia	Bateman (1986)
Lavukaleve	Lavukaleve	Lavukaleve	Solomon Islands	Terrill (2003)
Left May	Left May	Ama	Papua New Guinea	Årsjö (1999)
Limilngan-Wulna	Limilngan	Limilngan	Australia	Harvey (2001)

Appendix 1. Languages investigated in the study

Family	Genus	Language	Country	Source
Mande	Western Mande	Mauka (Mahou)	Côte d'Ivoire	Ebermann (1986)
Mangarrayi-Maran	Mangarrayi	Mangarrayi	Australia	Merlan (1982)
Mangarrayi-Maran	Warndarang	Warndarang	Australia	Heath (1980)
Maningrida	Burarran	Burarra	Australia	Green (1987)
Maningrida	Nakkara	Nakkara (Nakara)	Australia	Eather (1990)
Maningrida	Ndjébbana	Ndjébbana (Djeebbana)	Australia	McKay (2000)
Mayan	Mayan	Jakaltek (Popti')	Guatemala	Craig (1977)
Maybrat	North-Central Bird's Head	Maybrat (Maybrat-Karon)	Indonesia	Dol (1999)
Mirndi	Jaminjungan	Jaminjung (Jaminjung-Ngaliwurru)	Australia	Schultze-Berndt (2000)
Miwok-Costanoan	Costanoan	Mutsun (Southern Ohlone)	United States	Okrand (1977)
Mixe-Zoque	Mixe-Zoque	Chimalapa Zoque	Mexico	Johnson (2000)
Movima	Movima	Movima	Bolivia	Haude (2006)
Mpur	Kebar	Mpur	Indonesia	Odé (2002)
Muskogean	Muskogean	Choctaw	United States	Broadwell (2006)
Nambiquaran	Nambikuaran	Mamaindé	Brazil	Eberhard (2009)
Ndu	Middle Sepik	Ambulas	Papua New Guinea	Wilson (1980)
Ndu	Middle Sepik	Iatmul	Papua New Guinea	Jendraschek (2012)
Nilotic	Nilotic	Lango	Uganda	Noonan (1992)
Nilotic	Nilotic	Turkana	Kenya, Uganda	Dimmendaal (1983)
Nimboranic	Nimboran	Nimboran	Indonesia	May (1997)
North Bougainville	West Bougainville	Rotokas	Papua New Guinea	Robinson (2011)
North Halmahera	North Halmaheran	Tidore	Indonesia	Van Staden (2000)

Appendix 1c. Languages without participles

Family	Genus	Language	Country	Source
Northern Daly	Northern Daly	Malakmalak (Mullukmul-luk)	Australia	Birk (1976)
Nuclear Torricelli	Kombio-Arapesh	Mountain Arapesh (Bukiyip)	Papua New Guinea	Conrad and Wogiga (1991)
Nuclear Torricelli	Urim	Urim	Papua New Guinea	Wood (2012)
Nuclear Torricelli	Wapei-Palei	Olo	Papua New Guinea	Staley (2007)
Nuclear Trans New Guinea	Awju-Dumut	Korowai	Papua New Guinea	de Vries and van Enk (1997)
Nuclear Trans New Guinea	Binanderean	Suena	Papua New Guinea	Wilson (1974)
Nuclear Trans New Guinea	Chimbu	Golin	Papua New Guinea	Evans et al. (2005)
Nuclear Trans New Guinea	Dani	Lower Grand Valley Dani	Indonesia	Bromley (1981)
Nuclear Trans New Guinea	Eastern Highlands	Gahuku (Alekano)	Papua New Guinea	Deibler (1976)
Nuclear Trans New Guinea	Finisterre-Huon	Nankina	Papua New Guinea	Spaulding and Spaulding (1994)
Nuclear Trans New Guinea	Mek	Kosarek Yale	Indonesia	Heeschen (1992)
Nuclear Trans New Guinea	Ok	Mian	Papua New Guinea	Fedden (2011)
Nuclear Trans New Guinea	Wissel Lakes-Kemandoga	Ekari	Indonesia	Doble (1987)
Nuclear-Macro-Je	Ge-Kaingang	Canela-Krahô	Brazil	Popjes and Popjes (1986)
Nuclear-Macro-Je	Jabutí	Jabutí (Djeoromitxî)	Brazil	Campbell (2012)
Nuclear-Macro-Je	Karajá	Karajá	Brazil	Ribeiro (2012)
Nyulnyulan	Nyulnyulan	Bardi	Australia	Bowern (2012)
Nyulnyulan	Nyulnyulan	Warrwa	Australia	McGregor (1994)
Otomanguean	Chichimec	Chichimeca-Jonaz	Mexico	Lastra de Suárez (1984)
Otomanguean	Chinantecan	Comaltepec Chinantec	Mexico	Anderson (1989)

Appendix 1. Languages investigated in the study

Family	Genus	Language	Country	Source
Otomanguean	Mixtecan	Chalcatongo Mixtec	Mexico	Macaulay (1996)
Otomanguean	Otomian	Mezquital Otomí	Mexico	Hess (1968)
Otomanguean	Popolocan	San Juan Atzingo Popoloca	Mexico	Austin and Pickett (1974)
Otomanguean	Subtiaba-Tlapanec	Tlapanec (Acatepec Me'phaa)	Mexico	Wichmann (2007)
Otomanguean	Zapotecan	Teotitlán del Valle Zapotec	Mexico	Kalivoda and Zyman (2015)
Pama-Nyungan	Western Pama-Nyungan	Djaru (Jaru)	Australia	Tsunoda (1981)
Pano-Tacanan	Tacanan	Cavineña	Bolivia	Guillaume (2008)
Peba-Yagua	Peba-Yaguan	Yagua	Peru	Payne and Payne (1990)
Pomoan	Pomoan	Kashaya	United States	Olsson (2010)
Puinave	Puinave	Puinave	Colombia, Venezuela	Girón Higuita (2008)
Sahaptian	Sahaptian	Nez Perce	United States	Deal (2016)
Saharan	Eastern Saharan	Beria	Chad, Sudan	Jakobi and Crass (2004)
Salishan	Bella Coola	Bella Coola	Canada	Davis and Saunders (1978), Beck (1995)
Salishan	Central Salish	Lushootseed (Northern Lushootseed)	United States	Hess and Hilbert (1980), Beck (1995)
Salishan	Central Salish	Saanich (Northern Straits Salish)	Canada	Montler (1993)
Sandawe	Sandawe	Sandawe	Tanzania	Eaton (2008)
Senagi	Senagi	Menggwa Dla (Dera)	Papua New Guinea	De Sousa (2006)
Sentani	Sentani	Sentani	Indonesia	Cowan (1965)
Sepik	Ram	Awtuw	Papua New Guinea	Feldman (1986)
Sepik	Sepik Hill	Alamblak	Papua New Guinea	Bruce (1984)

Appendix 1c. Languages without participles

Family	Genus	Language	Country	Source
Sepik	Yellow River	Namia	Papua New Guinea	Feldpausch and Feldpausch (1992)
Sino-Tibetan	Bai	Yunnan Bai	China	Wiersma (2003)
Sino-Tibetan	Burmese-Lolo	Lahu	China, Thailand, Myanmar	Matisoff (2003)
Sino-Tibetan	Chinese	Mandarin Chinese	China	personal knowledge
Sino-Tibetan	Digaroan	Digaro (Tawra)	India	Sastry (1984)
Sino-Tibetan	Karen	Geba Karen	Myanmar	Shee (2008)
Sino-Tibetan	Kuki-Chin	Bawm (Bawm Chin)	Bangladesh, India, Myanmar	Reichle (1981)
Sino-Tibetan	Nungish	Dulong (Drung)	China	LaPolla (2003)
Siouan	Core Siouan	Lakhota (Lakota)	United States	Van Valin (1977)
Sko	Krisa	I'saka	Papua New Guinea	Donohue and San Roque (2002)
Sko	Warapu	Barupu (Bauni)	Papua New Guinea	Corris (2006)
Sko	Western Skou	Skou	Indonesia	Donohue (2004)
Songhay	Songhay	Tadaksahak	Mali	Christiansen-Bolli (2010)
Southern Daly	Murrinh-Patha	Murrinh-Patha (Murriny Patha)	Australia	Walsh (1976)
Southern Daly	Ngankiku-rungkurr	Ngankiku-rungkurr (Nangikurrunggurr)	Australia	Hoddinott and Kofod (1988)
Sulka	Sulka	Sulka	Papua New Guinea	Tharp (1996), Reesink (2005)
Surmic	Surmic	Murle	South Sudan	Arensen (1982)
Tai-Kadai	Kam-Tai	Thai	Thailand	Chingduang Yurayong (p.c.)
Teberan	Teberan	Folopa	Papua New Guinea	Anderson (2010)
Tequistlatecan	Tequistlatecan	Lowland Oaxaca Chontal	Mexico	O'Connor (2004)

Family	Genus	Language	Country	Source
Timor-Alor-Pantar	Greater Alor	Abui	Indonesia	Kratochvíl (2007)
Timor-Alor-Pantar	Makasae-Fataluku-Oirata	Makasae (Makasae-Makalero)	East Timor	Huber (2008)
Tiwi	Tiwian	Tiwi	Australia	Osborne (1974)
Tor-Orya	Tor	Berik	Indonesia	Westrum (1988)
Totonacan	Totonacan	Upper Necaxa Totonac	Mexico	Beck (2004)
Trumai	Trumai	Trumai	Brazil	Guirardello (1999)
Tsimshian	Tsimshianic	Coast Tsimshian (Southern-Coastal Tsimshian)	Canada United States	Dunn (1979)
Tupian	Arikem	Karitiâna	Brazil	Everett (2006)
Tupian	Monde	Gavião of Rondônia	Brazil	Moore (2012)
Tupian	Ramarama	Karó (Karo)	Brazil	Gabas (1999)
Tupian	Tupari	Mekens	Brazil	Galucio (2001)
Tuu	=|Hoan	=|Hoan (East Taa)	Botswana	Berthold (2012)
Tuu	Tu	!Xóõ (West !Xoon)	Botswana	Güldemann (2013)
Uru-Chipaya	Uru-Chipaya	Uru	Bolivia	Hannß (2011)
Uto-Aztecan	Aztecan	Huasteca Nahuatl	Mexico	Beller and Beller (1977)
Uto-Aztecan	Cahita	Yaqui	Mexico	Álvarez González (2012)
Wageman	Wagiman	Wagiman (Wageman)	Australia	Cook (1987)
Wakashan	Southern Wakashan	Nuuchahnulth (Nuu-chah-nulth)	Canada	Nakayama (2001)
Warao	Warao	Warao	Venezuela	Romero-Figueroa (1997)
Western Daly	Wagaydy	Emmi (Ami)	Australia	Ford (1998)
Worrorran	Worrorran	Worora (Worrorra)	Australia	Clendon (2001)
Yale	Yale	Nagatman (Yale)	Papua New Guinea	Campbell and Campbell (1987)
Yangmanic	Yangmanic	Wardaman	Australia	Merlan (1994)

Family	Genus	Language	Country	Source
Yanomam	Yanomam	Sanuma	Brazil, Venezuela	Borgman (1990)
Yele	Yele	Yelî Dnye (Yele)	Papua New Guinea	Henderson (1995)
Yuchi	Yuchi	Yuchi	United States	Linn (2001)
Yuracaré	Yuracare	Yuracare (Yuracaré)	Bolivia	van Gijn (2006, 2011)
Zamucoan	Zamucoan	Ayoreo	Paraguay	Bertinetto (2009)

Appendix 2. Properties of the languages in the core sample

This appendix provides some general information on the languages of the sample, which can be relevant for the discussion of individual participles or participial paradigms: morphosyntactic alignment (case marking of full noun phrases and verbal person marking), basic order of verb and object, presence of finite relative clauses, and presence of adjectival agreement. The information on alignment and word order comes either from WALS (Comrie 2013a; Siewierska 2013; Dryer 2013a), or from descriptions of individual languages. The alignment types distinguished in the table are accusative ("ACC", A=S≠P), ergative and split ergative ("(split) ERG", A≠S=P), neutral (A=S=P), tripartite (A≠S≠P), active ("ACT", A=S_A≠S_P=P), and hierarchical ("hier", marking conditioned by referential and/or ontological hierarchies). For word order, the options are object-verb ("OV"), verb-object ("VO"), and no dominant order ("no dom"). The information on the presence of finite relative clauses and adjectival agreement comes from descriptions of individual languages. If a language has finite relative clauses as a secondary relativization strategy, the value in the column is "sec". Languages for which the notion of adjectival agreement is not applicable for some reason (e.g. they do not have primary adjectives) are marked with "n/a".

Language	Alignment (case)	Alignment (person)	Word order	Finite RCs	Adjectival agreement
Aguaruna	ACC	ACC	OV	+	−
Albanian	ACC	ACC	VO	+	+
Apatani	ACC	neutral	OV	−	−
Apsheron Tat	ACC	ACC	OV	sec	−
Barasano	ACC	ACC	no dom	−	n/a
Basque	ACT	ERG	OV	+	−
Beng	neutral	ERG	OV	+	−
Beserman Udmurt	ACC	ACC	OV	sec	−
Burushaski	ERG	ERG	OV	+	+
Chimariko	neutral	ACT	OV	−	n/a
Coahuilteco	neutral	ACC	OV	−	−
Cocama	neutral	neutral	VO	−	n/a
Cofán	ACC	ACC	no dom	+	−
Dhimal	ACC	ACC	OV	sec	−

https://doi.org/10.1515/9783110633382-010

Appendix 2. Properties of the languages in the core sample — 273

Language	Alignment (case)	Alignment (person)	Word order	Finite RCs	Adjectival agreement
Dolakha Newar	ERG	ACC	OV	–	–
Eastern Armenian	ACC	ACC	no dom	+	–
Erzya	ACC	ACC	VO	+	–
Even	ACC	ACC	OV	sec	+
Finnish	ACC	ACC	VO	+	+
Fula	neutral	ACC	VO	+	+
Garo	ACC	neutral	OV	–	–
Garrwa	ERG	neutral	no dom	+	+
Georgian	act	ACC	OV	+	+
German	ACC	ACC	VO	+	+
Guarijío	neutral	neutral	no dom	–	–
Hinuq	ERG	ERG	OV	–	+
Hopi	ACC	ACC	OV	–	n/a
Hungarian	ACC	ACC	no dom	+	–
Hup	ACC	neutral	OV	–	–
Imbabura Quechua	ACC	ACC	OV	–	–
Ingush	ERG	ERG	OV	–	+
Irish	neutral	ACC	VO	+	+
Italian	ACC	ACC	VO	+	+
Japhug rGyalrong	ERG	hier	OV	–	–
Kalmyk	ACC	ACC	OV	sec	–
Kamaiurá	neutral	act	OV	–	n/a
Kambaata	ACC	ACC	OV	–	+
Kayardild	ACC	neutral	no dom	+	+
Ket	neutral	act	OV	+	–
Kharia	ACC	ACC	no dom	+	–
Kobon	neutral	ACC	OV	+	–
Kolyma Yukaghir	ACC	ACC	OV	–	n/a
Komi-Zyrian	ACC	ACC	VO	sec	–
Koorete	ACC	ACC	OV	–	–
Korean	ACC	neutral	OV	–	–
Koryak	ERG	ERG	OV	+	+
Krongo	neutral	neutral	VO	–	n/a
Lezgian	ERG	ERG	OV	sec	–
Lithuanian	ACC	ACC	VO	+	+

Language	Alignment (case)	Alignment (person)	Word order	Finite RCs	Adjectival agreement
Luiseño	ACC	ACC	no dom	−	+
Maba	ACC	ACC	OV	+	+
Ma'di	neutral	ACC	no dom	−	+
Malayalam	acc	acc	OV	sec	−
Manange	ERG	neutral	OV	−	−
Mapudungun	neutral	hier	VO	−	−
Marathi	split ERG	split ERG	OV	sec	+
Maricopa	ACC	ACC	OV	+	n/a
Martuthunira	ACC	neutral	VO	+	+
Matsés	ERG	ACC	OV	−	−
Meadow Mari	ACC	ACC	OV	sec	−
Mẽbengokre	ACC	ACC	OV	−	−
Middle Egyptian	neutral	neutral	VO	sec	+
Mochica	neutral	ACC	VO	−	−
Modern Greek	ACC	ACC	no dom	+	+
Modern Standard Arabic	ACC	ACC	VO	+	+
Motuna	ERG	tripartite	OV	+	−
Muna	neutral	ACC	VO	−	−
Nanai	ACC	ACC	OV	−	−
Nanga	ACC	ACC	OV	−	−
Nevome	neutral	ACC	OV	−	−
Nias	ERG	split ERG	VO	+	−
Nivkh	neutral	neutral	OV	−	−
North Saami	ACC	ACC	VO	+	−
Northern Khanty	ACC	ACC	OV	sec	−
Panare	neutral	split ERG	VO	+	n/a
Pitta Pitta	split ERG	neutral	no dom	−	+
Rif Berber	ACC	ACC	VO	+	+
Ronghong Qiang	neutral	ACC	OV	−	−
Russian	ACC	ACC	VO	+	+
Santiam Kalapuya	neutral	ACC	VO	+	−
Savosavo	ACC	ACC	OV	−	−
Seri	neutral	ACC	OV	−	n/a
Sheko	ACC	ACC	OV	+	+

Appendix 2. Properties of the languages in the core sample

Language	Alignment (case)	Alignment (person)	Word order	Finite RCs	Adjectival agreement
Tamil	ACC	ACC	OV	sec	–
Tanti Dargwa	ERG	ERG	OV	–	–
Tariana	ACC	ACC	OV	–	+
Tarma Quechua	ACC	ACC	OV	–	–
Telugu	ACC	ACC	OV	sec	–
Tsafiki	ACC	ACC	OV	–	–
Tümpisa Shoshone	ACC	ERG	OV	–	+
Tundra Nenets	ACC	ACC	OV	sec	–
Urarina	neutral	ACC	OV	–	n/a
Wambaya	ERG	tripartite	no dom	+	+
Wan	neutral	neutral	OV	–	–
Wappo	ACC	neutral	OV	–	+
West Greenlandic	ERG	ACC	OV	–	n/a
Wikchamni	ACC	neutral	no dom	–	n/a
Wolio	neutral	ACC	VO	+	–
Yakut	ACC	ACC	OV	–	–
Yimas	neutral	ERG	no dom	+	+

Appendix 3. Forms considered in the study

The three tables in this appendix present different properties of the individual participial forms considered in the study. The table in Appendix 3a shows the relativizing capacity of all forms (for the relevant discussion see Chapter 3, in particular Section 3.2). The table in Appendix 3b focuses primarily on morphosyntactic signs of desententialization (see Chapter 5), while the table in Appendix 3c provides information on argument marking in participial relative clauses (see Chapter 6). All the forms in the tables are represented by affixes. In case a form does not have an easily identifiable affix, it is simply referred by the gloss.

Appendix 3a. Relativizing capacity

This table shows intrinsic relativizing capacity of all the forms considered in the study: "+" means "can be relativized", "–" means "cannot be relativized", "?" means "not enough data". If a participle can relativize only a subset of participants belonging to a particular column (e.g. only instruments or locatives among obliques), it is mentioned explicitly in the table. Brackets used with specific option mean that relativization of the respective participant is possible in the language, but rare. As discussed in Section 3.6, some of the forms can extend their orientation by means of specific affixes or resumptive elements, or under specific pragmatic conditions. These possibilities are marked separately: "aff" stands for extension by means of an affix, "res" stands for extension by means of a resumptive pronoun, "pragm" stands for pragmatically conditioned extension.

Language	Form	A	S	P	IO	OBL	POSS
Aguaruna	REL.SUBJ -*u*	+	+	–	–	–	–
Aguaruna	REL.NS -*mau*	–	–	+	+	+	?
Aguaruna	REL.NEG -*tʃau*	+	+	–	–	–	–
Albanian	PTCP -*rë*/-*r*/-*ur*/-*ë*	–	+	+	–	–	–
Apatani	NMZ -*nɨ*	+	+ (?)	+	+	–	–
Apatani	NMZ.INS -*nanɨ*	–	–	–	–	INS	–
Apsheron Tat	PTCP -*de*/-*re*	+	+	+	+	+	res
Barasano	NMZ (system)	+	+	+	?	?	?
Barasano	PTCP -*ri*	+	+	aff	?	aff	?
Basque	PTCP.PFV -*tu*/ (*e-*)V-*i*	–	+	+	–	–	–

Appendix 3a. Relativizing capacity — 277

Language	Form	A	S	P	IO	OBL	POSS
Beng	NMZ -lɛ	–	+	+	–	–	–
Beserman Udmurt	PTCP.PRS -š'	+	+	–	–	–	–
Beserman Udmurt	PTCP.PST -m	+	+	+	+	+	–
Beserman Udmurt	PTCP.NPST -n	–	–	+	+	+	–
Burushaski	PTCP -um	+	+	+	?	+ (?)	+ (?)
Chimariko	DEP -rop/-rot/-lop/-lot	+	+	+	?	?	?
Coahuilteco	SUB p-/pa-	+	+	+	+	INS	–
Cocama	NMZ.A -tara	+	–	–	–	–	–
Cocama	NMZ.S/P -n	–	+	+	–	–	–
Cocama	NMZ.LOC -tupa	–	–	–	(+)	LOC	–
Cofán	PTCP -'su	+	+	–	–	–	–
Dhimal	NMZ -ka	+	+	+	+	+	?
Dolakha Newar	NMZ.SUBJ -gu/-ku/-u	+	+	–	–	–	–
Dolakha Newar	NMZ.NS -e/-a	–	–	+	+	+	–
Eastern Armenian	PTCP.SUBJ -oł	+ (?)	+	–	–	–	–
Eastern Armenian	PTCP.RES -ac	–	+	+	–	–	–
Eastern Armenian	PTCP.FUT -ik'	–	– (?)	+	–	–	–
Erzya	PTCP.PRS -i(c'a)	+	+	–	–	–	–
Erzya	PTCP.PFV -z'	–	+	+	–	–	–
Erzya	PTCP.PST -vt	–	+	+	–	–	–
Even	PTCP.NFUT -ri/-i/-si/-di	+	+	+	+	+	res
Even	PTCP.PRF -ča/-če	+	+	+	+	+	res
Even	PTCP.PST -daŋ/-deŋ	+ (?)	+ (?)	+	+	+	res
Even	PTCP.NEC -nna/-nne	+	+	+	+	+	res
Even	PTCP.HYP -d'iŋa/-d'iŋe	+	+	+	+	+	res
Finnish	PTCP.PST.ACT -nut	+	+	–	–	–	–
Finnish	PTCP.PRS.ACT -va	+	+	–	–	–	–
Finnish	PTCP.PST.PASS -tu	–	–	+	–	–	–
Finnish	PTCP.PRS.PASS -tava	–	–	+	–	–	–
Finnish	PTCP.A -ma	–	–	+	–	–	–

Appendix 3. Forms considered in the study

Language	Form	A	S	P	IO	OBL	POSS
Finnish	PTCP.NEG -*maton*	+	+	+	–	some	–
Fula	PTCP.PST.ACT -*u*/-Ø	+	+	–	–	–	–
Fula	PTCP.PST.MID -*ii*/-*i*	–	+	–	–	–	–
Fula	PTCP.PST.PASS -*aa*/-*a*	–	–	+	–	–	–
Fula	PTCP.FUT.ACT -*oo*/-*ay*	+	+	–	–	–	–
Fula	PTCP.FUT.MID -*otoo*/-*oto*	–	+	–	–	–	–
Fula	PTCP.FUT.PASS -*etee*/-*ete*	–	–	+	–	–	–
Garo	NMZ -*gipa*	+	+	+	+	+	– (?)
Garrwa	NMZ.CHAR -*warr*	+	+	–	–	–	–
Georgian	PTCP.ACT *m-V(-el)*	+	+	–	–	–	–
Georgian	PTCP.PST -*ul*/-*il*/*m-V-ar*	–	+	+	–	–	–
Georgian	PTCP.FUT *sa-V(-el)*	–	–	+	–	–	–
Georgian	PTCP.PRIV *u-V(-el)*	–	+	+	–	–	–
German	PTCP.PRS -*end*	+	+	–	–	–	–
German	PTCP.PST	–	+	+	–	–	–
Guarijío	NMZ.S/A -*me*	+	+	–	–	–	–
Guarijío	NMZ.P/OBL -*a*	–	–	+	+	INS	–
Guarijío	NMZ.LOC -*ači*	–	–	–	–	LOC	–
Hinuq	PTCP -*o goła*	+	+	+	+	+	+
Hinuq	PTCP.PST -*(y)oru*	+	+	+	+	+	+
Hinuq	PTCP.HAB -*ƛ'os*	+	+	+	+	+	+
Hinuq	PTCP.RES -*s*	(+)	+	+	(+)	(+)	(+)
Hinuq	PTCP.LOC -*a*	–	–	–	–	LOC	–
Hopi	REL -*qa*	+	+	+	+	+, res if PP	?
Hungarian	PTCP.ACT -*ó*	+	+	–	–	–	–
Hungarian	PTCP.PST -*ott*	–	+	+	–	–	–
Hup	DEP -*Vp*	+	+	+	+	+	–
Imbabura Quechua	NMZ.PST -*shka*	+	+	+	+	+	–
Imbabura Quechua	NMZ.PRS -*j*	+	+	+	+	+	–
Imbabura Quechua	NMZ.FUT -*na*	+	+	+	+	+	–
Ingush	PTCP.PST -*aa*/-*na*	+	+	+	+	+	+, INAL

Appendix 3a. Relativizing capacity — **279**

Language	Form	A	S	P	IO	OBL	POSS
Ingush	PTCP.PRS -*a*	+	+	+	+	+	+, INAL
Ingush	CVB.SIM -*(a)zh*	+	+	+	+	+	+, INAL
Irish	PTCP.PST -*tha*/-*the*	–	+	+	–	–	–
Italian	PTCP.PST -*t*-	–	+	+	–	–	–
Japhug rGyalrong	NMZ.S/A *kɯ*-	+	+	–	–	–	res, POSS of S/A
Japhug rGyalrong	NMZ.P *kɤ*-	–	–	+	if =P	–	res, POSS of P
Japhug rGyalrong	NMZ.OBL *sɤ*-	–	–	–	+	+	–
Kalmyk	PTCP.PST -*sən*	+	+	+	+	+, res if PP	res
Kalmyk	PTCP.FUT-*xə*	+	+	+	+	+, res if PP	res
Kalmyk	PTCP.HAB -*dəg*	+	+	+	+	+, res if PP	res
Kalmyk	PTCP.PASS -*ata*	–	–	+	–	–	–
Kamaiurá	NMZ.A -*tat*	+	–	–	–	–	res, POSS of A
Kamaiurá	NMZ.S -*ama'e*	–	+	–	–	–	res, POSS of S
Kamaiurá	NMZ.P -*ipyt*	–	–	+	–	–	res, POSS of P
Kamaiurá	NMZ.OBJ -*emi*	–	–	+	–	–	res, POSS of P
Kamaiurá	NMZ.OBL -*tap*	–	–	–	+	+	res, poss of OBL
Kamaiurá	NMZ.NEG.S -*uma'e*	–	+	–	–	–	res, POSS of S
Kambaata	REL	+	+	+	+	+	res
Kambaata	PTCP.NEG -*umb*	+	+	+	+	+	res
Kayardild	NMZ-CONS -*n-ngarrba*	+	+	aff	–	aff	–
Kayardild	RES-NMZ -*thirri-n*-	–	?	+	–	–	–
Ket	NMZ	+	+	+	+	+	–
Kharia	PTCP	+	+	+	?	+	–
Kobon	NMZ/ADJR -*eb*/-*ep*	+	+	–	–	–	–
Kolyma Yukaghir	ATTR.ACT -*je*	+	+	+	+	?	res, POSS of S
Kolyma Yukaghir	NMZ -*l*	+	(+)	+	+	+	res, POSS of S
Kolyma Yukaghir	NMZ.RES -*ōl*	–	–	+	–	LOC	–
Kolyma Yukaghir	ATTR.PASS -*me*	–	–	+	+	+	–
Komi-Zyrian	PTCP.ACT -*iš'*	+	+	–	–	–	–
Komi-Zyrian	PTCP.PFV -*əm(a)*	+	+	+	?	+	POSS of P
Komi-Zyrian	PTCP.HAB -*an(a)*	(+)	(+)	+	+	+	?

Language	Form	A	S	P	IO	OBL	POSS
Komi-Zyrian	PTCP.NEG -tam	+	+	+	+	+	?
Koorete	PTCP.IPFV -e	+	?	+	?	?	?
Koorete	PTCP.PFV.SUBJ -a	+	+	−	−	−	−
Koorete	PTCP.PFV.NS -o	−	−	+	?	+	?
Korean	REL -n	+	+	+	+	+	+
Korean	REL.PRS -nɨn	+	+	+	+	+	+
Korean	REL.FUT -l	+	+	+	+	+	+
Koryak	NMZ -lʕ-	−	+	+	−	−	−
Koryak	NMZ-NOMFUT -jo-lqal	−	+	+	−	−	−
Krongo	CONN ŋ-	?	+	res (?)	res	res	?
Lezgian	PTCP -j	+	+	+	+	+	+, INAL
Lithuanian	PTCP.PST.ACT -us- HAB-PTCP.PST.ACT -dav-us-	+	+	−	−	−	−
Lithuanian	PTCP.PRS.ACT -nt- FUT-PTCP.PRS.ACT -si-ant-	+	+	−	−	−	−
Lithuanian	PTCP.PST.PASS -t-	−	−	+	−	−	−
Lithuanian	PTCP.PRS.PASS -m- FUT-PTCP.PRS.PASS -si-m-	−	−	+	−	−	−
Luiseño	REL (system)	+	+	+	+	+	−
Maba	PTCP n-	+	+	−	−	−	−
Ma'di	SR.S/A -rɛ̄ (SG)/ -ɓá (PL)	+	+	−	−	res, COM	res, POSS of S/A
Ma'di	SR.P -lɛ́	−	−	+	−	−	res, POSS of P
Ma'di	SR.INS -dʒɔ́	−	−	−	−	INS, PURP	res, POSS of INS/PURP
Malayalam	PTCP -a	+	+	+	+	+	+, INAL
Malayalam	PTCP.NEG -aatta	+	+	+	+	+	+, INAL
Manange	NMZ -pʌ	+	+	+	?	+	?
Mapudungun	PTCP.ACT -lu	+	+	−	−	−	−
Mapudungun	PTCP.PASS -el	−	−	+	if =P	−	−
Marathi	PTCP (system)	+	+	+	+	+, if not PP	−
Maricopa	REL kw-	+	+	−	−	−	pragm
Maricopa	NMZ.NS	−	−	+	+	+	?

Appendix 3a. Relativizing capacity — **281**

Language	Form	A	S	P	IO	OBL	POSS
Martuthunira	REL.PRS -nyila	+	+	–	–	–	–
Matsés	NMZ.A/S -quid	+	+, REC	–	–	–	–
Matsés	NMZ.P -aid	–	+, REC	+, not FUT	+, not FUT	+, not FUT, not INS in PRS	–
Matsés	NMZ.INS -te/ -tequid	–	–	+, FUT	+, FUT	INS, not REC	–
Matsés	NMZ (system)	+	+	+	+	+	–
Matsés	NMZ.NEG.S/A.HAB -esa	+	+	–	–	–	–
Matsés	NMZ.NEG.P/INS.PFV -acmaid	–	–	+	–	INS	–
Matsés	NMZ.NEG.P/INS.HAB -temaid	–	–	+	–	INS	–
Meadow Mari	PTCP.ACT -še	+	+	–	–	–	–
Meadow Mari	PTCP.FUT -šaš	+	+	+	+	+	res
Meadow Mari	PTCP.NS -me	–	–	+	+	+	res
Meadow Mari	PTCP.NEG -dəme	+	+	+	+	+	res
Mēbengokre	NMZ	+	+	+	+	+	+
Middle Egyptian	PTCP.SUBJ	+	+	–	–	–	–
Middle Egyptian	PTCP.NS	–	–	+	res	res (?)	–
Mochica	NMZ.STAT -d.o	–	+	+	–	–	–
Modern Greek	PTCP.PST -ménos	–	+	+	–	–	–
Modern Standard Arabic	PTCP.ACT	+	+	(res)	(res)	(res)	(res)
Modern Standard Arabic	PTCP.PASS	–	–	+	(res)	(res)	(res)
Motuna	PTCP -(wa)h	+	+	+	?	+	res
Muna	PTCP.ACT mo-V-no	+	+	–	–	–	pragm/res, POSS of S/A
Muna	PTCP.PASS ni-	–	–	+	aff	–	–
Muna	NMZ ka-	–	–	+	–	–	–
Muna	NMZ-V-LOC ka-V-ha	–	–	–	–	LOC	–
Nanai	PTCP.PST -xan/ -kin/-čin	+	+	+	+	+	res

Appendix 3. Forms considered in the study

Language	Form	A	S	P	IO	OBL	POSS
Nanai	PTCP.NPST -j/-ri/-di/-či	+	+	+	+	+	res
Nanga	PTCP.PFV -sɛ̀	+	+	+	+	+	+
Nanga	PTCP.IPFV -mì	+	+	+	+	+	+
Nevome	NMZ -cama	+ (?)	+	?	?	?	?
Nevome	NMZ.FUT -cugai	?	?	+	?	?	?
Nevome	NMZ.LOC.PRS -cami	–	–	–	–	LOC	–
Nevome	NMZ.LOC.HAB -carhami	–	–	–	–	LOC	–
Nevome	NMZ.LOC.PST -parhami	–	–	–	–	LOC	–
Nevome	NMZ.LOC.FUT -aicami	–	–	–	–	LOC	–
Nias	PTCP.PASS ni-	–	–	+	(+)	–, (DAT)	–
Nivkh	PTCP	+	+	+	+	+	– (?)
North Saami	PTCP.PRS -i/-(jead)dji	+	+	–	–	–	–
North Saami	PTCP.PST -n	+	+	–	–	–	–
North Saami	PTCP.A -n	–	–	+	–	–	–
North Saami	PTCP.NEG -keahtes	+	+	+	–	–	–
Northern Khanty	PTCP.PST -m	+	+	+	+	+	res
Northern Khanty	PTCP.NPST -ti	+	+	+	+	+	res
Northern Khanty	PTCP.NEG -li	– (?)	+	+	– (?)	– (?)	–
Panare	PTCP.A -jpo	+	– (?)	–	–	–	–
Panare	PTCP.PST -sa'	–	+	+	–	–	–
Pitta Pitta	PST -ka	+	+	+	+	+	+
Rif Berber	PTCP.ACT	+	+	–	–	–	–
Ronghong Qiang	NMZ.AN -m	+	+	–	+	?	+
Ronghong Qiang	NMZ.INS -s	–	–	–	–	INS, (LOC)	–
Russian	PTCP.PST.ACT -vš-/-š-	+	+	–	–	–	–
Russian	PTCP.PRS.ACT -ušč-/-ašč-	+	+	–	–	–	–
Russian	PTCP.PST.PASS -n-/-t-	–	–	+	–	–	–

Appendix 3a. Relativizing capacity — **283**

Language	Form	A	S	P	IO	OBL	POSS
Russian	PTCP.PRS.PASS -em-/-im-	–	–	+	–	–	–
Santiam Kalapuya	INF gi-	+	+ (?)	?	– (?)	– (?)	– (?)
Savosavo	REL -tu	+	+	+	+	+	res
Seri	NMZ.SUBJ	+	+	–	–	–	POSS of S/A
Seri	NMZ.OBJ	–	–	+	=P	–	POSS of P
Seri	NMZ.OBL	–	–	–	–	+	POSS of OBL
Sheko	REL -əb, -əbe (F.SG)	+	+	+	+	+	res
Tamil	PTCP -a	+	+	+	+	+	–
Tamil	PTCP.FUT -um	+	+	+	+	+	–
Tanti Dargwa	PRET[PTCP]/ATTR -se	+	+	+	+	+	+
Tanti Dargwa	PRS[PTCP]/ATTR -se	+	+	+	+	+	+
Tanti Dargwa	PTCP.POT -an	+	+	+	+	+	+
Tariana	REL ka-	+	+	–	–	–	–
Tariana	REL.PST ka-V-kari (M)/ ka-V-karu (F)/ ka-V-kani (PL)	+	+	–	–	–	–
Tariana	REL.FUT ka-V-pena	+	+	–	–	–	–
Tariana	NMZ.P -nipe	–	–	+	–	–	–
Tariana	NMZ.NS -mi	–	–	+	?	LOC	–
Tarma Quechua	NMZ.SUBJ -q	+	+	–	–	–	–
Tarma Quechua	NMZ.STAT -sha	–	+	+	–	–	–
Tarma Quechua	NMZ.NFUT -nqa	–	–	+	+	+	?
Tarma Quechua	NMZ.FUT -na	–	–	+	+	+	?
Telugu	PTCP.PST -ina	+	+	+	+	some	?
Telugu	PTCP.FUT -ee	+	+	+	+	some	?
Telugu	PTCP.DUR -tunna	+	+	+	+	some	?
Telugu	PTCP.NEG -ani	+	+	+	+	some	?
Tsafiki	PTCP.IPFV -min	+	+	(+)	–	–	–
Tsafiki	PTCP.PFV -ka	(+)	+	+	–	–	–
Tsafiki	NMZ.INS/LOC -nun	–	–	–	–	INS, LOC	–
Tümpisa Shoshone	PTCP.PRS -tün	+	+	–	–	–	–
Tümpisa Shoshone	PTCP.PST -ppüh	–	–	+	+	res	–
Tümpisa Shoshone	INF -nna	–	–	+	+	res	–

Appendix 3. Forms considered in the study

Language	Form	A	S	P	IO	OBL	POSS
Tundra Nenets	PTCP.PFV -mia/-me	+	+	+	–	–	res, POSS of S/A
Tundra Nenets	PTCP.IPFV -n(')a/-t(')a	+	+	+	–	–	res, POSS of S/A
Tundra Nenets	PTCP.FUT -mənta	+	+	+	–	–	res, POSS of S/A
Tundra Nenets	NMZ.PFV -(o)qm(')a	–	–	–	+	+	res, POSS of non-S/A
Tundra Nenets	NMZ.IPFV -m(')a	–	–	–	+	+	res, POSS of non-S/A
Tundra Nenets	CVB.MOD -s'ə/-ə	–	–	–	+	+	res, POSS of non-S/A
Tundra Nenets	PTCP.NEG -mədawe(y(ə))	+	+	+	–	–	?
Urarina	NMZ.A -era	+	–	–	–	–	–
Urarina	NMZ.S/P -i	–	+	+	–	–	–
Wambaya	NMZ.A	+	+	–	–	–	–
Wan	NMZ.ATTR -ŋ	–	–	+	+	+	–
Wappo	DEP (system)	+	+	+	+	?	?
West Greenlandic	PTCP.ACT -soq	aff	+	–	–	–	res, POSS of S/A
West Greenlandic	PTCP.PASS -saq	–	–	+	–	aff	res, POSS of P
Wikchamni	VN.SUBJ {-ač/}/{-ič/}	+	+	–	–	–	–
Wikchamni	VN.PASS {-ʔaṅa/}/{-ʔ...aṅa/}	–	–	+	–	–	–
Wolio	PTCP.ACT mo-	+(?)	+	–	–	–	–
Wolio	PTCP.PASS i-	–	–	+	–	–	–
Yakut	PTCP.PST -bït	+	+	+	+	+	res
Yakut	PTCP.PRS -ar/-ïr	+	+	+	+	+	res
Yakut	PTCP.FUT -ïax	+	+	+	+	+	res
Yakut	PTCP.NEG.PST -batax	+	+	+	+	+	res
Yakut	PTCP.NEG.PRS -bat	+	+	+	+	+	res
Yakut	PTCP.NEG.FUT -(ï)mïax	+	+	+	+	+	res
Yimas	NF -ru	+	+	–	–	–	–
Yimas	NF.NEG -kakan	+	+	+	–	–	–

Appendix 3b. Position and desententialization

This table contains information on the position of participial relative clauses introduced by individual forms, and on the morphosyntactic signs of desententialization these forms show. The positional types of relative clauses represented in the table are prenominal ("pre"), postnominal ("post"), free (either pre- or postnominal), internally headed ("int.h."), and adjoined ("adj."); see Dryer (2013b). The rest of the columns (from left to right) show:
- whether the form is +TAM or –TAM;
- whether it can take additional inflectional TAM markers, and if yes, then which;
- what TAM meaning the form has (e.g. past or present), or what determines its TAM meaning (e.g. context);
- how the form is negated ("nom" here means that a nominal negative marker is used; "spec" means that a specialized affix or construction is available; "n/a" stands for "not applicable", and it means that the form itself is negative);
- whether the form shows nominal agreement with the modified noun, and if yes, then with respect to which nominal categories (e.g. case and number).

The information presented in this table comes primarily from descriptions of individual languages, and in most cases, TAM meanings are labelled in the way they are referred to in the sources. Brackets used with specific option mean "possible, but rare".

Language	Form	Position	TAM (+/–)	TAM markers	TAM meaning	Negation	Nominal agreement
Aguaruna	REL.SUBJ -*u*	pre/post	–	aspect. stem	stem	REL.NEG	–
Aguaruna	REL.NS -*mau*	pre/post/int.h.	–	aspect. stem	stem	none	–
Aguaruna	REL.NEG -*tʃau*	pre/post	–	aspect./ unmarked stem	stem/ context	n/a	–
Albanian	PTCP -*rë*/-*r*/-*ur*/-*ë*	post	+	no	PFV	reg	case, number, gender
Apatani	NMZ -*nɨ*	pre	?	no (?)	PST (?)	?	–
Apatani	NMZ.INS -*nanɨ*	pre	?	no (?)	PRS (?)	?	–

Appendix 3. Forms considered in the study

Language	Form	Position	TAM (+/−)	TAM markers	TAM meaning	Negation	Nominal agreement
Apsheron Tat	PTCP -de/-re	pre	−	no	context, factual	?	−
Barasano	NMZ	post/pre	+	yes	marker	reg (?)	number, gender
Barasano	PTCP -ri	post/pre	−	no	context (?)	reg (?)	noun class
Basque	PTCP.PFV -tu/(e-)V-i	pre/(post)	+	no	PFV, RES	?	−
Beng	NMZ -lɛ	int.h.	+	no	RES	?	−
Beserman Udmurt	PTCP.PRS -š'	pre/(post)	+	no	SIM	CAR -tem	−
Beserman Udmurt	PTCP.PST -m	pre/(post)	+	no	PFV, ANT	spec -te	−
Beserman Udmurt	PTCP.NPST -n	pre/(post)	+	no	NPST, HAB	CAR -tem	−
Burushaski	PTCP -um	pre	+	IPFV	PFV	?	number (optional)
Chimariko	DEP -rop/-rot/-lop/-lot	int.h.	−	no	context	?	−
Coahuilteco	SUB p-/pa-	post	−	no	context	?	−
Cocama	NMZ.A -tara	pre/post	−	no	AUX marker	reg	−
Cocama	NMZ.S/P -n	pre/post	−	no	AUX marker	reg	−
Cocama	NMZ.LOC -tupa	pre/post	−	no	AUX marker	reg	−
Cofán	PTCP -'su	pre	−	no	?	?	−
Dhimal	NMZ -ka	pre	−	no (?)	context (?)	reg	−
Dolakha Newar	NMZ.SUBJ -gu/-ku/-u	pre	−	no (?)	context (?)	reg	−
Dolakha Newar	NMZ.NS -e/-a	pre	−	no (?)	context (?)	reg	−
Eastern Armenian	PTCP.SUBJ -oł	pre	+	no	SIM, HAB	?	−
Eastern Armenian	PTCP.RES -ac	pre	+	no	RES	?	−

Appendix 3b. Position and desententialization

Language	Form	Position	TAM (+/−)	TAM markers	TAM meaning	Negation	Nominal agreement
Eastern Armenian	PTCP.FUT -ik'	pre	+	no	FUT, DEB	?	–
Erzya	PTCP.PRS -i(c'a)	pre	+	no	SIM, HAB	reg	–
Erzya	PTCP.PFV -z'	pre	+	no	ANT	apak	–
Erzya	PTCP.PST -vt	pre	+	no	ANT	apak	–
Even	PTCP.NFUT -ri/ -i/-si/-di	pre/ int.h.	+	aspect	ANT, SIM	?	case, number
Even	PTCP.PRF -ča/ -če	pre/ int.h.	+	aspect	PFV, ANT	?	case, number
Even	PTCP.PST -daŋ/ -deŋ	pre/ int.h.	+	aspect	PST, ANT	?	case, number
Even	PTCP.NEC -nna/ -nne	pre/ int.h.	+	aspect	NEC	?	case, number
Even	PTCP.HYP -d'iŋa/-d'iŋe	pre/ int.h.	+	aspect	POT	?	case, number
Finnish	PTCP.PST.ACT -nut	pre	+	no	PST	PTCP.NEG	case, number
Finnish	PTCP.PRS.ACT -va	pre	+	no	PRS	PTCP.NEG	case, number
Finnish	PTCP.PST.PASS -tu	pre	+	no	PST	PTCP.NEG	case, number
Finnish	PTCP.PRS.PASS -tava	pre	+	no	PRS, DEB	PTCP.NEG	case, number
Finnish	PTCP.A -ma	pre	+	no	PFV, PST	PTCP.NEG	case, number
Finnish	PTCP.NEG -maton	pre	−	no	context	n/a	case, number
Fula	PTCP.PST.ACT -u/-Ø	post	+	yes	PST	none	noun class
Fula	PTCP.PST.MID -ii/-i	post	+	yes	PST, (PRS)	none	noun class
Fula	PTCP.PST.PASS -aa/-a	post	+	yes	PST	none	noun class
Fula	PTCP.FUT.ACT -oo/-ay	post	+	yes	PRS, FUT	none	noun class
Fula	PTCP.FUT.MID -otoo/-oto	post	+	yes	PRS, FUT	none	noun class

Appendix 3. Forms considered in the study

Language	Form	Position	TAM (+/−)	TAM markers	TAM meaning	Negation	Nominal agreement
Fula	PTCP.FUT.PASS -etee/-ete	post	+	yes	HAB, FUT	none	noun class
Garo	NMZ -gipa	pre	−	aspect	marker/ context	nom. -gija	–
Garrwa	NMZ.CHAR -warr	post	+	no	HAB	?	case
Georgian	PTCP.ACT m-V(-el)	pre/ (post)	−	no	context	none	nominal
Georgian	PTCP.PST -ul/ -il/m-V-ar	pre/ (post)	+	no	PFV	PTCP. PRIV	nominal
Georgian	PTCP.FUT sa-V(-el)	pre/ (post)	+	no	FUT, DEB	PTCP. PRIV	nominal
Georgian	PTCP.PRIV u-V(-el)	pre/ (post)	+	no	PFV, POT	n/a	nominal
German	PTCP.PRS -end	pre	+	no	SIM, HAB	reg	case, number, gender
German	PTCP.PST	pre	+	no	RES	reg	case, number, gender
Guarijío	NMZ.S/A -me	post	−	some	marker	?	–
Guarijío	NMZ.P/OBL -a	post	−	some	marker	?	–
Guarijío	NMZ.LOC -ači	post	−	some	marker	?	–
Hinuq	PTCP -o goła	pre/ (post)	+	no	PST, PRS (relative)	(reg)	–
Hinuq	PTCP.PST -(y)oru	pre/ (post)	+	no	PST (relative)	(reg)	–
Hinuq	PTCP.HAB -ƛ'os	pre/ (post)	+	no	PRS, FUT (relative), HAB	(reg)	–
Hinuq	PTCP.RES -s	pre/ (post)	+	no	PST (relative), RES	(reg)	–
Hinuq	PTCP.LOC -a	pre/ (post)	−	no	context	(reg)	–
Hopi	REL -qa	post	−	no (?)	context (?)	?	number
Hungarian	PTCP.ACT -ó	pre	+	no	SIM, HAB	reg	–
Hungarian	PTCP.PST -ott	pre	+	no	PFV	reg	–
Hup	DEP -Vp	pre	−	inner suffixes	marker	reg	–

Language	Form	Position	TAM (+/−)	TAM markers	TAM meaning	Negation	Nominal agreement
Imbabura Quechua	NMZ.PST -shka	pre/int.h.	+	some	PST	none	case if post
Imbabura Quechua	NMZ.PRS -j	pre/int.h.	+	some	PRS	none	case if post
Imbabura Quechua	NMZ.FUT -na	pre	+	some	FUT	none	case if post
Ingush	PTCP.PST -aa/-na	pre	+	no	PST	NF cy= lexical	reduced case
Ingush	PTCP.PRS -a	pre	+	no	PRS	NF cy=	reduced case
Ingush	CVB.SIM -(a)zh	pre	+	no	PROG	NF cy=	–
Irish	PTCP.PST -tha/-the	post	+	no	RES	?	–
Italian	PTCP.PST -t-	post	+	no	RES	reg	number, gender
Japhug rGyalrong	NMZ.S/A kɯ-	pre/int.h.	–	restricted	marker	reg	–
Japhug rGyalrong	NMZ.P kɤ-	pre/int.h.	–	restricted	marker	reg	–
Japhug rGyalrong	NMZ.OBL sɤ-	pre	–	IPFV	marker	reg	–
Kalmyk	PTCP.PST -sən	pre	+	PROG	PFV	NF esə	–
Kalmyk	PTCP.FUT -xə	pre	+	PROG	FUT	NF esə	–
Kalmyk	PTCP.HAB -dəg	pre	+	no	HAB	NF esə	–
Kalmyk	PTCP.PASS -ata	pre	+	no	RES	?	–
Kamaiurá	NMZ.A -tat	post	–	yes	marker	nom.	–
Kamaiurá	NMZ.S -ama'e	post	–	yes	marker	nom.	–
Kamaiurá	NMZ.P -ipyt	post	–	yes	marker	nom.	–
Kamaiurá	NMZ.OBJ -emi	post	–	yes	marker	nom.	–
Kamaiurá	NMZ.OBL -tap	post	–	yes	marker	nom.	–
Kamaiurá	NMZ.NEG.S -uma'e	post	–	yes	marker	nom.	–
Kambaata	REL	pre	–	PFV, IPFV, PROG	marker	PTCP.NEG	–
Kambaata	PTCP.NEG -umb	pre	–	no	context	n/a	case, gender
Kayardild	NMZ-CONS -n-ngarrba	pre/post	+	no	ANT	none	case

Language	Form	Position	TAM (+/−)	TAM markers	TAM meaning	Negation	Nominal agreement
Kayardild	RES-NMZ -thirri-n-	pre/post	+	no	RES	none	case
Ket	NMZ	pre	−	no	PRS (SUBJ) PST (DO)	?	−
Kharia	PTCP	pre	−	no	context	?	−
Kobon	NMZ/ADJR -eb/ -ep	pre	+	no	hab (?)	reg (?)	−
Kolyma Yukaghir	ATTR.ACT -je	pre	−	no	(FUT)	context, marker	reg	−
Kolyma Yukaghir	NMZ -l	pre	−	no	(FUT)	context, marker	?	−
Kolyma Yukaghir	NMZ.RES -ōl	pre	+	no	RES	?	−
Kolyma Yukaghir	ATTR.PASS -me	pre	−	no	(FUT)	context, marker	reg	−
Komi-Zyrian	PTCP.ACT -iš'	pre/(post)	+	no	SIM, PRS, HAB	PTCP. NEG	case, number if post
Komi-Zyrian	PTCP.PFV -am(a)	pre/(post)	+	no	PFV, PST	PTCP. NEG	case, number if post
Komi-Zyrian	PTCP.HAB -an(a)	pre/(post)	+	no	PST, HAB	PTCP. NEG	case, number if post
Komi-Zyrian	PTCP.NEG -təm	pre/(post)	−	no	context	n/a	case, number if post
Koorete	PTCP.IPFV -e	pre	+	no (?)	IPFV	reg	−
Koorete	PTCP.PFV.SUBJ -a	pre	+	no (?)	PFV	reg	−
Koorete	PTCP.PFV.NS -o	pre	+	no (?)	PFV	reg	−
Korean	REL -n	pre	+	RET, PST	PST, PRS	reg	−
Korean	REL.PRS -nɨn	pre	+	no	PRS	reg	−
Korean	REL.FUT -l	pre	+	PST, (FUT)	FUT, HYP	reg	−
Koryak	NMZ -lʕ-	post/pre	+	no	PRS, PST	?	case, number
Koryak	NMZ-NOMFUT -jo-lqəl	post/pre	+	no	FUT	?	case, number
Krongo	CONN ŋ-	post	−	yes	marker	?	gender
Lezgian	PTCP -j	pre	−	some	marker	NF te-	−
Lithuanian	PTCP.PST.ACT -us-	free	+	HAB	PST	reg (?)	case, number, gender

Language	Form	Position	TAM (+/−)	TAM markers	TAM meaning	Negation	Nominal agreement
Lithuanian	PTCP.PRS.ACT -nt-	free	+	FUT	PRS	reg (?)	case, number, gender
Lithuanian	PTCP.PST.PASS -t-	free	+	HAB	PST	reg (?)	case, number, gender
Lithuanian	PTCP.PRS.PASS -m-	free	+	FUT	PRS	reg (?)	case, number, gender
Luiseño	REL (system)	post	+	n/a	many	?	case, number
Maba	PTCP n-	post	−	some	marker	reg	number
Ma'di	SR.S/A -rɛ̃ (SG)/ -bá (PL)	post	−	no	context	reg	−
Ma'di	SR.P -lɛ́	post	−	no	context	reg	−
Ma'di	SR.INS -dʒɔ́	post	−	no	context	reg	−
Malayalam	PTCP -a	pre	−	some	marker	PTCP.NEG	−
Malayalam	PTCP.NEG -aatta	pre	−	aspect	marker, context	n/a	−
Manange	NMZ -pʌ	pre	−	no	context	?	−
Mapudungun	PTCP.ACT -lu	post	−	yes	marker	NF -no-	−
Mapudungun	PTCP.PASS -el	post	−	yes	marker	NF -no-	−
Marathi	PTCP (system)	pre	+	n/a	many	PTCP.NEG	number, gender
Maricopa	REL kw-	int.h.	−	irrealis	context, marker	reg	matrix clause
Maricopa	NMZ.NS	int.h.	−	irrealis	context, marker	reg	matrix clause
Martuthunira	REL.PRS -nyila	post	+	no	PRS	?	case
Matsés	NMZ.A/S -quid	free	−	no	context	NMZ.NEG	case
Matsés	NMZ.P -aid	free	−	no	context, NFUT	NMZ.NEG	case
Matsés	NMZ.INS -te/ -tequid	free	−	no	context, NPST	NMZ.NEG	case
Matsés	NMZ (system)	free	+	n/a	many	NMZ.NEG	case
Matsés	NMZ.NEG.S/A. HAB -esa	free	+	no	HAB	n/a	case

Language	Form	Position	TAM (+/−)	TAM markers	TAM meaning	Negation	Nominal agreement
Matsés	NMZ.NEG.P/INS.PFV -acmaid	free	+	no	PFV	n/a	case
Matsés	NMZ.NEG.P/INS.HAB -temaid	free	+	no	HAB	n/a	case
Meadow Mari	PTCP.ACT -še	pre/(post)	−	no	context	PTCP.NEG	case, number if post
Meadow Mari	PTCP.FUT -šaš	pre/(post)	+	no	FUT, HAB, MOD	PTCP.NEG	case, number if post
Meadow Mari	PTCP.NS -me	pre/(post)	−	no	context	PTCP.NEG	case, number if post
Meadow Mari	PTCP.NEG -dəme	pre/(post)	−	no	context	n/a	case, number if post
Mēbengokre	NMZ	int.h.	−	some	marker, context	reg	–
Middle Egyptian	PTCP.SUBJ	post	−	no (?)	verb root	reg	number, gender
Middle Egyptian	PTCP.NS	post	−	no (?)	verb root	reg	number, gender
Mochica	NMZ.STAT -d.o	pre	+	no (?)	RES	?	–
Modern Greek	PTCP.PST -ménos	post	+	no	PFV	verbal adj.	case, number, gender
Modern Standard Arabic	PTCP.ACT	post	−	no	context	adj. ghayr	case, definiteness
Modern Standard Arabic	PTCP.PASS	post	−	no	context	adj. ghayr	case, definiteness
Motuna	PTCP -(wa)h	post/pre	−	no	context	?	(number)
Muna	PTCP.ACT mo-V-no	post	−	FUT	context, marker	NF pata	–
Muna	PTCP.PASS ni-	post	−	FUT	context, marker	NF pata	–
Muna	NMZ ka-	post	−	no	context	nom. suano	–
Muna	NMZ-V-LOC ka-V-ha	post	−	no	context	nom. suano	–
Nanai	PTCP.PST -xan/-kin/-čin	pre	+	aspect	PST	?	–
Nanai	PTCP.NPST -j/-ri/-di/-či	pre	+	aspect	NPST	?	–

Appendix 3b. Position and desententialization — **293**

Language	Form	Position	TAM (+/−)	TAM markers	TAM meaning	Negation	Nominal agreement
Nanga	PTCP.PFV -sɛ̀	int.h.	+	AUX only	PFV	reg	−
Nanga	PTCP.IPFV -mì	int.h.	+	AUX only	IPFV	reg	−
Nevome	NMZ -cama	post	+	no (?)	HAB	reg	−
Nevome	NMZ.FUT -cugai	post	+	no (?)	FUT.RES	reg	−
Nevome	NMZ.LOC.PRS -cami	post	+	no (?)	PRS	reg	−
Nevome	NMZ.LOC.HAB -carhami	post	+	no (?)	HAB	reg	−
Nevome	NMZ.LOC.PST -parhami	post	+	no (?)	PST	reg	−
Nevome	NMZ.LOC.FUT -aicami	post	+	no (?)	FUT	reg	−
Nias	PTCP.PASS ni-	post	+	no	IPFV	spec	−
Nivkh	PTCP	pre	−	yes	marker	reg	−
North Saami	PTCP.PRS -i/-(jead)dji	pre	+	no	SIM, HAB	PTCP.NEG	−
North Saami	PTCP.PST -n	pre	+	no	ANT	PTCP.NEG	−
North Saami	PTCP.A -n	pre	+	no	ANT	PTCP.NEG	−
North Saami	PTCP.NEG -keahtes	pre	−	no	context	n/a	−
Northern Khanty	PTCP.PST -m	pre	+	no	PST	PTCP.NEG	−
Northern Khanty	PTCP.NPST -ti	pre	+	no	NPST	PTCP.NEG	−
Northern Khanty	PTCP.NEG -li	pre	−	no	context	n/a	−
Panare	PTCP.A -jpo	post	+	no (?)	PST.IMM	?	−
Panare	PTCP.PST -sa'	post	+	no (?)	PST	?	−
Pitta Pitta	PST -ka	post	+	no (?)	PST	?	case
Rif Berber	PTCP.ACT	post	−	no	stem	reg	−
Ronghong Qiang	NMZ.AN -m	pre	−	no	context	?	−
Ronghong Qiang	NMZ.INS -s	pre	−	no	context	?	−
Russian	PTCP.PST.ACT -vš-/-š-	free	+	no	PST	reg	case, number, gender

Appendix 3. Forms considered in the study

Language	Form	Position	TAM (+/−)	TAM markers	TAM meaning	Negation	Nominal agreement
Russian	PTCP.PRS.ACT -*ušč-*/-*ašč-*	free	+	no	PRS	reg	case, number, gender
Russian	PTCP.PST.PASS -*n-*/-*t-*	free	+	no	PST	reg	case, number, gender
Russian	PTCP.PRS.PASS -*em-*/-*im-*	free	+	no	PRS	reg	case, number, gender
Santiam Kalapuya	INF *gi-*	post	−	no	context	?	−
Savosavo	REL -*tu*	pre	−	no	context	?	−
Seri	NMZ.SUBJ	int.h.	−	no	context	nom. *i-*	−
Seri	NMZ.OBJ	int.h.	−	no	context	nom. *Ø-*	−
Seri	NMZ.OBL	int.h.	−	no	context	none	−
Sheko	REL -*əb*, -*əbe* (F.SG)	pre/post	−	realis	marker	reg	gender
Tamil	PTCP -*a*	pre	−	no (?)	marker	NEG + PTCP -*a*	−
Tamil	PTCP.FUT -*um*	pre	+	no (?)	FUT	NEG + PTCP -*a*	−
Tanti Dargwa	PRET[PTCP]	pre	+	some	PRET	reg	−
Tanti Dargwa	PRS[PTCP]	pre	+	some	PRS	reg	−
Tanti Dargwa	PTCP.POT -*an*	pre	+	some	POT	reg	−
Tariana	REL *ka-*	post	+	no (?)	SIM	spec *ma-V-kade-*	−
Tariana	REL.PST *ka-V-kari* (M)/ *ka-V-karu* (F)/ *ka-V-kani* (PL)	post	+	no (?)	ANT	spec *ma-V-kade-*	number, gender
Tariana	REL.FUT *ka-V-pena*	post	+	no (?)	POSTER	spec *ma-V-kade-*	−
Tariana	NMZ.P -*nipe*	free	+	no (?)	SIM	?	−
Tariana	NMZ.NS -*mi*	free	+	no (?)	ANT	?	−
Tarma Quechua	NMZ.SUBJ -*q*	pre/post	+	no (?)	ongoing, PST	?	−

Appendix 3b. Position and desententialization — 295

Language	Form	Position	TAM (+/−)	TAM markers	TAM meaning	Negation	Nominal agreement
Tarma Quechua	NMZ.STAT -sha	pre/post	+	(EVD)	RES, STAT	?	–
Tarma Quechua	NMZ.NFUT -nqa	pre/post	+	no (?)	ongoing, accompl.	?	–
Tarma Quechua	NMZ.FUT -na	pre/post	+	no (?)	non-accompl.	?	–
Telugu	PTCP.PST -ina	pre	+	no	PST	PTCP.NEG	–
Telugu	PTCP.FUT -ee	pre	+	no	FUT	PTCP.NEG	–
Telugu	PTCP.DUR -tunna	pre	+	no	DUR	PTCP.NEG	–
Telugu	PTCP.NEG -ani	pre	−	no	context	n/a	–
Tsafiki	PTCP.IPFV -min	pre/(post)	+	PROG	IPFV	reg (?)	–
Tsafiki	PTCP.PFV -ka	pre/(post)	+	PROG	PFV	reg (?)	–
Tsafiki	NMZ.INS/LOC -nun	pre/(post)	?	PROG	?	reg (?)	–
Tümpisa Shoshone	PTCP.PRS -tün	free	+	no	PRS, SIM	reg	case
Tümpisa Shoshone	PTCP.PST -ppüh	free	+	no	PST, PFV	reg	case
Tümpisa Shoshone	INF -nna	free	+	no	PRS, SIM	reg	case
Tundra Nenets	PTCP.PFV -miə/-me	pre	+	no	ANT	PTCP.NEG	(case, number)
Tundra Nenets	PTCP.IPFV -n(')a/-t(')a	pre	+	no	SIM	spec	(case, number)
Tundra Nenets	PTCP.FUT -mənta	pre	+	no	FUT, MOD	spec	(case, number)
Tundra Nenets	NMZ.PFV -(o)qm(')a	pre	+	(FUT)	ANT	spec	(case, number)
Tundra Nenets	NMZ.IPFV -m(')a	pre	+	(FUT)	SIM	spec	(case, number)
Tundra Nenets	CVB.MOD -s'ə/-ə	pre	+	no	SIM	spec	(case, number)
Tundra Nenets	PTCP.NEG -madawe(y(ə))	pre	+	no	ANT	n/a	(case, number)

Appendix 3. Forms considered in the study

Language	Form	Position	TAM (+/−)	TAM markers	TAM meaning	Negation	Nominal agreement
Urarina	NMZ.A -era	pre	−	no	context	?	−
Urarina	NMZ.S/P -i	pre	−	no	context	?	−
Wambaya	NMZ.A	post/adj.	+ (?)	no	HAB	?	case, noun class
Wan	NMZ.ATTR -ŋ	pre	−	no	context	?	−
Wappo	DEP (system)	int.h./adj.	+	n/a	many	DEP -lah	−
West Greenlandic	PTCP.ACT -soq	post	−	some	marker	?	case, number
West Greenlandic	PTCP.PASS -saq	post	−	some	marker	?	case, number
Wikchamni	VN.SUBJ {-ač̓/}/{-ič̓/}	post	?	no (?)	factive, HAB	?	case
Wikchamni	VN.PASS {-ʔaṅa/}/{-ʔ...aṅa/}	post	?	no (?)	factive, PST	?	case
Wolio	PTCP.ACT mo-	post	−	no (?)	?	?	−
Wolio	PTCP.PASS i-	post	−	no (?)	?	?	−
Yakut	PTCP.PST -bït	pre	+	?	PST	PTCP.NEG	−
Yakut	PTCP.PRS -ar/-ïr	pre	+	?	PRS	PTCP.NEG	−
Yakut	PTCP.FUT -ïax	pre	+	?	FUT	PTCP.NEG	−
Yakut	PTCP.NEG.PST -batax	pre	+	?	PST	n/a	−
Yakut	PTCP.NEG.PRS -bat	pre	+	?	PRS	n/a	−
Yakut	PTCP.NEG.FUT -(ï)mïax	pre	+	?	FUT	n/a	−
Yimas	NF -ru	post	+	no	HAB	NF.NEG	noun class
Yimas	NF.NEG -kakan	post	+	no	HAB	n/a	noun class

Appendix 3c. Argument expression

This table contains information concerning the way different arguments are expressed in participial relative clauses introduced by individual forms. "N/a" ("not applicable") stands for cases where a particular participant is the one towards which the participle is inherently oriented (subject for active participles, direct object for passive and absolutive participles). "Reg" ("regular") stands for cases where a particular participant in participial relative clauses is expressed in the same way as in independent clauses. If there is any deviation in expressing a specific participant, the table indicates the means used in this case. Brackets used with specific option mean that the expression of a particular participant is possible, but rare. Many grammars do not explicitly discuss the encoding of arguments and adverbial modifiers in participial clauses. In such cases, I try, whenever possible, to infer this information from the examples or some other parts of the grammatical descriptions. In unclear cases, the value in the table is accompanied by a question mark.

Language	Form	Subject	Object	Adverbials
Aguaruna	REL.SUBJ -u	n/a	reg	reg
Aguaruna	REL.NS -mau	reg	reg	reg
Aguaruna	REL.NEG -tʃau	n/a	reg	reg
Albanian	PTCP -rë/-r/-ur/-ë	prep. nga/prej	n/a	reg
Apatani	NMZ -nɨ	GEN (POSS)	reg/GEN (?)	reg (?)
Apatani	NMZ.INS -nanɨ	GEN	reg (?)	reg (?)
Apsheron Tat	PTCP -de/-re	reg (+ATTR)	reg	reg
Barasano	NMZ	reg	reg	reg
Barasano	PTCP -ri	reg	reg	reg
Basque	PTCP.PFV -tu/(e-)V-i	reg	n/a	reg (?)
Beng	NMZ -lɛ	impossible (?)	n/a	?
Beserman Udmurt	PTCP.PRS -š'	n/a	reg	reg
Beserman Udmurt	PTCP.PST -m	POSS/GEN/NOM/INS	reg	reg
Beserman Udmurt	PTCP.NPST -n	GEN (?)	reg	reg
Burushaski	PTCP -um	reg (?)	reg (?)	reg (?)
Chimariko	DEP -rop/-rot/-lop/-lot	reg	reg	reg
Coahuilteco	SUB p-/pa-	POSS	reg	reg
Cocama	NMZ.A -tara	n/a	reg	reg
Cocama	NMZ.S/P -n	reg	n/a	reg

Appendix 3. Forms considered in the study

Language	Form	Subject	Object	Adverbials
Cocama	NMZ.LOC -*tupa*	reg	reg	reg
Cofán	PTCP -*'su*	n/a	reg	reg
Dhimal	NMZ -*ka*	POSS	reg (?)	reg (?)
Dolakha Newar	NMZ.SUBJ -*gu*/-*ku*/-*u*	n/a	reg	reg
Dolakha Newar	NMZ.NS -*e*/-*a*	reg	reg	reg
Eastern Armenian	PTCP.SUBJ -*oł*	n/a	reg	reg (?)
Eastern Armenian	PTCP.RES -*ac*	DAT/POSS	n/a	reg (?)
Eastern Armenian	PTCP.FUT -*ik'*	DAT/POSS	n/a	reg (?)
Erzya	PTCP.PRS -*i(c'a)*	n/a	reg	reg
Erzya	PTCP.PFV -*z'*	GEN	n/a	reg
Erzya	PTCP.PST -*vt*	GEN	n/a	reg
Even	PTCP.NFUT -*ri*/-*i*/-*si*/-*di*	POSS	reg	reg
Even	PTCP.PRF -*ča*/-*če*	POSS	reg	reg
Even	PTCP.PST -*daŋ*/-*deŋ*	POSS	reg	reg
Even	PTCP.NEC -*nna*/-*nne*	POSS	reg	reg
Even	PTCP.HYP -*d'iŋa*/-*d'iŋe*	POSS	reg	reg
Finnish	PTCP.PST.ACT -*nut*	n/a	reg	reg
Finnish	PTCP.PRS.ACT -*va*	n/a	reg	reg
Finnish	PTCP.PST.PASS -*tu*	impossible	n/a	reg
Finnish	PTCP.PRS.PASS -*tava*	impossible	n/a	reg
Finnish	PTCP.A -*ma*	POSS	n/a	reg
Finnish	PTCP.NEG -*maton*	POSS	reg (PTV)	reg
Fula	PTCP.PST.ACT -*u*/-*Ø*	n/a	reg	reg
Fula	PTCP.PST.MID -*ii*/-*i*	n/a	n/a	reg
Fula	PTCP.PST.PASS -*aa*/ -*a*	?	n/a	reg
Fula	PTCP.FUT.ACT -*oo*/-*ay*	n/a	reg	reg
Fula	PTCP.FUT.MID -*otoo*/-*oto*	n/a	n/a	reg
Fula	PTCP.FUT.PASS -*etee*/-*ete*	?	n/a	reg
Garo	NMZ -*gipa*	GEN (POSS)	reg	reg
Garrwa	NMZ.CHAR -*warr*	n/a	DAT	?
Georgian	PTCP.ACT *m-V(-el)*	n/a	GEN	DAT > GEN
Georgian	PTCP.PST -*ul*/-*il*/*m-V-ar*	post. *mier*/ GEN (?)	n/a	reg (?)
Georgian	PTCP.FUT *sa-V(-el)*	post. *mier*/ GEN (?)	n/a	reg (?)

Appendix 3c. Argument expression — **299**

Language	Form	Subject	Object	Adverbials
Georgian	PTCP.PRIV *u-V(-el)*	?	n/a	reg (?)
German	PTCP.PRS *-end*	n/a	reg	reg
German	PTCP.PST	prep. *von*	n/a	reg
Guarijío	NMZ.S/A *-me*	n/a	reg	reg
Guarijío	NMZ.P/OBL *-a*	reg/NS/POSS	reg	reg
Guarijío	NMZ.LOC *-ači*	reg/NS/POSS	reg	reg
Hinuq	PTCP *-o goła*	reg	reg	reg
Hinuq	PTCP.PST *-(y)oru*	reg	reg	reg
Hinuq	PTCP.HAB *-ƛ'os*	reg	reg	(reg)
Hinuq	PTCP.RES *-s*	(reg)	reg	(reg)
Hinuq	PTCP.LOC *-a*	reg	reg	reg
Hopi	REL *-qa*	reg	reg	reg
Hungarian	PTCP.ACT *-ó*	n/a	reg	reg
Hungarian	PTCP.PST *-ott*	post. *által*	n/a	reg
Hup	DEP *-Vp*	reg	reg	reg
Imbabura Quechua	NMZ.PST *-shka*	reg	reg/incorp.	reg
Imbabura Quechua	NMZ.PRS *-j*	reg	reg/incorp.	reg
Imbabura Quechua	NMZ.FUT *-na*	reg	reg/incorp.	reg
Ingush	PTCP.PST *-aa/-na*	reg	reg	reg
Ingush	PTCP.PRS *-a*	reg	reg	reg
Ingush	CVB.SIM *-(a)zh*	reg	reg	reg
Irish	PTCP.PST *-tha/-the*	impossible (?)	n/a	(reg)
Italian	PTCP.PST *-t-*	prep. *da*	n/a	reg
Japhug rGyalrong	NMZ.S/A *kɯ-*	n/a	POSS	reg
Japhug rGyalrong	NMZ.P *kɤ-*	POSS	n/a	reg
Japhug rGyalrong	NMZ.OBL *sɤ-*	POSS (S/A or P)	POSS (S/A or P)	reg
Kalmyk	PTCP.PST *-sən*	POSS/reg	reg	reg
Kalmyk	PTCP.FUT *-xə*	POSS/reg	reg	reg
Kalmyk	PTCP.HAB *-dəg*	POSS/reg	reg	reg
Kalmyk	PTCP.PASS *-ata*	INS	n/a	some
Kamaiurá	NMZ.A *-tat*	n/a	POSS	reg
Kamaiurá	NMZ.S *-ama'e*	n/a	n/a	reg
Kamaiurá	NMZ.P *-ipyt*	DAT	n/a	reg
Kamaiurá	NMZ.OBJ *-emi*	POSS	n/a	reg
Kamaiurá	NMZ.OBL *-tap*	POSS	POSS	reg
Kamaiurá	NMZ.NEG.S *-uma'e*	n/a	n/a	reg

Appendix 3. Forms considered in the study

Language	Form	Subject	Object	Adverbials
Kambaata	REL	reg	reg	reg
Kambaata	PTCP.NEG -umb	reg	reg	reg
Kayardild	NMZ-CONS -n-ngarrba	POSS/ABL/CONS	CONS	CONS
Kayardild	RES-NMZ -thirri-n-	POSS/ABL/CONS/ORIG	depending on aspect/polar.	impossible
Ket	NMZ	POSS	reg/incorp.	reg
Kharia	PTCP	GEN (POSS)	reg	reg
Kobon	NMZ/ADJR -eb/-ep	n/a	reg	reg
Kolyma Yukaghir	ATTR.ACT -je	POSS	spec. DOM	reg
Kolyma Yukaghir	NMZ -l	POSS	spec. DOM	reg
Kolyma Yukaghir	NMZ.RES -ōl	POSS	n/a	reg
Kolyma Yukaghir	ATTR.PASS -me	POSS	spec. DOM	reg
Komi-Zyrian	PTCP.ACT -iš'	n/a	reg	reg
Komi-Zyrian	PTCP.PFV -am(a)	POSS/GEN/NOM/INS	reg	reg
Komi-Zyrian	PTCP.HAB -an(a)	POSS/GEN/NOM/INS	reg	reg
Komi-Zyrian	PTCP.NEG -təm	POSS/GEN/NOM/INS	reg	reg
Koorete	PTCP.IPFV -e	reg	reg	reg
Koorete	PTCP.PFV.SUBJ -a	reg	reg	reg
Koorete	PTCP.PFV.NS -o	reg	reg	reg
Korean	REL -n	reg	reg	reg
Korean	REL.PRS -nɨn	reg	reg	reg
Korean	REL.FUT -l	reg	reg	reg
Koryak	NMZ -lʕ-	GEN/reg	n/a	reg
Koryak	NMZ-NOMFUT -jo-lqəl	GEN/reg	n/a	reg
Krongo	CONN ŋ-	POSS/spec. pronouns	reg	reg
Lezgian	PTCP -j	reg	reg	reg
Lithuanian	PTCP.PST.ACT -us-	n/a	reg	reg
Lithuanian	PTCP.PRS.ACT -nt-	n/a	reg	reg
Lithuanian	PTCP.PST.PASS -t-	GEN	n/a	reg
Lithuanian	PTCP.PRS.PASS -m-	GEN	n/a	reg
Luiseño	REL (system)	POSS	reg	reg
Maba	PTCP n-	n/a	reg (?)	reg (?)
Ma'di	SR.S/A -rɛ̃ (SG)/-ɓá (PL)	(POSS)	reg	reg

Appendix 3c. Argument expression — **301**

Language	Form	Subject	Object	Adverbials
Ma'di	SR.P -lɛ́	POSS	(reg)	reg
Ma'di	SR.INS -dʒɔ́	POSS	reg	reg
Malayalam	PTCP -a	reg	reg	reg (?)
Malayalam	PTCP.NEG -aatta	reg	reg	reg (?)
Manange	NMZ -pʌ	GEN (POSS)	reg	reg
Mapudungun	PTCP.ACT -lu	n/a	reg	reg
Mapudungun	PTCP.PASS -el	reg	n/a	reg
Marathi	PTCP (system)	reg	reg	reg
Maricopa	REL kw-	n/a	reg	reg
Maricopa	NMZ.NS	unmarked	reg	reg
Martuthunira	REL.PRS -nyila	n/a	reg (?)	reg
Matsés	NMZ.A/S -quid	n/a	reg	reg
Matsés	NMZ.P -aid	reg	reg	reg
Matsés	NMZ.INS -te/-tequid	reg	reg	reg
Matsés	NMZ (system)	reg	reg	reg
Matsés	NMZ.NEG.S/A.HAB -esa	n/a	reg	reg
Matsés	NMZ.NEG.P/INS.PFV -acmaid	reg	reg	reg
Matsés	NMZ.NEG.P/INS.HAB -temaid	reg	reg	reg
Meadow Mari	PTCP.ACT -še	n/a	reg	reg
Meadow Mari	PTCP.FUT -šaš	POSS/GEN/NOM/INS	reg	reg
Meadow Mari	PTCP.NS -me	POSS/GEN/NOM/INS	reg	reg
Meadow Mari	PTCP.NEG -dəme	POSS/GEN/NOM/INS	reg	reg
Mēbengokre	NMZ	erg. alignm.	erg. alignm.	reg
Middle Egyptian	PTCP.SUBJ	n/a	reg (?)	reg (?)
Middle Egyptian	PTCP.NS	prep. jn	reg (?)	reg (?)
Mochica	NMZ.STAT -d.o	GEN (POSS)	n/a	reg
Modern Greek	PTCP.PST -ménos	prep. apo	n/a	reg
Modern Standard Arabic	PTCP.ACT	n/a	reg	reg
Modern Standard Arabic	PTCP.PASS	reg	n/a	reg
Motuna	PTCP -(wʌ)h	reg	reg	reg

302 — Appendix 3. Forms considered in the study

Language	Form	Subject	Object	Adverbials
Muna	PTCP.ACT *mo-V-no*	n/a	reg	reg
Muna	PTCP.PASS *ni-*	POSS	n/a	reg
Muna	NMZ *ka-*	poss/prep. *ne*	POSS (for IO)	reg
Muna	NMZ-V-LOC *ka-V-ha*	POSS	reg	reg
Nanai	PTCP.PST *-xan/-kin/-čin*	POSS	reg	reg
Nanai	PTCP.NPST *-j/-ri/-di/-či*	POSS	reg	reg
Nanga	PTCP.PFV *-sɛ̀*	reg	reg	reg
Nanga	PTCP.IPFV *-mì*	reg	reg	reg
Nevome	NMZ *-cama*	n/a	?	reg
Nevome	NMZ.FUT *-cugai*	POSS	n/a	reg
Nevome	NMZ.LOC.PRS *-cami*	?	?	reg
Nevome	NMZ.LOC.HAB *-carhami*	?	?	reg
Nevome	NMZ.LOC.PST *-parhami*	?	?	reg
Nevome	NMZ.LOC.FUT *-aicami*	?	?	reg
Nias	PTCP.PASS *ni-*	POSS/mutated	reg (for IO)	reg (?)
Nivkh	PTCP	reg	reg	reg
North Saami	PTCP.PRS *-i/-(jead)dji*	n/a	reg	(reg)
North Saami	PTCP.PST *-n*	n/a	reg	(reg)
North Saami	PTCP.A *-n*	GEN	n/a	(reg)
North Saami	PTCP.NEG *-keahtes*	impossible (?)	reg	(reg)
Northern Khanty	PTCP.PST *-m*	LOC/POSS	reg	reg
Northern Khanty	PTCP.NPST *-ti*	LOC/POSS	reg	reg
Northern Khanty	PTCP.NEG *-li*	reg (?)	n/a	reg
Panare	PTCP.A *-jpo*	n/a	reg (?)	reg (?)
Panare	PTCP.PST *-sa'*	DAT	n/a	reg (?)
Pitta Pitta	PST *-ka*	reg	reg	reg
Rif Berber	PTCP.ACT	n/a	reg	reg
Ronghong Qiang	NMZ.AN *-m*	reg	reg	reg
Ronghong Qiang	NMZ.INS *-s*	reg	reg	reg
Russian	PTCP.PST.ACT *-vš-/-š-*	n/a	reg	reg
Russian	PTCP.PRS.ACT *-ušč-/-ašč-*	n/a	reg	reg
Russian	PTCP.PST.PASS *-n-/-t-*	INS	n/a	reg
Russian	PTCP.PRS.PASS *-em-/-im-*	INS	n/a	reg
Santiam Kalapuya	INF *gi-*	n/a	reg (?)	reg (?)
Savosavo	REL *-tu*	GEN (POSS)	reg	reg

Appendix 3c. Argument expression — **303**

Language	Form	Subject	Object	Adverbials
Seri	NMZ.SUBJ	n/a	reg	reg
Seri	NMZ.OBJ	POSS	reg (for IO)	reg
Seri	NMZ.OBL	POSS	reg	reg
Sheko	REL -*əb*, -*əbe* (F.SG)	reg	reg	reg
Tamil	PTCP -*a*	reg	reg	reg
Tamil	PTCP.FUT -*um*	reg	reg	reg
Tanti Dargwa	PRET[PTCP]	reg	reg	reg
Tanti Dargwa	PRS[PTCP]	reg	reg	reg
Tanti Dargwa	PTCP.POT -*an*	reg	reg	reg
Tariana	REL *ka-*	n/a	reg (?)	reg
Tariana	REL.PST *ka-V-kari* (M)/ *ka-V-karu* (F)/ *ka-V-kani* (PL)	n/a	reg (?)	reg
Tariana	REL.FUT *ka-V-pena*	n/a	reg (?)	reg
Tariana	NMZ.P -*nipe*	reg	n/a	reg
Tariana	NMZ.NS -*mi*	reg	reg (?)	reg
Tarma Quechua	NMZ.SUBJ -*q*	n/a	reg	reg
Tarma Quechua	NMZ.STAT -*sha*	ABL	n/a	reg
Tarma Quechua	NMZ.NFUT -*nqa*	reg	reg	reg
Tarma Quechua	NMZ.FUT -*na*	reg	reg	reg
Telugu	PTCP.PST -*ina*	reg	reg	reg
Telugu	PTCP.FUT -*ee*	reg	reg	reg
Telugu	PTCP.DUR -*tunna*	reg	reg	reg
Telugu	PTCP.NEG -*ani*	reg	reg	reg
Tsafiki	PTCP.IPFV -*min*	reg (?)	reg (?)	?
Tsafiki	PTCP.PFV -*ka*	reg (?)	reg (?)	?
Tsafiki	NMZ.INS/LOC -*nun*	reg (?)	reg (?)	?
Tümpisa Shoshone	PTCP.PRS -*tün*	n/a	reg	reg
Tümpisa Shoshone	PTCP.PST -*ppüh*	POSS/POSS.REFL	reg	reg
Tümpisa Shoshone	INF -*nna*	POSS/POSS.REFL	reg	reg
Tundra Nenets	PTCP.PFV -*miə*/-*me*	POSS	reg	reg
Tundra Nenets	PTCP.IPFV -*n(')a*/-*t(')a*	POSS	reg	reg
Tundra Nenets	PTCP.FUT -*mənta*	POSS	reg	reg
Tundra Nenets	NMZ.PFV -*(o)qm(')a*	POSS	reg	reg
Tundra Nenets	NMZ.IPFV -*m(')a*	POSS	reg	reg
Tundra Nenets	CVB.MOD -*s'ə*/-*ə*	POSS	reg	reg

Appendix 3. Forms considered in the study

Language	Form	Subject	Object	Adverbials
Tundra Nenets	PTCP.NEG -*mədawe(y(ə))*	POSS	reg	reg
Urarina	NMZ.A -*era*	n/a	reg	reg
Urarina	NMZ.S/P -*i*	?	n/a	reg
Wambaya	NMZ.A	n/a	reg	reg (?)
Wan	NMZ.ATTR -*ŋ*	POSS, INAL/AL	POSS, INAL/AL	POSS, INAL/external
Wappo	DEP (system)	ACC -*Ø*	reg	reg
West Greenlandic	PTCP.ACT -*soq*	n/a	n/a	reg (?)
West Greenlandic	PTCP.PASS -*saq*	POSS/ABL	n/a	reg (?)
Wikchamni	VN.SUBJ {-*ač̓/*}/{-*ič̓/*}	n/a	?	reg (?)
Wikchamni	VN.PASS {-*ʔaṅa/*}/{-*ʔ...aṅa/*}	GEN	n/a	reg (?)
Wolio	PTCP.ACT *mo-*	n/a	?	reg (?)
Wolio	PTCP.PASS *i-*	reg (?)	n/a	reg (?)
Yakut	PTCP.PST -*bït*	POSS	reg	reg
Yakut	PTCP.PRS -*ar/-ïr*	POSS	reg	reg
Yakut	PTCP.FUT -*ïax*	POSS	reg	reg
Yakut	PTCP.NEG.PST -*batax*	POSS	reg	reg
Yakut	PTCP.NEG.PRS -*bat*	POSS	reg	reg
Yakut	PTCP.NEG.FUT -*(ï)mïax*	POSS	reg	reg
Yimas	NF -*ru*	n/a	reg	reg
Yimas	NF.NEG -*kakan*	reg	reg	reg

References

General references

Abraham, P. T. 1985. *Apatani grammar* (Central Institute of Indian Languages Grammar Series 12). Manasagangotri, Mysore: Central Institute of Indian Languages.

Adelaar, Willem F. H. (with Pieter Muysken). 2004. *The languages of the Andes* (Cambridge Language Surveys). Cambridge: Cambridge University Press.

Adelaar, Willem F. H. 2011. Participial clauses in Tarma Quechua. In Rik van Gijn, Katharina Haude & Pieter Muysken (eds.), *Subordination in native South American languages* (Typological Studies in Language 97), 267–280. Amsterdam: John Benjamins.

Aikhenvald, Alexandra Y. 2000. *Classifiers: A typology of noun categorization devices* (Oxford Studies in Typology and Linguistic Theory). Oxford: Oxford University Press.

Aikhenvald, Alexandra Y. 2003. *A grammar of Tariana, from Northwest Amazonia* (Cambridge Grammatical Descriptions). Cambridge: Cambridge University Press.

Aikhenvald, Alexandra Y. 2006. Serial verb constructions in typological perspective. In Alexandra Y. Aikhenvald & R. M. W. Dixon (eds.), *Serial verb constructions: A cross-linguistic typology* (Explorations in Linguistic Typology), 1–68. Oxford: Oxford University Press.

Aikhenvald, Alexandra Y. & R. M. W. Dixon 2011. Non-ergative associations between S and O. In Alexandra Y. Aikhenvald & R. M. W. Dixon (eds.), *Language at large: Essays on syntax and semantics* (Empirical Approaches to Linguistic Theory 2), 143–169. Leiden: Brill.

Altieri, Radamés A. 1939. *Fernando de la Carrera, Arte de la lengua Yunga (1644)*. Tucumán: Universidad Nacional de Tucumán, Instituto de Antropología.

Ambrazas, Vytautas (ed.). 2006. *Lithuanian grammar*. Vilnius: Baltos Lankos.

Anagnostopoulou, Elena. 2003. Participles and voice. In Artemis Alexiadou, Monika Rathert & Arnim von Stechow (eds.), *Perfect explorations* (Interface Explorations 2), 1–36. Berlin: Mouton de Gruyter.

Anceaux, Johannes Cornelis. 1952. *The Wolio language: Outline of grammatical description and texts*. Leiden: Rijksuniversiteit te Leiden doctoral dissertation.

Andrews, Avery D. 2007. Relative clauses. In Timothy Shopen (ed.), *Language typology and syntactic description*, 2nd edn., Vol. 2: *Complex constructions*, 206–236. Cambridge: Cambridge University Press.

Applegate, Richard Brian. 1972. *Ineseño Chumash grammar*. Berkeley, CA: University of California doctoral dissertation.

Aralova, N. B. & M. M. Brykina. 2012. Finitnye otnositelnye predloženija v marijskom i èrzja-mordovskom jazykax [Finite relative clauses in Mari and Erzya Mordvin]. In Kuznecova, A. I. (ed.), *Finno-ugorskie jazyki: Fragmenty grammatičeskogo opisanija. Formal'nyj i funkcional'nyj podxody* [Finno-Ugric languages: fragments of a grammatical description. Formal and functional approaches] (Studia Philologica), 521–542. Moscow: Rukopisnye pamjatniki Drevnej Rusi.

Arkadiev, Peter. 2014a. Kriterii finitnosti i morfosintaksis litovskix pričastij [Finiteness criteria and the morphosyntax of Lithuanian participles]. *Voprosy jazykoznanija* 5. 68–96.

Arkadiev, Peter. 2014b. (Non-)finiteness, constructions, and participles in Lithuanian. Talk given at the Max Planck Institute for Evolutionary Anthropology, Leipzig, 10 October 2014.

Arnott, D. W. 1970. *The nominal and verbal systems of Fula*. Oxford: Oxford University Press.
Årsjö, Britten. 1999. Words in Ama. (Manuscript.)
Asher, R. E. & T. C. Kumari. 1997. *Malayalam* (Routledge Descriptive Grammars). London: Routledge.
Authier, Gilles. 2012. New strategies for relative clauses in Azeri and Apsheron Tat. In Volker Gast & Holger Diessel (eds.), *Clause linkage in cross-linguistic perspective: Data-driven approaches to cross-clausal syntax* (Trends in Linguistics 249), 225–252. Berlin: Mouton de Gruyter.
Auwera, Johan van der & Vladimir A. Plungian. 1998. Modality's semantic map. *Linguistic Typology* 2 (1). 79–124.
Avrorin, V. A. 1961. *Grammatika nanajskogo jazyka* [A grammar of Nanai], Vol. 2, *Morfologija glagol'nyx i narečnyx častej reči, meždometij, služebnyx slov i častic* [The morphology of verbal and adverbial parts of speech, interjections, function words, and particles]. Moscow: Izdatel'stvo Akademii nauk SSSR.
Badawi, Elsaid, Michael G. Carter & Adrian Gully. 2004. *Modern Written Arabic: A comprehensive grammar* (Routledge Comprehensive Grammars). London: Roultledge.
Banks, Jonathan. 2007. The verbal morphology of Santiam Kalapuya. *Northwest Journal of Linguistics* 1 (2). 1–98.
Bartens, Raija. 1999. *Mordvalaiskielten rakenne ja kehitys* (Mémoires de la Société Finno-Ougrienne 232). Helsinki: Suomalais-Ugrilainen Seura.
Bartsch, Renate. 1973. "Negative Transportation" gibt es nicht. *Linguistische Berichte* 27. 1–7.
Berg, Helma van den. 1995. *A grammar of Hunzib (with texts and lexicon)* (Lincom Studies in Caucasian Linguistics 1). München: Lincom Europa.
Berg, René van den. 2013 [1989]. *A grammar of the Muna language* (Summer Institute of Linguistics e-Books 52). Summer Institute of Linguistics International.
Berger, Hermann. 1998. *Die Burushaski-Sprache von Hunza und Nager* (Neuindische Studien 13), Vol. 1–3. Wiesbaden: Harrassowitz.
Bergsland, Knut. 1997. *Aleut grammar (Unangam tunuganaan achixaasix̂)* (Research Paper 10). Fairbanks, AK: Alaska Native Language Center.
Bhat, D. N. S. 1994. *The adjectival category: Criteria for differentiation and identification* (Studies in Language Companion Series 24). Amsterdam: John Benjamins.
Bickel, Balthasar. 2007. Typology in the 21st century: Major current developments. *Linguistic Typology* 11 (1). 239–251.
Bickel, Balthasar. 2008. A refined sampling procedure for genealogical control. *Language Typology and Universals* 61 (3). 221–233.
Bickel, Balthasar. 2013. Linguistic diversity and universals. In Nick J. Enfield, Paul Kockelman & Jack Sidnell (eds.), *The Cambridge handbook of linguistic anthropology* (Cambridge Handbooks in Language and Linguistics), 102–127. Cambridge: Cambridge University Press.
Birk, D. B. W. 1976. *The Malakmalak language, Daly River (Western Arnhem Land)* (Pacific Linguistics B-45). Canberra: Australian National University.
Bisang Walter. 2001. Finite vs. non-finite languages. In Martin Haspelmath, Ekkehard König, Wulf Oesterreicher & Wolfgang Raible (eds.), *Language Typology and Language Universals. An International Handbook*, Vol. 2, 1400–1413. Berlin: Mouton de Gruyter.
Bisang Walter. 2007. Categories that make finiteness: discreetness from a functional perspective and some of its repercussions. In Irina Nikolaeva (ed.), 2007: 115–137.

Blackings, Mairi & Nigel Fabb. 2003. *A grammar of Ma'di* (Mouton Grammar Library 32). Berlin: Mouton de Gruyter.
Blake, Barry J. 1979. Pitta-Pitta. In R. M. W. Dixon & Barry J. Blake (eds.), *Handbook of Australian languages*, Vol. 1, 183–242. Amsterdam: John Benjamins.
Bläsing, Uwe. 2003. Kalmuck. In Juha Janhunen (ed.), *The Mongolic languages* (Routledge Language Family Series), 229–247. London: Routledge.
Bresnan, Joan. 1982. The passive in lexical theory. In Joan Bresnan (ed.), *The mental representation of grammatical relations*, 3–86. Cambridge, MA: MIT Press.
Brown, Lea. 2001. *A grammar of Nias Selatan*. Sydney: University of Sydney doctoral dissertation.
Brown, Lea. 2005. Nias. In Alexander Adelaar & Nikolaus P. Himmelmann (eds.), *The Austronesian Languages of Asia and Madagascar* (Routledge Language Family Series), 562–589. London: Routledge.
Brown, Dunstan, Marina Chumakina & Greville G. Corbett (eds.). 2013. *Canonical morphology and syntax*. Oxford: Oxford University Press.
Brugmann K. 1892. *Grundriss der vergleichenden Grammatik der Indogermanischen Sprachen. II. Bd. Wortbildungslehre (Stammbildungs- und Flexionslehre)*. Strassburg: Karl J. Trübner.
Brykina, M. M. & N. B. Aralova. 2012. Sistemy pričastij v marijskom i permskix jazykax [The systems of participles in Mari and Permic]. In A. I. Kuznecova (ed.), *Finno-ugorskie jazyki: fragmenty grammatičeskogo opisanija. Formal'nyj i funkcional'nyj podxody* [Finno-Ugric languages: fragments of a grammatical description. Formal and functional approaches] (Studia Philologica), 476–520. Moscow: Rukopisnye pamjatniki Drevnej Rusi.
Buchholz, Oda & Wilfried Fiedler. 1987. *Albanische Grammatik*. Leipzig: Verlag Enzyklopädie.
Burling, Robins 2004. *The language of the Modhupur Mandi (Garo)*, Vol. 1: *Grammar*. New Delhi: Bibliophile South Asia.
Bybee, Joan. 1985. Morphology: A study of the relation between meaning and form (Typological Studies in Language 9). Amsterdam: John Benjamins.
Bybee, Joan. 1988. Tbe diachronic dimension in explanation. In John A. Hawkins (ed.), *Explaining language universals*, 350–379. Oxford: Basil Blackwell.
Bybee, Joan. 2003. Mechanisms of change in grammaticization: The role of frequency. In Brian D. Joseph and Richard D. Janda (eds.), *The handbook of historical linguistics* (Blackwell Handbooks in Linguistics), 602–623 Oxford: Blackwell.
Bybee, Joan. 2008. Formal universals as emergent phenomena: The origins of structure preservation. In Jeff Good (ed.), *Linguistic universals and language change*, 108–121. Oxford: Oxford University Press.
Bybee, Joan, Revere Perkins & William Pagliuca. 1994. *The evolution of grammar*. Chicago, IL: The University of Chicago Press.
Čeremisina, M. I. (ed.). 1995. *Grammatika sovremennogo jakutskogo literaturnogo jazyka: Sintaksis* [A grammar of Modern Standard Yakut: Syntax]. Novosibirsk: Nauka.
Cinque, Guglielmo. 1999. *Adverbs and functional heads: A cross-linguistic perspective* (Oxford Studies in Comparative Syntax). Oxford: Oxford University Press.
Cole, Peter. 1985. *Imbabura Quechua* (Croom Helm Descriptive Grammars). London: Croom Helm.
Comrie, Bernard. 1976a. *Aspect*. Cambridge: Cambridge University Press.
Comrie, Bernard. 1976b. The syntax of action nominals: a cross-language study. *Lingua* 40 (2–3). 177–201.

Comrie, Bernard. 1981. *Language universals and linguistic typology: Syntax and morphology*. Oxford: Basil Blackwell.
Comrie, Bernard. 1985. *Tense* (Cambridge Textbooks in Linguistics). Cambridge: Cambridge University Press.
Comrie, Bernard. 1998. Rethinking the typology of relative clauses. *Language Design* 1. 59–86.
Comrie, Bernard. 2013a. Alignment of case marking of full noun phrases. In Matthew S. Dryer & Martin Haspelmath (eds.), *The World Atlas of Language Structures Online*. Leipzig: Max Planck Institute for Evolutionary Anthropology. http://wals.info/chapter/98 (accessed 16 June 2016).
Comrie, Bernard. 2013b. Alignment of case marking of pronouns. In Matthew S. Dryer & Martin Haspelmath (eds.), *The World Atlas of Language Structures Online*. Leipzig: Max Planck Institute for Evolutionary Anthropology. http://wals.info/chapter/99 (accessed 16 June 2016).
Comrie, Bernard & Sandra A. Thompson. 2007. Lexical nominalization. In Timothy Shopen (ed.), *Language typology and syntactic description*, 2nd edn., Vol. 3: *Grammatical categories and the lexicon*, 334–410. Cambridge: Cambridge University Press.
Comrie, Bernard & Tania Kuteva. 2013a. Relativization on obliques. In Matthew S. Dryer & Martin Haspelmath (eds.), *The World Atlas of Language Structures Online*. Leipzig: Max Planck Institute for Evolutionary Anthropology. http://wals.info/chapter/123 (accessed 30 January 2015).
Comrie, Bernard & Tania Kuteva. 2013b. Relativization strategies. In Matthew S. Dryer & Martin Haspelmath (eds.), *The World Atlas of Language Structures Online*. Leipzig: Max Planck Institute for Evolutionary Anthropology. http://wals.info/chapter/s8 (accessed 5 September 2016).
Cook, Anthony R. 1987. *Wagiman Matyin: A description of the Wagiman language of the Northern Territory*. Melbourne: La Trobe University doctoral dissertation.
Corbett, Greville G. 1987. The morphology/syntax interface: Evidence from possessive adjectives in Slavonic. *Language* 63 (2). 299–345.
Corbett, Greville G. 1991. *Gender* (Cambridge Textbooks in Linguistics). Cambridge: Cambridge University Press.
Corbett G.G. 2005. The canonical approach to typology. In Zygmunt Frajzyngier, Adam Hodges & David S. Rood (eds.), *Linguistic diversity and language theories* (Studies in Language Companion Series 72), 25–49. Amsterdam: John Benjamins.
Corbett, Greville G. 2013. Number of genders. In Matthew S. Dryer & Martin Haspelmath (eds.), *The World Atlas of Language Structures Online*. Leipzig: Max Planck Institute for Evolutionary Anthropology. http://wals.info/chapter/30 (accessed 7 March 2017).
Craig, Colette. 1977. *The structure of Jacaltec*. Austin, TX: University of Texas Press.
Creissels, Denis. 2009. Participles and finiteness: The case of Akhvakh. *Linguistic Discovery* 7 (1). 106–130.
Crevels, Mily & Hein van der Voort. 2008. The Guaporé-Mamoré region as a linguistic area. In Pieter Muysken (ed.), *From linguistic areas to areal linguistics* (Studies in Language Companion Series 90), 151–179. Amsterdam: John Benjamins.
Cristofaro, Sonia. 1998. Deranking and balancing in different subordination relations: a typological study. *Sprachtypologie und Universalienforschung* 51 (1). 3–42.
Cristofaro, Sonia. 2003. *Subordination* (Oxford Studies in Typology and Linguistic Theory). Oxford: Oxford University Press.

Cristofaro, Sonia. 2007. Deconstructing categories: Finiteness in a functional-typological perspective. In Irina Nikolaeva (ed.), *Finiteness: Theoretical and empirical foundations,* 91–114. Oxford: Oxford University Press.
Cristofaro, Sonia. 2012. Cognitive explanations, distributional evidence, and diachrony. In Nikolas Gisborne & Willem B. Hollmann (eds.), Theory and data in cognitive linguistics [Special issue], *Studies in Language* 36 (3), 645–670.
Cristofaro, Sonia. 2014. Competing motivation models and diachrony: What evidence for what motivations? In Brian MacWhinney, Andrej L. Malchukov & Edith A. Moravcsik (eds.), *Competing motivations in grammar and usage,* 282–298. Oxford: Oxford University Press.
Cristofaro, Sonia. 2017. Implicational universals and dependencies. In Nick J. Enfield (ed.), *Dependencies in language: On the causal ontology of linguistic systems* (Studies in Diversity Linguistics 14), 9–22. Berlin: Language Science Press.
Croft, William. 1990. *Typology and universals.* Cambridge: Cambridge University Press.
Croft, William. 1991. *Syntactic categories and grammatical relations: The cognitive organization of information.* Chicago, IL: University of Chicago Press.
Croft, William. 1995. Autonomy and functionalist linguistics. *Language* 71 (3). 490–532.
Croft, William. 2001. *Radical Construction Grammar: Syntactic theory in typological perspective.* Oxford: Oxford University Press.
Crystal, David. 2003. *A dictionary of linguistics and phonetics,* 5th edn. Oxford: Basil Blackwell.
Daguman, Josephine S. 2004. *A grammar of Northern Subanen.* Melbourne: La Trobe University doctoral dissertation.
Dahl, Östen. 1985. *Tense and aspect systems.* Oxford: Basil Blackwell.
Dahl, Östen & Viveka Velupillai. 2013. Tense and aspect. In Matthew S. Dryer & Martin Haspelmath (eds.), *The World Atlas of Language Structures Online.* Leipzig: Max Planck Institute for Evolutionary Anthropology. http://wals.info/chapter/s7 (accessed 9 September 2016).
Davies, John. 1981. *Kobon* (Lingua Descriptive Studies, 3). Amsterdam: North-Holland.
Davis, John. 1973. *A partial grammar of simplex and complex sentences in Luiseño.* Los Angeles, CA: University of California doctoral dissertation.
Dayley, Jon P. 1989. *Tümpisa (Panamint) Shoshone grammar* (University of California Publications in Linguistics 115). Berkeley, CA: University of California Press.
DeLancey, Scott. 1981. An interpretation of split ergativity and related patterns. *Language* 57 (3). 626–657.
DeLancey, Scott. 1982. Aspect, Transitivity, and Viewpoint. In Paul J. Hopper (ed.), *Tense-Aspect: Between semantics and pragmatics* (Typological Studies in Language 1), 167–183. Amsterdam: John Benjamins.
DeLancey, Scott. 1986. Relativization as nominalization in Tibetan and Newari. Talk given at the 19th International Conference on Sino-Tibetan Languages and Linguistics. Ohio State University, Columbus, OH.
DeLancey, Scott. 1990. Ergativity and the cognitive model of event structure in Lhasa Tibetan. *Cognitive Linguistics* 1 (3), 289–321.
DeLancey, Scott. 1999. Relativization in Tibetan. In Yogendra P. Yadava & Warren W. Glover (eds.), *Topics in Nepalese Linguistics,* 231–249. Kathmandu: Royal Nepal Academy.
DeLancey, Scott. 2002. Relativization and nominalization in Bodic. In Patrick Chew (ed.), *Proceedings of the Annual Meeting of the Berkeley Linguistics Society* 22, 55–72. Berkeley, CA: University of California.

Dench, Alan & Nicholas Evans. 1988. Multiple case-marking in Australian languages. *Australian Journal of Linguistics* 8 (1). 1–47.
Dench, Alan. 1994. *Martuthunira: A language of the Pilbara region of Western Australia* (Pacific Linguistics C-125). Canberra: Australian National University.
Dench, Alan. 2009. Case in an Australian language: Distribution of case and multiple case marking in Nyamal. In Andrej L. Malchukov & Andrew Spencer (eds.), *The Oxford handbook of case* (Oxford Handbooks in Linguistics), 756–769. Oxford: Oxford University Press.
Depuydt, Leo. 1996. Twixt relative verb form and passive participle in Egyptian. *Zeitschrift der Deutschen Morgenländischen Gesellschaft* 146 (1). 1–24.
Dhongde, Ramesh Vaman & Kashi Wali. 2009. *Marathi* (London Oriental and African Language Library 13). Amsterdam: John Benjamins.
Dickinson, Connie. 2002. *Complex predicates in Tsafiki*. Eugene, OR: University of Oregon doctoral dissertation.
Diessel, Holger & Michael Tomasello. 2005. A new look at the acquisition of relative clauses. *Language* 81 (4). 882–906.
Di Garbo, Francesca. 2014. *Gender and its interaction with number and evaluative morphology: An intra- and intergenealogical typological survey of Africa*. Stockholm: Stockholm University doctoral dissertation.
Dik, Simon C. 1991. Functional Grammar. In Flip G. Droste & John E. Joseph (eds.), *Linguistic theory and grammatical description: Nine current approaches* (Current Issues in Linguistic Theory 75), 247–274. Amsterdam: John Benjamins.
Dik, Simon C. 1997. *The theory of Functional Grammar*, Part 2: *Complex and derived constructions* (Functional Grammar Series 21). Berlin: Mouton de Gruyter.
Dixon, R. M. W. 1979. Ergativity. *Language* 55 (1). 59–138.
Dixon, R. M. W. 1994. *Ergativity* (Cambridge Studies in Linguistics 69). Cambridge: Cambridge University Press.
Dixon, R. M. W. 2004a. Adjective classes in typological perspective. In R. M. W. Dixon & Alexandra Y. Aikhenvald (eds.), *Adjective classes: A cross-linguistic typology* (Explorations in Linguistic Typology 1), 1–49. Oxford: Oxford University Press.
Dixon, R. M. W. & Alexandra Y. Aikhenvald. 1999. Introduction. In R. M. W. Dixon & Alexandra Y. Aikhenvald (eds.), *The Amazonian languages* (Cambridge Language Surveys), 1–22. Cambridge: Cambridge University Press.
Dixon, R. M. W. & Alexandra Y. Aikhenvald. 2000. Introduction. In R. M. W. Dixon & Alexandra Y. Aikhenvald (eds.), *Changing valency: Case studies in transitivity*, 1–29. Cambridge: Cambridge University Press.
Doron, Edit & Reintges, Chris H. 2005. On the syntax of participial modifiers. (Manuscript.) http://pluto.huji.ac.il/~edit/papers/DORON&REINTGES2.pdf (accessed 8 August 2019).
Driem, George van. 1987. *A grammar of Limbu* (Mouton Grammar Library 4). Berlin: Mouton de Gruyter.
Dryer, Matthew S. 1986. Primary objects, secondary objects, and antidative. *Language* 62 (4). 808–845.
Dryer, Matthew S. 1989. Large linguistic areas and language sampling. *Studies in Language* 13 (2). 257–292.
Dryer, Matthew S. 1997. Are grammatical relations universal? In Joan Bybee, John Haiman & Sandra A. Thompson (eds.), *Essays on language function and language type: Dedicated to T. Givón*, 115–143. Amsterdam: John Benjamins.

Dryer, Matthew S. 2006. Functionalism and the metalanguage – Theory confusion. In Grace Wiebe, Gary Libben, Tom Priestly, Ron Smyth & Sam Wang (eds.), *Phonology, morphology, and the empirical imperative: Papers in honour of Bruce Derwing*, 27–259. Taipei: Crane Publishing Company.

Dryer, Matthew S. 2013a. Order of object and verb. In Matthew S. Dryer & Martin Haspelmath (eds.), *The World Atlas of Language Structures Online*. Leipzig: Max Planck Institute for Evolutionary Anthropology. http://wals.info/chapter/83 (accessed 20 March 2019).

Dryer, Matthew S. 2013b. Order of relative clause and noun. In Matthew S. Dryer & Martin Haspelmath (eds.), *The World Atlas of Language Structures Online*. Leipzig: Max Planck Institute for Evolutionary Anthropology. http://wals.info/chapter/90 (accessed 1 September 2015).

Dryer, Matthew S. & Martin Haspelmath (eds.). 2013. *The World Atlas of Language Structures Online*. Leipzig: Max Planck Institute for Evolutionary Anthropology. http://wals.info (accessed 11 August 2019).

Du Bois, John W. 1987. The discourse basis of ergativity. *Language* 63 (4). 805–855.

Dum-Tragut, Jasmine. 2009. *Armenian: Modern Eastern Armenian* (London Oriental and African Language Library 14). Amsterdam: John Benjamins.

Durie, Mark. 1986. The grammaticization of number as a verbal category. *Proceedings of the Annual Meeting of the Berkeley Linguistics Society* 12. 355–370. Berkeley, CA: University of California.

Edygarova, Svetlana. 2015. Negation in Udmurt. In Matti Miestamo, Anne Tamm & Beáta Wagner-Nagy (eds.), *Negation in Uralic languages* (Typological Studies in Language 108), 265–291. Amsterdam: John Benjamins.

Epps, Patience. 2008. *A grammar of Hup* (Mouton Grammar Library 43). Berlin: Mouton de Gruyter.

Epps, Patience. 2012. Between headed and headless relative clauses. In Bernard Comrie & Zarina Estrada-Fernández (eds.), *Relative clauses in languages of the Americas: A typological overview* (Typological Studies in Language 102), 191–211. Amsterdam: John Benjamins.

Evans, Nicholas. 1995. *A grammar of Kayardild: with historical-comparative notes on Tangkic* (Mouton Grammar Library 15). Berlin: Mouton de Gruyter.

Evans, Nicholas. 2007. Insubordination and its uses. In Irina Nikolaeva (ed.), *Finiteness: Theoretical and empirical foundations*, 366–431. Oxford: Oxford University Press.

Evans, Nicholas & Honoré Watanabe. 2016. The dynamics of insubordination. In Nicholas Evans & Honoré Watanabe (eds.), *Insubordination* (Typological Studies in Language 115), 1–38. Amsterdam: John Benjamins.

Félix Armendáriz, Rolando Gpe. 2005. *A grammar of River Warihio*. Houston, TX: Rice University doctoral dissertation.

Fillmore, Charles J. 1963. The position of embedding transformations in a grammar. *WORD* 19 (2). 208–231.

Fischer, Rafael & Eva van Lier. 2011. Cofán subordinate clauses in a typology of subordination. In Rik van Gijn, Katharina Haude & Pieter Muysken (eds.), *Subordination in native South American languages* (Typological Studies in Language 97), 221–249. Amsterdam: John Benjamins.

Fleck, David William. 2003. *A grammar of Matsés*. Houston, TX: Rice University doctoral dissertation.

Foley, William Auguste. 1976. *Comparative syntax in Austronesian*. Berkeley, CA: University of California doctoral dissertation.

Foley, William Auguste. 1980. Toward a universal typology of the noun phrase. *Studies in Language* 4 (2). 171–199.
Foley, William Auguste. 1991. *The Yimas language of Papua New Guinea*. Stanford, CA: Stanford University Press.
Foley, William Auguste & Van Valin, Robert D. 1984. *Functional syntax and universal grammar* (Cambridge Studies in Linguistics 38). Cambridge: Cambridge University Press.
Forker, Diana. 2013. *A grammar of Hinuq* (Mouton Grammar Library 63). Berlin: Mouton de Gruyter.
Fortescue, Michael. 1984. *West Greenlandic* (Croom Helm Descriptive Grammars). London: Croom Helm.
Fortescue, Michael. 1992. Morphophonemic complexity and typological stability in a polysynthetic language family. *International Journal of American Linguistics* 58 (2). 242–248.
Fox, Barbara A. 1987. The noun phrase accessibility hierarchy reinterpreted: Subject primacy or the absolutive hypothesis? *Language* 63 (4). 856–870.
Fox, Barbara A. & Sandra A. Thompson. 1990. A discourse explanation of the grammar of relative clauses in English conversation. *Language* 66 (2). 297–316.
Furby, E. S. & C. E. Furby. 1977. *A preliminary analysis of Garawa phrases and clauses* (Pacific Linguistics B-42). Canberra: Australian National University.
Gamble, Geoffrey. 1978. *Wikchamni grammar* (University of California Publications in Linguistics 89). Berkeley, CA: University of California Press.
Gast, Volker & Holger Diessel. 2012. The typology of clause linkage: status quo, challenges, prospects. In Volker Gast & Holger Diessel (eds.), *Clause linkage in cross-linguistic perspective: Data-driven approaches to cross-clausal syntax* (Trends in Linguistics 249), 1–36. Berlin: Mouton de Gruyter.
Generalova, Valeriia. 2016. *Aktanty motivirujuščego glagola v semantike russkix otglagol'nyx prilagatel'nyx* [Actants of the motivating verb in the semantics of Russian adjectives]. Saint Petersburg: Saint Petersburg State University BA thesis.
Genetti, Carol. 2007. *A grammar of Dolakha Newar* (Mouton Grammar Library 40). Berlin: Mouton de Gruyter.
Genetti, Carol, A. R. Coupe, Ellen Bartee, Kristine Hildebrandt & You-Jing Lin. 2008. Syntactic aspects of nominalization in five Tibeto-Burman languages of the Himalayan area. *Linguistics of the Tibeto-Burman Area* 31 (2). 97–144.
Georg, Stefan. 2007. *A descriptive grammar of Ket (Yenisei-Ostyak)* (Languages of Asia Series 1), Vol. 1: *Introduction, phonology, morphology*. Folkestone: Global Oriental.
Gijn, Rik van. 2014. Subordination strategies in South America: nominalization. In Loretta O'Connor & Pieter Muysken (eds.), *The native languages of South America: Origins, development, typology*, 274–296. Cambridge: Cambridge University Press.
Gildea, Spike. 1992. *Comparative Cariban morphosyntax: On the genesis of main clause morphosyntax*. Eugene, OR: University of Oregon doctoral dissertation.
Gildea, Spike. 1998. *On reconstructing grammar: Comparative Cariban morphosyntax* (Oxford Studies in Anthropological Linguistics). Oxford: Oxford University Press.
Givón, Talmy. 2001. *Syntax: An introduction*. Amsterdam: John Benjamins.
Givón, T. 2012. Toward a diachronic typology of relative clause. In Bernard Comrie & Zarina Estrada-Fernández (eds.), *Relative clauses in languages of the Americas: A typological overview* (Typological Studies in Language 102), 3–26. Amsterdam: John Benjamins.

Golluscio, Lucía A. 2012. Ditransitives in Mapudungun. In Andrej L. Malchukov, Martin Haspelmath & Bernard Comrie (eds.), *Studies in ditransitive constructions: A comparative handbook*, 710–756. Berlin: Mouton de Gruyter.

Gordon, Lynn. 1980. Relative clauses in Maricopa. *Occasional Papers on Linguistics* 7. 15–24. Carbondale: Southern Illinois University.

Gordon, Lynn. 1986. *Maricopa morphology and syntax* (University of California Publications in Linguistics 108). Berkeley, CA: University of California Press.

Greenberg, Joseph H. 1963. Some universals of grammar with particular reference to the order of meaningful elements. In Joseph H. Greenberg (ed.), *Universals of language*, 73–113. Cambridge, MA: MIT Press.

Grimes, Barbara F. (ed.). 2000. *Ethnologue*, 14th edn. Dallas, TX: Summer Institute of Linguistics International.

Grjunberg, A. L. 1966. Tatskij jazyk [The Tat language]. In V. V. Vinogradov (ed.), *Jazyki narodov SSSR* (Languages of the USSR), Vol. 1: *Indoevropejskie jazyki* (Indo-European languages), 281–301. Moscow: Nauka.

Gruzdeva, Ekaterina. 1998. *Nivkh* (Languages of the world/Materials 111). München: Lincom Europa.

Haig, Geoffrey. 1998. *Relative constructions in Turkish* (Turcologica 33). Wiesbaden: Harrassowitz.

Hale, Kenneth. 1976. The adjoined relative clause in Australia. In R. M. W. Dixon (ed.), *Grammatical categories in Australian languages* (Linguistic Series 22), 78–105. Canberra, Australia: Australian Institute of Aboriginal Studies.

Hamari, Arja & Niina Aasmäe. 2015. Negation in Erzya. In Matti Miestamo, Anne Tamm & Beáta Wagner-Nagy (eds.), *Negation in Uralic languages* (Typological Studies in Language 108), 293–324. Amsterdam: John Benjamins.

Hammarström, Harald, Robert Forkel & Martin Haspelmath. 2019. *Glottolog* 4.0. Jena: Max Planck Institute for the Science of Human History. http://glottolog.org (accessed 8 August 2019).

Harris, Alice C. 1981. *Georgian syntax: A study in relational grammar* (Cambridge Studies in Linguistics 33). Cambridge: Cambridge University Press.

Harris, Alice C. 2002. *Endoclitics and the origins of Udi morphosyntax*. Oxford: Oxford University Press.

Harris, Alice C. & Lyle Campbell. 1995. *Historical syntax in cross-linguistic perspective* (Cambridge Studies in Linguistics 74). Cambridge: Cambridge University Press.

Hartmann, R. R. K. & F. C. Stork. 1972. *Dictionary of language and linguistics*. London: Applied Science Publishers Ltd.

Haspelmath, Martin. 1989. From purposive to infinitive – a universal path of grammaticization. *Folia Linguistica Historica* 10 (1–2). 287–310.

Haspelmath, Martin. 1990. The grammaticization of passive morphology. *Studies in Language* 14 (1). 25–72.

Haspelmath, Martin. 1993. *A grammar of Lezgian* (Mouton Grammar Library 9). Berlin: Mouton de Gruyter.

Haspelmath, Martin. 1994. Passive participles across languages. In Barbara A. Fox & Paul J. Hopper (eds.), *Voice: Form and function* (Typological Studies in Language 27), 151–177. Amsterdam: John Benjamins.

Haspelmath, Martin. 1995. The converb as a cross-linguistically valid category. In Martin Haspelmath & Ekkehard König (eds.), *Converbs in cross-linguistic perspective* (Empirical Approaches to Language Typology 13), 1–55. Berlin: Mouton de Gruyter.

Haspelmath, Martin. 1996. Word-class-changing inflection and morphological theory. In Geert Booij & Jaap van Marle (eds.), *Yearbook of morphology 1995*, 43–66. Dordrecht: Kluwer Academic Publishers.

Haspelmath, Martin. 2001. The European linguistic area: Standard Average European. In Martin Haspelmath, Ekkehard König, Wulf Oesterreicher & Wolfgang Raible (eds.), *Language typology and language universals: An international handbook* (Handbooks of Linguistics and Communication Science 20), Vol. 2, 1492–1510. Berlin: Walter de Gruyter.

Haspelmath, Martin. 2010. Comparative concepts and descriptive categories in cross-linguistic studies. *Language* 86 (3). 663–687.

Haspelmath, Martin. 2011a. On S, A, P, T, and R as comparative concepts for alignment typology. *Linguistic Typology* 15 (3). 535–567.

Haspelmath, Martin. 2011b. The indeterminacy of word segmentation and the nature of morphology and syntax. *Folia Linguistica* 45 (1). 31–80.

Haspelmath, Martin. 2014. Comparative syntax. In Andrew Carnie, Yosuke Sato & Dan Siddiqi (eds.), *The Routledge handbook of syntax* (Routledge Handbooks in Linguistics), 490–508. London: Routledge.

Haspelmath, Martin. 2015. A grammatical overview of Egyptian and Coptic. In Eitan Grossman, Martin Haspelmath & Tonio Sebastian Richter (eds.), *Egyptian-Coptic linguistics in typological perspective* (Empirical Approaches to Language Typology 55), 103–144. Berlin: Mouton de Gruyter.

Haspelmath, Martin & Andrea D. Sims. 2010. *Understanding morphology* (Understanding Language Series), 2nd edn. London: Hodder Education.

Hayward, R. J. 1982. Notes on the Koyra language. *Afrika und Übersee* 65. 211–268.

Hazout, Ilan. 2001. Predicate formation: The case of participial relatives. *The Linguistic Review* 18 (2). 97–123.

Heath, Jeffrey. 2008. A grammar of Nanga. (Manuscript.)

Hellenthal, Anne-Christie. 2010. *A grammar of Sheko* (LOT Dissertation Series 258). Utrecht: LOT.

Hendery, Rachel. 2012. *Relative clauses in time and space: A case study in the methods of diachronic typology* (Typological Studies in Language 101). Amsterdam: John Benjamins.

Hengeveld, Kees. 1989. Layers and operators in Functional Grammar. *Journal of Linguistics* 25 (1). 127–157.

Hengeveld, Kees. 1992. *Non-verbal predication: Theory, typology, diachrony* (Functional Grammar Series 15). Berlin: Mouton de Gruyter.

Herrmann, Tanja. 2003. *Relative clauses in dialects of English: A typological approach*. Albert-Ludwigs-Universität Freiburg doctoral dissertation.

Hewitt, Brian George. 1978. The Armenian relative clause. *International Review of Slavic Linguistics* 3 (1–2). 99–138.

Hewitt, Brian George. 1979. *Abkhaz* (Lingua Descriptive Studies 2). Amsterdam: North-Holland.

Hewitt, Brian George. 1995. *Georgian: A structural reference grammar* (London Oriental and African Language Library 2). Amsterdam: John Benjamins.

Hildebrandt, Kristine A. 2004. A grammar and glossary of the Manange language. In Carol Genetti (ed.), *Tibeto-Burman languages of Nepal: Manange and Sherpa* (Pacific Linguistics 557), 2–189. Canberra: Australian National University.

Hoffmann, Carl. 1963. *A grammar of the Margi language*. London: Oxford University Press.
Hopper, Paul J. (ed.). *Tense-Aspect: Between semantics and pragmatics* (Typological Studies in Language 1). Amsterdam: John Benjamins.
Hopper, Paul J. & Sandra A. Thompson. 1984. The discourse basis for lexical categories in Universal Grammar. *Language* 60 (4). 703–752.
Horn, L. R. 1978. Remarks on neg-raising. In Peter Cole (ed.), *Syntax and semantics*, Vol. 9: *Pragmatics*, 129–220. New York, NY: Academic Press.
Hualde, José Ignacio & Jon Ortiz de Urbina. 2003. *A grammar of Basque* (Mouton Grammar Library 26). Berlin: Mouton de Gruyter.
Huang, Chenglong. 2008. Relativization in Qiang. *Language and Linguistics* 9 (4). 735–768.
Huttar, George L. & Mary L. Huttar 1994. *Ndyuka* (Routledge Descriptive Grammars). London: Routledge.
Jacques, Guillaume. 2013. Relativization in Japhug Rgyalrong. (Manuscript.)
Jacques, Guillaume. 2016. Subjects, objects and relativization in Japhug. *Journal of Chinese Linguistics* 44 (1). 1–28.
Jany, Carmen. 2008. Relativization versus nominalization strategies in Chimariko. In Joye Kiester & Verónica Muñoz-Ledo (eds.), *Proceedings from the Eleventh Workshop on American Indigenous Languages* (Santa Barbara Papers in Linguistics 19), 40–50. Santa Barbara, CA: University of California.
Jany, Carmen. 2009. *Chimariko grammar: Areal and typological perspective* (University of California Publications in Linguistics 142). Berkeley, CA: University of California Press.
Jeanne, LaVerne Masayesva. 1978. *Aspects of Hopi grammar*. Cambridge, MA: Massachusetts Institute of Technology doctoral dissertation.
Jendraschek, Gerd. 2012. *A grammar of Iatmul*. Regensburg: Universität Regensburg Habilitationsschrift.
Johnson, D. E. 1974. On the role of grammatical relations in linguistic theory. In Michael W. La Galy, Robert A. Fox & Anthony Bruck (eds.), *Papers from the Tenth Regional Meeting of the Chicago Linguistic Society*, 269–283. Chicago, IL: Chicago Linguistic Society.
Jones, Wendell & Paula Jones. 1991. *Barasano syntax* (Studies in the Languages of Colombia 2; Summer Institute of Linguistics Publications in Linguistics 101). Arlington, TX: Summer Institute of Linguistics and the University of Texas at Arlington.
Josephs, Lewis S. 1975. *Palauan reference grammar*. Honolulu, HI: The University Press of Hawaii.
Kalinina, E. Yu. 1998. Razgraničenie finitnyx i nefinitnyx form glagola v tipologičeskom aspekte [Distinguishing between finite and non-finite verb forms from a typological point of view]. *Voprosy jazykoznanija* 4. 82–110.
Kalinina, E. Yu. 2001. *Nefinitnye skazuemye v nezavisimom predloženii* [Non-finite predicates as heads of independent sentences]. Moscow: IMLI RAN.
Kazenin, Konstantin I. 1994. Split syntactic ergativity: toward an implicational hierarchy. *Sprachtypologie und Universalienforschung* 47 (2). 78–98.
Keenan, Edward L. 1984. Semantic correlates of the ergative/absolutive distinction. *Linguistics* 22 (2). 197–223.
Keenan, Edward L. 1985. Relative clauses. In Timothy Shopen (ed.), *Language typology and syntactic description*, Vol. 2: *Complex constructions*, 141–170. Cambridge: Cambridge University Press.
Keenan, Edward L. & Bernard Comrie. 1977. Noun phrase accessibility and universal grammar. *Linguistic Inquiry* 8 (1). 63–99.

Keenan, Edward L. & Bernard Comrie. 1979. Noun phrase accessibility revisited. *Language* 55 (3). 649–664.
Kenesei, István, Robert M. Vago & Anna Fenyvesi. 1998. *Hungarian* (Routledge Descriptive Grammars). London: Routledge.
King, John T. 2009. *A grammar of Dhimal* (Brill's Tibetan Studies Library 5/8). Leiden: Brill.
Kirjanov, Denis & Shagal, Ksenia. 2011. Dejstvitel'noe pričastie buduščego vremeni soveršennogo vida v russkom jazyke [Future active perfective participle in Russian]. In D. V. Gerasimov, N. M. Zaika, V. A. Krylova, S. A. Oskol'skaja, S. S. Saj, M. A. Kholodilova & K. A. Shagal (eds.), *Acta linguistica Petropolitana: Transactions of the Institute for Linguistic Studies RAS* (*Studies in Typology and Grammar*), Vol. 7 (3), 93–98. Saint Petersburg: Nauka.
Kiss, Katalin É. 2015. Negation in Hungarian. In Matti Miestamo, Anne Tamm & Beáta Wagner-Nagy (eds.), *Negation in Uralic languages* (Typological Studies in Language 108), 219–238. Amsterdam: John Benjamins.
Klein, Wolfgang. 1994. *Time in language*. London: Routledge.
Klein, Wolfgang. 1998. Assertion and finiteness. In Norbert Dittmar & Zvi Penner (eds.), *Issues in the theory of language acquisition: Essays in honor of Jürgen Weissenborn*, 225–245. Bern: Peter Lang.
Klimov, G. A. & D. I. Èdel'man. 1970. *Jazyk burušaski* [The Burushaski language]. Moscow: Nauka.
Koehn, Edward & Sally Koehn. 1986. Apalai. In Desmond C. Derbyshire & Geoffrey K. Pullum (eds.), *Handbook of Amazonian languages*, Vol. 1, 33–127. Berlin: Mouton de Gruyter.
Koptjevskaja-Tamm, Maria. 1993. *Nominalizations*. London: Routledge.
Koptjevskaja-Tamm, Maria. 1999. Finiteness. In Keith Brown & Jim Miller (eds.), *Concise encyclopedia of grammatical categories*, 146–149. Amsterdam: Elsevier.
Kossmann, Maarten. 2000. *Esquisse grammaticale du rifain oriental* (Société d'Études Linguistiques et Antropologiques de France 387). Paris: Peeters.
Kossmann, Maarten. 2003. The origin of the Berber 'participle'. In M. Lionel Bender, Gábor Takács & David L. Appleyard (eds.), *Selected comparative-historical Afrasian linguistic studies in memory of Igor M. Diakonoff* (Lincom Studies in Afroasiatic Linguistics 14), 27–40. München: Lincom Europa.
Kossmann, Maarten. 2007. Berber morphology. In Alan S. Kaye (ed.), *Morphologies of Asia and Africa*, Vol. 1, 429–446. Winona Lake, IN: Eisenbrauns.
Kramer, Ruth. 2003. *(Virtual) relative clauses in Middle Egyptian*. Providence, RI: Brown University BA thesis.
Krapivina, K. A. 2007. Valentnostno-aktantnye xarakteristiki russkix glagolov [Argument structure of Russian verbs]. *Aničkovskij vestnik* 60. 23–39.
Krapivina, K. A. 2009a. Pričastie v roli skazuemogo otnositel'nogo oborota v kalmyckom jazyke [Participle as the head of relative clause in Kalmyk]. In S. S. Saj, V. V. Baranova & N. V. Serdobolskaya (eds.), *Issledovanija po grammatike kalmyckogo jazyka* [Studies in the grammar of Kalmyk], 497–524. Saint Petersburg: Nauka.
Krapivina, K. A. 2009b. *Pričastnyj taksis v russkom jazyke* [Participial taxis in Russian]. Saint Petersburg: Saint Petersburg State University BA thesis.
Krishnamurti, Bh. & J. P. L. Gwynn. 1985. *A grammar of Modern Telugu*. Oxford: Oxford University Press.

Kurebito, Megumi. 2011. How is Taro=wa asu ku-ru hazu-da expressed in Koryak: Comparing Koryak agentive/patientive nominal with Japanese MMC. 富山大学人文学部紀要 55. 19–36.
König, Ekkehard & Johan van der Auwera. 1990. Adverbial participles, gerunds and absolute constructions in the languages of Europe. In Johannes Bechert, Giuliano Bernini & Claude Buridant (eds.), *Toward a typology of European languages* [Empirical Approaches to Language Typology 8], 337–355. Berlin: Mouton de Gruyter.
Lander, Yury A. 2008. Pričastnye konstrukcii ili nekategorial'noe podčinenie? [Participial constructions or non-categorial subordination?]. In Mikhail E. Alekseev & Timur A. Maisak (eds.), *Udinskij sbornik: grammatika, leksika, istorija jazyka* [The Udi collection: Grammar, lexicon, the history of the language], 54–95. Moscow: Academia.
Lander, Yury A. 2012. *Reljativizacija v polisintetičeskom jazyke: adygejskie otnositel'nye konstrukcii v tipologičeskoj perspective* [Relativization in a polysynthetic language: Adyghe relative constructions in a typological perspective]. Moscow: Institute of Oriental Studies of the Russian Academy of Sciences doctoral (k.f.n.) dissertation.
Lander, Yury A. 2014. Tipologija nemarkirovannogo klauzal'nogo podčinenija: otnositel'nye konstrukcii [Typology of unmarked clausal subordination: Relative constructions]. *Voprosy jazykoznanija* 1. 3–20.
Langacker, Ronald W. 1972. *Fundamentals of linguistic analysis*. New York, NY: Harcourt Brace Jovanovich.
Langacker, Ronald W. 1987a. *Foundations of cognitive grammar*, Vol. 1: Theoretical prerequisites. Stanford, CA: Stanford University Press.
Langacker, Ronald W. 1987b. Nouns and verbs. *Language* 63 (1). 53–94.
LaPolla, Randy J. with Chenglong Huang. 2003. *A grammar of Qiang with annotated texts and glossary* (Mouton Grammar Library 31). Berlin: Mouton de Gruyter.
Ledgeway, Adam. 1998. Variation in the Romance infinitive: The case of the southern Calabrian inflected infinitive. *Transactions of the Philological Society* 96 (1). 1–61.
Lee, Hansol H. B. 1994. *Korean grammar*, 2nd edn. Oxford: Oxford University Press.
Lefebvre, Claire & Pieter Muysken. 1988. *Mixed categories: Nominalizations in Quechua*. Dordrecht: Kluwer Academic Publishers.
Lehmann, Christian. 1984. *Der Relativsatz*. Tübingen: Gunter Narr.
Lehmann, Christian. 1986. On the typology of relative clauses. *Linguistics* 24 (4). 663–680.
Lehmann, Christian. 1988. Towards a typology of clause linkage. In John Haiman & Sandra A. Thompson (eds.), *Clause combining in grammar and discourse* (Typological Studies in Language 18), 181–225. Amsterdam: John Benjamins.
Lehmann, Christian & Edith Moravcsik. 2000. Noun. In G. Booij, C. Lehmann & J. Mugdan (eds.), *Morphology: An international handbook on inflection and word-formation*, Vol. 1, 732–757. Berlin: Mouton de Gruyter.
Lehmann, Thomas. 1993. *A grammar of Modern Tamil*. Pondicherry: Institute of Language and Culture.
Li, Charles N. (ed.). 1976. *Subject and Topic*. New York, NY: Academic Press.
Li, Charles N. & Sandra A. Thompson. 1978. Relativization strategies in Wappo. *Proceedings of the Annual Meeting of the Berkeley Linguistics Society* 4. 106–113. Berkeley, CA: University of California.
Lier, Eva van. 2009. *Parts of speech and dependent clauses: A typological study* (LOT Dissertation Series 221). Utrecht: LOT.

Lindsey, Geoffrey & Janine Scancarelli. 1985. Where have all the adjectives come from? The case of Cherokee. *Proceedings of the Annual Meeting of the Berkeley Linguistics Society* 11. 207–215. Berkeley, CA: University of California.

Lyons, John. 1968. *Introduction to theoretical linguistics*. Cambridge: Cambridge University Press.

Mackridge, Peter. 1985. *The Modern Greek language: A descriptive analysis of standard Modern Greek*. Oxford: Oxford University Press.

Maiden, Martin & Robustelli, Cecilia. 2000. *A reference grammar of modern Italian*. London: Arnold.

Maisak, Timur A. 2008. Glagol'naja paradigma udinskogo jazyka [The Udi verbal paradigm]. In Mikhail E. Alekseev & Timur A. Maisak (eds.), *Udinskij sbornik: grammatika, leksika, istorija jazyka* [The Udi collection: Grammar, lexicon, the history of the language], 96–161. Moscow: Academia.

Malchukov, Andrej L. 1995. *Even* (Languages of the World/Materials 12). München: Lincom Europa.

Malchukov, Andrej L. 2004. *Nominalization/verbalization: Constraining a typology of transcategorial operations* (Lincom Studies in Language Typology 8). München: Lincom Europa.

Malchukov, Andrej L. 2008. *Sintaksis èvenskogo jazyka: strukturnye, semantičeskie, kommunikativnye aspekty* [The syntax of Even: Structural, semantic, and communicative aspects]. Saint Petersburg: Nauka.

Marlett, Stephen A. 2012. Relative clauses in Seri. In Bernard Comrie & Zarina Estrada-Fernández (eds.), *Relative clauses in languages of the Americas: A typological overview* (Typological Studies in Language 102), 213–241. Amsterdam: John Benjamins.

Maslova, Elena. 2003. *A grammar of Kolyma Yukaghir* (Mouton Grammar Library 27). Berlin: Mouton de Gruyter.

Matisoff, James A. 1972. Lahu nominalization, relativization, and genetivization. In John P. Kimball (ed.), *Syntax and Semantics*, 237–257. New York, NY: Academic Press.

Matras, Yaron & Jeanette Sakel. 2007. Introduction. In Yaron Matras & Jeanette Sakel (eds.), *Grammatical borrowing in cross-linguistic perspective* (Empirical Approaches to Language Typology 38), 1–13. Berlin: Mouton de Gruyter.

Matsumoto, Yoshiko, Bernard Comrie & Peter Sells. 2017. Noun-modifying clause constructions in languages of Eurasia: Rethinking theoretical and geographical boundaries. In Yoshiko Matsumoto, Bernard Comrie & Peter Sells (eds.), *Noun-modifying clause constructions in languages of Eurasia: Rethinking theoretical and geographical boundaries*, 3–21. Amsterdam: John Benjamins.

Mattissen, Johanna. 2002. Dependent-head synthesis in Nivkh – with an outlook on polysynthesis in the Far Northeast. In Nicholas Evans & Hans-Jürgen Sasse (eds.), *Problems of polysynthesis*, 136–166. Berlin: Akademie Verlag.

Mattissen, Johanna. 2003. *Dependent-head synthesis in Nivkh: A contribution to a typology of polysynthesis* (Typological Studies in Language 57). Amsterdam: John Benjamins.

Maxwell, Dan. 1982. Implications of NP accessibility for diachronic syntax. *Folia Linguistica Historica* 3 (2). 135–152.

McGregor, William B. 2009. Typology of ergativity. *Language and Linguistics Compass* 3 (1). 480–508.

Mel'čuk, Igor A. 1988. *Dependency syntax: Theory and practice*. Albany, NY: State University of New York Press.

Miestamo, Matti. 2003. *Clausal negation: A typological study*. Helsinki: University of Helsinki doctoral dissertation.
Miestamo, Matti. 2005. *Standard negation: The negation of declarative verbal main clauses in a typological perspective*. (Empirical Approaches to Language Typology 31). Berlin: Mouton de Gruyter.
Miestamo, Matti, Anne Tamm & Beáta Wagner-Nagy. 2015. Negation in Uralic languages – Introduction. In Matti Miestamo, Anne Tamm & Beáta Wagner-Nagy (eds.), *Negation in Uralic languages* (Typological Studies in Language 108), 1–44. Amsterdam: John Benjamins.
Miller, Marion. 1999. *Desano grammar* (Studies in the Languages of Colombia 6; Summer Institute of Linguistics Publications in Linguistics 132). Dallas, TX: Summer Institute of Linguistics and University of Texas at Arlington.
Mithun, Marianne. 1984. The evolution of noun incorporation. *Language* 60 (4). 847–894.
Mithun, Marianne & Wallace Chafe. 1999. What are S, A, and O? *Studies in Language* 23 (3). 569–596.
Mushin, Ilana. 2012. *A grammar of (Western) Garrwa* (Pacific Linguistics 637). Berlin: Mouton de Gruyter.
Nagasaki, Iku. 2014. Relative clauses in Kolyma Yukaghir. *Asian and African Languages and Linguistics* 8. 79–98.
Narrog, Heiko. 2009. *Modality in Japanese: The layered structure of the clause and hierarchies of functional categories* (Studies in Language Companion Series 109). Amsterdam: John Benjamins.
Nedjalkov, Vladimir P. & Galina A. Otaina. 2013. *A syntax of the Nivkh language: The Amur dialect* (Studies in Language Companion Series 139). Amsterdam: John Benjamins.
Nefedov, Andrey. 2012. Relativization in Ket. In Volker Gast & Holger Diessel (eds.), *Clause linkage in cross-linguistic perspective: Data-driven approaches to cross-clausal syntax* (Trends in Linguistics 249), 191–224. Berlin: Mouton de Gruyter.
Newmark, Leonard, Philip Hubbard & Peter Prifti. 1982. *Standard Albanian: A reference grammar for students*. Stanford, CA: Stanford University Press.
Nichols, Johanna. 1992. *Linguistic diversity in space and time*. Chicago, IL: The University of Chicago Press.
Nichols, Johanna. 2011. *Ingush grammar* (University of California Publications in Linguistics 143). Berkeley, CA: University of California Press.
Nikitina, Tatiana 2007. Nominalization/verbalization: Constraining a typology of transcategorial operations (Review of Malchukov 2004). *Linguistic Typology* 11 (3). 605–614.
Nikitina, Tatiana. 2009. The function and form of action nominalization in Wan. *Mandenkan* 45. 17–28.
Nikolaeva, Irina. 1997. *Yukagir texts* (Specimina Sibirica 13). Szombathely: Savariae.
Nikolaeva, Irina. 1999. *Ostyak* (Languages of the World/Materials 305). München: Lincom Europa.
Nikolaeva, Irina. 2007a. Introduction. In Irina Nikolaeva (ed.), *Finiteness: Theoretical and empirical foundations,* 1–19. Oxford: Oxford University Press.
Nikolaeva, Irina. 2007b. Constructional Economy and non-finite independent clauses. In Irina Nikolaeva (ed.), *Finiteness: Theoretical and empirical foundations,* 138–180. Oxford: Oxford University Press.

Nikolaeva, Irina. 2013. Unpacking finiteness. In Dunstan Brown, Marina Chumakina & Greville G. Corbett (eds.), *Canonical morphology and syntax*, 99–122. Oxford: Oxford University Press.

Nikolaeva, Irina. 2014. *A grammar of Tundra Nenets* (Mouton Grammar Library 65). Berlin: Mouton de Gruyter.

Noonan, Michael. 1985. Complementation. In Timothy Shopen (ed.), *Language typology and syntactic description*, Vol. 2: *Complex constructions*, 42–140. Cambridge: Cambridge University Press.

Noonan, Michael. 1997. Versatile nominalizations. In Joan Bybee, John Haiman & Sandra A. Thompson (eds.), *Essays on language function and language type: Dedicated to T. Givón*, 373–394. Amsterdam: John Benjamins.

Nordlinger, Rachel. 1998. *A grammar of Wambaya, Northern Territory (Australia)* (Pacific Linguistics C-140). Canberra: Australian National University.

Nordlinger, Rachel. 2002. Non-finite subordinate verbs in Australian Aboriginal languages. In Cynthia Allen (ed.), *Proceedings of the 2001 Conference of the Australian Linguistic Society*. http://www.als.asn.au/proceedings/als2001/nordlinger.pdf (accessed 10 August 2019).

Nordlinger, Rachel. 2006. Spearing the emu drinking: Subordination and the adjoined relative clause in Wambaya. *Australian Journal of Linguistics* 26 (1). 5–29.

Nuyts, Jan. 2000. *Epistemic modality, language and conceptualization* (Human Cognitive Processing 5). Amsterdam: John Benjamins.

Ó Baoill, Dónall P. 2009. Irish. In Martin J. Ball & Nicole Müller (eds.), *The Celtic languages* (Routledge Language Family Series), 2nd edn., 163–229. London: Routledge.

Olawsky, Knut J. 2006. *A grammar of Urarina*. (Mouton grammar library 37). Berlin: Mouton de Gruyter.

Onishi, Masayuki. 1994. *A grammar of Motuna (Bougainville, Papua New Guinea)*. Australian National University doctoral dissertation.

Overall, Simon. 2007. *A grammar of Aguaruna*. Melbourne: La Trobe University doctoral dissertation.

Overall, Simon & Marine Vuillermet. 2015. The Eastern foothills as a contact zone: Evidence from non-canonical switch-reference. Talk given at the European Network for the Study of Andean Languages (REELA), Centre for Linguistics, Leiden University, 7 September 2015.

Pakendorf, Brigitte. 2012. Patterns of relativization in North Asia: Towards a refined typology of prenominal participial relative clauses. In Volker Gast & Holger Diessel (eds.), *Clause linkage in cross-linguistic perspective: Data-driven approaches to cross-clausal syntax* (Trends in Linguistics 249), 253–284. Berlin: Mouton de Gruyter.

Palmer, Frank Robert. 1986. *Mood and Modality* (Cambridge Textbooks in Linguistics). Cambridge: Cambridge University Press.

Pandharipande, Rajeshwari V. 1997. *Marathi* (Routledge Descriptive Grammars). London: Routledge.

Paperno, Denis. 2014. Grammatical sketch of Beng. *Mandenkan* 51. 7–130.

Payne, Thomas E. 1997. *Describing morphosyntax: A guide for field linguists*. Cambridge: Cambridge University Press.

Payne, Thomas E. & Doris L. Payne. 2013. *A typological grammar of Panare: A Cariban language of Venezuela* (Brill's Studies in the Indigenous Languages of the Americas 5). Leiden: Brill.

Pengitov, N. T. 1951. *Pričastija v marijskom jazyke* [Participles in Mari]. Moscow: Institute of Linguistics of the Academy of Sciences of the USSR doctoral (k.f.n.) dissertation.
Peterson, John. 2011. *A grammar of Kharia: A South Munda language* (Brill's Studies in South and Southwest Asian Languages 1). Leiden: Brill.
Plank, Frans. 1991. Inflection and derivation. *EUROTYP Working Papers* VII (10).
Plank, Frans. 1994. Inflection and derivation. In R. E. Asher (ed.), *The encyclopedia of language and linguistics*, Vol. 3, 1671–1681. Oxford: Pergamon Press.
Plungian, Vladimir A. & Ekaterina V. Raxilina. 1990. Sirkonstanty v tolkovanii? In Zygmunt Saloni (ed.), *Metody formalne w opisie jezykow slovianskich* [Formal methods in the description of Slavic languages] (Rozprawy Uniwersytetu Warszawskiego 399), 201–210. Białystok: University of Warsaw.
Plungian, Vladimir A. 2010. Pričastija i psevdopričastija v russkom jazyke. [Participles and pseudoparticiples in Russian]. Talk given at the University of Oslo, 26 February 2010.
Press, Margaret L. 1979. *Chemehuevi: A grammar and lexicon* (University of California Publications in Linguistics 92). Berkeley, CA: University of California Press.
Reh, Mechthild. 1985. *Die Krongo-Sprache (Nìinò Mó-Dì): Beschreibung, Texte, Wörterverzeichnis* (Kölner Beiträge zur Afrikanistik 12). Berlin: Dietrich Reimer.
Reuse, Willem J. de. 1994. Noun incorporation. In R. E. Asher (ed.), *The encyclopedia of language and linguistics*, Vol. 9, 2842–2847. Oxford: Pergamon Press.
Rijkhoff, Jan. 1992. *The noun phrase: A typological study of its form and function*. Amsterdam: Vrije Universiteit Amsterdam doctoral dissertation.
Rijkhoff, Jan. 2016. Crosslinguistic categories in morphosyntactic typology: Problems and prospects. *Linguistic Typology* 20 (2). 333–363.
Rijkhoff, Jan, Dik Bakker, Kees Hengeveld & Peter Kahrel. 1993. A method of language sampling. *Studies in Language* 17 (1). 169–203.
Rijkhoff, Jan & Dik Bakker. 1998. Language sampling. *Linguistic Typology* 2 (3). 263–314.
Robins, R. H. 1958. *The Yurok language: Grammar, texts, lexicon* (University of California Publications in Linguistics 15). Berkeley, CA: University of California Press.
Ross, John Robert. 1972. The category squish: Endstation Hauptwort. In Paul M. Peranteau, Judith N. Levi & Gloria C. Phares (eds.), *Proceedings of the Eighth Regional Meeting of the Chicago Linguistic Society*, 316–328. Chicago, IL: University of Chicago.
Ross, John Robert. 1973. Slifting. In Maurice Gross, Morris Halle & Marcel-P. Schützenberger (eds.), *The formal analysis of natural languages: Proceedings of the first international conference, Paris, April 27–29, 1970* (Janua Linguarum. Series Maior 62), 133–169. The Hague: Mouton.
Ross, Daniel. 2016. Expressing adverbial relations in clause linkage with converbs: Definitional and typological considerations. Talk given at the Syntax of the World's Languages VII conference, Mexico City, 20 August 2016.
Ryding, Karin C. 2005. *A reference grammar of Modern Standard Arabic*. Cambridge: Cambridge University Press.
Saj, Sergej. 2016. Pričastie [Participle]. In Vladimir A. Plungian (ed.), *Materialy k korpusnoj grammatike russkogo jazyka* [Materials for a corpus-based grammar of Russian], Part 1: *Glagol* [Verb], 341–388. Saint Petersburg: Nestor-Istorija.
Salanova, Andrés Pablo. 2011. Relative clauses in Mẽbengokre. In Rik van Gijn, Katharina Haude & Pieter Muysken (eds.), *Subordination in native South American languages* (Typological Studies in Language 97), 45–78. Amsterdam: John Benjamins.

Sat, Š. Č. 1980. *Sintaksičeskie funkcii pričastij v tuvinskom jazyke* [Syntactic functions of participles in Tuvinian]. Kyzyl: Tuvinskoe knižnoe izdatel'stvo.

Scalise, Sergio. 1988. Inflection and derivation. *Linguistics* 26 (4). 561–582.

Schmidtke-Bode, Karsten. 2012. The performance basis of grammatical constraints on complex sentences: A preliminary survey. In Volker Gast & Holger Diessel (eds.), *Clause linkage in cross-linguistic perspective: Data-driven approaches to cross-clausal syntax* (Trends in Linguistics 249), 415–448. Berlin: Mouton de Gruyter.

Schuh, Russell G. 1998. *A grammar of Miya* (University of California Publications in Linguistics 130). Berkeley, CA: University of California Press.

Seki, Lucy. 1990. Kamaiurá (Tupí-Guaraní) as an active–stative language. In Doris L. Payne (ed.), *Amazonian linguistics: Studies in lowland South American languages*, 367–391. Austin, TX: University of Texas Press.

Seki, Lucy. 2000. *Gramatica do Kamaiurá: Língua Tupi-Guarani do Alto Xingu*. Campinas: Editora da Unicamp.

Serdobolskaya, Natalia. 2005. *Sintaksičeskij status aktantov zavisimoj nefinitnoj predikacii* [Syntax of core arguments in non-finite dependent clauses]. Moscow: Moscow State University doctoral (k.f.n.) dissertation.

Serdobolskaya, Natalia. 2009. Akkuzativ sub"ekta v zavisimoj predikacii: za i protiv pod"ema argumenta v kalmyckom jazyke [Accusative subject in dependent clause: pro et contra argument raising in Kalmyk]. In S. S. Saj, V. V. Baranova & N. V. Serdobolskaya (eds.), *Issledovanija po grammatike kalmyckogo jazyka* [Studies in the grammar of Kalmyk], 581–621. Saint Petersburg: Nauka.

Serdobolskaya, Natalia & Denis Paperno. 2006. The polysemy of relativizing and nominalizing markers. (Manuscript.) https://www.academia.edu/8483668/The_polysemy_of_relativizing_and_nominalizing_markers (accessed 10 August 2019).

Serdobolskaya, Natalia & Svetlana Toldova. 2017. Oformlenie prjamogo dopolnenija v finno-ugorskix jazyax: meždu predikaciej i diskursom [Direct object marking in Finno-Ugric languages: between sentence and discourse]. *Ural-Altaic Studies* 27 (4). 92–112.

Shagal, Ksenia. 2011. O kategorii vremeni u russkix pričastij [Russian participles and category of tense] In Anton Kjunal', Grigorij Utgof & Inna Adamson (eds.), *Studia Slavica* X, 346–357. Tallinn: OÜ Vali Press.

Shagal, Ksenia. 2016. Relative clauses in the languages of Sakhalin as an areal feature. In Ekaterina Gruzdeva & Juha Janhunen (eds.), *Linguistic crossings and crosslinguistics in Northeast Asia* (Studia Orientalia 117), 153–170. Helsinki: Finnish Oriental Society.

Shagal, Ksenia. 2017. *Towards a typology of participles*. Helsinki: University of Helsinki doctoral dissertation.

Shagal, Ksenia. 2018. Participial systems in Uralic languages: An overview. In Gerson Klumpp, Lidia Federica Mazzitelli & Fedor Rozhanskiy (eds.), Typology of Uralic languages: current views and new perspectives [Special issue], *Journal of Estonian and Finno-Ugric Linguistics* 9 (1), 55–84.

Shagal, Ksenia & Anna Volkova. 2018. Participiális főnév módosítás a hegyi mariban [Participial modification in Hill Mari]. *Általános nyelvészeti tanulmányok* 30. Uralisztikai tanulmányok [General Linguistics Studies 30. Uralic Studies], 207–232.

Shaul, David Leedom. 1986. *Topics in Nevome syntax* (University of California Publications in Linguistics 109). Berkeley, CA: University of California Press.

Shibatani, Masayoshi. 2009. Elements of complex structures, where recursion isn't: The case of relativization. In T. Givón & Masayoshi Shibatani (eds.), *Syntactic complexity: Diachrony, acquisition, neuro-cognition, evolution* (Typological Studies in Language 85), 163–198. Amsterdam: John Benjamins.

Shin, Kyu-Suk. 2003. *Characteristics of the relative clause in Korean and the problems second language learners experience in acquiring the relative clause*. Perth: Curtin University of Technology doctoral dissertation.

Siewierska, Anna. 1984. *The passive: A comparative linguistic analysis* (Croom Helm Linguistics Series). London: Croom Helm.

Siewierska, Anna. 2013. Alignment of verbal person marking. In Matthew S. Dryer & Martin Haspelmath (eds.), *The World Atlas of Language Structures Online*. Leipzig: Max Planck Institute for Evolutionary Anthropology. http://wals.info/chapter/100 (accessed 16 June 2016).

Silverstein, Michael. 1976. Hierarchy of features and ergativity. In R. M. W. Dixon (ed.), *Grammatical Categories in Australian Languages* (Linguistic Series 22), 112–171. Canberra, Australia: Australian Institute of Aboriginal Studies.

Smeets, Ineke. 2008. *A grammar of Mapuche* (Mouton Grammar Library 41). Berlin: Mouton de Gruyter.

Spencer, Andrew. 2013. *Lexical relatedness: A paradigm-based model*. Oxford: Oxford University Press.

Stassen, Leon. 1985. *Comparison and universal grammar*. Oxford: Basil Blackwell.

Sumbatova, Nina R. & Yury A. Lander. 2014. *Darginskij govor selenija Tanty: Grammatičeskij očerk. Voprosy sintaksisa* [The Dargwa variety of the Tanti village: A grammatical sketch. Aspects of syntax]. Moscow: Jazyki slav'anskoj kul'tury.

Sun, Jackson T.-S. 2003. Tani languages. In Graham Thurgood & Randy J. LaPolla (eds.), *The Sino-Tibetan languages* (Routledge Language Family Series), 456–466. London: Routledge.

Sunik, O. P. 1947. *Očerki po sintaksisu tunguso-man'čžurskix jazykov* [Essays on the syntax of Tungusic languages]. Leningrad: Učpedgiz.

Thompson, Sandra A., Joseph Sung-Yul Park & Charles N. Li. 2006. *A reference grammar of Wappo* (University of California Publications in Linguistics 138). Berkeley, CA: University of California Press.

Thomson, Robert W. 1975. *An introduction to Classical Armenian*. Delmar, NY: Caravan Books.

Toldova, Svetlana & Natalia Serdobolskaya. 2002. Nekotorye osobennosti oformlenija prjamogo dopolnenija v marijskom jazyke [Some peculiarities of direct object marking in Mari]. In Tatiana B. Agranat & Olga A. Kazakevič (eds.), *Lingvističeskij bespredel. The volume dedicated to the 70th anniversary of A. I. Kuznetsova*, 106–125. Moscow: Izdatel'stvo Moskovskogo universiteta.

Torero Fernández de Cordoba, Alfredo. 2002. *Idiomas de los Andes: Lingüística e historia*. Lima: Editorial Horizonte.

Trask, Robert Lawrence. 1993. *A dictionary of grammatical terms in linguistics*. London: Routledge.

Treis, Yvonne. 2008. Relativization in Kambaata (Cushitic). In Zygmunt Frajzyngier & Erin Shay (eds.), *Interaction of morphology and syntax: Case studies in Afroasiatic* (Typological Studies in Language 75), 161–206. Amsterdam: John Benjamins.

Troike, Rudolph C. 1996. Sketch of Coahuilteco, a language isolate of Texas. In Ives Goddard (ed.), *Handbook of North American Indians*, Vol. 17: *Languages*, 644–665. Washington, DC: Smithsonian Institution.
Troike, Rudolph C. 2010. Relative clauses in Coahuilteco, an Indian language of Texas. (Manuscript.)
Ubrjatova, Elizaveta Ivanovna. 1976. *Issledovanija po sintaksisu jakutskogo jazyka: Složnoe predloženie* [Studies in the syntax of Yakut: Complex sentence]. Novosibirsk: Nauka.
Ubrjatova, Elizaveta Ivanovna (ed.). 1982. *Grammatika sovremennogo jakutskogo jazyka: Fonetika i morfologija* [A grammar of Modern Yakut: Phonetics and morphology]. Moscow: Nauka.
Urban, Greg. 1985. Ergativity and accusativity in Shokleng (Ge). *International Journal of American Linguistics* 51 (2). 164–187.
Uusikoski, Risto. 2016. *The concept of tense*. Helsinki: University of Helsinki doctoral dissertation.
Vallejos Yopán, Rosa. 2010. *A grammar of Kokama-Kokamilla*. Eugene, OR: University of Oregon doctoral dissertation.
Vallejos Yopán, Rosa. 2016. *A grammar of Kukama-Kukamiria* (Brill's Studies in the Indigenous Languages of the Americas 13). Leiden: Brill.
Van Valin, Robert D. 1977. *Aspects of Lakhota syntax*. Berkeley, CA: University of California doctoral dissertation.
Van Valin, Robert D. & Randy J. LaPolla. 1997. *Syntax: Structure, meaning and function* (Cambridge Textbooks in Linguistics). Cambridge: Cambridge University Press.
Vlaxov, Andrian. 2010. *Pričastija buduščego vremeni v russkom jazyke* [Future participles in Russian]. Saint Petersburg: Saint Petersburg State University BA thesis.
Voort, Hein van der. 1991. *Relative clauses in West Greenlandic*. Amsterdam: University of Amsterdam. (Master's thesis.)
Vries, Mark de. 2002. *The syntax of relativization* (LOT Dissertation Series 53). Amsterdam: LOT.
Wegener, Claudia. 2012. *A grammar of Savosavo* (Mouton Grammar Library 61). Berlin: Mouton de Gruyter.
Weiss, Doris. 2009. *Phonologie et morphosyntaxe du Maba*. Université Lumière Lyon 2 doctoral dissertation.
Woodbury, Anthony C. 1975. *Ergativity of grammatical processes: A study of Greenlandic Eskimo*. Chicago, IL: University of Chicago MA thesis.
Wu, Tong. 2011. The syntax of prenominal relative clauses: a typological study. *Linguistic Typology* 15 (3). 569–623.
Xalipov, S. G. 1997. *Kratkaja grammatika irlandskogo jazyka* [A concise grammar of Irish]. Saint Petersburg: Notabene.
Ylikoski, Jussi. 2009. *Non-finites in North Saami* (Mémoires de la Société Finno-Ougrienne 257). Helsinki: Suomalais-Ugrilainen Seura.
Yoshioka, Noboru. 2012. *A reference grammar of Eastern Burushaski*. Tokyo: Tokyo University of Foreign Studies doctoral dissertation.
Zhukova, Alevtina Nikodimovna. 1972. *Grammatika korjakskogo jazyka* [A grammar of Koryak]. Leningrad: Nauka.
Zúñiga, Fernando. 2000. *Mapudungun* (Languages of the World/Materials 376). München: Lincom Europa.

References on languages outside the core sample

Abbott, Clifford. 2000. *Oneida* (Languages of the World/Materials 301). München: Lincom Europa.
Adelaar, Willem & Simon van de Kerke. 2009. Puquina. In Mily Crevels & Pieter Muysken (eds.), *Lenguas de Bolivia*, Vol. 1: *Ámbito andino*, 125–146. La Paz: Plural Editores.
Ahland, Colleen Anne. 2012. *A grammar of Northern and Southern Gumuz*. Eugene, OR: University of Oregon doctoral dissertation.
Aikhenvald, Alexandra Y. & R. M. W. Dixon. 1999. Other small families and isolates. In R. M. W. Dixon & Alexandra Y. Aikhenvald (eds.), *The Amazonian languages* (Cambridge Language Surveys), 341–381. Cambridge: Cambridge University Press.
Ajíbóyè, Ọládiípọ̀ Jacob. 2005. *Topics on Yorùbá nominal expressions*. Vancouver: The University of British Columbia doctoral dissertation.
Alphonse, Ephraim S. 1956. *Guaymí grammar and dictionary with some ethnological notes* (Smithsonian Institution: Bureau of American Ethnology Bulletin 162). Washington, D. C.: United States Goverment Printing Office.
Álvarez González, Albert. 2012. Relative clauses and nominalizations in Yaqui. In Bernard Comrie & Zarina Estrada-Fernández (eds.), *Relative clauses in languages of the Americas: A typological overview* (Typological Studies in Language 102), 67–96. Amsterdam: John Benjamins.
Ameka, Felix K. 1991. *Ewe: Its grammatical constructions and illocutionary devices*. Canberra: Australian National University doctoral dissertation.
Anderson, Carol. 2010. *Beginning Folopa language lessons and simple glossary*. Summer Institute of Linguistics International.
Anderson, Judi Lynn. 1989. *Comaltepec Chinantec syntax* (Studies in Chinantec Languages 3; Summer Institute of Linguistics Publications in Linguistics 89). Dallas, TX: Summer Institute of Linguistics.
Andrade, Manuel J. 1933. Quileute. In Franz Boas (ed.), *Handbook of American Indian Languages* 3, 151–292. New York, NY: Columbia University Press.
Andronov, Mikhail S. 1980. *The Brahui language* (Languages of Asia and Africa). Moscow: Nauka.
Angulo, Jaime de & L. S. Freeland. 1930. The Achumawi language. *International Journal of American Linguistics* 6 (2). 77–120.
Applegate, Richard Brian. 1972. *Ineseño Chumash grammar*. Berkeley, CA: University of California doctoral dissertation.
Armbruster, Charles Hubert. 1960. *Dongolese Nubian: A grammar*. Cambridge: Cambridge University Press.
Årsjö, Britten. 1999. Words in Ama. (Manuscript.)
Arensen, Jon. 1982. *Murle grammar* (Occasional Papers in the Study of Sudanese Languages 2). Juba: Summer Institute of Linguistics and University of Juba.
Austin, Jeanne & Velma B. Pickett. 1974. Popoloca clause and sentence. *Summer Institute of Linguistics Mexico Workpapers* 1. 59–92.
Bateman, Janet. 1986. *Iau verb morphology* (NUSA 26). Jakarta: Badan Penyelenggara Seri Nusa, Universitas Katolik Indonesia Atma Jaya.
Beaton, A. C. 1968. *A grammar of the Fur language* (Linguistics Monograph Series 1). Khartoum: University of Khartoum, Sudan Research Unit.

Beck, David James. 1995. *A comparative conceptual grammar of Bella Coola and Lushootseed.* Greater Victoria: University of Victoria MA thesis.
Beck, David. 2004. *Upper Necaxa Totonac* (Languages of the World/Materials 432). München: Lincom Europa.
Beller, Richard & Patricia Beller. 1977. *Huasteca Nahuatl.* In Ronald W. Langacker (ed.), *Studies in Uto-Aztecan grammar*, Vol. 2: *Modern Aztec grammatical sketches* (Summer Institute of Linguistics Publications in Linguistics 56), 199–306. Dallas, TX: Summer Institute of Linguistics and the University of Texas at Arlington.
Bender, M. Lionel. 1989. The Eastern Jebel languages. In M. Lionel Bender (ed.), *Topics in Nilo-Saharan linguistics*, 151–179. Hamburg: Helmut Buske.
Bender, M. Lionel. 1996. *Kunama* (Languages of the World/Materials 59). München: Lincom Europa.
Bendor-Samuel, John, Donna Skitch & Esther Cressman. 1973. *Duka sentence, clause and phrase* (Studies in Nigerian Languages 3). Zaria: Institute of Linguistics and Centre for the Study of Nigerian Languages.
Bergman, Richard. 1981. *An outline of Igede grammar* (Language Data Africa Series 15) Dallas, TX: Summer Institute of Linguistics.
Bergsland, Knut. 1997. *Aleut grammar (Unangam tunuganaan achixaasix̂)* (Research Paper 10). Fairbanks, AK: Alaska Native Language Center.
Berthiaume, Scott Charles. 2012. *A phonological grammar of Northern Pame* (Summer Institute of Linguistics e-Books 37). Summer Institute of Linguistics International.
Berthold, Falko. 2012. Relativization in ǂHoan. Talk given at the Max Planck Institute for Evolutionary Anthropology, 7 August 2012.
Bertinetto, Pier Marco 2009. *Ayoreo (Zamuco): A grammatical sketch* (Quaderni del Laboratorio di Linguistica della Scuola Normale Superiore, Pisa 8). http://linguistica.sns.it/QLL/QLL09/Bertinetto_1.pdf (accessed 11 August 2019).
Birk, D. B. W. 1976. *The Malakmalak language, Daly River (Western Arnhem Land)* (Pacific Linguistics B-45). Canberra: Australian National University.
Black, Keith & Elizabeth Black. 1971. *The Moro language grammar and dictionary.* (Linguistics Monograph Series 6). Khartoum: University of Khartoum, Sudan Research Unit.
Boas, Franz. 1947. Kwakiutl grammar, with a glossary of the suffixes. *Transactions of the American Philosophical Society* 37. 203–377.
Böhm, Gerhard. 1984. *Grammatik der Kunama-Sprache* (Beiträge zur Afrikanistik 22). Wien: Institut für Afrikanistik und Ägyptologie der Universität Wien.
Borgman, Donald M. 1990. Sanuma. In Desmond C. Derbyshire & Geoffrey K. Pullum (eds.), *Handbook of Amazonian languages*, Vol. 2, 15–248. Berlin: Mouton de Gruyter.
Bowden, John. 2005. Taba. In Alexander Adelaar & Nikolaus P. Himmelmann (eds.), *The Austronesian languages of Asia and Madagascar* (Routledge Language Family Series), 769–792. London: Routledge.
Bowern, Claire. 2012. *A grammar of Bardi* (Mouton Grammar Library 57). Berlin: Mouton de Gruyter.
Boyeldieu, Pascal. 2008. Dadjo-Sila. In Holger Tröbs, Eva Rothmaler & Kerstin Winkelmann (eds.), *La qualification dans les langues africaines* (Topics in African Studies 9), 57–70. Köln: Rüdiger Köppe.
Bright, William. 1957. *The Karok language* (University of California Publications in Linguistics 13). Berkeley, CA: University of California Press.

Briley, David. 1997. Four grammatical marking systems in Bauzi. In Karl J. Franklin (ed.), *Papers in Papuan Linguistics* 2, 1–131. Canberra: Australian National University.
Broadwell, George Aaron. 2006. *A Choctaw reference grammar*. (Studies in the Anthropology of North American Indians). Lincoln, NE: University of Nebraska Press.
Bromley, H. Myron. 1981. *A grammar of Lower Grand Valley Dani* (Pacific Linguistics C-63). Canberra: Australian National University.
Bruce, Les. 1984. *The Alamblak language of Papua New Guinea (East Sepik)* (Pacific Linguistics C-81). Canberra: Australian National University.
Bugaeva, Anna. 2017. Noun-modifying clause constructions in Ainu. In Yoshiko Matsumoto, Bernard Comrie & Peter Sells (eds.), *Noun-Modifying clause constructions in languages of Eurasia: Reshaping theoretical and geographical boundaries* (Typological Studies in Language 116), 203–250 Amsterdam: John Benjamins.
Burenhult, Niclas. 2005. *A grammar of Jahai* (Pacific Linguistics 566). Canberra: Australian National University.
Campbell, Carl & Jody Campbell. 1987. Yade grammar essentials. Summer Institute of Linguistics. (Manuscript.)
Campbell, Lyle. 2012. Typological characteristics of South American indigenous languages. In Lyle Campbell & Verónica Grondona (eds.), *The indigenous languages of South America: A comprehensive guide* (The World of Linguistics 2), 259–330. Berlin: Mouton de Gruyter.
Carpio, María Belén & Marisa Censabella. 2012. Clauses as noun modifiers in Toba (Guaycuruan). In Bernard Comrie & Zarina Estrada-Fernández (eds.), *Relative clauses in languages of the Americas: A typological overview* (Typological Studies in Language 102), 173–190. Amsterdam: John Benjamins.
Chapman, Shirley & Desmond C. Derbyshire. 1991. Paumarí. In Desmond C. Derbyshire & Geoffrey K. Pullum (eds.), *Handbook of Amazonian languages*, Vol. 3, 161–352. Berlin: Mouton de Gruyter.
Childs, G. Tucker. 1995. *A grammar of Kisi: A southern Atlantic language* (Mouton Grammar Library 16). Berlin: Mouton de Gruyter.
Christiansen-Bolli, Regula. 2010. *A grammar of Tadaksahak, a northern Songhay language of Mali* (Berber Studies 31). Leiden: Universiteit Leiden doctoral dissertation.
Clendon, Mark. 2001. *A grammar of Worrorra*. Halls Creek: Kimberley Language Resource Centre.
Comrie, Bernard. 1998. Rethinking the typology of relative clauses. *Language Design* 1. 59–86.
Conrad, Robert J. & Kepas Wogiga. 1991. *An outline of Bukiyip grammar* (Pacific Linguistics C-113). Canberra: Australian National University.
Corris, Miriam. 2006. *A grammar of Barupu, a language of Papua New Guinea*. Sydney: University of Sydney doctoral dissertation.
Cowan, H. K. J. 1965. *Grammar of the Sentani language with specimen texts and vocabulary* (Verhandelingen van het Koninklijk Instituut voor Taal-, Land- en Volkenkunde 47). The Hague: Martinus Nijhoff.
Craig, Colette. 1977. *The structure of Jacaltec*. Austin, TX: University of Texas Press.
Crevels, Mily. 2010. Ditransitives in Itonama. In Andrej L. Malchukov, Martin Haspelmath & Bernard Comrie (eds.), *Studies in ditransitive constructions: A comparative handbook*, 678–709. Berlin: Mouton de Gruyter.
Crippen, James A. 2012. Exploring Tlingit relative clauses: Morphology and syntax. (Manuscript.) http://tlingitlanguage.com/wp-content/uploads/2015/01/Crippen-2012-relative-clauses.pdf (accessed 11 August 2019).

Crowell, Thomas Harris. 1979. *A grammar of Bororo*. Ithaca: Cornell University doctoral dissertation.
Danielsen, Swintha. 2011. Clause embedding strategies in Baure (Arawakan). In Rik van Gijn, Katharina Haude & Pieter Muysken (eds.), *Subordination in native South American languages* (Typological Studies in Language 97), 79–108. Amsterdam: John Benjamins.
Davis, Philip W. & Ross Saunders. 1978. Bella Coola syntax. In Eung-Do Cook & Jonathan Kaye (eds.), *Linguistic Studies of Native Canada*, 37–65. Vancouver: University of British Columbia Press.
Deal, Amy Rose. 2016. Cyclicity and connectivity in Nez Perce relative clauses. *Linguistic Inquiry* 47 (3). 427–470.
Deibler, Ellis W. 1976. *Semantic relationships of Gahuku verbs* (Summer Institute of Linguistics Publications in Linguistics and Related Fields 48). Norman, OK: Summer Institute of Linguistics of the University of Oklahoma.
De Sousa, Hilário. 2006. *The Menggwa Dla language of New Guinea*. Sydney: University of Sydney doctoral dissertation.
Derbyshire, Desmond C. 1986. Comparative survey of morphology and syntax in Brazilian Arawakan. In Desmond C. Derbyshire & Geoffrey K. Pullum (eds.), *Handbook of Amazonian languages*, Vol. 1, 469–566. Berlin: Mouton de Gruyter.
Dickens, Patrick. 1991. Relative clauses in Juǀ'hoan. In W. H. G. Haacke & E. D. Elderkin (eds.), *Namibian languages: Reports and papers* (Namibian African Studies 4), 107–116. Köln: Rüdiger Köppe.
Dimmendaal, Gerrit Jan. 1983. *The Turkana language*. Dordrecht: Foris Publications.
Dixon, R. M. W. 2004b. *The Jarawara language of Southern Amazonia*. Oxford: Oxford University Press.
Doble, Marion. 1987. A description of some features of Ekari language structure. *Oceanic Linguistics* 26. 55–113.
Dol, Philomena Hedwig. 1999. *A grammar of Maybrat: A language of the Bird's Head, Irian Jaya, Indonesia*. Leiden: Universiteit Leiden doctoral dissertation.
Donohue, Mark & Lila San Roque. 2002. I'saka. (Manuscript.)
Donohue, Mark. 2004. A grammar of the Skou language of New Guinea. (Manuscript.) http://hdl.handle.net/11858/00-001M-0000-0012-7AAC-9 (accessed 11 August 2019).
Dunn, John Asher. 1979. *A reference grammar for the Coast Tsimshian language* (National Museum of Man, Mercury Series: Canadian Ethnology Service Paper 55). Ottawa: National Museums of Canada.
Dunn, Phyllis and Charles Peck. 1988. Noun phrases in Tatana'. In Charles Peck (ed.), *Borneo language studies*, Vol. 1: *Sabah syntax papers* (Language Data, Asian-Pacific Series 14), 206–227. Dallas, TX: Summer Institute of Linguistics.
Eather, Bronwyn. 1990. *A grammar of Nakkara (Central Arnhem Land coast)*. Canberra: Australian National University doctoral dissertation.
Eaton, Helen. 2008. *A Sandawe grammar* (Summer Institute of Linguistics e-Books 20). Summer Institute of Linguistics International.
Eberhard, David Mark. 2009. *Mamaindê Grammar: A Northern Nambikwara language and its cultural context* (LOT Dissertation Series 236). Utrecht: LOT.
Ebermann, Erwin. 1986. *Die Sprache der Mauka: Eine Kleine Grammatik der Sprache eines noch kleineren westafrikanischen Volkes im Nordwesten der Elfenbeinküste* (Dissertationen der Universität Wien 181). Wien: Universität Wien doctoral dissertation.

Ebert, Karen H. 1979. *Sprache und Tradition der Kera (Tschad)*, Part 3: *Grammatik*. Berlin: Dietrich Reimer.
Edgar, John. 1989. *A Masalit grammar*. Berlin: Dietrich Reimer.
Egli, Hans. 1990. *Paiwangrammatik*. Wiesbaden: Otto Harrassowitz.
Elfenbein, Josef. 1998. Brahui. In Sanford B. Steever (ed.), *The Dravidian languages*, 388–414. New York, NY: Routledge.
Emenanjo, E. Nolue. 1987. *Elements of modern Igbo grammar: A descriptive approach*. Ibadan: University Press Limited.
Emeneau, M. B. 1955. *Kolami: A Dravidian language*. (University of California Publications in Linguistics 12). Berkeley, CA: University of California Press.
England, Nora C. 1983. *A grammar of Mam, a Mayan language*. Austin, TX: University of Texas Press.
Enrico, John. 2003. *Haida syntax*. Lincoln, NE: University of Nebraska Press.
Escalante, Roberto Hernández. 1962. *El cuitlateco*. Mexico City: Instituto Nacional de Antropología e Historia.
Evans, Nicholas. 2003. *Bininj Gun-wok: A pan-dialectal grammar of Mayali, Kunwinjku and Kune* (Pacific Linguistics 541). Canberra: Australian National University.
Evans, Nicholas, Jutta Besold, Hywel Stoakes & Alan Lee (eds.). 2005. *Materials on Golin: Grammar, texts and dictionary*. Parkville: University of Melbourne.
Everett, Caleb. 2006. *Patterns in Karitiana: Articulation, perception, and grammar*. Houston, TX: Rice University doctoral dissertation.
Everett, Daniel L. 1986. Pirahã. In Desmond C. Derbyshire & Geoffrey K. Pullum (eds.), *Handbook of Amazonian languages*, Vol. 1, 200–325. Berlin: Mouton de Gruyter.
Everett, Daniel L. & Barbara Kern. 1997. *Wari: The Pacaas Novos language of western Brazil* (Routledge Descriptive Grammars). London: Routledge.
Fabre, Anne Gwenaëlle. 2003. *Le samba leko, langue Adamawa du Cameroun* (Studies in African Linguistics 56). München: Lincom Europa.
Facundes, Sidney da Silva. 2000. *The language of the Apurinã people of Brazil (Maipure/Arawak)*. Buffalo, NY: State University of New York doctoral dissertation.
Fedden, Sebastian. 2011. *A grammar of Mian* (Mouton Grammar Library 55). Berlin: Mouton de Gruyter.
Feldman, Harry. 1986. *A grammar of Awtuw* (Pacific Linguistics B-94). Canberra: Australian National University.
Feldpausch, Tom & Becky Feldpausch. 1992. Namia grammar essentials. In John Roberts (ed.), *Namia and Amanab grammar essentials*, 3–97. Ukarumpa via Lae: Summer Institute of Linguistics.
Fleming, Harold. 1990. A grammatical sketch of Dime (Dim-Af). In Richard J. Hayward (ed.), *Omotic Language Studies*, 494–583. London: School of Oriental and African Studies, University of London.
Foley, William Auguste. 1980. Toward a universal typology of the noun phrase. *Studies in Language* 4 (2). 171–199.
Ford, Lysbeth Julie. 1998. *A description of the Emmi language of the Northern Territory of Australia*. Canberra: Australian National University doctoral dissertation.
Fortier, Joseph. 1971. *Grammaire mbaye-moissala (Tchad – groupe sara)* (Afrique et Langage Documents 6). Lyon: Afrique et Langage.
Foster, Mary Lecron. 1969. *The Tarascan language* (University of California Publications in Linguistics 56). Berkeley, CA: University of California Press.

Frajzyngier, Zygmunt. 2012. *A grammar of Wandala* (Mouton Grammar Library 47). Berlin: De Gruyter Mouton.
Frank, Paul Stephen. 1985. *A grammar of Ika*. Philadelphia, PA: University of Pennsylvania doctoral dissertation.
Gabas, Nilson, Jr. 1999. *A Grammar of Karo, Tupí (Brazil)*. Santa Barbara, CA: University of California doctoral dissertation.
Galucio, Ana Vilacy. 2001. *The morphosyntax of Mekens (Tupi)*. Chicago, IL: University of Chicago doctoral dissertation.
Geary, Elaine. 1977. *Kunimaipa grammar: Morphophonemics to discourse* (Workpapers in Papua New Guinea Languages 23). Ukarumpa: Summer Institute of Linguistics.
Gijn, Rik van. 2006. *A grammar of Yurakaré*. Nijmegen: Radboud Universiteit Nijmegen doctoral dissertation.
Gijn, Rik van. 2011. Semantic and grammatical integration in Yurakaré subordination. In Rik van Gijn, Katharina Haude & Pieter Muysken (eds.), *Subordination in native South American languages* (Typological Studies in Language 97), 169–192. Amsterdam: John Benjamins.
Girón Higuita, Jesús Mario. 2008. *Una gramática del Wãnsöjöt (Puinave)*. Amsterdam: Vrije Universiteit Amsterdam doctoral dissertation.
Gossner, Jan David. 1994. *Aspects of Edolo grammar*. Arlington, TX: University of Texas MA thesis.
Granberry, Julian. 2004. *Modern Chitimacha (Sitimaxa)* (Languages of the World/Materials 438). München: Lincom Europa.
Green, Rebecca. 1987. *A sketch grammar of Burarra*. Canberra: Australian National University Honours thesis.
Grinevald, Colette. 1990. A grammar of Rama. (Manuscript.)
Guillaume, Antoine. 2008. *A grammar of Cavineña* (Mouton Grammar Library 44). Berlin: Mouton de Gruyter.
Guirardello, Raquel. 1999. *A reference grammar of Trumai*. Houston, TX: Rice University doctoral dissertation.
Güldemann, Tom. 2013. Syntax: Southern Khoesan (Tuu). In Rainer Vossen (ed.), *The Khoesan Languages* (Routledge Language Family Series), 408–431. London: Routledge.
Hagman, Roy Stephen. 1973. *Nama Hottentot grammar*. New York, NY: Columbia University doctoral dissertation.
Hamlin, Newton Burgess. 1998. *Nai verb morphology*. Columbia, SC: University of South Carolina MA thesis.
Hannß, Katja. 2011. Complex sentences in Uchumataqu in a comparative perspective with Chipaya. In Rik van Gijn, Katharina Haude & Pieter Muysken (eds.), *Subordination in native South American languages* (Typological Studies in Language 97), 281–306. Amsterdam: John Benjamins.
Hantgan, Abbie. 2013. *Aspects of Bangime phonology, morphology and morphosyntax*. Bloomington, IN: Indiana University doctoral dissertation.
Harvey, Mark. 1986. *Ngoni Waray Amungal-Yang: The Waray language from Adelaide River*. Canberra: Australian National University MA thesis.
Harvey, Mark. 2001. *A grammar of Limilngan: A language of the Mary River Region, Northern Territory, Australia* (Pacific Linguistics 516). Canberra: Australian National University.
Harvey, Mark. 2002. *A grammar of Gaagudju* (Mouton Grammar Library 24). Berlin: Mouton de Gruyter.

Haude, Katharina. 2006. *A grammar of Movima*. Nijmegen: Radboud Universiteit Nijmegen doctoral dissertation.
Hayward, Richard J. 1990. Notes on the Aari language. In Richard J. Hayward (ed.), *Omotic Language Studies*, 425–493. London: School of Oriental and African Studies, University of London.
Heath, Jeffrey. 1978. *Ngandi grammar, texts, and dictionary*. Canberra: Australian Institute of Aboriginal Studies.
Heath, Jeffrey. 1980. *Basic materials in Warndarang: Grammar, texts, and dictionary* (Pacific Linguistics B-72). Canberra: Australian National University.
Heeschen, Volker. 1992. *A dictionary of the Yale (Kosarek) language (with sketch of grammar and English index)* (Mensch, Kultur und Umwelt im Zentralen Bergland von West-Neuguinea 22). Berlin: Dietrich Reimer.
Henderson, James. 1995. *Phonology and grammar of Yele, Papua New Guinea* (Pacific Linguistics B-112). Canberra: Australian National University.
Hess, H. Harwood. 1968. *The syntactic structure of Mezquital Otomi* (Janua Linguarum. Series Practica 43). The Hague: Mouton.
Hess, Thom & Vi Hilbert. 1980. *Lushootseed: The language of the Skagit, Nisqually, and other tribes of Puget Sound*, Part 2. Seattle: Daybreak Star Press.
Hewitt, Brian George. 1979. *Abkhaz* (Lingua Descriptive Studies 2). Amsterdam: North-Holland.
Himmelmann, Nikolaus P. & John U. Wolff. 1999. *Toratán (Ratahan)* (Languages of the World/Materials 130). München: Lincom Europa.
Hoddinott, W. G. & F. M. Kofod. 1988. *The Ngankikurungkurr language (Daly River area, Northern Territory)* (Pacific Linguistics D-77). Canberra: Australian National University.
Hoffmann, Carl. 1963. *A grammar of the Margi language*. London: Oxford University Press.
Holt, Dennis. 1999. *Pech (Paya)* (Languages of the World/Materials 366). München: Lincom Europa.
Huang, Lillian M. 1995. *A study of Mayrinax syntax*. Taipei: Crane.
Huber, Juliette. 2008. *First steps towards a grammar of Makasae: A language of East Timor* (Languages of the World/Materials 195). München: Lincom Europa.
Hudson, Richard. A.1974. A structural sketch of Beja. *African Languages Studies* 15. 111–142.
Hyman, Larry M. & Daniel J. Magaji. 1970. *Essentials of Gwari grammar* (Occasional Publication 27). Ibadan: University of Ibadan, Institute of African Studies.
Jakobi, Angelika. 1990. *A Fur grammar: Phonology, morphophonology and morphology* (Nilo-Saharan Linguistic Analyses and Documentation 5). Hamburg: Helmut Buske.
Jakobi, Angelika & Joachim Crass (with Bakhit Seby Abdoulaye). 2004. *Grammaire du beria (langue saharienne): Avec un glossaire français – beria* (Nilo-Saharan Linguistic Analyses and Documentation 18). Köln: Rüdiger Köppe.
Jendraschek, Gerd. 2012. *A grammar of Iatmul*. Regensburg: Universität Regensburg Habilitationsschrift.
Jenny, Mathias, Tobias Weber & Rachel Weymuth. 2014. The Austroasiatic languages: A typological overview. In Mathias Jenny & Paul Sidwell (eds.), *The Handbook of Austroasiatic languages*, Vol. 1, 13–143. Leiden: Brill.
Jensen, John Thayer. 1977. *Yapese reference grammar*. (PALI Language Texts: Micronesia). Honolulu, HI: University of Hawaii Press.
Johnson, Heidi Anna. 2000. *A grammar of San Miguel Chimalapa Zoque*. Austin, TX: University of Texas doctoral dissertation.

Josephs, Lewis S. 1975. *Palauan reference grammar*. Honolulu, HI: The University Press of Hawaii.
Jukes, Anthony. 2005. Makassar. In Alexander Adelaar & Nikolaus P. Himmelmann (eds.), *The Austronesian languages of Asia and Madagascar* (Routledge Language Family Series), 649–682. London: Routledge.
Jun, Akamine. 2005. Sama (Bajaw). In Alexander Adelaar & Nikolaus P. Himmelmann (eds.), *The Austronesian languages of Asia and Madagascar* (Routledge Language Family Series), 377–396. London: Routledge.
Kalivoda, Nick & Erik Zyman. 2015. On the derivation of relative clauses in Teotitlán del Valle Zapotec. *Proceedings of the Annual Meeting of the Berkeley Linguistics Society* 41. 219–243. Berkeley, CA: University of California.
Kari, Ethelbert E. 1997. *Degema* (Languages of the World/Materials 180). München: Lincom Europa.
Kari, Ethelbert E. 2000. *Ogbronuagum (The Bukuma language)* (Languages of the World/Materials 329). München: Lincom Europa.
Keenan, Edward L. 1972. Relative clause formation in Malagasy (and some related and some not so related languages). In Paul M. Peranteau, Judith N. Levi & Gloria C. Phares (eds.), *The Chicago which hunt: Papers from the Relative Clause Festival, April 13, 1972*, 169–189. Chicago, IL: Chicago Linguistic Society.
Kiessling, Roland. 1994. *Eine Grammatik des Burunge* (Afrikanistische Forschungen 13). Hamburg: Research and Progress.
Kim, Yuni. 2008. *Topics in the phonology and morphology of San Francisco del Mar Huave*. Berkeley, CA: University of California doctoral dissertation.
Kimball, Geoffrey. 2005. Natchez. In Heather Kay Hardy & Janine Scancarelli (eds.), *Native languages of the Southeastern United States* (Studies in the Anthropology of North American Indians), 385–453. Lincoln, NE: University of Nebraska Press.
Klamer, Marian. 1998. *A grammar of Kambera* (Mouton Grammar Library 18). Berlin: Mouton de Gruyter.
Koehn, Edward & Sally Koehn. 1986. Apalaí. In Desmond C. Derbyshire & Geoffrey K. Pullum (eds.), *Handbook of Amazonian languages*, Vol. 1, 33–127. Berlin: Mouton de Gruyter.
Kofod, Frances M. 1978. *The Miriwung language (East Kimberley): A phonological and morphological study*. Armidale: University of New England MA thesis.
Koopman, Hilda. 1984. *The syntax of verbs: From verb movement rules in the Kru languages to Universal Grammar* (Studies in Generative Grammar 15). Dordrecht: Foris Publications.
Kratochvíl, František. 2007. *A grammar of Abui: A Papuan language of Alor*. Leiden: Universiteit Leiden doctoral dissertation.
Kulick, Don & Christopher Stroud. 1992. The structure of the Taiap (Gapun) language. In Tom Dutton, Malcolm Ross & Darrell Tryon (eds.), *The language game: Papers in memory of Donald C. Laycock*, 203–226. Canberra: Australian National University.
Kumar, Pramod. 2012. *Descriptive and typological study of Jarawa*. New Delhi: Jawaharlal Nehru University doctoral dissertation.
Kutsch Lojenga, Constance. 1994. *Ngiti: a Central Sudanic language of Zaire* (Nilo-Saharan Linguistic Analyses and Documentation 9). Köln: Rüdiger Köppe.
Landaburu, Jon. 1979. *La langue des andoke (Amazonie colombienne): Grammaire* (Langues et Civilisations a Tradition Orale 36). Paris: Société d'Études Linguistiques et Anthropologiques de France.

LaPolla, Randy J. 2003. Dulong. In Graham Thurgood & Randy J. LaPolla (eds.), *The Sino-Tibetan languages* (Routledge Language Family Series), 674–682. London: Routledge.
Lastra de Suárez, Yolanda. 1984. Chichimeco Jonaz. In Munro S. Edmonson (ed.), *Supplement to the Handbook of Middle American Languages*, Vol. 2: *Linguistics*, 20–42. Austin, TX: University of Texas Press.
Lefebvre, Claire & Anne-Marie Brousseau. 2002. *A grammar of Fongbe* (Mouton Grammar Library 25). Berlin: Mouton de Gruyter.
Lindsey, Geoffrey & Janine Scancarelli. 1985. Where have all the adjectives come from? The case of Cherokee. *Proceedings of the Annual Meeting of the Berkeley Linguistics Society* 11. 207–215. Berkeley, CA: University of California.
Lindström, Eva. 2002. *Topics in the grammar of Kuot, a non-Austronesian Language of New Ireland, Papua New Guinea*. Stockholm: Stockholm University doctoral dissertation.
Linn, Mary Sarah. 2001. *A grammar of Euchee (Yuchi)*. Lawrence, KS: University of Kansas doctoral dissertation.
Lukas, Johannes. 1937. *A study of the Kanuri language: Grammar and vocabulary*. London: The Oxford University Press.
Macaulay, Monica. 1996. *A grammar of Chalcatongo Mixtec* (University of California Publications in Linguistics 127). Berkeley, CA: University of California Press.
Mak, Pandora. 2012. *Golden Palaung: A grammatical description* (SEAsian Mainland Languages E-Series). Canberra: Australian National University. http://hdl.handle.net/1885/9558 (accessed 11 August 2019).
Maring, Joel Marvyl. 1967. *Grammar of Acoma Keresan*. Bloomington, IN: Indiana University doctoral dissertation.
Matisoff, James A. 2003. Lahu. In Graham Thurgood & Randy J. LaPolla (eds.), *The Sino-Tibetan languages* (Routledge Language Family Series), 208–221. London: Routledge.
May, Kevin. 1997. *A study of the Nimboran language: Phonology, morphology, and phrase structure*. Melbourne: La Trobe University MA thesis.
McGinn, Richard. 1982. *Outline of Rejang syntax* (NUSA 14). Jakarta: Badan Penyelenggara Seri Nusa, Universitas Katolik Indonesia Atma Jaya.
McGregor, William. 1990. *A Functional Grammar of Gooniyandi*. Amsterdam: John Benjamins.
McGregor, William. 1994. *Warrwa* (Languages of the World/Materials 89). München: Lincom Europa.
McKay, Graham R. 1975. *Rembarnga, a language of central Arnhem Land*. Canberra: Australian National University doctoral dissertation.
McKay, Graham. 2000. Ndjébbana. In R. M. W. Dixon & Barry J. Blake (eds.), *Handbook of Australian languages*, Vol. 5, 154–354. Oxford: Oxford University Press.
Melis, Antonino. 1999. *Description du Masa (Tchad): Phonologie, syntaxe et dictionnaire encyclopedique*. Tours: Université François Rabelais doctoral dissertation.
Merlan, Francesca C. 1982. *Mangarayi* (Lingua Descriptive Studies 4). Amsterdam: North-Holland.
Merlan, Francesca C. 1983. *Ngalakan grammar, texts and vocabulary* (Pacific Linguistics B-89). Canberra: Australian National University.
Merlan, Francesca C. 1994. *A grammar of Wardaman: A language of the Northern Territory of Australia* (Mouton Grammar Library 11). Berlin: Mouton de Gruyter.
Mihas, Elena. 2010. *Essentials of Asheninka Perene grammar*. Milwaukee, WI: University of Wisconsin-Milwaukee doctoral dissertation.

Mirikitani, Leatrice T. 1972. *Kapampangan syntax* (Oceanic Linguistics Special Publication 10). Honolulu, HI: University of Hawaii Press.
Montler, Timothy. 1993. Relative clauses and other attributive constructions in Saanich. In Anthony Mattina & Timothy Montler (eds.), *American Indian linguistics and ethnography in honor of Laurence C. Thompson* (University of Montana Occasional Papers in Linguistics 10), 241–262. Missoula: University of Montana.
Moore, Denny. 2012. Relative clauses in Gavião of Rondônia. In Bernard Comrie & Zarina Estrada-Fernández (eds.), *Relative clauses in languages of the Americas: A typological overview* (Typological Studies in Language 102), 243–252. Amsterdam: John Benjamins.
Morgan, Lawrence Richard. 1991. *A description of the Kutenai language*. Berkeley, CA: University of California doctoral dissertation.
Mous, Martinus Petrus Gerardus Maria. 1992. *A grammar of Iraqw*. Rijksuniversiteit te Leiden doctoral dissertation.
Murane, Elizabeth. 1974. *Daga grammar: From morpheme to discourse* (Summer Institute of Linguistics Publications in Linguistics and Related Fields 43). Norman: Summer Institute of Linguistics.
Nakayama, Toshihide. 2001. *Nuuchahnulth (Nootka) morphosyntax* (University of California Publications in Linguistics 134). Berkeley, CA: University of California Press.
Nettle, Daniel. 1998. *The Fyem language of Northern Nigeria* (Languages of the World/Materials 136). München: Lincom Europa.
Noonan, Michael. 1992. *A grammar of Lango* (Mouton Grammar Library 7). Berlin: Mouton de Gruyter.
Obata, Kazuko. 2003. *A grammar of Bilua: A Papuan language of the Solomon Islands* (Pacific Linguistics 540). Canberra: Australian National University.
O'Connor, Loretta Marie. 2004. *Motion, transfer, and transformation: The grammar of change in Lowland Chontal*. Santa Barbara, CA: University of California doctoral dissertation.
Odé, Cecilia. 2002. A sketch of Mpur. In Ger Reesink (ed.), *Languages of the Eastern Bird's Head* (Pacific Linguistics 524), 45–107. Canberra: Australian National University.
Ogloblin, Alexander K. 2005. Javanese. In Alexander Adelaar & Nikolaus P. Himmelmann (eds.), *The Austronesian languages of Asia and Madagascar* (Routledge Language Family Series), 590–624. London: Routledge.
Okrand, Marc. 1977. *Mutsun grammar*. Berkeley, CA: University of California doctoral dissertation.
Olsson, Bruno. 2010. *Subordinate clauses in Kashaya Pomo*. Stockholm: Stockholm University BA thesis.
Osborne, Charles R. 1974. *The Tiwi language* (Australian Aboriginal Studies 55, Linguistic Series 21). Canberra: Australian Institute of Aboriginal Studies.
Payne, Doris L. & Thomas Payne. 1990. Yagua. In Desmond C. Derbyshire & Geoffrey K. Pullum (eds.), *Handbook of Amazonian languages*, Vol. 2, 249–474. Berlin: Mouton de Gruyter.
Piper, Nick. 1989. *A sketch grammar of Meryam Mir*. Canberra: Australian National University MA thesis.
Popjes, Jack & Jo Popjes. 1986. Canela-Krahô. In Desmond C. Derbyshire & Geoffrey K. Pullum (eds.), *Handbook of Amazonian languages*, Vol. 1, 128–199. Berlin: Mouton de Gruyter.
Purnell, Herbert C. (ed.). 1972. *Miao and Yao linguistic studies: Selected articles in Chinese* (Southeast Asia Data Papers 88). Ithaca: Cornell University.

Queixalós, Francesc. 2010. Grammatical relations in Katukina-Kanamari. In Spike Gildea & Francesc Queixalós (eds.), *Ergativity in Amazonia* (Typological Studies in Language 89), 235–284. Amsterdam: John Benjamins.
Queixalós, Francesc. 2011. Nominalization in Sikuani. *Amerindia* 35. 155–188.
Quesada, J. Diego. 2000. *A grammar of Teribe* (Lincom Studies in Native American Linguistics 36). München: Lincom Europa.
Quesada Pacheco, Miguel Ángel. 2008. *Gramática de la lengua guaymí (ngäbe)* (Languages of the World/Materials 474). München: Lincom Europa.
Reesink, Ger P. 1999. *A grammar of Hatam, Bird's Head Peninsula, Irian Jaya* (Pacific Linguistics C-146). Canberra: Australian National University.
Reesink, Ger. 2002. A grammar sketch of Sougb. In Ger Reesink (ed.), *Languages of the Eastern Bird's Head* (Pacific Linguistics 524), 181–275. Canberra: Australian National University.
Reesink, Ger. 2005. Sulka of East New Britain: A mixture of Oceanic and Papuan traits. *Oceanic Linguistics* 44 (1). 145–193.
Reichle, Verena. 1981. *Bawm language and lore: Tibeto-Burman area* (Europäische Hochschulschriften Reihe 21, Linguistik 14). Bern: Peter Lang.
Reid, Lawrence Andrew. 1966. *An Ivatan syntax* (Oceanic Linguistics Special Publications 2). Honolulu, HI: University of Hawaii Press.
Rennison, John R. 1997. *Koromfe* (Routledge Descriptive Grammars). London: Routledge.
Ribeiro, Eduardo Rivail. 2012. *A grammar of Karajá*. Chicago, IL: University of Chicago doctoral dissertation.
Robins, R. H. 1958. *The Yurok language: Grammar, texts, lexicon* (University of California Publications in Linguistics 15) Berkeley, CA: University of California Press.
Robinson, Stuart. 2011. *Intransitivity in Rotokas, a Papuan language of Bougainville*. Nijmegen: Radboud Universiteit Nijmegen doctoral dissertation.
Rojas Berscia, Luis Miguel. 2014. *A heritage reference grammar of Selk'nam*. Nijmegen: Radboud Universiteit Nijmegen MA thesis.
Romero-Figueroa, Andrés. 1997. *A reference grammar of Warao* (Lincom Studies in Native American Linguistics 6). München: Lincom Europa.
Sakel, Jeanette. 2004. *A grammar of Mosetén* (Mouton Grammar Library 33). Berlin: Mouton de Gruyter.
Salamanca, Danilo. 1988. *Elementos de gramática del miskito*. Cambridge, MA: Massachusetts Institute of Technology doctoral dissertation.
Samarin, William J. 1966. *The Gbeya language: Grammar, texts and vocabularies* (University of California Publications in Linguistics 44). Berkeley, CA: University of California Press.
Santandrea, Stefano. 1976. *The Kresh group, Aja and Baka languages (Sudan): A linguistic contribution*. Naples: Istituto Universitario Orientale.
Sastry, G. Devi Prasada. 1984. *Mishmi grammar* (Central Institute of Indian Languages Grammar Series 11). Mysore: Central Institute of Indian Languages.
Schuh, Russell G. 1998. *A grammar of Miya* (University of California Publications in Linguistics 130). Berkeley, CA: University of California Press.
Schultze-Berndt, Eva. 2000. *Simple and complex verbs in Jaminjung: A study of event categorisation in an Australian language*. Nijmegen: Katholieke Universiteit Nijmegen doctoral dissertation.
Seiler, Walter. 1985. *Imonda, a Papuan language* (Pacific Linguistics B-93). Canberra: Australian National University.

Serzisko, Fritz. 1989. The Kuliak languages: A structural comparison. In M. Lionel Bender (ed.), *Topics in Nilo-Saharan linguistics*, 385–404. Hamburg: Helmut Buske.
Shaul, David L. 1995. The Huelen (Esselen) language. *International Journal of American Linguistics* 61. 191–239.
Shee, Naw Hsar. 2008. *A descriptive grammar of Geba Karen*. Chiang Mai: Payap University MA thesis.
Singer, Ruth. 2006. *Agreement in Mawng: Productive and lexicalised uses of agreement in an Australian language*. Melbourne: University of Melbourne doctoral dissertation.
Sneddon, James N. 1975. *Tondano phonology and grammar* (Pacific Linguistics B-38). Canberra: Australian National University.
Spaulding, Craig & Pat Spaulding. 1994. *Phonology and grammar of Nankina* (Data Papers on Papua New Guinea Languages 41). Ukarumpa: Summer Institute of Linguistics.
Staden, Miriam van. 2000. *Tidore: A linguistic description of a language of the North Moluccas*. Leiden: Rijksuniversiteit te Leiden doctoral dissertation.
Staley, William E. 2007. *Referent management in Olo: A cognitive perspective* (Summer Institute of Linguistics e-Books 5). Summer Institute of Linguistics International.
Stevenson, Roland C. 1981. Adjectives in Nyimang, with special reference to k- and t- prefixes. In Thilo Schadeberg & M. Lionel Bender (eds.), *Nilo-Saharan: Proceedings of the First Nilo-Saharan Linguistics Colloquium, Leiden, September 8–10, 1980*, 151–165. Dordrecht: Foris.
Sunee, Kamnuansin. 2003. Syntactic characteristics of Kasong: An endangered language of Thailand. *Mon-Khmer Studies* 33. 167–182.
Teeter, Karl V. 1964. *The Wiyot language* (University of California Publications in Linguistics 37). Berkeley, CA: University of California Press.
Terrill, Angela. 2003. *A grammar of Lavukaleve* (Mouton Grammar Library 30). Berlin: Mouton de Gruyter.
Tharp, Douglas. 1996. Sulka grammar essentials. In John M. Clifton (ed.), *Two non-Austronesian grammars from the islands* (Data Papers on Papua New Guinea Languages 42), 77–179. Ukarumpa: Summer Institute of Linguistics.
Thiesen, Wesley & David Weber. 2012. *A grammar of Bora with special attention to tone* (Summer Institute of Linguistics International Publications in Linguistics 148). Summer Institute of Linguistics International.
Thomas, David D. 1971. *Chrau grammar* (Oceanic Linguistics Special Publication 7). Honolulu, HI: University of Hawaii Press.
Thornell, Christina. 1997. *The Sango language and its lexicon (Sêndâ-yângâ tî sängö)* (Travaux de l'Institut de Linguistique de Lund 32). Lund: Lund University Press.
Topping, Donald M. (with the assistance of Bernadita C. Dungca). 1973. *Chamorro reference grammar*. Honolulu, HI: University of Hawaii Press.
Triulzi, A., A. A. Dafallah & Lionel M. Bender. 1976. Berta. In M. Lionel Bender (ed.), *The non-Semitic languages of Ethiopia* (Committee on Ethiopian Studies: Occasional Papers Series 5), 513–532. East Lansing, MI: African Studies Center, Michigan State University.
Tsukida, Naomi. 2005. Seediq. In Alexander Adelaar & Nikolaus P. Himmelmann (eds.), *The Austronesian languages of Asia and Madagascar* (Routledge Language Family Series), 291–325. London: Routledge.
Tsunoda, Tasaku. 1981. *The Djaru language of Kimberley, Western Australia* (Pacific Linguistics B-78). Canberra: Australian National University.

Tucker, A. N. & M. A. Bryan. 1966. *Linguistic analyses: The non-Bantu languages of North-Eastern Africa*. London: Oxford University Press.
Van Valin, Robert D. 1977. *Aspects of Lakhota syntax*. Berkeley, CA: University of California doctoral dissertation.
Vogel, Alan. 2009. Covert tense in Jarawara. *Linguistic Discovery* 7 (1). 43–105.
Volodin, Aleksandr P. 1976. *Itel'menskij jazyk* [The Itelmen language]. Leningrad: Nauka.
Voort, Hein van der. 2004. *A grammar of Kwaza* (Mouton Grammar Library 29). Berlin: Mouton de Gruyter.
Vries, James A. de & Sandra A. de Vries. 1997. An overview of Kwerba morphology. In Andrew Pawley (ed.), *Papers in Papuan linguistics* 3 (Pacific Linguistics A-87), 1–35. Canberra: Australian National University.
Vries, Lourens de. 1996. Notes on the morphology of the Inanwatan language. In Ger P. Reesink (ed.), *Studies in Irian Languages* 1 (NUSA 40), 97–127. Jakarta: Universitas Katolik Indonesia Atma Jaya.
Vries, Lourens de & Gerrit J. van Enk 1997. *The Korowai of Irian Jaya: Their language and its cultural context* (Oxford Studies in Anthropological Linguistics 9). Oxford: Oxford University Press.
Wal, Jenneke van der. 2010. Makhuwa non-subject relatives as participial modifiers. *Journal of African Languages & Linguistics* 31 (2). 205–231.
Walker, Dale F. 1976. *A grammar of the Lampung language: the Pesisir dialect of Way Lima* (Linguistic Studies of Indonesian and Languages in Indonesia 2). Jakarta: Badan Penyelenggara Seri Nusa.
Walsh, Michael James. 1976. *The Murinypata language of North-West Australia*. Canberra: Australian National University doctoral dissertation.
Wang, Shan-Shan. 2004. *An ergative view of Thao syntax*. Honolulu, HI: University of Hawaii doctoral dissertation.
Watkins, Laurel J. (with the assistance of Parker McKenzie). 1984. *A grammar of Kiowa* (Studies in the Anthropology of North American Indians). Lincoln, NE: University of Nebraska Press.
Westrum, Peter. 1988. Berik grammar sketch. *Irian* 16. 133–181.
Whitehead, Carl R. 2004. *A reference grammar of Menya, an Angan language of Papua New Guinea*. Winnipeg: University of Manitoba doctoral dissertation.
Wichmann, Søren. 2007. The reference-tracking system of Tlapanec: Between obviation and switch-reference. *Studies in Language* 31 (4). 801–827.
Wier, Thomas. 2014. A sketch grammar of Tonkawa. (Manuscript.) https://www.academia.edu/9242027/A_Sketch_Grammar_of_Tonkawa (accessed 11 August 2019).
Wiersma, Grace. 2003. Yunnan Bai. In Graham Thurgood & Randy J. LaPolla (eds.), *The Sino-Tibetan languages* (Routledge Language Family Series), 651–673. London: Routledge.
Wilhelm, Andrea. 2014. Nominalization instead of modification. In Ileana Paul (ed.), *Cross-linguistic investigations of nominalization patterns* (Linguistik Aktuell 210), 51–81. Amsterdam: John Benjamins.
Williamson, Kay. 1965. *A grammar of the Kolokuma dialect of Ịjọ* (West African Language Monographs 2). Cambridge: Cambridge University Press.
Wilson, Darryl. 1974. *Suena grammar* (Workpapers in Papua New Guinea Languages 8). Ukarumpa: Summer Institute of Linguistics.
Wilson, Patrizia R. 1980. *Ambulas grammar* (Workpapers in Papua New Guinea Languages 26). Ukarumpa: Summer Institute of Linguistics.

Wise, Mary Ruth. 1986. Grammatical characteristics of PreAndine Arawakan languages of Peru. In Desmond C. Derbyshire & Geoffrey K. Pullum (eds.), *Handbook of Amazonian languages*, Vol. 1, 567–642. Berlin: Mouton de Gruyter.

Wood, Joyce Kathleen. 2012. *Valence-increasing strategies in Urim syntax*. Dallas, TX: Graduate Institute of Applied Linguistics MA thesis.

Woollams, Geoff. 2005. Karo Barak. In Alexander Adelaar & Nikolaus P. Himmelmann (eds.), *The Austronesian languages of Asia and Madagascar* (Routledge Language Family Series), 534–561. London: Routledge.

Wu, Jing-lan Joy. 2006. *Verb classification, case marking, and grammatical relations in Amis*. Buffalo, NY: State University of New York doctoral dissertation.

Zamponi, Raoul. 2003. *Betoi* (Languages of the World/Materials 428). München: Lincom Europa.

Zandvoort, Franklin D. 1999. *A grammar of Matngele*. Armidale: University of New England BA thesis.

Zeitoun, Elizabeth. 2005. Tsou. In Alexander Adelaar & Nikolaus P. Himmelmann (eds.), *The Austronesian languages of Asia and Madagascar* (Routledge Language Family Series), 259–290. London: Routledge.

Index of subjects

ablative 199, 201, 203, 213
absolutive 54, 184–185, 207
Absolutive Hypothesis 123
absolutive participle 75–76, 78–85, 122–123, 199–200, 204, 216, 238
Accessibility Hierarchy 52–58, 86, 91, 95, 102, 115, 202, 218, 237
accusative 134, 190, 198–199, 206, 208, 210
accusative alignment 53, 60, 65, 85, 123, 194
active participle 1, 51, 58, 62–67, 110–111, 113, 122, 211, 216, 238
– specialized in S relativization 63–64
adjacency 11, 191–192
adjective 14–15, 17–20, 134, 137, 175–177, 186, 190, 214, 248–250, *see also* verbal adjective
– verb-like 18–19
adjectivization 131, 214
adverbial clause 5–6, 15–17, 145
adverbial participle 17, *see also* converb
adverbialization 131
Africa 11, 72, 216
agent demotion 68, 70, 154, 204, 213–214, 245
agentive participle 75–77, 122–123, 125
Aktionsart 146
alienable possession 96, 205, 211, *see also* inalienable possession
ambiguity 22, 69, 87, 92, 193, 209, 212
animacy 124, 201, 203, 224, 235
Animacy Hierarchy 202, 204
applicative 59, 106
Asia 10, 196
aspect 80, 132, 134, 136, 140, 146, 149, 159–160, 172, 180, 213, 220
– grammatical 146
– lexical 146
assertion 143–145
associations between core participants
– S and A 60–61
– S and P 61
Australia 11, 17, 44, 207, 216

balancing 2, 38–39, 129

blocking effects 141–142
borrowing 217, 251

canonical typology 142–143
caritive 177
case 20, 131, 134, 153, 180, 186–188, 190–191
case marking 133–137, 145, 153, 191–192, 209
causative 59, 107
comparative concept 7, 20, 21, 237
complement clause 5–6, 15–17, 41, 44, 133, 134, 147, 150, 196, 198, 224, 250
complementizer 26, 31, 226, *see also* subordinating conjunction
consequential case 203, 213
contextually oriented participle *see* orientation
control 61, 123, 128
converb 6, 169
coordination 60, 85
coreference 197–198, 248

dative 54, 200, 203, 207, 211
decategorization 130
definiteness 131, 186–188, 208, 210, 234–235
deranking 2, 4, 38–39, 129, 154
derivation 31, 36, 248
descriptive category 7, 12
desententialization 131–135, 194, 204, 213
detransitivization 59, 63, 109
deverbalization 130, 141
diachrony 7, 26, 37, 44, 79, 81, 126, 142, 179, 182, 220, 222–223, 238, 250
differential object marking 204, 207–210, 214
differential subject marking 201, 207
direct object expression 133, 194, 204, 211–213
– regular 204
– as a possessor 204–206, 214
– as a non-core participant 204, 207
– variation in ~ 204, 207

discourse 61, 123, 210, 223
discourse prominence 208

economy 137–138, 142
ergative 65, 73, 207
ergative alignment 53, 60, 76, 123, 194
ergativity 65, 73, 80, 84–85, 122, 194, 238, 247
Eurasia 10–11, 25, 72, 251
Europe 1–2, 5, 17, 28, 45, 51, 61, 68, 83, 167, 216–217, 221, see also Standard Average European
evidentiality 102–103, 143–144, 148, 167–168, 233
expression of non-core participants 194, 210–214
expression of participants 133, 135–136, 153

finiteness 2, 129, 135, 249
– canonical approach 142–144
– constructional approach 36, 39, 41, 250
– scalar approaches 130
– traditional (binary) approach 129
Functional Grammar 139, 150
functional typology 6–7, 129, 138–139
future 148–149, 159, 170, 172
future participle 34, 148–149, 159, 162, 170–174, 181, 231

gap strategy 56, 93, 95–96, 114, 138, 154
gender 26, 69, 134, 153, 155, 180, 186–190, 235
general noun-modifying clause constructions (GNMCC) 25
Generalized Scale Model 141–142
genitive 44, 116, 195, 198, 202–203, 205–206, 211, 213–214, 224
geographical distribution of participles 7, 10–11
glossing 12
gradual "headedness" 24
grammaticalization 23, 81, 123, 124, 153, 189–190

habitual 166–167, 181, 210, 214, 228, 238
head noun 21, 23, 195–196, 203, 206
humanness 61, 70, 123, 128, 202–203, 207

illocutionary force 131, 134, 139–140, 143, 148
inalienable possession 96, 114, 205, 211 see also alienable possession
incorporation 61, 209–210, 214
indirect object 54–55, 93, 201, 210
infinitive 6, 14, 29–30, 34
inflection 31, 36, 248
– word-class-changing 37
inherently oriented participle see orientation
instrumental 44, 63, 68, 200, 203, 208
instrumental participle 87–91, 93, 111, 119, 124, 224
insubordination 39
intonation 23

juxtaposition 43, 153, 196

language contact 126, 221, 251
layering 139–140
lexicalization 30, 38, 71, 210
ligature 26–27
linking particle 11, 27
locative 34, 200–201
locative participle 86–91, 124, 224, 233, 237

middle 64, 108
middle participle 64, 227
modality 131, 148, 168
– epistemic 148, 168
– root 148, 168
modified noun see head noun
mood 131, 134, 136, 140, 143, 148, 169, 170
morphosyntactic alignment 60, 62, 122, 238, 247
multifunctionality 5, 16, 17, 44, 212, 224, 246, 250

negation 41, 132, 150, 175–184, see also negative participle
– nominal 175–178
– non-finite 175–178
– unavailable 183
negative participle 65, 81, 92, 94, 107, 159, 172, 178, 180–182, 186, 215
Neg-Raising 150
neutralization 159, 180–181, 229

Index of subjects — **341**

nominal agreement 20, 69, 134, 145, 152, 180, 185–187, 249
– obligatory 187–191
– conditional 191–193
nominal hierarchy 140–141
nominalization 11, 24, 131, 138, 194, 213–214, 249
– action 6, 42, 155, 211, 249
– participant 24, 42, 88, 249
nominative 44, 80, 143, 152, 154, 197, 202–203, 207, 208
non-aprioristic approach 6
non-finite verb forms 6, 14
North America 11, 39, 72, 246
noun class 187–188
number 20, 61, 69, 129–130, 134, 140–141, 151, 153, 155, 184, 186–191, 235

object agreement 140–141, 151
object of comparison 53, 57
oblique 56–57, 93, 95
operator 139
orientation 1, 4, 51, 122, 124
– inherent 1, 51, 58–59, 86, 122–123, 126, 199, 216
– contextual 1, 51, 58, 91, 126, 200, 218
– full contextual 91, 96–97, 125, 218
– limited contextual 91, 100, 104–105, 125, 220
orientation extension 71, 94, 105
– by specialized affixes 106–109
– by resumptive elements 109–113
– pragmatic 113–114
origin case 203, 213

Papunesia 11, 72, 177, 216, 246
participant nominalization 24
participial marker 32, 158
– suffix 32
– prefix 32–33
– circumfix 32–33
– non-segmental 34–36
– +TAM 158
– –TAM 158

participial paradigm 4, 65, 73, 76, 84, 102, 126, 161, 179, 215, 238
– orientation-based 221, 239
– TAM-based 225, 239
– orientation and TAM-based 226, 239
participle (definition) 1, 6, 14, 46
participle/nominalization syncretism 41–44, 89, 152
participles oriented towards non-core participants 86–91, 124, see also instrumental participle, locative participle
passive 5, 68–69, 72, 200, 214
passive participle 1, 5, 51, 59, 68–74, 78–79, 94, 106, 110–111, 122, 124, 199, 200, 204, 214, 217
past 78, 149, 168, 220
perfectivity 80, 149, 238
periphrastic participle 33–34, 107, 169
periphrastic verb form 5, 14, 68, 162
person agreement 129–130, 132, 135–137, 151, 184, 186, 217
personal pronoun 203, 223
politeness 143–144
polysynthesis 28
possessive marker 56, 70, 110, 114, 184, 195, 197, 201, 203, 205, 210
possessor 57, 197, 213
– of a subject 57, 111, 114
– of a direct object 57, 111
– of a non-core participant 111
present 149, 172
primary relativization strategy 2, 25, 125, 171, 196
privative 177
proper name 202–203
pseudoparticiple 37–38
purpose 29, 30, 137, 169, 224, 247
purposive clause 60, 85, 147, 248

raising 198–199
recategorization 131
recoverability 94–96, 114, 118–119, 142, 223
reduplication 34, 82, 84
reflexive 61, 64, 115, 197, 198

relative clause 5–6, 16–17, 21–22, 30
- adjoined 11
- restrictive 22–23
- non-restrictive 22–23
- correlative 22, 55, 221
- headed 23–24
- headless 23, 43, 71, 89, 183
- externally headed 24, 95, 103
- internally headed 24–25, 71, 95, 104, 119, 154, 174
- finite 26–27, 125–126, 183, 218
- infinitival 29–30
relative pronoun 2, 26, 28, 31, 126, 171, 218, 221
relativization
- of subjects 53–54, 68
- of direct objects 53–54
- of locatives 71, 93–94, 116
- of temporal adverbials 94–95, 101–102
- of adpositional phrases 202
- of possessors 95, 110, 113, 116
relativization strategy 153, 202
relevance 136, 174
resultative participle 79, 80, 83, 166–167, 204, 212–213, 228, 232, 238
resumptive element 55, 95, 109, 115, 119, 120–121, 154, 202
Role and Reference Grammar 139, 150

sample 8–12, 47–50, 250
satellite 139
scale of desententialization 134
single participle in a language 65, 73, 83, 102, 164, 166–167, 216–220, 238–239
South America 11, 61, 72, 75, 80, 83, 153, 216, 246
specificity 210
split ergativity 75–76, 85, 194, 233
Standard Average European 62, 218, 221, 251
stative verb 18, 37

structural factors in desententialization 141, 172–175
subject agreement 40, 116, 140–141, 143, 151–152, 184–187, *see also* person agreement
subject expression 69, 133, 194–195, 212–213
- as a non-core participant 195, 199–201, 204
- as a possessor 195–199, 201, 204, 214
- obligatory 70
- regular 204
- unavailable 70, 195, 204
- variation in ~ 195–196, 201–204
subjunctive 131, 169, 170
subordinating conjunction 31–32, *see also* complementizer
subordination 5, 11, 135
switch-reference 143, 145, 247

TAM 135–136, 146, 157, 164, 225, 238
telicity 79, 146, 165
tense 132, 134, 136, 140, 147, 170
- absolute 147, 225
- relative 147, 149, 225

unmarked relative subordination 40

valency rule 93, 95–96
valency-changing operation 59, 63, 106, 109
verbal adjective 30–31, 34, 36–38, 71, 82, 166, 248
verbal hierarchy 139–141, 148
verbal noun 6, 31, 51, 134
verbal valency 30, 59, 71, 93, 140, 151
verbalization 138
volition 123, 155

word order 18, 41, 191–193, 246

zero-marking 161, 197, 199, 207–210, 214

Index of languages

Abkhaz 28, 46
Abkhaz-Adyge 28
Adyghe 28, 46
Afro-Asiatic 11
Aguaruna 65–66, 105, 182, 184, 223, 241
Akhvakh 40, 46
Albanian 80, 84–85, 167, 188, 200, 217, 240
Aleut 147
Altaic 17, 41, 212
Ama 177
Ao *see* Mongsen Ao
Apalaí 24
Apatani 54–55, 87, 91, 93, 98, 124, 159, 206, 222, 224, 241
Apsheron Tat 99, 121, 164, 165, 208–209, 219–220, 240
Arabic *see* Gulf Arabic, Modern Standard Arabic
Armenian *see* Classical Armenian, Eastern Armenian
Austroasiatic 11
Austronesian 11, 26–27, 106
Azeri 111

Baltic 251
Barasano 66, 108, 235–236, 243
Basque 80, 84–85, 217, 240
Batak *see* Karo Batak
Beng 9, 80, 84–85, 204, 217, 240
Berber 190, *see also* Rif Berber
Beserman Udmurt 67, 99, 105, 149, 176–177, 191, 203, 231, 242
Bura 34
Burushaski 220, 243

Canela-Krahô 9
Cariban 81, 194
Celtic 9
Chantyal 42
Cherokee 39, 46
Chimariko 92, 97, 220, 240
Chumash *see* Ineseño Chumash
Cibak 34
Classical Armenian 26, 46

Classical Greek 17
Coahuilteco 98, 115, 121, 220, 240
Cocama 75, 77, 80, 85–86, 90, 123, 197, 224, 241, 247–248
Cofán 31–32, 46, 64, 66, 157, 197, 216, 239
Cuzco Quechua 142

Dargwa *see* Tanti Dargwa
Desano 153
Dhimal 99, 220, 240
Dolakha Newar 67, 105, 123, 216, 223, 241
Dongwang Tibetan 24, 46
Dravidian 1, 10, 32, 159, 195, 221

Eastern Armenian 17, 26, 46, 67, 72, 74, 80, 85, 148, 203, 207, 228, 242
Eastern Mande 9
English 1, 12, 15, 28–29, 46, 51, 53–54, 78, 125, 133–134, 155, 200, 216, 221
Erzya 12, 67, 80, 85, 123, 228, 242
Even 9, 93–94, 99, 121, 146, 163, 165, 170, 197, 225, 242
Evenki 190, 197

Finnish 1, 12, 15, 20, 51, 67, 70–72, 74, 94–95, 99, 126, 159, 176, 181–182, 204, 216, 221, 224, 231, 242, 251
Fula 63–64, 67, 72, 74, 183, 188, 227, 242

Garo 19, 20, 37, 45–46, 99, 160, 176, 219, 240
Garrwa 17, 64–66, 166, 207, 216, 239
Ge-Kaingang 9
Georgian 32–33, 46, 67, 72, 74, 80, 85, 148, 181–182, 201, 205, 211, 214, 228, 242
German 12, 51, 53, 67, 79–80, 84–85, 162, 188, 200, 216, 221, 228, 242
Germanic 9, 251
Greek *see* Classical Greek, Modern Greek
Greenlandic *see* West Greenlandic
Guarijío 66, 86, 90, 105, 161, 172, 203, 224, 241
Gulf Arabic 129

Hinuq 25, 83, 86, 88–89, 91, 100, 118, 121, 122, 184, 185, 204, 213, 233, 237, 242
Hopi 98, 117, 121, 220, 240
Hungarian 62–63, 67, 80, 84–85, 199, 216, 221, 228, 243, 251
Hunzib 60
Hup 18, 23–24, 98, 219, 240

Iatmul 177
Imbabura Quechua 9, 25, 46, 57–58, 98, 103, 134, 183, 191–193, 209, 225, 242
Indic 5, see also Old Indic
Indo-European 9, 10, 32, 62, 79–80, 126, 151, 162, 184, 188, 190, 199–200, 221, 251
Ineseño Chumash 39
Ingush 29, 46, 96, 100, 170, 176, 195, 225, 242
Iranian 5
Irish 80, 84–85, 167, 204, 217, 240
Italian 29, 80, 84–85, 167, 188, 200, 217, 221, 240

Jakaltek 132–133, 150, 194
Japhug rGyalrong 67, 70–72, 74, 102, 105, 122, 160, 205, 224, 241
Jiwarli 207

Kalapuya see Santiam Kalapuya
Kalmyk 2–3, 5, 12, 56–57, 72–74, 93, 99, 111, 121, 151, 162–163, 176, 198, 200, 202, 212, 232–233, 242
Kamaiurá 63–64, 66, 72, 74–77, 102, 105, 111, 122, 161, 182, 200, 224, 241
Kambaata 35, 46, 98, 117, 121, 180–182, 186, 187, 219, 240
Karo Batak 9
Kayardild 16, 66, 80, 108, 167, 183, 203, 213–214, 228, 242
Ket 82, 99, 123–124, 165–167, 210, 220, 240
Khanty see Northern Khanty
Kharia 11, 34, 46, 98, 195–196, 220, 240
Kilba 34
Kobon 64, 66, 132, 216, 239
Kolyma Yukaghir 57, 99, 105, 121, 169, 195, 196, 208, 234, 243
Komi-Zyrian 41–42, 67, 99–100, 159, 181–182, 191, 200, 203, 231, 243

Koorete 67, 105, 169, 184, 229, 242
Korean 25, 95–96, 100, 121, 154, 159, 225, 242
Koryak 80, 84–85, 226, 241
Krongo 16, 34, 64, 67, 110, 122, 184, 189, 216, 239

Lakhota 18
Latin 17, 59, 79, 131–132, 217
Lezgian 51–52, 93, 96, 100, 118, 122, 168, 175, 219, 240
Limbu 141
Lithuanian 62–63, 67–68, 72, 74, 134, 162, 187, 214, 216, 227, 242
Luiseño 98, 121, 195–196, 225, 242

Ma'di 67, 72–74, 87–88, 90, 111, 119, 122, 124, 179, 224, 241
Maba 65, 67, 173, 216, 239
Malakmalak 17
Malayalam 96, 100, 158, 160, 166, 172, 180–182, 219, 240
Manange 99, 220, 240
Mande 217
Mapudungun 66, 72–74, 151, 176, 184, 222, 241
Marathi 22–23, 46, 99, 179, 188, 225, 242
Margi 34
Mari 43, 210, see also Meadow Mari
Maricopa 66, 105, 114, 141, 168, 216, 223, 241
Martuthunira 65–66, 172, 216, 239
Matsés 66, 75–77, 98, 100, 102–103, 105, 124, 148, 153, 168, 181–183, 192–193, 233–234, 242
Meadow Mari 67, 99–101, 105, 115, 121, 125, 148, 181, 183, 191, 203, 210, 229–231, 243
Mēbengokre 9, 99, 119–120, 122, 174, 194, 219, 240
Middle Egyptian 67, 72–74, 110, 122, 222, 241
Miya 25–26
Mochica 80, 84–85, 217, 240
Modern Greek 80, 84–85, 141, 188, 200, 217, 240

Modern Standard Arabic 67, 69, 73–74, 109–110, 122, 155, 176, 186, 188, 228, 242
Mongolic 1, 10, 32
Mongsen Ao 24, 46
Motuna 98, 121, 164, 220, 240
Muka Qiang 87
Muna 32–33, 46, 66, 72, 74, 86, 90, 106, 113–114, 122, 124, 176–178, 201–202, 210, 235, 243, 250

Nakh-Daghestanian 1, 10, 40, 118, 195
Nanai 9, 12, 17, 99, 121, 159, 162, 170, 173, 190, 197, 225, 241
Nanga 33–34, 46, 95, 100, 107, 121, 158, 225, 241
Ndyuka 82
Nenets *see* Tundra Nenets
Nevome 66, 80, 86, 90, 233, 242
Newar *see* Dolakha Newar
Nias 9, 69, 70, 72–74, 183, 217–218, 220, 240
Nivkh 12, 35–36, 46, 99, 160, 219, 240
North Saami 67, 73–74, 92, 97, 159, 181, 183, 216, 228, 243
Northern Khanty 81, 85, 99, 121, 126, 159, 170, 181, 183, 200–201, 225, 241, 251
Northwest Sumatra-Barrier Islands 9
Nyamal 207

Old Indic 79
Old Neapolitan 142
Old Persian 222

Pabir 34
Palauan 26–27, 46
Panare 75–78, 80, 84–85, 168, 200, 222–223, 241, 247
Permic 44
Pitta Pitta 44, 99, 220, 240
Portuguese 142
Proto-Indo-European 79

Qiang 87, 224, *see also* Muka Qiang, Qugu Qiang, Ronghong Qiang
Quechuan 9, 131, 134, 148, 184 *see also* Cuzco Quechua, Imbabura Quechua, Tarma Quechua

Qugu Qiang 87

rGyalrong *see* Japhug rGyalrong, Zhuokeji rGyalrong
Rif Berber 65, 67, 190, 216, 239
Ronghong Qiang 87, 91, 100, 122, 124, 222, 224, 241
Russian 1, 3, 5, 12, 28, 34, 37–38, 46, 51, 59–60, 67–68, 71–74, 79, 126, 134, 147, 162, 168–171, 173, 188, 200, 216, 218, 221, 224, 227, 231, 242

Sanskrit, 79
Santiam Kalapuya 32–33, 216, 243
Savosavo 98, 116, 121, 220, 240
Seri 19, 20, 45, 66, 72–74, 102, 105, 224, 241
Sheko 55, 98, 117, 121, 189–190, 219, 240
Sino-Tibetan 81, 87, 160, 206, 221, 224
Slavic 9, 251

Tamil 29–30, 46, 55, 98, 159, 171, 225, 241
Tanti Dargwa 35, 100, 115, 118, 121, 163, 225, 242
Tariana 32–33, 66, 72, 74, 105, 234, 243
Tarma Quechua 9, 66, 80, 85, 105, 123, 168, 228, 242
Tashelhiyt 190
Tat 222, *see also* Apsheron Tat
Telugu 98, 149, 159, 181, 183, 225, 242
Tibetan *see* Dongwang Tibetan
Tibeto-Burman 25, 42
Touareg 190
Tsafiki 66, 80, 85, 88, 90, 149, 159, 228, 242
Tümpisa Shoshone 66, 105, 115, 117, 121, 198, 228–229, 242
Tundra Nenets 25, 92–94, 97, 101, 105, 107, 112–113, 147, 169, 176, 181–183, 195–196, 231, 243, 251
Tungusic 9–10, 32, 43, 190, 197
Turkic 1, 10, 32, 251
Turkish 17, 22
Tuvan 43

Udi 40–41, 46
Udmurt *see* Beserman Udmurt
Uilta 12, 190

Uralic 10, 32, 41, 126, 150, 159, 181, 190, 193, 203, 231, 251
Urarina 75–77, 80, 84–85, 222, 241, 247

Vedic 79

Wagiman 17
Wambaya 65–66, 188, 207, 216, 239
Wan 9, 102, 105, 205, 210–212, 220, 240
Wappo 93, 98, 176, 199, 225, 242
Warlpiri 207
West Greenlandic 19–20, 45, 59, 63, 66, 72–74, 109, 111, 122–123, 199, 201, 214, 222, 241

Wikchamni 66, 72, 74, 153, 159, 222, 228, 241
Wolio 27, 46, 66, 72, 74, 222, 241

Xokleng 194

Yakut 41–42, 99, 110–111, 121, 179, 183, 225, 242
Yeniseian 251
Yimas 65–66, 92, 97, 166, 180, 183, 188, 216, 239
Yukaghir *see* Kolyma Yukaghir
Yurok 39, 46

Zhuokeji rGyalrong 24, 46

www.ingramcontent.com/pod-product-compliance
Lightning Source LLC
Chambersburg PA
CBHW031753220426
43662CB00007B/382